Praise for *Street Gang*

"As joyfully compelling as *Sesame Street* itself."　　　　　*—People*

"*Street Gang* is informative, heartbreaking, hilarious, and often eye-opening, even for the most *Sesame Street*-wise."
—The Philadelphia Inquirer

"It was a pleasure to spend some time back where everything's A-OK."
—Los Angeles Times

"A fascinating page-turner chock full of juicy revelations."
—The Atlanta Journal-Constitution

"Davis writes with such vivid details that one can almost see the brownstone houses and the furry, feathery, fresh-faced Muppets."
—The Baltimore Sun

"Davis culls insights from the show's creators and cast to serve up this painstakingly detailed history of television's most famous address."
—Time.com

"The author's swift narrative—the product of hundreds of interviews—is essentially a Dumpster dive into Oscar's trash can of cast stories. . . . A sensitive, honest account that could jog fond memories even from the amnesiac *Street* denizen Forgetful Jones."
—Drew Toal, TimeOut New York

"Well-researched details and an unflinching eye make Davis's book continuously fascinating."　　　　*—Publishers Weekly*

"Anyone who has ever seen *Sesame Street* as parent or child—or both—will love the detail and exuberance of this book."　　　*—Booklist*

ABOUT THE AUTHOR

Michael Davis was an editor and family television columnist for *TV Guide* from 1998 to 2007. A Nieman fellow, he has also worked for *The Baltimore Sun*, *The Evening Sun*, and the *Chicago Sun-Times*. He lives in Yardley, Pennsylvania. To learn more, please visit www.streetgangbook.com.

STREET GANG

The Complete History
of
Sesame Street

Michael Davis

PENGUIN BOOKS

To Dave, Jeff, Jim, Joe, Jon, and Richard

PENGUIN BOOKS
Published by the Penguin Group
Penguin Group (USA) Inc., 375 Hudson Street, New York, New York 10014, U.S.A. • Penguin Group
(Canada), 90 Eglinton Avenue East, Suite 700, Toronto, Ontario, Canada M4P 2Y3 (a division of Pearson
Penguin Canada Inc.) • Penguin Books Ltd, 80 Strand, London WC2R 0RL, England • Penguin
Ireland, 25 St Stephen's Green, Dublin 2, Ireland (a division of Penguin Books Ltd) • Penguin Group
(Australia), 250 Camberwell Road, Camberwell, Victoria 3124, Australia (a division of Pearson Australia
Group Pty Ltd) • Penguin Books India Pvt Ltd, 11 Community Centre, Panchsheel Park, New Delhi –
110 017, India • Penguin Group (NZ), 67 Apollo Drive, Rosedale, North Shore 0632, New Zealand (a
division of Pearson New Zealand Ltd) • Penguin Books (South Africa) (Pty) Ltd, 24 Sturdee Avenue,
Rosebank, Johannesburg 2196, South Africa

Penguin Books Ltd, Registered Offices: 80 Strand, London WC2R 0RL, England

First published in the United States of America by Viking Penguin,
a member of Penguin Group (USA) Inc. 2008
Published in Penguin Books 2009

1 3 5 7 9 10 8 6 4 2

Grateful acknowledgment is made for permission to reprint excerpts from the following copyrighted
works:
"One of These Things" from *Sesame Street*. Words by Bruce Hart and Joe Raposo, music by Joe Raposo.
Copyright © 1970 Instructional Children's Music, Inc. Copyright renewed. Rights in the U.S.A.
administered by Stage Harbor Publishing, Inc. Rights outside the U.S.A. administered by Instructional
Children's Music, Inc. International copyright secured. All rights reserved.
"Somebody Come and Play," words and music by Joe Raposo. Copyright © 1970 Jonico Music, Inc.
Copyright renewed. Rights in the U.S.A. adminstered by Green Fox Music, Inc. Rights outside the U.S.A.
administered by Jonico Music, Inc. International copyright secured. All rights reserved.

Illustration credits appear on page 380.

THE LIBRARY OF CONGRESS HAS CATALOGED THE HARDCOVER EDITION AS FOLLOWS:
Davis, Michael, date.
Street gang: the complete history of Sesame Street/by Michael Davis.
p. cm.
Includes bibliographical references and index.
ISBN 978-0-670-01996-0 (hc.)
ISBN 978-0-14-311663-9 (pbk.)
1. Sesame Street (Television program) I. Title.
PN1992.77.S43D38 2009
791.43'72—dc 2008035498

Printed in the United States of America
Set in Adobe Garamond   Designed by Francesca Belanger

Prologue

Joan Ganz Cooney walked toward the corner of Amsterdam Avenue and 112th Street, lost in a fog of grief. Ahead were the crenelated parapets that crown the Cathedral of St. John the Divine, a Gothic Revival glory on Manhattan's Upper West Side. Black limousines lined the curbside, clogging the street, as NYPD officers waved their arms in a futile effort to get vehicles moving. The sidewalks were overrun by pedestrians, hundreds of them, all moving toward the cathedral steps. Cooney walked alongside mothers with toddlers clutching Ernie dolls, students playing hooky from school, executives in crisp suits, Midtown secretaries in heels, Latinas in scoop-necked tops, and bohemian types sporting jeans, running shoes, and long ponytails.

It was May 21, 1990, five days after Jim Henson, her friend and creative partner since 1969, had died at fifty-three from a runaway strep infection gone stubbornly, foolishly untreated. There was no other word to describe his passing other than *shocking*, and it was played just that way in the papers and on the nightly news. People who didn't know him wept as if a favorite uncle had died, that subversive adult who sat with the adults at Thanksgiving but would have preferred dinner at the kids' table. They came out in force for the public memorial, filling the vast, vaulted sanctuary, even more than the organizers of the event had anticipated. Some five thousand attendees filled the pews, standing in the antechambers and spilling into the aisles. The overflow was so great that people had simply dropped their backpacks, folded up their strollers, and sat on the hard stone floor.

Clustered row upon row near them were mourners bound by their years together working for and with the Children's Television Workshop (CTW), the nonprofit corporation Cooney helped build. Cooney took a seat next to Christopher Cerf, one of the founding fathers of *Sesame Street*.

From the altar, the congregation was an impressionistic canvas, dappled with a profusion of spring green. That was to be expected. Just as teams, tribes, and nations have representative colors, Jim Henson owned Kermit green.

Cooney's thoughts wandered to Kermit and the early days of *Sesame Street*. Reminders of that time were everywhere. Sitting nearby was Frank Oz, who in 1969—*Sesame*'s debut year—became a Henson protégé, having joined the Muppets right out of high school. For more than twenty years,

Oz had been uptight Bert to Henson's mischievous Ernie, the straight man of the odd-couple comedy duo. On *The Muppet Show*, their roles had reversed; Oz was outrageously pushy Miss Piggy to Henson's pushed-to-the-brink Kermit.

At no time had Jim Henson's disparate worlds collided quite as markedly as at this memorial. Over to one side was Henson's friend Harry Belafonte. A humanitarian and artist, Belafonte had appeared on *The Muppet Show*, where he introduced "Turn the World Around," a joyous, syncopated African folk melody that would be part of the day's program.

Not far away was Lorne Michaels, who gave the Muppets a weekly showcase during the audacious first season (1975) of *Saturday Night Live* at a time when the ambitious Henson feared he might be trapped for eternity in children's television. Henson's talent manager, Bernie Brillstein, saw to it that that never happened. Brillstein, who signed John Belushi, Dan Ackroyd, and Gilda Radner, was like a second father to Henson, a Jewish one.

In the late 1980s, Henson had separated from his wife, Jane, the mother of his five children. For most of his career, he had been more married to his work than to Jane, and a relationship that began when they met as students at the College Park campus of the University of Maryland withered. Henson was known to work around the clock in the studio when a production deadline loomed, and his travel schedule and list of business commitments would have seemed unreasonable to most. He seemed happier and more fulfilled away from home, but he craved time with his two sons and three daughters.

As a single man, Henson had had his pick of staggeringly beautiful companions. Daryl Hannah, who had flown in from California for the service on a private jet and now wept softly in a pew, had been one of them. Henson went through a Hollywood stage in his late forties and early fifties, shedding his signature bohemian wardrobe for goods from Rodeo Drive. His beard was neatly trimmed and his hair styled for an appearance he'd made with Kermit on the late-night *Arsenio Hall Show*, just twelve days before he died. Complaining of a sore throat in the greenroom that night, he was uncharacteristically flat and slow on the uptake during an interview segment. Henson used the occasion to plug an upcoming special shot at Disney World in Orlando and to introduce Clifford, a new Muppet musician working with Dr. Teeth and the Electric Mayhem, the house band from *The Muppet Show*. African American puppeteer Kevin Clash gave voice and performance to Clifford, he of the fuchsia dreadlocks, sunglasses, and vocal delivery that was distinctly urban contemporary. Clash was sensational, bantering with the black comic as the audience howled.

Henson seemed to enjoy it as much as anyone, and he looked relieved to have Clash carry the load. It was Henson's final televised interview.

Chris Cerf lost a dear friend and comic collaborator in Henson. Walking into the memorial, he was numb with grief, but being surrounded by his CTW colleagues was a comfort. Only months earlier, *Sesame Street* composer-arranger extraordinaire Joe Raposo had been laid to rest, dead at age fifty-one from complications of lymphoma.

Cerf composed tunes for *Sesame Street* as well, half-silly, half-sophisticated parody numbers. As the son of Bennett Cerf, the witty cofounder of Random House, Chris had used his book-world DNA to create the first paperback library of *Sesame Street* books. He was also sly and unpredictable, which made him a perfect fit for Henson's extended family of mirth makers. Cerf provided many good times in *Sesame*'s freewheeling formative days, when an elaborate prank would reduce Henson to a puddle.

Cooney knew that everything about *Sesame Street* had been unalterably turned upside down the minute Jim Henson was declared dead at 1:30 a.m. on Wednesday, May 16.

In his final hour, he twice went into cardiac arrest, as the raging infection shut down his organs and left him struggling for air, surrounded by strangers. The cause of his death was Group A streptococcal pneumonia, an infection that probably started with that sore throat he complained about in Los Angeles the night of the *Arsenio* taping. A timely course of penicillin would have saved him, but he chose not to seek medical help until it was too late. Henson, whose mother was a practicing Christian Scientist, had considered calling in a faith healer, but, after hours of feverish decline, he finally acceded to be taken to the hospital. Around 4 a.m., Henson's publicist Arthur Novell received a phone call in San Francisco. "Oh, Arthur, I'm not feeling well," Henson rasped. Sensing danger, Novell arranged for a Manhattan car service to pick up Henson at the Sherry-Netherland Hotel. Henson, whose organs were failing, walked to the lobby and got into the limo. Precious minutes were lost as the driver pulled up to a door at New York Hospital that was three-quarters of a block away from the emergency entrance. More time was lost when Henson sent the driver on his way, insisting he could walk to the ER. There was no arguing with him. For all his exceptional attributes, Henson was a willful, unyielding man who almost always got his way. This served him well in business, where he could wear people down.

Jim Henson was a genius, and not only for reinventing puppetry for the television age and for inspiring a raft of characters that make you smile just thinking about them. Henson was a genius businessman, as well. His only flaws might have been an inability to stay within budget for his feature-length films and his unwillingness to fire people when prudence would have suggested he should do so. He always found someone else to take that responsibility.

"Puppetry," he once said, "is a way of hiding." At six foot three and perpetually bearded to cover acne scars, Henson was defined by bemusing and often baffling contradictions. He was shy by nature, yet his creations were explosively silly and spontaneous. Often reticent and contemplative, at times he eagerly played the Pied Piper, organizing one of New York's most outrageous annual costume parties. He spoke of simple pleasures but had a taste for European casinos, coastal vacation homes, and four-star dining. He lived large but, as a proto-environmentalist, talked of protecting a small planet's shrinking resources. He embraced and celebrated life exuberantly and spread acres of joy but suffered through at least one major depression after his fantasy film, *The Dark Crystal,* bombed at the box office and was dismissed by critics.

Henson was deeply unhappy and fatigued in the months leading up to his death. Many believed he sensed that he would not live to see grandchildren, pointing to a plan he had drawn up five years earlier for the public memorial service as evidence that he believed the end was near. It was included in letters left behind for each of his children, in which Henson indicated a burning curiosity about the afterlife and an eagerness to reconnect with the dead, and assured the children that he would be waiting for them "on the other side." He also asked his survivors to bring everyone together for a few songs and stories, insisting that guests avoid wearing funereal black. As a son of the South and a jazz fancier, he requested that a New Orleans–style band play "When the Saints Go Marching In." He requested that the proceedings be entertaining and light, hoping that friends and colleagues would provide laughter in large doses and silliness worthy of the Muppets.

Henson wrote the letter three years before he began working—without a contract—for The Walt Disney Company. Doing so, some believe, was the beginning of the end.

Disney CEO Michael D. Eisner waited for the proceedings to begin alongside Frank Wells, his No. 2 at the company. In the late 1980s, Eisner had been clever enough to see that Disney's cast of classic characters aimed at the very young, such as Mickey Mouse and Goofy, were being slowly supplanted in children's hearts by fresher, hipper icons. Eisner and Wells had pledged a huge pile of Disney dollars—a sum estimated to be between $100 million and $150 million—to purchase Henson's production company and library of film and television properties. The price included ownership of the boisterous, satirical, and sometime sardonic puppet ensemble that had made *The Muppet Show* a worldwide sensation, but it did not—and would not—include the Muppets Henson had specifically created for *Sesame Street*.

Henson believed there was no entertainment company better suited than Disney to perpetuate such multidimensional characters as Miss Piggy, the porcine diva; Fozzie Bear, the clueless comic; and hectoring balcony critics Statler and Waldorf. Disney's litigious history of protecting its characters is the stuff of Hollywood legend. Under Eisner, the company once sued the Academy of Motion Picture Arts and Sciences over an unauthorized Oscar appearance by an actress portraying Snow White.

Cooney knew Eisner to be cold, arrogant, and insistent when he was in pursuit of a creative property. She was not pleased with his predatory forays into *Sesame Street*. Her gut churned as she considered how miserable Eisner had made things for Henson in his final months. Henson's gentle manner masked a steely shrewdness—you could not budge him if he didn't want to be budged—but Eisner had been surprisingly relentless in the Henson campaign. Cooney—a courteous woman who had persuaded senators and top philanthropists to do her bidding, who had stared down cancer, and who was married to a private-equity mogul who could quite possibly arrange to buy the entire Disney company if push came to shove—was not intimidated by his tactics.

Cooney held Disney in high regard but regarded the company's merchandising arms as competitors in the marketplace of character-licensed toys, games, and consumer goods. She was convinced that Eisner would not be satisfied until his deal with Henson was sweetened by ownership of the Sesame Muppets, which generated an estimated $15 million to $17 million annually in licensing and merchandising fees split between Sesame Workshop and Henson Associates, Inc. In 1969, Henson had waived his performance fee for *Sesame Street* in exchange for full ownership of his characters, agreeing later to split any revenue generated by them.

In time, both organizations depended on that revenue for survival. By 1990, CTW had long shed its dependence on government and philanthropic grants, gaining its financial independence by building and sustaining a formidable endowment. Henson Associates, notorious for going over budget on productions, stayed afloat thanks to the huge popularity of its characters and the public's hunger for Muppet-licensed bed linens, apparel, computer games, action figures, books, CDs, and other products.

By 1989, after building his company from a husband-and-wife operation out of the trunk of his car into one of the world's most recognized entertainment brands, Henson was eager to return to a simpler existence of creating and performing. Disney had offered a way to cash out, and a letter of intent, by which he would have sold his privately held company to the California-based entertainment and media colossus, was already signed.

But after months of legal process, during which Henson had commenced working for Disney without a consummated deal, lingering doubts began to plague him. As media analysts were hailing the merger-in-progress as "a business association made in entertainment heaven," discord bubbled just beneath the surface at Disney Studios in Florida and California. Henson's employees, accustomed to his benevolence, creative freedom, and camaraderie, were suffering massive culture shock in their day-to-day dealings within Disney's rapacious negotiate-everything hierarchy. They referred to their new working environment as Mauschwitz.

Beyond that, Henson was beginning to chafe at provisions in the deal for his exclusive personal services and for the rights to any future characters he might create. These were not unreasonable demands from a company about to dump an armored carload of cash at his door. But regret clearly was setting in for a man who valued creative freedom and independence above all else. "Trapped" was the only word Cooney could use to describe how Henson felt, and she believed the whole situation was causing him immense grief and contributing to his lack of physical resistance. Henson felt that he would be Disney's highly compensated but indentured servant for the rest of his life.

What the business-page pundits and entertainment insiders never quite sniffed out about the stalled marriage had its roots in Eisner's covetous yen for the Sesame Muppets. Despite Henson's refusals to discuss the matter, Eisner wouldn't let up. Cooney recalled how early in the winter of 1990, Henson had invited her to attend what he described as a peace luncheon with Eisner, at which he wanted to put the matter to rest once and for all. She remembered how charming Eisner had been, how well the lunch was proceeding, until she looked over at Henson and saw that he had become upset over a stray remark of Eisner's in which he discussed the Sesame Muppets as if he might own them. "There you go again," Henson said to Eisner, blood rising up his neck. Cooney had never seen Henson that agitated.

It was that day that the dispute became bitterly personal. "It wasn't about business anymore," recalled Frank Oz, Henson's longtime creative partner. "It was about what Jim believed in, the simplicity and purity of the characters. There was a bit of anger in him about this, and he was not an angry man."

Henson believed that even though he owned the trademark to them, the *Sesame* characters really belonged to children, and he did not want those Muppets to be exploited. In his mind, they were in a special protected category and he was their caretaker. The thought of Eisner trying to hijack them bred no small amount of mistrust and ill will. "There was no way in hell that was going to happen," recalled Oz.

According to Cooney, Henson came up with a plan in late winter and early spring of 1990, vowing to her that he would change all the paperwork necessary to ensure that ownership of the *Sesame Street* Muppets would be transferred to CTW upon his death. The split in licensing and merchandising would continue, but the trademark would rest with Cooney's nonprofit corporation.

That Henson died before his intentions could be codified in a legally binding document was a bitter pill for Cooney to swallow. She knew that a time would come, very soon, when she would have to engage in a blink-first showdown with Eisner and the Disney machine over this issue. But today was not the day to dwell on that, no matter how the fear kept impinging on her mind.

Today was a day to remember and celebrate Jim.

Just then, the service began, not with an invocation but rather with the howling, growling strains of the Dirty Dozen Brass Band, a Dixieland band flown in especially from New Orleans for the occasion—just the way Jim wanted. To the measured refrain of the old Negro spiritual "Just a Closer Walk with Thee," Jane Henson and her children led a twelve-minute processional as the dirge filled the cavernous holy space with the *blat* of a tuba, the *squawk* of a muted trumpet, the *squeal* of a clarinet. It was music meant to send the spirit of James Maury Henson soaring to that great good place.

Sesame Street began as a flash of brilliance that struck like a bolt from the gods. Cooney was its mother of invention, while Lloyd N. Morrisett, a well-connected vice president at the Carnegie Corporation, was its financial godfather. *Sesame's* moment of conception occurred at a dinner party at Cooney's apartment, when Morrisett and his wife were discussing how their three-year-old daughter, Sarah, had become transfixed by television. She would sit in front of a test pattern at 6:30 a.m., waiting for the cartoons to appear at 7:00. It was the same thing millions of kids were doing all across the country, an image that confounded Cooney.

Within days of that dinner, Cooney, Morrisett, and three other contributors engaged in an outpouring of ideas on how to master the addictive qualities of television and do something good with them. "What if?" became their operative phrase. "What if you could create content for television that was both entertaining and instructive? What if it went down more like ice cream than spinach? What if we stopped complaining about the banality we are allowing our children to see and did something about it?"

Over the summer of 1967, Cooney would crisscross the country testing the idea of a daily show for preschoolers that would teach basic school-readiness concepts. With her confident and persuasive writing style, the former reporter, drew up a proposal that, with Morrisett's skillful maneuvering and networking, secured a $1 million grant from Carnegie and millions more from the federal government, the Corporation for Public Broadcasting, and the Ford Foundation.

Then, with her funds secured, Cooney began to assemble her team, a talent roundup that would, after *Sesame*'s first season, result in three Emmys, a Peabody, and the cover of *Time*.

Henson loped in to provide the missing alchemy in the summer of 1969. Test audiences of preschoolers in Philadelphia had rejected live-action sequences shot on a mock urban street, with trash cans on the curb and laundry hanging from tenement windows. But that was before Henson began sketching a bird puppet that would be so oversized that a six-foot-tall man, hiding within it, would be required to work its long neck and mouth with an outstretched arm. And that was before the idea arose to have a contrarian, ornery puppet pop up from inside one of those trash cans and provide a grouch's view of everyday life. And that was before the idea arose to allow two best-friend puppets—one playful and upbeat, one overearnest and square—to provide comedy in the classic mode of Laurel and Hardy, Burns and Allen, Martin and Lewis. In the history of show business, there probably never was a straighter straight man than banana-yellow Bert, the paper clip collector and pigeon fancier.

It was Henson who helped the grandest and most ambitious experiment in children's television find its legs. That those legs were yellow and attached to a curious eight-foot canary is not the oddest part of the story, by a long shot.

Henson's touch helped definitively establish *Sesame Street*'s "delicate balance between fun and learning," as he once described it. Cooney understood from the show's earliest days, back before it became a brand of excellence here and around the globe, that using television to teach the alphabet and counting to twenty would have been a noble effort, but not nearly as much fun, without him. Henson's influence also helped to create the two-tiered audience that was essential to *Sesame*'s vast and immediate appeal. Kids watched in rapture, but parents watched, too, often laughing to the winking references to pop culture, song parodies, and outrageous puns that came out of the mouths of the Muppets.

Henson was the key, but he wasn't the only visionary among the early architects of *Sesame Street*. There was a whole gang of them, many of whom, curiously, had first names beginning with *J,* the letter that has acquired a near-mystical stature through the thirty-nine years the show has aired on PBS.

Besides Joan Cooney and Jim Henson there was the seductively handsome, multitalented Jon Stone, who as writer, director, and producer drew the cast and crew under his spell and established a creative atmosphere of risk and trust.

There was scriptwriter-composer-lyricist-poet Jeff Moss, a sometimes difficult but always passionate contributor to the show.

Finally, there was Joe Raposo, the musical prodigy who provided *Sesame Street* with its signature sound and sing-along melodies that endure to this day.

In those early years there was an Arthurian round table of other remarkable souls—logicians and artists, dreamers and pragmatists, folksingers, storybook illustrators, and bow-tied PhDs—all gathered with a singular purpose. They came together at a star-crossed moment in American life when people of means who lived in comfort chose to dedicate their energies to the less fortunate and the forgotten, the rural poor and the underprivileged of the urban ghettos. *Sesame* succeeded beyond their wildest imaginings and, in doing so, changed the world, one child at a time.

These memories, and memories of Henson in particular, washed over Cooney as the service got under way. She was consoled by the knowledge that Henson respected her as he respected no other woman in his professional life. Their affectionate, trusting bond was mixed into the mortar that held together every brick of *Sesame Street*. She smiled as she recalled what Henson had said once about their relationship: "What we had was like a marriage. Lots of valuable time together and no sex."

Now, for the second time in less than a year, she was burying one of her "originals." The previous February had seen the death of Raposo, the gregarious, name-dropping, often bewildering talent whose final, tortured years were cursed by cancer. In a twist that seemed almost too much to bear, a television tribute to Raposo was scheduled to air on PBS hours after Henson died. Cooney watched it in bed and cried throughout.

She had also been in tears listening to Jon Stone earlier in the day, speaking about Henson from the pulpit. "I don't remember exactly how Jim and I met," said Stone. "It was in nineteen sixty-three or sixty-four. But from the moment we met, we were never very far apart. For me, the early hours of May sixteenth were a living nightmare. One by one, all of us heard the unhearable. And we all must have had the same reaction: This is an epic mistake."

Stone, overwhelmed, barely made it through his brief remarks. As he walked off, all eyes were on Big Bird, who walked toward a grand piano. Through the years, Stone, a stickler for preparation and prompt rehearsal, had grown impatient with Caroll Spinney, a puppeteer who could easily access his inner child. Spinney, who since Day One of *Sesame Street* had provided voice and movement for sweetly quizzical Big Bird and hypercritical Oscar, was marvelous on his feet. But he had an antipathy for studying his lines, preferring to read them fresh, often after he had already stepped into Bird's awkward and confining costume.

But on this day, there would be détente between director and performer, and Spinney left no dry eyes with Bird's aching rendition of "Bein' Green," the anthem to self-acceptance written by Raposo.

Just before Big Bird trudged off, he looked skyward and said, "Thank you, Kermit."

Chapter One

On a Sunday morning in December 1965, three-year-old Sarah Morisett awoke to streams of soft light on her pillow. She pulled herself upright on the bed and blinked. Zipped into pink footie pajamas, Sarah hopped down to the edge of the mattress and stretched across the bedspread to grab her "nockey," a faded, frayed security blanket she had been dragging around since taking her earliest steps.

Her parents, Lloyd and Mary, slept soundly, only steps away in the master bedroom of the family's ranch-style home in Irvington, New York. Built along the Hudson, Irvington was a quiet refuge of workaday villagers, shopkeepers, and a smattering of commuters who worked downriver in Manhattan. The Morrisetts had hoped to sleep in that morning, or, with the Almighty's good graces, stay under the covers until at least 8:00 a.m. An early walker and a chatterbox, Sarah had light brown, slightly wavy hair and a propensity for whirling about in a tutu, repeating jingles she had memorized from television. Like Sarah, it was, her parents thought, adorable.

To be three is to be absorbent, kinetic, inquisitive, exuberant, determined, malleable, and uninhibited. Sarah was a boundlessly energetic entertainer and, at bedtime, an attentive listener who enjoyed storybooks, her blanket close at hand. Because her parents believed in the social benefits of nursery school, Sara attended a private nondenominational one situated in a church hall. Though Sarah was smaller than most of the other children, she thrived in the play-school atmosphere.

Her nimble little hands had no problem popping open the doors to the cabinet-style TV set in the living room, transforming an idle and inert piece of furniture into an electronic theater that came to life at her command.

As she sat cross-legged on the floor there was nothing much to watch on local TV so early on a Sunday, beyond a test pattern. Sarah cupped her hands over her ears to block out the test's constant shrill tone, transfixed by a picture of an ascetic Indian chief in full headdress on a field of geometric shapes.[1]

Sarah understood that if she waited patiently, the Indian would soon vanish. An unseen announcer would then begin the broadcast day with a recitation of FCC-mandated station-identification drone, followed by the National Anthem, played over a film that panned Mount Rushmore, the

Statue of Liberty, and, depending on whether you owned a color or a black-and-white set, either amber waves of grain or amorphous waves of gray.

Roused from a sound sleep that December morning, Lloyd Morrisett followed the trail of TV noise to find Sarah spellbound in front of the Indian. The clock had not struck seven.

For a moment, Morrisett stood in wonder as Sarah stared blankly at the TV. "It struck me there was something fascinating to Sarah about television," said her father, an experimental psychologist with a PhD from Yale, much later. "What is a child doing watching the station identification signal? What does this mean?"

Morrisett's search for meaning in a preschool child's enthrallment with television would have far-reaching implications for preschool children in America and beyond. In a real sense, one could say there may not have been a *Sesame Street* had Morrisett not been intrigued that morning, watching his preschooler watch television.

A few months later, Morrisett offered the test-pattern story as a conversational gambit during a dinner party held at the Manhattan apartment of Tim and Joan Cooney. The Morrisetts and the Cooneys had been indirectly introduced by Joan's cousin and Morrisett's boyhood friend, Julian Ganz, who operated successful furniture stores in Southern California. When the Morrisetts moved East from Berkeley in 1958, Julian had suggested to Morrisett that he look up Joan, but it took him until 1961 to do so. Lloyd and Joan shared the occasional lunch thereafter, and the couples met socially from time to time.

Though the Cooneys were childless urban professionals and the Morrisetts were mortgage-holding suburban parents, the couples had been swept up in the tide of the times and shared the core beliefs of left-leaning Democrats. Disciples of President John Fitzgerald Kennedy, they were ardent supporters of the Great Society initiatives of his successor, Lyndon Baines Johnson. They saw the expansion of federally funded social programs as a remedy to the nation's ills, and they believed that a more racially tolerant and compassionate nation would unite to offer not a handout but a hand up to the dispossessed.

While the Cooneys were vocal reformists and civil-rights activists, the Morrisetts were more quietly committed to issues of social justice. "We would term ourselves *progressive*," Morrisett said. "Our support was more intellectual than action oriented."

Manhattan in those days was a bastion of sixties liberalism, so naturally true believers had their own television station, WNDT, Channel Thirteen. Before there was a PBS, and before Thirteen's call letters were changed to WNET, there was a loose confederation of local channels that offered *educational television* (ETV). In many homes, that term brought to mind programming that was as unimaginative as it was unwatchable, especially the torturous classroom-of-the-air lectures that filled weekday-morning schedules.

At the time Morrisett was telling his test-pattern story, Cooney had become one of the brighter lights at Thirteen, a producer of high-minded, low-rated public service programs and thirty-minute documentaries.

Neither Lewis Freedman, the station's program manager and Joan's brilliant mentor[2], nor Anne Bower, Cooney's producer colleague at Thirteen, had met the Morrisetts before arriving at the Cooneys' high-rise apartment building at Twenty-first Street and Third Avenue. It was only a half block shy of being considered within the boundaries of sedate, stately Gramercy Park.[3]

Joan said that she and her husband—medium-income earners, at best—were literally on the outside looking in. "People always looked at me blankly when I said where we lived, but everyone got it when I would say, 'It's a *block* from Gramercy Park,' which had, and still has, a bit of cachet. Rents were low enough in those days, and apartments plentiful, so even those with low incomes could get a pretty good deal, if it was out of Midtown. We had what seemed like a palace after my having lived in a small one-bedroom on Sixty-sixth Street for eight years. We had two good-size bedrooms and a kitchen in which two people could actually eat at a small table. In the L-shaped dining area was a small table, but there weren't six chairs to go around it."

For parties, dinner was served buffet-style. Cooney would set out the heavy handmade sterling silver place settings that came as wedding gifts from friends and relatives. "We ended up eating on trays and tables in the living room," she said.

In 1966, Cooney was caught up in the still-bubbling American craze for French food, a change in the American palate inspired, in part, by the haute cuisine of Rene Verdon, White House chef during the Kennedy years.[4]

A second impetus for the sharp rise in interest for—and demystification of—French food could be traced to another New Englander, an oddly affecting, altitudinous matron from Cambridge named Julia Child, who lived a short walk away from JFK's beloved Harvard campus. After studying at Le Cordon Bleu in Paris, Child coauthored the first volume of *Mastering the Art of French Cooking*. The cookbook found its way into hundreds of thousands of home kitchens, including that of Madame Cooney. A second volume was published in 1970.

The French Chef, Child's spin-off television program, was made available to viewers nationwide by the good offices of Boston's pioneering educational station, WGBH. When it debuted in February 1963, *The French Chef* helped to popularize an entire genre of television, the studio-based cooking show built around the talents—and recipes—of a stove-top auteur. The show's producers strove for such authenticity that they virtually duplicated the kitchen design of Child's work area, sink, and cabinetry in Cambridge.

According to Morrisett, on the evening of the dinner party, Cooney served up a delectable boeuf bourguignon, beef stew in red wine with bacon, onions, and mushrooms, a traditional French country recipe—which, as it happens, appears on page 315 of the first volume of *Mastering the Art of French Cooking*. Let history note, then, that Julia Child, public television's grande dame, provided the savory sauce poured on the night *Sesame Street* was conceived.

After dinner, the Cooneys' guests lingered over coffee and conversation. The topic was TV.

"Lewis Freedman was holding forth on the educational potential of television," Cooney recalls. "He would dramatize and mesmerize, and I was always in his thrall. He could have been a revival minister, an Elmer Gantry." Freedman bemoaned the awesome, unfulfilled potential of television, wondering aloud what it might take for the network program lords to strive higher for America's children. That void was part of the "vast wasteland" famously described by the then FCC chairman Newton N. Minow in a 1961 speech. On the receiving end of that stinging critique was the duly chastised membership of the National Association of Broadcasters. Minow told the assembly, "It used to be said that there were three great influences on a child: home, school, and church. Today there is a fourth great influence, and you, ladies and gentlemen, control it. If parents, teachers, and ministers conducted their responsibilities by following the ratings, children would have a steady diet of ice cream, school holidays, and no Sunday school. What about your responsibilities? There are some fine children's shows, but they are drowned out in the massive doses of cartoons, violence, and more violence. Must these be your trademarks?"[5]

The Morrisetts acknowledged the failings of children's television, but they did allow Sarah to watch certain shows. In their view, the best of the lot was *Captain Kangaroo*, the gently comedic, sweetly soothing, good-hearted early-morning program on CBS. *Captain Kangaroo* was network television's first sustained attempt to provide preschoolers with consistent quality entertainment and stimulation for growing intellects. It clicked with children who enjoyed picture books, puppets, music, and animation—kids like Sarah.

At one point in the discussion, Morrisett, the psychologist, turned to Joan, the television professional, and asked aloud, "Do you think television could be used to teach young children?" The question hung in the air for several long seconds.

Unbeknownst to everyone in the room but Mary Morrisett, Lloyd had more than a parent's concern in asking the question. Her husband was on the forefront of a quiet revolution being led by researchers in education and child development and funded by private foundations and the federal government. Morrisett was then a vice president for the Carnegie Corporation, the foundation instituted by Andrew Carnegie in 1911 to advance knowledge and spread it globally. In that role Morrisett had helped award between $500,000 and $1 million in grants for programs meant to stimulate the intellect of preschoolers. "Carnegie had begun to take an interest in what you could do to enrich the preschool curriculum, in particular to overcome the disadvantages that poor children and children from minority groups were suffering when they entered school," Morrisett said. "The results indicated you could teach children a great deal before they entered school in first grade. And the children who had that advantageous education early did better in the early school years. I thought that the evidence was pretty clear.

"But one of the problems was that despite the money, [Carnegie was] only reaching a few hundred children. The problem was far greater than we were able to deal with on an experimental basis. There was really no mechanism for spreading this kind of activity. There was a dissonance, if you will, between the goals we were trying to achieve and the [distribution] mechanisms available."

In short, there were some powerful new strategies emerging to help disadvantaged children arrive at the school door better prepared for kindergarten and first grade, but too few means available to distribute and apply them. Listening to Freedman, Morrisett realized that perhaps television might provide an ideal electronic delivery system for some of these ideas.

If Morrisett had been inspired by Freedman, so, too, did Cooney get knocked back a bit listening to Morrisett go on about Carnegie's commitment to help children learn more. What he did not know is that Cooney had produced *A Chance at the Beginning,* a documentary for Channel Thirteen about an intervention experiment in Harlem for at-risk preschoolers.

Cooney was already well versed in the ideas that had led to Head Start, the federal program initiated in 1965 that helped communities meet the needs of disadvantaged children. Its supporters believed the tyranny of America's poverty cycle could be broken if the emotional, social, health, nutritional, and psychological needs of poor children could be met.[6]

Before good nights were exchanged, the fates of Joan Ganz Cooney and Lloyd Morrisett had become entwined like strands of DNA. A professional relationship that spanned five decades started with Morrisett's ostensibly simple question, "Do you think television could be used to teach young children?"

"I don't know," Cooney replied, "but I'd like to talk about it."

Within a week, Morrisett had invited Freedman and Cooney to Carnegie to do just that.

Chapter Two

As autumn turned to winter in 1929, a direful shadow crossed the continent, like biblical darkness falling upon Egypt. Indeed, it was as if God Almighty had unleashed an eleventh plague, one of pessimism and despair.

In early December, President Herbert Hoover announced on radio that the worst of the financial crisis was over, but Sylvan Ganz knew too much about economics—and human nature—to believe it. As executive vice president of the First National Bank of Arizona, Ganz was obliged to assume an air of calm and confidence, and his upbeat veneer never faltered at work. But at night, his thoughts turned to what measures he might need to take to protect the bank should the nation's economy reach a danger point.

In the final weeks of 1929, the Ganz household was going through diapers at an astonishing rate. Three children had been born in a thirty-nine-month span to Ganz's wife, Pauline. Baby Joan arrived on November 30, a month and a day after Black Tuesday, the third and most disastrous day of record losses on Wall Street. Across the nation, billions in assets had been wiped out in less than a week.

The new sibling joined older brother Emil Paul, named for his grandfather and mother, and older sister Sylvia Rose, named for her father and maternal grandmother. "By the time I came along, Mother had run out of steam—and names," Joan Ganz Cooney explained years later. "The joke in our family was they barely had time to name me at all, and it was after no one, except, possibly, Joan Crawford."

While Cooney's father had not amassed the wealth of some of his neighbors, he was well off, and well thought of, a civic-minded, progressive commercial banker following in the path of his father, Emil Ganz, one of the first mayors of Phoenix. Sylvan attended college, but shortly before graduation, his mother died and he failed to complete his finals and earn a degree. But as the son of a city father, Ganz was still considered one of the town's more prominent bachelors when he met dark-haired, dark-eyed Pauline. He was thirty-five; she twenty-two. Pauline had moved as a teen from Jackson, Michigan, to Arizona along with her sister and mother. Her father had been killed in a train wreck when she was two, and her mother had to take in sewing to make ends meet. After graduating from secretarial school, Pauline headed west with her family, "for the warmer weather and, I suspect, the adventure," Cooney said.

After a five-year courtship, Pauline and Sylvan finally made it to the altar, but not easily. She wanted to be married in the church, but to do so, Sylvan had to promise their children would be raised Roman Catholic. Though Ganz was agnostic, he feared taking vows from a priest would be seen as a denial of his Jewish roots. Despite his indifference to the religious tenets and obligations of Judaism, Ganz remained culturally identified with his heritage. But ultimately he relented, "because [marriage to Pauline] just wasn't going to happen without it," Cooney said. "He was by then forty, or close to it, and he desperately wanted to get married and have children, and he'd been in love with this woman for five years."

To be sure, there were Jews among the earliest settlers of Phoenix, not the least of whom was papa Emil, an immigrant tailor from Walldorf, Germany. Emil Ganz, a nonpracticing Jew and avowed atheist, came to the United States in 1858 or 1859. After stops in New York and Philadelphia, he established his trade in the unlikely locale of Cedartown, Georgia. Family speculation has it that Georgia reminded him—and a smattering of other German-Jewish settlers—of the "bucolic scenes from which they had come in Germany," Cooney said.

Convinced the South would prevail in the Civil War, Emil joined the Confederate army, served with distinction, and was wounded twice. His company participated in the battles of Antietam, Gettysburg, Fredericksburg, and the defense of Richmond. He was held for seven months at a notorious federal prison in Elmira, New York, but when the war ended, he signed a loyalty oath to the United States and was released. Emil headed west, with stops in Quincy, Illinois; Kansas City, Missouri; and Las Animas, Colorado, before settling in Arizona in the mid-1870s. After operating hotels in Prescott and Phoenix, he became bank president at the National Bank of Arizona (which later became First National) and served three mayoral terms.

Emil was a charter member of the Phoenix Country Club and enjoyed privileges there that were denied succeeding generations of Jews. It was almost as if the gates of the club briefly swung open for certain old-line families with German-Jewish bloodlines, only to close rapidly thereafter. Also making it through the country-club portal were the wealthy owners of a family-owned Phoenix department store, M. Goldwater & Sons—one of those sons being Barry Goldwater, the grandchild of Jewish immigrants from Poland. Raised in the Episcopalian tradition of his mother, Goldwater inherited the family business, attained wealth and stature, and went on to serve five terms in the United States Senate.

"The pioneering Jews of Phoenix were English and German, and they were treated as a separate class by the non-Jews," Cooney said. "My father *hated* that country club. It made him uncomfortable on almost every level. It let the Goldwaters and Ganzes in, but Eastern European Jews who had accents from the old country? I don't know if they even applied to get in, but if they had, they would not have been admitted. And these were my father's friends." Sylvan kept up his membership in the club, despite his objections to its tacit discriminatory policies. "My father didn't want to deprive his children of using the club, so he would occasionally go to dinner there, but he would be uncomfortable."

Sylvan and Pauline owned a pale pink one-story home on East Verde Lane, just a ten-minute walk from the country club. It had three bedrooms, a large high-ceilinged living room, a dining room, a family room, and a bedroom and bath for Eunice Turner, a black housekeeper the children called Turner.

In 1932, when Joan was three, a family crisis erupted. Sylvan was seeking buyers for First National, a difficult assignment during a national epidemic of bank failures. "He became extremely worried that the stockholders would be harmed if he couldn't get a sale," Cooney said, "and he began drinking heavily, using alcohol as self-medication the way people use Xanax or Valium today."

Sylvan and Pauline booked passage on an ocean liner, in the hope that time at sea would provide rest and relief from the pressure. But it was to no avail, as Sylvan began to unravel further onboard. "He had started to say some things that were off-kilter," Cooney said, "and while on the cruise, he became a little paranoid, convinced that one of the passengers was a detective. That's when my mother knew she'd better get him to a doctor."

Sylvan was having a nervous breakdown, a crushing case of depression. He needed uninterrupted rest, therapy, and a clean break from alcohol. "My mother moved all of us [temporarily] to California, where there was good psychiatric help," Cooney said. For Joan, leaving Phoenix meant leaving Turner, whom she adored. "With three children, each a year and a half apart, my mother really didn't have time to give to everybody . . . and a very demanding husband," Cooney said. "So it was Turner who taught me how to tie my shoes and the ABCs. She gave me the love that I really wanted. Family lore has it that I always said 'bye-bye' to my mother when she would go out, but I would just sob when it was Turner's day off. I'd go wandering back to her room, find her gone, and just throw a total tantrum."

Under proper care, Sylvan recovered within three months and was sent home with a stern recommendation: "The doctor said, 'I think you'd better drink less,' and Pop said, 'Well, I'll just stop'—and he did," Cooney said. "Alcohol was never a problem again."

Poverty was pandemic in the early 1930s, and a steady stream of homeless, jobless, hungry men arrived in Phoenix seeking work, their possessions balled in burlap and slung over a shoulder. "Arizona was right in the middle of the national malaise," said David Tatum, a curator with the Arizona Historical Society.[1] "Nobody was insulated from it. Farm workers from the Old South, Texas and Oklahoma looking for work in the cotton fields, along with immigrants from Mexico." And Pauline Ganz always tried to help those left unemployed by the Depression when they came to her door, often with a sandwich and a dollar bill.

Pauline's compassion was an expression of her living faith. Though later in life that faith would be tested severely, Christian teaching guided her through the Depression, and she assisted the less fortunate with an open heart. Her little girl, whom she favored and gave the nickname Ganzy-Bug, never forgot the small kindnesses dispensed by her devout Irish-Catholic mother.

The baby of the family, the most independent and adventurous of the three Ganz siblings, would venture far from Arizona during her long, fruitful, and celebrated public life. The specter of a household dogged by depression—and, later, cancer—informed Joan Ganz Cooney's own painful private life and prepared her for a string of setbacks that might have felled a lesser person.

In the summers of Joan Ganz's early elementary school years, after her father's recovery from his breakdown, the family retreated to the Hassayampa Mountain Club near Prescott, elevation 5,347 feet. That "cabin," as it was called, was set within a landscape of boulder outcroppings and ponderosa pines. It had a two-story living room with a balcony, Indian rugs, handmade rustic furniture, and a deck overlooking the Prescott National Forest. With the outbreak of World War II and the imposition of gasoline rationing, however, the Ganzes sold the summer home. That came as an especially great disappointment to Joan, for the cabin was, as she recalled, "sheer heaven" for an inquisitive, serious beanpole who was frequently sick with minor ailments.

"I was not a happy child," she said. "I was always trying to keep up with my brother and sister, and I never could be quite as good as they were. So I became a student, which they weren't. And I read a lot, which they didn't." She devoured *Anne of Green Gables*, *Gone With the Wind* (three times), and the Nancy Drew mystery series. "I would come home from school and go into a corner with a book. My mother was forever trying to get me to go outside." Cooney once told *Life* magazine[2] that her mother "was always trying to fatten me up. In those days, people thought being thin meant being unwell, though I was perfectly healthy. Her idea was to give me a good lunch and drive me back to school."

Joan was, in large measure, bookish and opinionated, "high-strung, but not nerdy. I was always reading and arguing about ideas," she said, "trying to find answers and forever being slapped down." She even took on the priests at school, questioning the catechism. "The priests were Jesuits, and they understood that I was just intellectually curious," she told a *People* magazine interviewer in 1977. "If there was an adult conversation, I moved right into the center of it." But at home, her father was unaccustomed to being challenged by a child and he was not amused.[3]

Sylvan reacted predictably: "It drove my father crazy because he didn't like intellectual women. Here was this peanut telling him he was wrong and showing less respect than his two older children. I didn't realize I sounded insubordinate. I saw myself as his peer, his friend."[4] There were times when Joan was put in her place. "If I argued with or contradicted my father, he often became enraged, leaving me hurt and puzzled."

Cooney recalled afternoons in 1938 and 1939 when her family was joined for Sunday dinner by pilot trainees from the British Royal Air Force, young men who were being readied for combat at Army Air Corps bases in Arizona. After the United States entered the war, American pilots would come for dinner, as well. "Our town was filled with armed services people," Cooney said. "War was everywhere. We listened to every Churchill speech on the radio, then every speech of Roosevelt's. My father was the neighborhood air-raid warden, and he had to go out every night and make sure all the blinds were down because Phoenix was thought to be a target with so many air force training fields around us. When I think about that period, World War II was the overriding event that turned me, and I suspect others, outward."

For young Joan, adolescence changed everything. "I just flowered," Cooney said. "I was a kind of grim, overwrought little kid, but the world's happiest adolescent. All that I was as a child suddenly became a plus. A psychiatrist once said to me, 'You're the only patient I've ever had who had a happy adolescence.'"

Breaking free from her siblings was like being reborn. Paul and Sylvia each attended ninth grade at North Phoenix High School but were sent to parochial St. Mary's High for grades ten through twelve. With no small sense of triumph, Cooney said, "They misbehaved and were sent there as punishment. After I had had a year at North High, my mother said it was time for me to transfer to St. Mary's, and I just said, 'You have *got* to be kidding.' The subject never came up again."

Coming into her own as a teen, Joan could be willful and intransigent. "My mother used to say to me, 'You want your own way at any cost,' and that was probably true. Though I don't look back and see any cost that was all that high."

She entered ninth grade in 1943, not entirely prepared for Bud Brown, a provocateur of a social studies teacher who challenged a disputatious, perspicacious, and altogether sheltered thirteen-year-old. "He was the first teacher I ever had who talked about injustice, and it absolutely inflamed me and totally changed my life," Cooney said. "At the time in Phoenix, minorities didn't have to sit in the back of the bus, but the schools were segregated and blacks had to sit up in the balcony at the movie theater. My first awareness of Jim Crow began with Turner in the 'crow's nest' at the movie house. I had taken segregation for granted, and my parents were not enlightened on the subject of race. My father liked many individual black people but he saw nothing wrong with segregation.

"I became very argumentative with him about all these issues. He was an enlightened man in that he wouldn't say, "Well, I'm going to go over to North High and find out who is teaching you.' It didn't bother him that I was getting this point of view."

Brown, a fancier of cowboy boots and Western wear, operated a weekend barn-dance center. But his worldview went well beyond the confines of the West. He used classroom time to discuss anti-Semitism in Europe, "which nobody was talking about," Cooney said.

Other teachers had provided instruction; Brown was the first to make Joan think beyond herself. "Bud would say that the only thing you can count on is change," Cooney said. "It got him—and another teacher at North Phoenix—investigated for being Communists in the 1950s."

At home, Joan's thoughts often turned to a relative in Germany, her father's first cousin, Elsie Wolf. Her letters from Berlin had depicted a horrific anti-Semitic display in the streets that most likely was Kristallnacht. Cooney said, "We knew that she was in trouble, and then my father's letters stopped being answered." It was a chilling thought for an adolescent, the idea of a blood relative being rounded up and transported to an internment camp simply for being a Jew.

It wasn't until after the war that the Red Cross informed Sylvan that his cousin had died of tuberculosis in a concentration camp.

While in high school, Joan appeared in school plays, small theater productions, and statewide drama contests. Her sights were set on Broadway, but before she entered college Sylvan squelched that plan, Cooney said. "He said he would never support me in any manner, shape, or form as an actress. 'You have got to find something else.'"

Although the refusal stung at the time, Cooney later came to see the wisdom in it. "I bless him every night for stopping me. I had a better life because of it."

Joan enrolled as a freshman at the Dominican College of San Rafael, a Catholic girls' school near San Francisco, but after a successful year transferred to the University of Arizona. "I didn't want to stay in a girls' college, and my sister was down at UA. It sounded like a lot of fun, which is what it was, a lot more fun than being in a Catholic girls' school. But I don't regret the year [at Dominican]. I had a better education in one year than I really had in the subsequent three years [at the University of Arizona]."

The sisters of Kappa Alpha Theta gave her the nickname Guts, a sobriquet that was bestowed without irony. Education major Joan Ganz was neither shy nor tentative, characteristics that made her attractive to young men on campus who were confident and secure. She briefly dated Dean Burch, whom she described as "this darling, wonderful, funny, interesting, smart man." After college, their lives would intersect in ways that neither could have imagined.

Though some of her sorority sisters married right out of college, matrimony was not one of Joan's priorities. She was similarly uninterested in finding an elementary school teaching job, which was the expected thing to do. Though she earned a B for a semester of student-teaching second-graders, "I wasn't a natural in the classroom," she confessed. "In those days, mothers said to daughters, 'Get a degree in education and get certified. If your husband dies, you will be able to get a job and be home when your children are home.'"

It was more out of a sense of adventure than defiance of her parents' wishes that newly graduated Joan Ganz decided to leave home and relocate to an entirely unfamiliar locale. Without a job, she landed in Washington, D.C., moving in with a college friend, Virginia Grose, and Virginia's mother and brother. In no time, she found a clerk-typist position at the State Department, working for a postwar program that brought Austrians and

Germans to the United States for a year of study. It was, in a sense, a reverse-flow Fulbright fellowship, a hands-across-the-water cultural exchange akin to the vaunted program that provides Americans a year of study abroad.

It was during her year in Washington that Ganz encountered another teacher who reshaped her views and intentions, the visionary Roman Catholic priest Father James Keller. In 1945, Father Keller founded the Christophers, an organization whose name is derived from the Greek word for "Christbearer." The embracing aim of the organization was to encourage believers to apply the teachings of the Gospel in everyday life.

In the early 1950s, at the peak of radio's power, Father Keller took to the airwaves to preach a message adapted from a Chinese proverb: "It's better to light one candle than to curse the darkness." This call to activism asked each individual to become a missionary within his or her profession. That notion was life altering for Joan. Father Keller was particularly keen to encourage not just Catholics but Christians of all denominations to take jobs in media, where he saw a bountiful opportunity. As his popularity spread, Keller himself became a multimedia exemplar, as author, newspaper columnist, radio host, newsletter publisher, and, ultimately, one of the first spiritual leaders to exploit television. Unlike others who would follow, Father Keller's approach was dignified, humble, and without pretense.

In 1952,[5] after "a wonderful year and one of the most fun, interesting, and memorable in my life," twenty-two-year-old Joan Ganz did an unexpected about-face, moving home to Phoenix, where she was determined to plunge into a career in the media. "Father Keller said that if idealists didn't go into media, nonidealists would," Cooney once told a reporter from *Forbes*.[6] "I walked into the *Arizona Republic* and got a job." While she had no formal training in journalism, she did have brainpower, good breeding, a well-respected surname in Phoenix, and an unbendable will. She also exuded credibility and self-confidence beyond her years. "Two weeks after I started [at the *Republic*] I got a byline. I moved up very fast."[7]

At first, Joan was assigned to write wedding announcements and social notes for the newspaper's Women's Department, often a dumping ground for female reporters back in an unenlightened age of journalism. Her weekly pay was fifty dollars. "But over time," she said, "I was given more interesting general assignments, covering events. I covered a lecture on the book *Witness* by Whittaker Chambers. After my piece appeared, Eugene Pulliam, the paper's owner and a passionate anti-Communist, called the city editor to ask who the Communist was on the women's page. Fortunately, the professor who gave the lecture called the city editor to thank him for sending such an accurate reporter. So I was off the hook," she said.

"Reporting is wonderful training because it is precise, it is detailed, and if you're good, you're getting exact quotes. I really cared about that, and that is why I did well as a reporter and later, a producer. I paid a lot of attention to detail and following through."[8]

Joan first saw television that year, at a neighbor's home. The experience left her weak in the knees, not because of the technology of the squawking box but because of who was speaking through it: a balding intellectual who was about to accept his party's nomination for president of the United States at the 1952 Democratic National Convention in Chicago. "It was the moment when I fell in love with Adlai Stevenson," Cooney recalls, still a little dreamy eyed.

After eighteen months at the *Republic*, Joan walked away from newspapering almost as quickly as she came to it, though her reporting and writing demonstrated promise. Had she persisted, she might have made an exceptional journalist, a woman who could have pushed aside gender barriers and proven herself the equal of any man in the newsroom, editor's suite, or perhaps even the publisher's office.

Instead, at twenty-three she started anew, relocating to New York, once again without any firm idea of what she might do once she got there. She moved in with Sallie Brophy, an actress friend from Phoenix who had urged her to move to Manhattan. Together they shared the top floor of a crumbling four-apartment brownstone off Beekman Place. Monthly rent was fifty dollars.

"The Brophys were the Kennedys of Arizona, a big, wealthy Irish family of eight children," Cooney said. "They had a fabulous house farther out than ours, and on Central Avenue. Big stars would come to visit in the winter, and the Brophys would be the ones to entertain them. But the Brophys themselves were glamorous. We were very close to the Brophy children because we all attended Saint Francis Xavier school together. My sister and I would spend parts of the summer on their fabulous ranch in Patagonia. I dated one of the Brophy sons when I was nineteen. My mother was still of that generation where you wanted to marry your daughters off to wealthy people. She was dying to have me marry him, making me crazy, actually."

Brophy was the near-perfect roommate, Cooney said. "She was one of my sister's and my closest friends. She attended the Royal Academy of Dramatic Art and moved back and forth between California and New York. In those days she got a lot of parts in television, and her being away so much was the reason our living together worked. The apartment had one bedroom, and when she was there, I slept in the living room."

In the 1950s, Brophy brought home directors the way ordinary people lug home groceries. Among her suitors were Sidney Lumet, Hal Prince, and Arthur Penn. Sometimes the roommates traded off, Cooney said. "I went out with Hal Prince when he produced his first Broadway show, *The Pajama Game*, and through him I met George Abbott, Richard Rodgers, Stephen Sondheim, Lena Horne, and Jerome Robbins. One night, Sallie and I went out with Spencer Tracy to the Stork Club. She was the doorway to it all, and I don't know what I would have done without her."

Penn once blithely suggested to Joan that she undergo psychoanalysis. "Everybody does [in show business]," she remembers him saying. "When I told him I couldn't afford it, he said, 'Don't worry. You'll make more money.' Then I said, 'Analysis works *that* well?' He laughed and said, 'No, you'll have to change jobs.'" With that encouragement, Cooney found a psychiatrist, someone who provided a needed safety net. "He was a real human liberationist [who] kept urging me to fly and reminding me that I didn't have to become a housewife and move to the suburbs."[9]

Brophy took Cooney along with her to the home of *New York World* executive editor Herbert Bayard Swope and his wife, Maggie.[10]

For the literary crowd that frequented the baronial estate at Sands Point, Long Island, the compound brought to mind *The Great Gatsby*, and for good reason. In his 1925 meditation on the sociology of wealth, F. Scott Fitzgerald patterned Jay Gatsby's fictional mansion after the Swope residence.

Cooney became a weekend regular at Sands Point, where on a summer's day, the Swopes might entertain a swirl of authors, statesmen, comedians, stage actors, and the wits and sages of the Algonquin Round Table. An afternoon guest list might include Averell Harriman; Robert Moses; Harpo Marx; Martin Gabel and his wife, the actress Arlene Francis; CBS founder William Paley; and his friend and chief competitor, RCA president General David Sarnoff.

At one weekend party, Maggie Swope urged Sarnoff to take notice of this new arrival in town. General, she said, "Joan is such a nice girl. You have to give her a job."

Joan, flattered and a bit embarrassed, suggested that she might be useful in the press department at RCA. "In those days, publicity departments were always hiring people who had been on newspapers," Cooney recalled.

"Fine," Sarnoff said. "Come interview at RCA."

A position quickly opened up for the fresh-faced friend-of-a-friend of the Swopes.[11] "My path was always marked by encounters with strong men," Cooney said. "No one could understand why the General had brought me in, and rumors attended me. The General had a twinkle in his eye, and he was rumored to be a ladies' man. And like so many great men, he was a real presence when he walked into a room. Men like that emanate some sort of electrical current. Everything stopped.

"But I was this innocent—a Candide, really—who was being thought of as an extremely sophisticated, manipulative, ambitious person, probably sleeping with the General."

Cooney wrote press releases to churn up coverage of Sarnoff's frequent speeches, many of which addressed advances in communications technology and the advent of color television. But while she may have cashed a paycheck from RCA during her early years in New York, it didn't provide enough earning power to actually buy a television, the very product she was paid to promote. When she needed to see something on TV, she borrowed a key to a downstairs neighbor's apartment. "Clyde was out most nights, and certainly wasn't around in the daytime," she recalls. "He'd say, 'When I'm not home, look at whatever you want.' So I started going down. It was not so long ago in my life that I had been an actress, so I still cared a lot about drama."

Her next professional move was, in essence, a company transfer, moving after nine months from the more corporate public relations responsibilities of the parent company to RCA's bourgeoning broadcasting wing, NBC Television. She wrote press releases about the network's frothy lineup of daily serials, euphemistically renamed "day dramas" by NBC's visionary programming chief, Sylvester "Pat" Weaver.[12]

Corporate parsimony and rigidity explain, in part, why Joan did not ultimately make a career of it at NBC. When she transferred over from RCA, company rules limited her new salary at the network to no more than 15 percent higher than what she had been making for the parent company. It did not take much sleuthing for Joan to discover that she "was making half of what everybody else was making [at NBC] and having a hard time [with my] living expenses." Her boss, Sid Igus, said, "I get it, but there's nothing I can do about it except to help you get out of here."

That he did. With a phone call to a friend at United States Steel Corporation, Joan Ganz had another one of those star-kissed employment moments, walking into a publicity job for the *United States Steel Hour*, CBS's twice-monthly live anthology series that won an Emmy for Best

Dramatic Series in 1955. The steel company itself, not CBS, had hired Joan—at a substantial raise in pay—to promote the show.

It was a dream job, she said later, and one that in time provided ample free time to pursue political causes. "I had done some volunteer work for the Democratic reform movement in New York that was led by Eleanor Roosevelt, Adlai Stevenson, and Herbert Lehman, and I would go to this political club, the Lexington Club, to write releases for them. But time still hung heavy on my hands. So I called a friend at the Theater Guild, a producer of *United States Steel Hour*. I said, 'There has to be someone in New York who could use a volunteer doing something interesting.' And he said, 'William Phillips of the *Partisan Review* could use some help.'"

In its history, the political and literary quarterly had provided a forum for T. S. Eliot, George Orwell, and other notable minds. "I was pulled—in my late twenties—into this incredible world. I helped William put on a fund-raising event at Columbia that included Norman Mailer, Mary McCarthy, and Lionel Trilling.

"This was incredibly heady stuff for me, far headier than the crowd at Sands Point. It was the New York intellectuals arguing, and I was a fly on the wall listening. It provided me with an education that was richer than anything I could have had at the best graduate school."

Not everyone from the *Partisan Review* crowd immediately embraced Cooney. "Television was a no-no among intellectuals," she said, "and Jason Epstein, a great editor at Random House of that time, had total contempt for me. Not only was I in television, but I was doing publicity for television. I mean, what could be lower?"

As the years passed though, Epstein and Cooney would forge a deep friendship, marked by wide avenues of mutual respect and a shared interest in the characters inhabiting *Sesame Street*.

At around 9:00 a.m on Monday, June 18, 1956, Sylvan Ganz reluctantly picked up the telephone receiver after repeated rings. It was just four days after he had returned home from a ten-day stay at Camelback Sanatorium in Phoenix. He had checked himself in, burdened by another bout of depression.

Joan's married sister, Sylvia Houle, was on the line, concern in her voice. Sylvia lived only streets away from her parents and was checking on her father's readjustment to being home. Sylvan kept the conversation short. "I'll see you later," he said.[13]

At a seemingly robust seventy-one, Sylvan had become an agent for Pacific Mutual Life Insurance Company and a director for the Butane

Corporation, following his retirement from the First National Bank of Arizona. Associates hailed him as a shrewd and judicious banker whose leadership guided the institution during years of steady growth. Ever civic-minded, he had also served as president of the Phoenix Chamber of Commerce and of the Arizona Bankers Association.

Pauline had left the house that morning to swim at the Phoenix Country Club, the place her husband endured more than accepted.

When she returned home just before 9:30, she discovered an empty shotgun scabbard on Sylvan's bed. Near panic, she set off to find her difficult, fragile, tormented husband.

Pauline discovered him in the backyard, dead by his own hand.

Across the continent in New York, her father's violent choice cut deeply into Joan Ganz. "I really had a terrible time for the next eight or ten months of being able to face what had happened," she recalled. "I just kept pushing it down. I was having dizzy spells and claustrophobia, headaches and neurological problems. I couldn't go to the theater. I couldn't get on a subway. I was able to go to work and go home, but I went out very little because of this kind of physical illness that overcame me. I felt like a marionette whose strings had been severed.

"I stayed in therapy and finally it got through," she said. Over long months, her strength and equilibrium were restored, and she emerged "a much strengthened person. My father's death was the event that most changed my life in terms of my inner self. I evolved in quite a different way after that."

Chapter Three

The stage manager barked "Ten seconds!" as Bob Keeshan found his mark, inhaled deeply, and smoothed the deep white-trimmed pockets of his navy blue jacket. It was Monday, October 3, 1955, and CBS was going live with the first episode of *Captain Kangaroo*, a hastily mounted breakfast-hour confection for young viewers. In contrast to the low-budget, locally produced cartoon caravans that defined much of morning television for children in that era, *Captain Kangaroo* would be a welcome departure. Its slower pace and idealism would reflect the better sensibilities of Keeshan, who was not only the series' star but at twenty-eight was its wise-beyond-his-years cocreator.

What mattered on the morning of the premiere for CBS programming executives and advertising salesmen was whether the new show would provide a ratings bounce. Though morning television had not yet evolved into the ferocious battleground it would one day become, network jobs were won and lost on the basis of which viewers—and how many of them— were tuned to programs at the top of any hour. The boys on the business side were hoping cereal eaters would flock to the TV set in such numbers that CBS would crush its competition at 8:00 a.m.

Applying the old show business adage, "If you can't beat 'em, steal 'em," CBS had convinced Keeshan to defect from *Tinker's Workshop*, a local children's show that had been hammering the network's New York City affiliate, WCBS, in the Nielsen morning ratings. Its deal with Keeshan and his business partner, Jack Miller, went something like this: Come up with a show pronto and we'll hand over a juicy plum of a time slot to you, with millions of kiddie eyeballs staring at you. We'll set you up at Lieder- kranz Hall on Fifty-eighth Street and Lexington Avenue, the same studio where those daytime-serial weepers *Secret Storm* and *Search for Tomorrow* originate. We'll need you to do two live shows every morning, five days a week. The first will be at 8:00 a.m. for Eastern affiliates. The second, at 9:00, will be for the Midwest. We'll give you forty seconds to pee between shows, *har, har, har*. And don't worry about the kids in California. We have a plan. They'll see the show on film delay, a couple of weeks late.[1]

CBS moved quickly, giving Keeshan and Miller only nine days to produce a pilot. With little time to deliberate, the pair went with gut impulses, relying on the basic formula that had worked so well on *Tinker's*

Workshop, which featured Keeshan costumed as an elderly Alpine toy maker. He would play a kindly older gentleman as host on the new show, the kind of courteous soul one might encounter on a sea voyage or train trip.[2] The Captain, as he would be called, would sport a bowl-cut gray wig, a bushy mustache, and walrus sideburns. Over a white shirt and black tie, he would don a four-button, three-quarter-length coat with a carnation flourish at the lapel. The deep pockets were piped in white. "When an artist drew the character as we described him, somebody said, 'Hey, he looks like a kangaroo. Hence *Captain Kangaroo*,'" Keeshan once told *TV Guide*.[3]

Each morning, the Captain would unlock a door to the knickknack-decorated Treasure House, "private wonderland of childhood," as described in a CBS press release.[4] Events both prosaic and fantastical could occur within and outside the Treasure House set. Mr. Green Jeans, a neighboring farmer and sidekick played by Hugh "Lumpy" Brannum, would drop by to show the Captain—and the "boys and girls at home"—a basket of baby chicks or a goat tethered to a rope. A slumbering grandfather clock could blink to life and share a riddle, or a life-sized teddy bear could dance around the studio. The Captain could read aloud from a storybook, the way a father or grandfather might at bedtime. Or he might dicker with a hand puppet named Bunny Rabbit, a mute, shrewd schemer in tiny eyeglasses who always found a way to scam a stash of fresh carrots from the Captain. Or Mr. Moose, a gentle punster-prankster with a voice that sounded as if the puppeteer who was manipulating him, Gus Allegretti, had been huffing helium, would find ingenious ways to rain Ping-Pong balls on the Captain's head. Anything could happen and did, within certain polite limits. Even before its premiere, CBS promoted *Captain Kangaroo* as "the gentlest children's show on the air."

Keeshan had all but fallen into show business. Two weeks prior to his eighteenth birthday, on Flag Day, 1945, he had been inducted into the United States Marine Corps Reserves and dispatched to Parris Island. "The marines were all training for the assault on the 'home islands' of Japan, which we knew we would be part of in a few short months. The atomic age changed all that as my boot camp days wound down," Keeshan said.[5]

To his great good fortune after being discharged, Keeshan was rehired by NBC, where, as a high school page, he had earned $13.50 a week for ushering radio audiences to their seats at the network studios. As part of his new responsibilities as a receptionist for NBC Radio, Keeshan had to scavenge research material for Bob Smith's chatty morning show. During a segment called "That Wonderful Year," Smith would sit at a piano and sing popular favorites from days past, using a script woven from Keeshan's notes.

At the time, Keeshan had been taking prelaw night courses at Fordham University, rebounding from an academic slide in high school following his mother's sudden death at age forty-five. A school guidance counselor, Gertrude Farley, interceded and "demanded that I find my way once again," Keeshan recalled. "Miss Farley saved my life."[6] In high school, Keeshan's pleasant voice and interests in broadcasting led him to produce plays over the school's public address system.

He abandoned a path toward law in 1947 after meeting Smith, a wavy-haired charmer who had leaped to popularity in his native Buffalo before landing a morning music-and-talk show in New York City. It was an answer to *Arthur Godfrey Time* on CBS, a variety show lorded over by a star-making, ukulele-plinking host who became a radio colossus, then later conquered TV. Smith's audience was minuscule compared to Godfrey's.

But Smith was also host of *Triple B Ranch*, a hit Saturday morning radio show for kids that aired on NBC's New York affiliate, WEAF. The three Bs in the self-referential title stood for Big Brother Bob. Affecting the voice of a rube ranch hand, Smith greeted listeners at the top of the show with an exuberant, "Oh, ho, ho, howdy doody!"[7]

Capitalizing on the radio show's popularity, Smith's agent, Martin Stone, sniffed out a possible move to television. NBC, hungry for programming and aware of the fan base for *Triple B Ranch*, bought Stone's pitch. Conceptualized for television as a cross between a one-ring circus and a Wild West show, the program got its start on the six stations that composed NBC's eastern television network: New York, Boston, Philadelphia, Washington, Baltimore, and Schenectady, epicenter of research and development for General Electric, manufacturer of the television picture tube.

The show's title was changed to *Howdy Doody* in recognition of its lead character, a freckled cowboy marionette that lived with a menagerie of characters, both human and wooden, in the video village of Doodyville, USA. Within a year, *Howdy Doody* would become television's first megahit children's show and a rollicking commercial success. By 1955, boxcars of *Howdy*-branded merchandise—hand puppets and marionettes, moccasins, RCA phonograph records, comic books, marbles, sleeping bags, cookie jars, and a small library of Little Golden Books—had found their way into display cases in toy stores, five-and-dimes, pharmacies, and neighborhood markets.

Howdy's impact on consumer culture was later astutely measured by

Miami Herald humorist extraordinaire Dave Barry in his book *Dave Barry Turns 50*: "We sang the *Howdy Doody* song, and we nagged our parents incessantly to buy the many items of Howdy Doody merchandise advertised on it. They could have advertised the official Howdy Doody edition of all sixteen volumes of *Remembrance of Things Past* by Marcel Proust in the original French, and we would have *begged* our parents for it."[8]

Perhaps the most extreme demonstration of the character's popularity came in the election year of 1948, when the show's writer, Eddie Kean, got the idea to mount a presidential campaign for Howdy. Smith recalled the stunt in a special issue of *People* magazine in the summer of 1989:

> We asked the kids to write in for buttons if they were going to vote for Howdy—send in a self-addressed stamped envelope and we'll send you a button. . . . I think that in the whole six cities [where *Howdy Doody* aired] there weren't more than 60,000 television sets. The response was overwhelming, like 150,000 returns after one mention on the air, and we had only ordered 10,000 buttons. We had no idea it would be that successful, but it turned out everybody was over at the neighbor's house watching *The Howdy Doody Show*. I thought, "Oh my God, I'm either fired or I've got to dig down and get more money for more buttons."[9]

On November 14, 1948, a week after Harry Truman's upset victory over Republican rival Thomas Dewey, *New York Times* writer Jack Gould[10] hailed the newly elected "president of the boys and girls of America," perhaps the most successful write-in candidate in American history:

> No mistake about it, it's Howdy Doody time. With a platform favoring double ice-cream sodas for a dime, school once a year, and plenty of movies, the earnest young boy who is the favorite of the Peanut Gallery finished third behind Truman and Dewey, racking up ten times the number of votes accorded [Progressive Party candidate Henry] Wallace.
>
> Howdy is reigning supreme on television each afternoon at 5:30 as he prances before the NBC cameras under the knowing guidance of Bob Smith. . . . In all the wonderful make-believe of puppet imagery [Howdy] is still the first exclusive and most amiable creation of video-land.
>
> Mr. Doody, as he is never called, is the handiwork almost exclusively of Mr. Smith, who in a twelve-month period has exhibited a gift for dealing with children that is truly phenomenal. Previously identified only as the proprietor of an early morning chatter and song show à la [Arthur] Godfrey, he proved upon exposure to Howdy to be that rarest of souls: a

man who avoids any hint of condescension toward the younger generation and makes the boys and girls feel partners in the spirited high jinks of
his wooden alter ego.

Thanks to Mr. Smith, those high jinks are sparked by one of the most
imaginative minds in broadcasting. For *The Howdy Doody Show* is blessed
with incredibly superb gadgets and, most importantly, a point of view
which always is wholesome yet never stuffy. . . .

Interlarded with the engaging nonsense and pure fantasy, however, is
an astonishing amount of information and education for the youngsters.
Last Tuesday the visitor to the show was an air force colonel, and of course
that old bothersome Mr. Y wanted to know what made an airplane get up
in the air. The resultant explanation was clear, succinct, and enlighten-
ing, even for an adult.

Or take Howdy's heroic victory over Mr. X in the election. Without
ever saying so, Mr. Smith offered what was a primer in democracy,
explaining how to mark a ballot and the rules of an election contest in a
free country. But it was all done with gaiety and harmless suspense so that
it did not seem like education at all.

On the show, Keeshan was at first a combination propmaster–child
wrangler, part gofer, part babysitter. Dressed in a smart blazer, he dutifully
dispensed prizes to the kiddies. But after donning a clown costume in one
episode, to the audience's glee, he became Clarabell Hornblow, a baggy-
pants prankster who had three thatches of hair sprouting from his pow-
dered dome, two above his ears, and one above the cranium. His mirthful
makeup choice, highlighted by an upturned grin and arched eyebrows, was
the antithesis of Weary Willy, Emmett Kelly's downcast, heavy-bearded
hobo clown, so popular in the 1940s. Like Willy, though, Clarabell was
mute. To make a point, he'd squeeze the rubber bulb of a bicycle-style horn
belted to his waist, honking in a style reminiscent of Harpo Marx. Clarabell's fizzy answer to most any comedic impasse was to douse a cast member
with a shower of seltzer from a spray canister, although once, as a special
guest on NBC's prime-time comedy cavalcade, *Texaco Star Theater*, Keeshan (as Clarabell) hit Milton Berle right in the kisser with a cream pie.

Second only to Berle's live show, *Howdy Doody* was the hottest ticket
in television. You had to know someone who knew someone who knew
someone to snag a ticket for your child. Smith told *People* magazine that
"Forty Peanut Gallery tickets were issued a day, and a sponsor got ten. I got
four, and each cast member got two or four a week. The station relations

department got all the rest. So actually, hardly anyone who wrote in for a ticket ever got one."[11]

On a half-dozen occasions or so, Sam Gibbon, a matinee-idol-handsome NBC production staff member, was assigned to keep an eye on the Peanut Gallery. He was, to say the least, overqualified. A Princeton grad and newly repatriated Rhodes Scholar, Gibbon had completed a study of children's theater in Europe before landing at NBC Studios. That his standards for children's entertainment were highly refined, while Buffalo Bob's were not, meant that Gibbon found *Howdy Doody* a deplorable waste of time. "The show was an abortion," he said. "The kids would come in dressed in their Sunday best and excited beyond measure, and they'd always leave cranky and crying. The mothers never understood why, but the reason was Smith. Before airtime, the kids would be saying, 'Where's Buffalo Bob?' When he finally came on, he would ignore them completely, except when he was on camera, and even then, he would sort of shove the kids aside to make room for himself in the Peanut Gallery. One time when a kid said something to him, he spun around and sort of kicked in the general direction of where the boy was sitting. Smith's moccasin flew off and skimmed up over the heads of the Peanut Gallery."

Years after *Howdy Doody* had completed its thirteen-season run (it ended September 24, 1960, after 2,343 shows), Smith admitted to some appalling off-camera behavior, citing two examples of his impatience with— and hostility toward—his overexuberant young fans.

One day I was doing a Tootsie Roll commercial. And this little kid kept interrupting with, "Buffalo Bob! Buffalo Bob!" I couldn't stop because it was all live back then. Finally, I turned around and said, "Yes, sonny, what is it?" He said, "I can't eat Tootsie Rolls 'cause I'm allergic to chocolate!" I went on with the show and thought, "Well, there goes our client." I was tempted to smack kids like that.

[Another] day, I was doing a commercial for Kellogg's Rice Krispies. Every time the camera would be on me with this box of cereal, this little kid behind me would say hello and wave his hand right in front of my face. When the commercial was over, I was so angry at this kid that I took the box and swung it around to the left—I just wanted to hit him in the face a little, to remind him not to do that anymore. As I did, he ducked, and the sweetest little girl got the box right in her face and got a bloody nose. The camera jiggled up and down because the cameraman was shaking, he laughed so hard. It looked like we had an earthquake in the studio.[12]

Gibbon, then a lowly studio hand, would later write and produce for three of the most acclaimed children's shows in television history: *Captain Kangaroo, Sesame Street,* and *The Electric Company.* He said many times that he learned a lot about what *not* to do on television from watching Buffalo Bob Smith.

NBC also was home to network television's first series targeted—and marketed—to preschoolers. Its history reads like a cautionary tale about advertising's corruptive influence on even the best-intentioned efforts of using television to teach.

One day in 1952 an arts editor at the *New York Times* answered the phone, only to hear a strange admission from Jules Herbuveaux, program director at NBC Television. "We've got a new show over here that's either the worst show we ever pitched up or the best," he said. "Right now, I just don't know."[13]

Days earlier, without any promotion or advance notice, the network added a children's show to its midmorning lineup, one that was initially produced at NBC's affiliate station in Chicago, WNBQ. On the occasion of its first day on the network, a cranky cameraman offered his sour assessment of the proceedings. "Where did they come up with *this* one?" he groused. Over on camera two, his buddy cracked, "This old gal won't last out the week—if that long."[14]

Though out of earshot, that old gal could decipher every word. Not only was Dr. Frances Horwich an accomplished educator, she also was a master lip-reader, a skill honed over twenty years in the classroom. And, like most teachers, she had grown eyes in the back of her head. Nothing got past her.

Within a matter of weeks, Dr. Horwich—as Miss Frances—would become a household name in the twenty-one major markets where the program aired. Miss Frances opened the show by ringing a handbell, like a teacher summoning students to a little red schoolhouse. That prompted the three-year-old-daughter of producer Reinald Werrenrath Jr. to suggest the title *Ding Dong School.* It stuck.

Billed as the "Nursery School of the Air," *Ding Dong School* was just that, a busy twenty-five minutes of stories and activities for three- to five-year-olds. The final five minutes of the half-hour show were directed to parents, after the children were dispatched to go find them. Miss Frances would then recap what the children had learned that day, like a teacher on back-to-school night.

NBC began receiving sacks of mail from pleased parents, sometimes as many as a thousand letters a day. *New York Times* writer Larry Wolters marveled at the phenomenon. "It's the only program NBC has ever devised that wins practically a hundred percent acclaim. . . . [Miss Frances] brings [children] a wide variety of experiences, through action, scenes, and events, which most mothers seem to be just too busy to give the youngsters."[15]

Dr. Horwich, chairman of the Education Department at Chicago's Roosevelt College, accomplished nothing less than inventing interactive children's television, five decades before *Blue's Clues*. Not surprisingly, her method combined equal parts show and tell. During activity segments, she would ask children to join along as she cut construction paper into five puzzle pieces or planted radish seeds in a Dixie Cup or made a doll from pipe cleaners and a shoehorn. The demonstrations moved at a child's pace, and Miss Frances paused frequently to encourage and question viewers, addressing them as if they were seated right in front of her, which, in a sense, they were.

At times, Miss Frances would even carry on as if the children were actually answering her. She would open a Monday broadcast: "How was your weekend? Did you go for a ride in the car? Oh! You went to see grandmother." Then, with a little gasp of surprise, she'd say, "Your cousin Billy was there! And his sister Susie?" To the adult ear, it was fruitcake nutty, but kids by the thousands began talking back to their sets.

The show's popularity spawned a line of *Ding Dong School* products, including long-playing albums on the RCA label (*Fun with Instruments*), a small library of Golden Books (*Your Friend the Policeman*), and finger-painting sets. It was reported that eight hundred offers were considered to extend the branded line of merchandise.

While commercialism built and sustained the show, it ultimately also eroded its credibility. For inasmuch as Miss Frances was a persuasive teacher, she also was a shameless huckster for *Ding Dong School*'s sponsors. Her live commercials for breakfast cereals, vitamins, and other consumables—along with her plugs for *Ding Dong School* products—were woven into the show and directed at children: "When you're going to the store, you help [mother] find the brand-new Wheaties box. I know you will!"

Critic Jack Gould gave Dr. Horwich quite a lecture in 1955. In a blistering column in the *Times*, he questioned the propriety of testimonial vitamin ads, re-creating one for his readers.

"You take [vitamins] every morning like I do?" Dr. Horwich inquired. "I hope so." Then came the demonstration. Out of the bottle she took two pills and put them on a cardboard plate. "They're a very pretty red color," said Dr. Horwich, later adding: "They're small. They're so easy to swallow."

First and foremost, there is the simple matter of safety. . . . Secondly, it is not for television to decide if tots do or do not need pills. Whether a child has a vitamin deficiency is better determined by a parent after consultation with a physician rather than the National Broadcasting Company.

Despite such criticism, in 1953 *Ding Dong School* won a George Foster Peabody Award for Outstanding Children's Program.[16] NBC nevertheless dropped the show after two years on the network in favor of a new game show called *The Price Is Right*. Stung by the cancellation, Dr. Horwich quit her position as NBC's supervisor for children's programming. "With the lack of teachers and shortage of schools, many boys and girls are attending school on a half-day basis," she said. "*Ding Dong School* filled a need."

Dr. Horwich retained the rights to *Ding Dong School*, which continued in syndication until 1965.

In 1952, after a tiff with Buffalo Bob, Keeshan ended his stint as Clarabell. The former page was cut loose, Clarabell was recast, and that was that. A year later, Keeshan resurfaced as Corny the Clown on *Time for Fun*, a local New York lunchtime show produced at WABC. Corny, less manic and mischievous than Clarabell, wore a bowler hat, a floppy tie, and a wide-striped jacket. From a park bench on the set, he would talk sweetly into the camera to the kids at home, his panting cocker spaniel Pudgy (a Keeshan family pet) perched on his lap. In 1954, Keeshan's character repertoire expanded again with *Tinker's Workshop*, which consistently won its early time slot in the weekly ratings, beating out news and information shows on rival stations.

If the local cartoon shows of the 1950s were the video equivalent of a bowl of Sugar Crisp with a chocolate-milk chaser, *Tinker's Workshop* was Irish oatmeal topped with a sensible sprinkle of cinnamon. It offered comfort, warmth, and reassurance to young viewers, some of whom were fastening their galoshes for school while younger siblings were settling in for a day with stay-at-home mom. Keeshan sensed he was on to something with his more soothing approach, one in which the host behaved as a welcomed guest might in the viewer's home. He quietly won over concerned mommies with his low-key tone and aversion to mayhem.

In 1954, the same year *Tinker's Workshop* came to local TV, WABC also launched *Uncle Lumpy's Cabin*, a half-hour program built around the multiple talents of Lumpy Brannum, an affable, lantern-jawed, bass-fiddleplunking professional musician turned children's performer. Famed orchestra and glee-club leader Fred Waring had featured Brannum, a small-town strummer and brass instrumentalist, on his popular radio program in the 1940s. Brannum, who had demonstrated a gift for mimicry, narration, and song, was given a few minutes on each radio broadcast to spin a folksy installment of *Little Orley*, the rural adventures of a farm boy with "hair the color of strawberry soda and a smile that could put the sun to shame."

When Keeshan jumped to CBS, he brought Brannum along to play the Captain's sidekick, the amiable agriculturalist Mr. Green Jeans. With a wide-brimmed straw hat, plaid shirt, and denim overalls, Brannum's character might have been Little Orley's uncle. In time, the Keeshan-Brannum duo would be to television what team teaching was to the classroom. Though neither had any training in education or child development, they both had sound pedagogical instincts and unshakable convictions about how young children should be entertained and instructed. Daily topics touched on basic science and nature, literature, music, art, geography, civics, and health. At the end of each broadcast, the Captain would often remind viewers to brush their teeth and to remember that it was "another Be Good to Mother Day."

Naturals before the camera, Keeshan and Brannum spoke to the "boys and girls" (never kids) with nary a hint of condescension, and they never lost sight of the vulnerability of their young audience. *Captain Kangaroo* thus became an especially valuable antidote to the commercial onslaught that was children's television in the 1950s and '60s—even as CBS kept continually trying to pull the rug out from under the Captain.

Until the frantic weeks leading up to the *Captain Kangaroo* debut, the show had no cast, no costumes, no set, not even a fully realized concept. What it did have was a time slot and a network hungering to claw out of the ratings rain cellar. In New York, CBS was dead last in a three-way ratings race and losing ground. The network was about to dump *The Morning Show*, a mélange of news and entertainment that, despite significant effort and expense, never captured the kind of attention enjoyed by its chief rival, the quirky morning mix called *Today* on NBC, hosted by Dave Garroway, a cool conversationalist imported from Chicago.

The Morning Show was originally built around the talents of Walter Cronkite, an Edward R. Murrow protégé from CBS News. As a United Press (UP) wire service reporter during World War II, Cronkite had parachuted into Holland with the 101st Airborne, flown along on bombing missions over Germany, and covered the Allied invasion on D-day. During the war, Murrow had tried unsuccessfully to persuade Cronkite to leave UP for CBS. But in 1950, Cronkite accepted a second offer from Murrow, a decision that ultimately led to a vaunted perch in broadcast journalism history.

On *The Morning Show*, Cronkite took time to discuss the day's events with Charlemagne, a lion puppet manipulated by Bil Baird, who appeared on early television with his puppeteer wife, Cora. In *A Reporter's Life*, Cronkite's 1996 autobiography, the newsman wrote: "A puppet can render opinions on people and things that a human commentator would not feel free to utter. It was one of the highlights of the show and I was, and am, proud of it." (For one teen viewer in Hyattsville, Maryland, watching Cronkite trade quips with a puppet was great sport. Young Jimmy Henson filed away the idea.)

Cronkite was succeeded in 1954 by thirty-six-year-old Jack Paar, a witty radio raconteur and movie actor who had been under contract with Howard Hughes's RKO Pictures. In 1955, Dick Van Dyke, a thirty-year-old comic from Danville, Illinois, joined *The Morning Show*.

In retrospect, if television titans Walter Cronkite, Jack Paar, and Dick Van Dyke couldn't move the ratings needle, euthanizing *The Morning Show* might have been the merciful decision. But that's not how the miffed network news staff at CBS viewed the situation. To them, waving a white flag at their *Today* competitors at Rockefeller Center was crushing and humiliating. For years to come, wounded news executives would seethe at this decision and vow to get back in the early morning game, an animus that plastered a target on Keeshan's back for almost all of his years at the network.

But on the morning of the new children's show's debut, as the announcer intoned, "Boys and girls, CBS Television presents Captain Kangaroo and his Treasure House," Keeshan had a geometrically expanded audience to serve and a business opportunity to exploit. Up came the musical theme, "Puffin' Billy," an obscure British instrumental piece written about a steam engine that Keeshan had snagged at the eleventh hour from a transcription library. Its playful opening bars provided a musical complement to accompany the Captain through the Treasure House threshold, an eventful stroll, to be sure.

Children took to the show in droves, parents hailed it, and at least one critic cheered. A *New York Times* review, written by radio and television editor John P. Shanley, praised "the delightful artistry of a television performer named Bob Keeshan" for a program that delivered "civilized and absorbing fun" to weekday mornings. "Not only does it keep little ones occupied, but it also does so without being noisy."[17]

By a quirk of fate, on the same day as the *Captain Kangaroo* debut, a highly anticipated show for school-age kids premiered on ABC's afternoon lineup. Jack Gould's review in the next morning's *Times* fairly boiled over with agitation.

Walt Disney's long-awaited afternoon show for children, *The Mickey Mouse Club*, had its premiere yesterday on Channel 7. Hopeful parents, who had assumed that Mr. Disney would bring about a long-needed revolution in adolescent TV programming, can only keep their fingers crossed. His debut bordered on the disastrous.

Not only was the opening show roughly on a par with any number of existing displays of juvenile precocity, but Mr. Disney and the American Broadcasting Company went commercial to a degree almost without precedent. . . . This viewer cannot recall ever having seen a children's program—or an adult's, for that matter—that was quite as commercial as Mr. Disney's, which is easily the new season's most distressing news. Apparently, even a contemporary genius is not immune to the virus of video.

Jon Stone approached a typewriter in the same way that a concert pianist approached a Steinway.

With a theatrical flourish, he snatched a fresh sheet of paper, fed it through the roller, lined the margins, cracked his knuckles, rubbed his hands, clapped once, and began.

One morning in 1955, not long after the *Captain Kangaroo* debut, Stone's hunting and pecking was impossible to ignore, as he was not so much tapping at the keys as he was attacking them, with percussion and purpose. An audience of sorts gathered outside the Olivetti showroom on Fifth Avenue to watch his performance.

With a forecast of fair skies, the typewriter company had proceeded with its plan to place a demonstration model outdoors, where it was bolted to a pedestal. Most who gave it a try pounded out high school typing-instruction inanities, but not Stone. He was furiously cranking out his résumé.

A self-described jack-of-all-trades, Stone had a well-deserved reputation for sidestepping calamity. He was doing just that as the minutes wound down toward a job interview at CBS Television and, possibly, the break of a lifetime. It would take all the luck and pluck a guy could muster to duplicate the résumé he had left behind in his apartment on West Fifteenth Street, six subway stops behind him.

Recently disentangled from a brief marriage and fresh out of the master's program at Yale Drama School, he was trying to make his way as an actor in New York, settling for walk-on parts in TV dramas and a commercial here and there. Prior to relocating to Manhattan, he had enjoyed a season of summer stock at a non-Equity theater on Cape Cod. While there, he crossed paths with a musician who would also soon relocate to New York. "I was directing a production of *Dream Girl*, a light little comedy which called for something like fifteen scene changes. In our tiny little theater there was limited machinery for segueing effortlessly from one set to another, and I desperately needed some entre'acte music to cover the transitions. One of the actresses in the company remembered that a friend of hers, a seventeen-year-old Harvard freshman, was playing cocktail piano across town at the Coonamessett Inn. She introduced me to Joe Raposo. He sat at his piano and asked how long each set change took, what happened at the close of the previous scene and what was the mood at the beginning of the next one. I started the tape recorder and Joe improvised a series of little compositions, each designed to lead the audience delicately out of one scene and into the next, and each precisely timed to cover the scenery change. I was blown away. He made it up on the spot."

By midautumn, the hard realities of competing for parts in New York had begun to sink in for Stone, who had yearned to live among the proto-beatniks of Greenwich Village. Then as now, it was a haven for performers, poets, painters, and street philosophers. Only one barrier separated him from moving into a blessed bohemian roost in the Village: a critical shortage of folding money in his pockets. And so, in the grand tradition of artsy immigrants to Manhattan, Stone dropped his bags in a less desirable neighborhood. His monthly rent was fifty-five dollars, and his fifth-floor walk-up had all the cold running water a guy could want. Beyond that, tenants were never at a loss for company. (In his hilarious and poignant unpublished memoir, Stone estimated the building had four thousand residents: "Me, about 10 mice, and 3,989 cockroaches.")[18]

That morning Jon Stone was on his way to meet Lou Stone—no relation, to his regret—a TV executive with the power to jump-start an eager young man's career. CBS had appointed him to oversee a two-track training program meant to develop producers and directors, and word had it that Ivy Leaguers and graduates of other well-regarded northeastern schools had a leg up.

Jon figured he had two check marks beside his name already, because he could boast of a bachelor's degree from Williams College, along with a Master of Fine Arts from Yale Drama School in New Haven, Connecticut, where he was raised.

CBS needed quick studies, men with theater backgrounds who had at least a basic understanding of stagecraft, lighting, sets, direction, costumes, and dealing with highly combustible egos. Another check.

He'd heard Lou Stone quickly weeded out candidates who would turn up their noses at a first assignment in the mailroom. There would be no special favors, and the assignments would become increasingly rigorous as trainees familiarized themselves with the production-process steps, in ascending order of importance.

That made perfect sense to Jon, who was not averse to toil and was almost born to be in that CBS training program. Stone had a musician's ear, an artist's eye (he had drawing talent and took photography seriously), and a bricklayer's stamina, despite a childhood bout of spina bifida that kept him out of the draft.

He blended well with people in show business, even—and maybe especially—with the oft-cantankerous union tradesmen offstage. Less a dreamer than a doer, Stone accomplished things, with energy, flair, and great good humor.

Though he had no television production experience, Stone sensed there was a place for him in the emerging entertainment field, and his desire to be a part of it was ignited after visiting Bob Myhrum, a Yale acquaintance, on the set of *The Robert Q. Lewis Show*, a live variety program broadcast each weekday from Maxine Elliot's Theater on Thirty-ninth Street. Myhrum, a bear of a man who had completed his studies at Yale before Stone and was already moving up the ranks in the CBS training program, was Robert Q's stage manager, and reveling in it.

It was almost unimaginably exciting to be in the theater as airtime neared. Stone recalled the moment in his memoir. "As I absorbed the electric atmosphere I realized that I was being drawn in minute by minute into its magnetic field."

When the end credits rolled, Stone glanced at his watch in disbelief. How could thirty minutes pass like ten? He grabbed Myhrum and they went off together. Over coffee, Myhrum explained the process of getting a shot at the training program. It was a simple game, he said. He needed to win over this guy Lou Stone.

That he did was a life-altering event for Stone and, eventually, nearly everyone connected with *Sesame Street*.

Stone joined *Captain Kangaroo* as a newly hired production assistant in the show's second month on the air. By December his fingers had turned purple from cranking script pages off the drum of a mimeograph machine, that fiendish mechanical duplicator of the 1950s and '60s rendered obsolete by the photocopier. He also had been assigned to mail a signed photograph to every child who sent a Christmas card to Captain Kangaroo. Stone recalled, "Keeshan had made up a card, on one side of which was a picture of the Captain holding up a baby lamb, and on the other side was a message saying, 'Dear friend, The little lamb and I thought you might like this picture of us. Sincerely.' All that was left to add was the Captain's signature. I must have written 'Captain Kangaroo' five thousand times that December. I thought my purple hand would fall off."

As much as Stone disliked the office detail as a PA, he reveled in the time spent in the studio. "I was transfixed," he said. "There was an energy and attitude and sense of shared purpose, and in that particular studio a delicious, dangerous, pungent sense of humor."

In his memoir, Stone related an example of what went on behind the cameras, describing a calamity involving incompatible mammals who had lodged at the Treasure House one murderous night.

The animal suppliers had left the next morning's animal visitors on the set overnight. In one cage were two spider monkeys and in another were two raccoons named Robbie and Rosie. Unfortunately, the cages were left too close together and at some point during the night the two raccoons, reaching through the mesh of the cages, caught the monkeys and killed them.

The carnage in the morning was horrible. The 'coons had eaten the monkeys' arms, and we were distraught. But the show had to go on, and on cue, Mr. Green Jeans brought the two raccoons out to show them to the audience. Now normally Keeshan used the animal spots for a cigarette break. He would welcome Mr. Green Jeans as Lumpy brought on the animal of the day, then wait for a close-up of the little visitor to say, "Tell us about it, Mr. Green Jeans." That was Lumpy's cue to fill for two or three minutes while Bob wandered off to smoke and joke with the stagehands. But on this day, Bob uncharacteristically stayed on camera, and the dialogue went something like this:

Keeshan: Look at those long tails on the raccoons, Mr. Green Jeans.
Brannum: Yes, indeed, Captain. They have long bushy tails.
Keeshan: Those tails are really long, Mr. Green Jeans, really, really long.
Brannum: Yup.
(*Pause*)
Keeshan: Mr. Green Jeans?

Brannum: Yes, Captain.

Keeshan: Do you suppose they have a little monkey in them?

The deafening collective groan from the stagehands and crew must have puzzled the little viewers at home.

In later years, associate producer Norton Wright had two major responsibilities on *Captain Kangaroo*: to carefully review advertising copy that Keeshan would read on the air and to book variety talent, including animal acts. "If it was a kitty or doggy or a parakeet, Bob would do the segment," Wright said. "But if it was a big animal or a dangerous one, he'd always give that task to Lumpy. Once, during a production rundown, Bob said, 'What's the animal today?' and you could just tell by the look on his face that he was not interested in picking up a seal. 'Lumpy, you handle it,' he would say. Well, the cuddly little seal—who had been so wonderful in rehearsal—came out and went berserk under the lights. The seal affixed its jaw on Lumpy's ear, and pretty soon, there was blood pouring down his neck," Wright said. "The seal was hanging on for dear life."

Keeshan could be a terrible tease and tormentor when it suited his mood. He liked to mock the high-wire tension of live television with an occasional practical joke during a live broadcast. This often happened while the control room was unspooling a four-minute episode of *The Adventures of Tom Terrific*, the delightfully spare animated shorts about an ingenious lad (Tom) and his sluggish pet (Mighty Manfred the Wonder Dog).

During *Tom Terrific*, the studio crew would typically head out to the hallways for a smoke. Stone recalled that Keeshan would remain behind and "stealthily pass from camera to camera, unplugging the headsets and slipping them into his oversized Kangaroo pockets. When the stage manager called for a warning that we were about to come back live, the cameramen would snuff out their cigarettes and return, only to realize that they had been cut off completely from any contact with the director in the control room. There was no recourse. We were back on the air, live. Keeshan would amble around the set and presently would take one of the headsets from his pocket and explain its function. 'This is called a headset, boys and girls. It's a lot like the ones airplane pilots wear when they're flying their big airplanes, and the pilots use them to talk to people on the ground. Why, if the pilots didn't have these headsets, they wouldn't know where to fly. There wouldn't be anyone to tell them where to go and they might get lost—or even crash!'"

While Keeshan would indulge himself with such mischief, he brooked little nonsense from those who worked with him and for him. "He did not want to be shown up," said associate producer Wright, who later served a term at Children's Television Workshop before moving to Hollywood to become a producer of made-for-television films.

Wright said, "Bob would never talk about anything that had to do with politics on the show and was surprised one day when our puppeteer, Gus Allegretti, with Mr. Moose on his hand, piped up with, "So what do you think about Red China, Captain?" Keeshan froze for a beat before Mr. Moose completed his thought. "Do you think it goes well with a red tablecloth?"

From Jon Stone's first days on the job, Keeshan's regard for his audience made an immediate positive impression, as did the producer-star's natural abilities to blend an ensemble while also excelling in his own on-camera role. "Bob was a brilliant performer, daily bringing to life the character he had so hastily but skillfully conceived," Stone said. "*Kangaroo* was created on two bases: imitation of elements in children's programming Bob admired and reaction to elements Bob detested."

That Keeshan all but barred children from the set was directly attributable to his experiences on *Howdy Doody*. Rather than play to a studio audience jacked up on Tootsie Pops, he instead peered into the camera and, in direct address, imagined speaking to one preschooler at a time. Often, the Captain would pose a question to his young viewer, providing a pause to allow the child to think and respond. There was time for that on *Captain Kangaroo*, as there was later on *Mister Rogers' Neighborhood*.

In the early days, before the advent of videotape, Stone said Keeshan "was full of fun. Humor pervaded everything that went out on the air, much of it directed deliberately over the heads of the preschool target audience and right at the parent who might be watching at that moment. I learned early that television for children did not have to cause adults to retch. It was quite possible to entertain parents and older siblings and caregivers, folks watching in appliance stores and station managers without compromising any of the appeal that the program might have for the [preschool] audience.

"[Keeshan] was working a backbreaking schedule in his dual role of performer and producer, overseeing all aspects of the program, making sure his ideals and caveats were instilled in all the people involved," Stone said. "And his ideals were exemplary."

Like Miss Frances on *Ding Dong School* and Buffalo Bob on *Howdy Doody*, Keeshan was obliged to pitch products on air, but he did so under strict, self-defined limits: he would not eat or drink products on camera and would not sell to parents through children. "If I came across copy that said, essentially, 'Hey kids, ask Mom and Dad to buy you . . .' no matter how wholesome the product, I would have to make immediate changes in the copy," Wright said. "The first thing Bob did each morning was read the cue cards. If I hadn't caught something, he would force us into high gear. It meant getting an advertising agency on the phone to work through changing the wording for the commercial, with only minutes to spare until airtime."

Keeshan would fly into a fury if he saw ad copy that asked a child to "Go get Mommy." Stone recalled Keeshan's "graphic and compelling" image to defend that rule: "Imagine a hapless mother being dragged from the toilet, panties around her ankles."

Keeshan banned some products outright. "When Kenner Toys and Hasbro would want to introduce a weapon product, be it a gun or sword or spear, Bob would not accept the ad," Wright said. "That put him on a collision course with the sales department, the lifeblood of the network. All hell would break loose."

A dramatic standoff occurred in the late fall of 1964, when Keeshan refused to accept ads during the run-up to Christmas for a toy that could have been called Combat in a Box. Topper's Johnny Seven O.M.A. (The One Man Army Gun) was a multiuse weapon that was at once a grenade and missile launcher, rifle, and tommy gun. It also had a removable pistol for whatever short-range warfare might erupt in the backyard.

The CBS sales department had signed a deal with Topper to air Johnny Seven commercials on Saturday morning shows, including *Captain Kangaroo*. When Keeshan refused to air them, he, along with his then executive producer, David D. Connell, was summoned to a meeting with representatives from Topper and CBS management. The network announced that it would be in violation of its contract if the spots did not air on *Captain Kangaroo*, and if Keeshan would not relent, his show would be canceled. "Bob, to his everlasting credit, stood firm," Stone said. "He and Dave turned to leave the conference room. Then Bob turned back to the assembly and said, 'Please remember that if the show is canceled, I will probably get a call from Jack Gould [of the *New York Times*]. As Captain Kangaroo would advise, I would have to tell the truth.'"

In the back of his mind, Keeshan knew that CBS chairman William Paley would likely have put a stop to any attempt to kill *Captain Kangaroo*. Paley had expressed his support of the show any number of times, in public and in private, and had shooed away the News Division every time it staged an attempt to commandeer the 8:00–9:00 a.m. hour.

Days after the tense meeting, the Johnny Seven battle ended with a victory for nonviolence. Not only were the commercials not going to air on *Captain Kangaroo*, but Keeshan was assured by CBS management that, in the future, standard advertising contracts would include a provision to allow individual shows to sign off on ads. "It was a true Frank Capra ending," Stone said.

Connell, a Clark Kent type in conservative dress and black glasses, was a steadying influence for Keeshan. It was as if he knew what Keeshan would want or need in a situation even before his boss did. A company man and organizational wonder who worked ungodly hours, Connell rose quickly through the ranks. Unlike most of his peers at *Captain Kangaroo*, Connell had a background in education, earning an undergraduate teaching degree at the University of Michigan. His parents were vastly disappointed when, after serving in the air force during the Korean War, he returned to Michigan to pursue a master's degree in speech. Their dream was for him to teach. His was to move to New York and find a job with a television network. Indeed, his thirty-two-page master's thesis—"Network Television Employment"—was virtually a how-to manual for breaking into television. By following his own advice, Connell got what he was after, landing a spot in Lou Stone's trainee program.

Regimented and dedicated to detail, to the point of being obsessive-compulsive, Connell was the production team's station master. Under his coordination, the train always stayed on the tracks and left the depot on time. Behind every long-running television series is a man like Connell, who owned a plaque that said, "There's no amount you can do so long as you don't care who gets the credit."

Character mattered to Keeshan. "It was no accident Bob surrounded himself with the people he did," Stone said. "[They all] shared [his] conscience and instincts. Bob knew this about each of them, and by assembling this particular team, they were free from conflicts of taste. Had any of them been called on to create a new children's program, as Bob had been, each one certainly would have come up with a show every bit as respectful of its audience as *Captain Kangaroo*.

"Then, too, Bob had a wonderful source of supply to augment this remarkable team: the CBS training program continually sent fresh young people to work on *Kangaroo*, and Bob scrutinized each new arrival, watched his performance, gauged his instincts and humor, then, when he found just the right person, plucked him out of the CBS program and put him on his own staff."

He found one such person in Samuel Gibbon, the young caretaker of the Peanut Gallery who thought Buffalo Bob was full of bull.

Edward R. Murrow looked out toward Madison Avenue, illuminated by a stream of morning sunlight. He was standing by a corner window in contemplative silence, considering the pages from a tome on foreign policy plucked from a wall of floor-to-ceiling bookshelves.

Sam Gibbon was shown in to Murrow's sanctum at CBS News on a spring afternoon in 1958, his arrival announced by Murrow's assistant.

The door shut and forty-five awkward seconds passed, leaving Gibbon to wonder whether he should clear his throat or otherwise indicate that Mr. Murrow was, indeed, not alone. Gibbon shifted his weight from right to left and began to feel a solitary bead of perspiration run down his lower spine and trickle to his waist, a sweat spot developing on his blue Oxford cloth shirt, just above the belt line.

Staring down at the book now, Murrow finished a passage, "showing me his noble profile," Gibbon said. "He then closed the book, put it back, and turned to me. It was just the most wonderfully theatrical moment, and I was in awe."

Murrow neither asked to see Gibbon's résumé nor engaged in pleasantries of any kind. "He really didn't take notice of me, choosing instead to offer what amounted to a lecture about the future of television, its importance to the culture," Gibbon recalled. "He said the role of television was to make the world aware of itself, the most prescient and sensible remark about television I've ever heard. I took that remark to have much wider significance than just news, and not many people were thinking that way back then. Murrow went on to describe the sort of person who would be necessary to carry the medium in that direction, and what he described was himself, a correspondent with an arsenal of abilities, including writing, performing, and directing."

Gibbon hoped spring would provide a freshening breeze to a career becalmed at NBC, where he was a low-paid page with no immediate hope of promotion. Just a week before this meeting with Murrow, arranged by a friend's father who was an executive at CBS Radio News, Gibbon had been shown the door at the CBS personnel office. It must have been a buyer's market in employment that spring, considering CBS was giving Fulbright Fellows the bum's rush.

"When Murrow was done speaking, he reached out for my résumé, attached a note, and signed his name. I took it back to the office that had turned me down for a production assistant's job just ten days before, with this note fluttering, and was hired instantly, much to the chagrin of the guy who had turned me down."

Like everyone else who ever worked on *Captain Kangaroo*, Sam Gibbon immediately clicked with Lumpy Brannum, by all accounts as genial, generous, and kind a man off camera as he was while playing Mr. Green Jeans. The son of a stern minister, Brannum was born in Sandwich, Illinois, west of Chicago. The family moved to California where young Hugh acquired the nickname Lumpy. (In his memoir, Jon Stone claims to be one of the few people who knew the story behind the sobriquet. Apparently, an appropriate telling of the tale concludes with a wink and a belly laugh. "I will only say that the truth is perfectly disgusting," Stone observed.)

As a child, Lumpy showed early promise in music and blossomed into a versatile instrumentalist, mastering tuba, trombone, and bass fiddle. On top of all that, he also played the guitar and had a pleasant singing voice. During the war, Brannum auditioned for a spot in a marine corps band and was shipped to the South Pacific with a gaggle of jazz musicians who had enlisted rather than wait to be drafted. Under the baton of Bob Crosby, Bing's brother, Brannum's lips were nearly worn out playing the marine corps hymn. "In relaxed moments in our studio, Lumpy told many tales about the reluctance of these musicians to play at parade-ground ceremonies or at officers club dances," Keeshan said.[19] It may have seemed like cushy duty for Brannum in the South Seas, but over time, the *Captain Kangaroo* crew and production team learned otherwise. "When they weren't playing for admirals and generals coming on and off aircraft carriers, the band members were assigned burial detail," Sam Gibbon said. When their instruments were packed away, the boys in the band shoveled graves for the often mutilated corpses.

"Lumpy was such a gentle soul, he would never inflict any discomfort on another person, even if it was just letting him know what a difficult time he had during the war," Stone said. "He saw the worst of the Pacific war and had come through it with humor and gentleness intact."

Though not quite a farmer like Mr. Green Jeans, Brannum was an inveterate gardener who would cart in fresh-picked vegetables to the studio on Monday mornings from his home in the Poconos. "Lumpy was a leader in the ecology movement back in the 1950s, long before 'environment' became a buzzword in the American lexicon," Keeshan said. "He would tell our audience about the need to share our Earth, protect our world, plan for the future. For these [segments], there was little, if any, preparation given to Lumpy; it all came from his mind and his heart. He had a genuine love for the Earth and all its creatures, great and small."[20]

Though each episode of *Captain Kangaroo* was meticulously scripted and timed, the writers understood that Keeshan and Brannum could—and would—improvise to good effect. Keeshan, who shunned rehearsal, reserved the right to ignore scripts altogether, sometimes dismissing them out of hand with only minutes to spare before airtime. "Bob hated rehearsals for a combination of reasons," Gibbon said. "It was partly laziness and partly because he loved winging it. He really enjoyed the aliveness of it and he felt that if he rehearsed it would take a lot of the freshness out of his performance. So he didn't rehearse. During my days as studio producer I would stand in for him at rehearsal, making changes in the scripts as we went, depending on how the segments timed out and knowing what Keeshan would hate and not hate."

The writer who might have been most in tune with Keeshan's needs as a performer was Connell, steady and supremely organized. His script pages were characteristically crisp, spare, and simple. "They seemed like they didn't have a hell of a lot of imagination in them. But Dave understood Keeshan and *Captain Kangaroo* at least as well as anybody, and when a Connell script came into the studio, everybody heaved a sigh of relief because you knew Keeshan would be happy and the show would go swimmingly," Gibbon said. "They were underwritten, which meant that if a bit went wrong that was fine, you didn't have to cut anything. Dave just had a wonderful sense of what Bob would do. This was important because we didn't know until five minutes before the show was to go on the air whether we would be doing it as written, with Bob in character and costume, or whether we were going to be winging it all the way with Lumpy, who never was particularly happy with that degree of uncertainty. He was the second banana and liked that role. He played off Keeshan absolutely beautifully. But he didn't ever like being the first banana. That was not his comfort zone or his role on the program."

However much Keeshan relied on Brannum, production colleagues believed the costar was granted too little respect. "Keeshan had a mean streak, in that he liked to let people dangle," said writer Tom Whedon, who wrote for *Kangaroo* before moving on to greater success as head writer for *The Electric Company* and writer-producer for a string of prime-time comedies, including *The Golden Girls*. "Lumpy was on a one-year contract the entire time he was with *Captain Kangaroo*, so that he never, ever knew whether he was going to be back the next year."

"Lumpy was always worried he wasn't doing well enough," said Bob Colleary, *Captain Kangaroo*'s head writer for twenty-three years. "He was insecure."

Whedon said, "We were always hoping [Keeshan would] be in a good mood. Sometimes, when he arrived in a bad mood and saw a writer's name on a script, he'd fire that writer on the spot. He did, after all, own the football."

Like all participants in the CBS directors' training program, Stone and Gibbon had to move on to other assignments to round out their experience and introduce new challenges.

Stone worked for two game shows that, as he recalled, bent the rules. On *Strike It Rich*, one of his duties "was to assist in providing the contestants with answers to questions they were likely to be asked." On that show, destitute people who needed medical care or a windfall to head off foreclosure would be asked simple quiz questions. If they answered them correctly, they'd win money. If they came up blank, the emcee would take donations from viewers calling in. *TV Guide* called *Strike It Rich* "a despicable travesty on the very nature of charity."

On *Stand Up and Be Counted*, another dubious sociology experiment, contestants would seek the advice of the audience to solve a real-life dilemma. "If you thought the poor soul should follow plan A, you stood up," Stone said. "A state-of-the-art electronic-scanning device immediately registered the exact number of standees. Those favoring plan B would then stand." The results would be calculated by a "computer," which Stone described as "a large board with electric lights all over it. Behind it stood a producer with two stagehands. When the first audience group rose to be counted, one of the stagehands would turn a crank that caused the lights to flash. Peeking through a hole, a producer would eyeball the standees and then whisper to the other stagehand. 'Call it thirty-nine.'"

Both Stone and Gibbon worked on the daytime *Jimmy Dean Show*, the easy-as-you-please afternoon variety series hosted by the likable Texan who would later become a baron of breakfast sausage. Dean, a boyish country singer with smooth skin and crossover appeal, concluded each show with a devotional. The stage lights would dim and, surrounded by the Noteworthys, a male-female singing group, Dean would offer a hymn and a homey benediction.

Gibbon dated one of the Noteworthys. "We used to get together and harmonize at the apartment of the group's married couples," he said. "Jimmy came over one evening, and we were all standing around the piano. He couldn't read a note of music. I could, and Jimmy noticed. 'You can read that shit?' he asked.

"A week later, at the end of a broadcast, Jimmy said, 'We've got a surprise for you and for our stage manager, Sam. He's going to sing with the Noteworthys next week.' I just about fell though the floor. I didn't have any desire to do this, had never performed in public, and was *not* a singer. I just did it for fun. I said to the executive producer, 'If you make me do this, I won't show up that day,' but my protests were to no avail. So I did a song, backed by the Noteworthys. And from that, fan mail began to show up, and I had to sing again. An entire fan club formed, and Jimmy would call me out on stage to his interview desk. He'd read the letters aloud while the camera stayed fixed on my face. It was absolutely awful.

"Then, the executive producer called me into his office one day and said, 'Listen, I could make you a star. I have connections in the music business.'

"I said, 'Forget it,' and went back to being a stage manager again."

In 1960, Gibbon took some needed time off. "I didn't let anyone know where I was going," he said, "not my parents, my friends, anybody. I was just going to go as far west as I could get, then turn around when half my vacation was gone." He got as far as Tahiti, a distance of nearly 5,500 nautical miles from Manhattan.

"I was living in a hotel that had thatched huts by the water, having an idyllic time. Then, one morning, one of the hotel employees came racing, saying there was a wire waiting for me at the local telegraph office. I jumped on a motorbike and raced through town, thinking anybody who had figured out where I was had to have some emergency reason to contact me."

Gibbon tore into the telegram, the first sentence of which read, "LAST CHANCE TO AVOID 42."

It was a mood-shattering reminder of what awaited Gibbon in New York. After a succession of enjoyable studio assignments in daytime television, progressing from production assistant to stage manager, his number had finally come up for duty at CBS, the network nerve center within an area of Grand Central Terminal. Like those lonely NATO outposts where faceless government drones monitor defense systems, associate directors (ADs) at Master Control—Studio 42—oversaw the network's precise, second-by-second system of program coordination. (Jon Stone described the first six months of service at Master Control as "the most terrifying, nerve-wracking responsibility imaginable.")[21]

The AD was responsible for making sure every program and commercial went on the air as scheduled. It was also his job during network-identification breaks to cue the always unseen studio announcer who would intone "This . . . is CBS."

"At the time I was on the job, President Eisenhower had had his first heart attack," Stone said. "Standing by, we had an extremely complicated obituary to be aired immediately in case a second heart attack should, without warning, fell the president. For six months I lived in dread that Eisenhower might die while I was on duty."

Gibbon dreaded the idea of being sequestered at Studio 42 altogether, tucked away in the broadcasting equivalent of a bunker. The first line of the telegram came like an abrupt tap on the shoulder. The second and third lines provided the *"Pssst."* They read: COME WORK ON CAPTAIN KANGAROO. WE HAVE AN OPENING ON THE STAFF.

It was signed DAVE CONNELL, EXECUTIVE PRODUCER, CAPTAIN KANGAROO.

Gibbon could not imagine how Connell had tracked him down and was furious that he had. "I was so annoyed at having gone through terrible anxiety, thinking that someone from my family had died," he recalled. "I sent him back a very rude telegram saying that I wasn't interested. I finished my vacation, came home, and went to work at Studio 42." After six months in the dark, Gibbon cooled off, and Connell renewed the offer. "By then, the charm of working all night and doing late, late movies had worn off," Gibbon said, sheepishly. He joined Robert Keeshan Associates, the production company responsible for *Captain Kangaroo*, as an associate producer and writer.

Not long after returning to the show, bachelor Gibbon became smitten with Connell's secretary, Carol Jorjorian. They kept their relationship secret, lest Keeshan learn of it and subject them to teasing.

Meanwhile Gibbon's roommate, Jon Stone, had his eye on Beverley Ogg, a fresh-faced blonde from the Midwest who looked as if she had just stepped out of a Tab Hunter movie.

Raised in Ottumwa, Iowa, Ogg came to New York City in 1959 after graduating from the University of Michigan. Upon arrival in the city, she stowed her bags, caught a cab, and was off to meet Dave Connell over at the production office of *Captain Kangaroo*. Months before, she had written a letter of introduction to Connell, on the advice of Ed Stasheff, a professor of television arts, under whom both she—and Connell, a few years earlier—had studied. Connell responded with a cordial letter that included the line, "When you're ready to come to New York, let me know."

In person, Connell shared the sad truth that even though Ogg had the academic credentials and experience in a college television studio, the gatekeepers of television in New York were not considering women for production jobs. "I had actually gotten into production at Michigan because my father insisted I had to earn a living," she said. "I had really wanted to be an actress."

Connell sent her to the CBS personnel office, where Ogg learned of a secretarial job in the casting department. Though her typing skills were questionable and she was untrained in dictation, she was hired for the position. It didn't take long for Ogg to realize that throughout CBS were overqualified secretaries just like herself, women whose ambitions were thwarted purely on the basis of gender. "We weren't trained to be secretaries," she said. "We had liberal arts degrees. We had come to New York to do something exciting, wanting to work in television. But they just weren't hiring women to do much."

Ogg was offered a job on a summer replacement series, where again her responsibilities were clerical and her performance subpar. "I had the production skills but I didn't type fast enough," Ogg said. She then became a secretary with the network's Sunday-night institution, *The Ed Sullivan Show*. That ended disastrously one Sunday afternoon during dress rehearsal, when Sullivan demanded that an introduction be revised and called out for secretarial assistance. The women of the secretarial pool worked Sundays on a rotating basis, and it was Ogg's week. "Can you take dictation?" Sullivan asked. "No, I can't," Ogg said. Furious, Sullivan steamed off, and on Monday morning Ogg was fired.

But thanks to the good graces of Dave Connell, her nine-lives secretarial career got a final reprieve when she filled an opening to type scripts for *Captain Kangaroo*. Having a seat in the bullpen among the irreverent, well-schooled wits of the production staff was like answering the phone at the *Harvard Lampoon*. One day, Ogg told Whedon and Stone she was considering ditching her Dutch surname and adopting a more neutral stage name. Unsure of what it should be, she asked for their help. After caucusing in the hallway, they returned with a suggestion. "We've got it!" Stone said. "Tuesday Ogg!"

The surname sweepstakes ended with Beverley adopting Owen as a stage name. She got an agent, took auditions, and snagged a small role on the daytime serial *As the World Turns*, working weekends at *Captain Kangaroo* to make up for acting time away from the office. Dave Connell, who had done some acting himself during his years in the air force, approved the flex hours.

One spring evening, while Beverley was returning home from a theater performance, she stepped off a bus just as Stone was pulling up to a stoplight in his Triumph TR3, top down. "He gave me a ride home and we ended up talking," Owen said.

With that a second secret workplace romance blossomed.

After four years the grind of pumping out two live daily shows and over-seeing the operation began to weigh heavily on Keeshan. But even when production of *Captain Kangaroo* went to videotape, eliminating the second show and the need for arriving for work before dawn, the more carefree, playful spirit that had once defined his studio demeanor curiously with-ered. "Bob had a hot Irish temper and he didn't mind using it," said Sam Gibbon, who became educational director of Robert Keeshan Associates. On a good day, working on the show "was like living through a very secure childhood an hour at a time. It was an enormous refuge. But there were lots of stormy periods, difficulties, and arguments."

Offstage, Keeshan had a quick-trigger temper and an acid tongue, and, as chief executive of Robert Keeshan Associates, his tightfisted, demand-ing managerial style spread enmity to a wounded staff. "He would never hold back on his feelings," said Bob Colleary, the longtime head writer. "There were days when he did not want to be on the set, and other days when he was happy to be there. We had all the ups and downs you might expect, working under those conditions."

The stress and uncertainties of dealing with Keeshan occurred particu-larly during what some say was a difficult period in his personal life. The boss's moods fused a bond among the writers, whose work Keeshan often dismissed as "crap." Colleary recalls that during a reception in Washington, he introduced the production team as his "unemployable staff." After work, the group would commiserate over cocktails. "There was a bar across the street from the studio that sold a triple martini for a dollar fifty and it got a lot of us in deep trouble," Whedon said. "It was the hardest-drinking crowd I ever worked with. The joke was, we loved the Captain but hated Keeshan."

On weekends, production staff members were dragooned into accompa-nying Keeshan to his frequent concert appearances with symphony orches-tras. Staff members were not paid for working these live "Fun with Music" shows; it was considered part of the job. "The concerts were difficult and you didn't get a weekend off, and we all grumbled and griped about hav-ing to go, but in the end it was like a reward," Gibbon said. "The direct contact with an audience was a real replenishment. You saw what Captain Kangaroo was doing for kids, and you felt gratified. To see Keeshan with fifteen hundred kids was just a revelation. His instincts as a performer were uncanny. He could turn an audience of kids on like nobody I've ever seen. His timing was brilliant. And also you learned how good simple stuff for kids could be. We'd get a bunch of cardboard boxes and paint them to look like train cars. Kids will get up onstage and be the train and we'll do it to this piece of train music. You'd first think to yourself [in rehearsal], 'Whoa, that's pretty stupid,' and then you'd see it in an auditorium with Keeshan orchestrating it and it would be the most exciting, exhilarating, theatrical thing. It was just perfectly wonderful."

These appearances, where he was showered with applause and squeals, were as a balm to Keeshan. The sharp edges that were so evident in the New York studio gave way to his softer, kinder influences.

One of the weekend workers was Norton Wright, who had been a light-weight boxing champion at Yale and had worked in Europe and North Africa for Armed Services Radio and Television. Wright recalled that after a performance, promoters would often ask Keeshan to visit a children's hospital. He would agree, but with a proviso: no press coverage. "Bob would be tired, but he would show up in his costume and reach inside oxygen tents to hold kids' hands," he said. "In Cincinnati, they came up to him and said, 'The kid that only had six weeks to live when you were here last year is still alive and wants to see you.' Bob said, 'Cancel the plane. I'm going out to see him.' It takes a certain amount of heart to do stuff like that, and I think Bob's heart was in the right place."

On the road, Keeshan enjoyed evenings out with his production staff and often treated them to the best restaurant in town. "He liked good wine and was generous with his Johnnie Walker Black Label scotch," said Tom Whedon. When properly lubricated, the boys would often seek out local entertainment, including burlesque shows. "If there's one real valuable lesson I learned from Keeshan, it was that a scotch sour on the rocks is a very good hangover drink," Whedon said.

Through good days and bad, the hand-selected team Keeshan assembled brought out the best in him. "Bob wanted to be more than what he was, but he didn't have the talent," said Wright. "His potential was modest. You were certainly not going to turn Bob Keeshan into Zero Mostel with the bright, witty script you had written. Our writers were from terrific schools, and they knew the Broadway stage, from Neil Simon to Gower Champion. They all harbored the desire to do infinitely more than what they were doing at *Captain Kangaroo* but they, like me, had fallen into a tender trap. It was a consistent job with health and pension benefits and a decent salary."

On the urging of her agent, staff secretary Beverley Owen auditioned for a spot in the Miss Rheingold beauty contest, a wildly successful promotion begun in 1941 by Liebmann Brewery. Once the sixth-ranking beer in terms of sales in New York, Rheingold shot to No. 1, thanks to a bevy of wholesome models who competed for the annual crown. Grace Kelly was famously turned down for a spot in the contest for being too thin. Owen, apparently, was not. As one of the six finalists in 1963, she made five hundred dollars a week.

Not long afterward, Owen signed a seven-year deal with Universal and filmed guest appearances on NBC's *Kraft Mystery Theater,* a summer replacement series in 1961, and *Wagon Train,* a dust-caked Western that first ran on NBC (1957–62) before jumping to ABC (1962–65). On *The Virginian* (1962–71), television's first ninety-minute Western, Owen played Doug McClure's chaste love interest in an episode in which a sudden storm forced the two to spend a night in a cave. They did nothing beyond kiss, but Owen's character skedaddled to a convent at the end of the story.

Stone, meanwhile, growing restless at *Kangaroo,* applied to enter the Actors Studio, Lee Strasberg's exclusive center for professional actors looking to expand their development. He made it past the initial audition before being cut. But after multiple callbacks, he won a role in *Money,* a musical satire cowritten by his *Kangaroo* colleague Whedon, with music by composer Sam Pottle. It was staged at the split-level cabaret known as Upstairs at the Downstairs, a hip performance space on Fifty-sixth Street that was a breeding ground for actors and comedians in the 1950s and '60s.

In the July 10, 1963, edition of the *New York Times,* critic Paul Gardner wrote, "Perhaps the best number is given to Jon Stone, an angular scarecrow, who readily admits to being the loser of the year. In 'Give a Cheer,' he holds back the tears and observes manfully: "I waited for years for opportunity to knock, but every time I open the door it's Avon calling."[22]

Stone, then a producer at *Kangaroo* who also wrote scripts, was already working a brutal schedule before he started moonlighting. Because there were two ninety-minute performances of *Money* each night, his new workday didn't end until 1:30 a.m., which meant he would often get less than four hours of sleep before having to be at *Captain Kangaroo* by 8:00 a.m. As *Money* stretched into a six-month run, his boss, Dave Connell, confronted him with an ultimatum: choose either his day job or acting. Stone, who could be petulant and defiant of authority, was leaning toward quitting *Captain Kangaroo* when another development arose. Bob Keeshan, who was also looking to stretch as a performer, was mounting a second children's show for Saturday mornings, a *Kangaroo* spinoff called *Mister Mayor*. Keeshan expected the writing staff to pump out material for the new show, without any additional compensation. This did not sit well with Stone and Whedon, and one night during a staff dinner at Christ Cella's steak house on Forty-sixth Street, with their tongues loosened by alcohol, they ignited an argument at the table. "If our work is such crap, why then do you want more of it?" Stone asked. It got testy, and sides were drawn. Executive producer Dave Connell and head writer Bob Colleary, while perhaps sympathetic to the writers' grievances, understandably lined up with the boss, which further enraged Stone and Whedon.

They unloaded all of their pent-up hurt and hostility, and then, like woozy tag-team wrestlers leaving the ring, arms over shoulders, walked out of the restaurant and off the show.

It's fair to say that in the late spring of 1961, executives at the nation's three broadcast networks were still stinging from the public approbations of FCC chairman Newton Minow. The withering phrase Minow had used in his May speech to industry leaders of the National Broadcasters Association, describing television as "a vast wasteland," branded the hides of the network overlords, especially those charged with programming for younger audiences. In his speech, Minow had described children's TV as little more than "massive doses of cartoons, violence, and more violence."

In response, the networks raced to be the first to launch a high-profile commercially viable children's project, if for no better reason than to get Minow, the JFK-appointed FCC chairman, off their backs. NBC devoted a year of development to *Exploring*, an hour-long noontime series designed to pique the curiosity and expand the knowledge of children age five to eleven. Its host was Dr. Albert R. Hibbs, a senior staff scientist at the California Institute of Technology's Jet Propulsion Laboratory.

For series producer, the network turned not to a rocket scientist but to an experienced newsman in Craig B. Fisher, who began his career with NBC as an associate producer of *Today* under Dave Garroway. It was Fisher who promoted staff writer Barbara Walters to her first on-air job, as the cheery "*Today* girl."

Fisher took the extraordinary step of bringing aboard an academic consultant for *Exploring* in Dr. Gerald S. Lesser, a Bigelow Professor of Education and Developmental Psychology at Harvard's Graduate School of Education. At the time, Lesser and his students had begun a serious inquiry into television's effects on child development. "I had had extensive opportunities starting in 1961 to observe young children watching television, and found these experiences to be an illuminating source of ideas about how children learn," Lesser once wrote.[23] "[Craig Fisher] asked if I would watch with groups of children as the show was being produced to see what I could learn that would improve the series from week to week. The arrangement provided him with immediate access to children's reactions and provided me with an opportunity to observe children closely and see how television programs were created."

In 1963, Encyclopedia Britannica purchased a half-sponsorship of the show, at the urging of the company's new vice president and general counsel, Newton Minow, who had resigned as FCC chairman.

In June of that year *Exploring* won a Peabody award for service to children, as did *Walt Disney's Wonderful World of Color*. As the Sunday primetime schedule began at 7:00 p.m., the NBC Peacock would appear in full plumage, reminding viewers that "the following program is in living color," and Disney himself would introduce each episode of the anthology series. That program was as much a showcase for the Disney entertainment brand as it was a campaign by NBC's parent company, RCA, to entice consumers to replace their aging black-and-white TVs with a color model.

Chapter Four

On the morning after the Cooneys' dinner party, thoughts were percolating for Joan, at Twenty-first and Third, and Lloyd Morrisett, out in suburbia. The two inspired opposites, the pragmatist and the experimentalist, the producer wired into the worlds of politics, celebrity, and issues and the social scientist plugged into educational research and philanthropy, were duly caffeinated and stirred.

Cooney had awakened prepared to undertake a mission, refreshed, energized, and determined. Years later, she said that almost overnight, she felt as though she had been summoned to a "television destiny" that would "test the power and the influence of the medium. I would have been interested if it had been a project to teach literacy to adults, or something for teenagers," she said. "Preschoolers were not necessarily my thing. It was using television in a constructive way that turned me on."

Lean, fit Morrisett, who rarely missed his rigorous daily workout, took a moment to watch Sarah scooting about in her pajamas. Thinking about the night before, he was fascinated by the notion of exploiting the technology of television to reach greater numbers of needy kids. "At that time, there were roughly four to four and a half million children entering school in a year, and our programs at the Carnegie Corporation were reaching perhaps a few hundred, maybe a couple thousand," he later said. "Of the four million, a conservative estimate of five hundred thousand needed help. There was a huge gap between what we were doing and what we were trying to achieve. And if you believe that the programs you're funding have potential value, and you find that you're only doing a very small part of the job, it creates a problem in your mind: how are you going to overcome it?"

They got to work on the problem—Cooney and Lewis Freedman at Channel Thirteen, Morrisett and two associates at Carnegie—and by mid-April, after an initial session at the foundation's offices, there already were a good number of dots to connect. Astonishingly, a primitive outline of a project that more than faintly resembles *Sesame Street* began to emerge as early as their second meeting.[1]

Cooney and Freedman proposed a daily program, "probably an hour long," telecast twice a day for a target audience of three- to five-year-olds. It would be shot in a studio on videotape, to give it a "live quality." There would be music, puppets, and stories. Filmed segments might venture beyond the set, visiting "firehouses, policemen, hospitals, zoos, and libraries."

What Cooney and Freedman had in mind is today referred to as "edutainment," a pleasurable—and often commercial—brand of pedagogy. Whatever the final format, they determined, the show would rise or fall on a single precept: it would need to be as engaging as it was informative. That would be no easy feat, considering that educational TV to that point had been well intentioned but stodgy, stiff, and colorless. If cartoons and Westerns were ice cream, educational TV was school lunch. What Cooney and Freedman hoped for would be more like raspberry yogurt, TV that was both tangy and nutritious.

Morrisett understood that any serious effort to explore such a program's viability would first necessitate researching whether anyone beyond the five people in the room thought it could work.[2] Certainly, there were educators, psychologists, child development specialists, and pediatricians whom they could tap for expert opinion. Not only could these advisers comment on the feasibility of the study, they might also offer guidance on age-appropriate content for the show.

There was buzz and a hum around the table. Morrisett had in mind a barnstorming tour of campuses and laboratories across the nation to test what only months before had been a simple question prompted by the story of a preschooler peering at an Indian chief.

Someone would have to be designated as researcher-scout, returning to the group after a few months with a report. He or she would need to be careful and inquisitive, resourceful and prepared, efficient and dependable. Cooney shifted in her seat.

The proposition of reaching out to a hit list of sages and scholars almost made Morrisett's ears wiggle. After all, they were his kind of people, especially those with a scientific bent toward cognitive matters. He was endlessly searching to find new ways to harness advances in science, technology, and media for the greater good.

Cooney recalled Morrisett saying, "*Maybe* we could do a little study for two or three months. *Maybe* we could let someone go around and talk to the various people about how they would view a television show to help with cognitive development."

That's when Freedman, the programming pro, piped up. "It's a good idea!" he blurted, as ever, ebullient. "Channel Thirteen could certainly run that study!" Within seconds, all eyes fell on Cooney, the obvious choice for the assignment, given her degree in education, her reporting background, and her tenure at Thirteen. It was as if she were born to the assignment, and in her mind, she started packing her valise.

Freedman cleared his throat. "Of course, Joan wouldn't be interested," he blurted. "She's a public affairs producer."

"Oh yes I would!" Cooney exclaimed, unwilling to let the comment stand for even a half second, even if it meant refuting her boss publicly. "I didn't know it until I said it," she later admitted.

Freedman shot Cooney a stern look, as he was understandably opposed to allowing one of his most reliable and levelheaded producers to go gallivanting to who-knows-where for three months. "Lewis was absolutely determined not to lose me on this," Cooney said, but she was equally adamant to be chosen. The meeting ended with the matter unresolved. Days passed.

By dint of good fortune, Tim Cooney had a scheduled lunch with Morrisett to discuss matters unrelated to the TV project. Before they met, Joan urged Tim to promote her cause. "Go ahead," she said. "It's never going to happen if we don't work around Lewis." Tim had no reservations about speaking up for his wife, and not only out of matrimonial allegiance. He might have done so for any capable woman attempting to lead in what was then a man's world. "Tim was a radical feminist, maybe the first feminist I ever knew," Cooney said. "He always felt that men and women should do what they want. I came late to the idea."[3]

When he was sober, thirty-four-year-old Tim Cooney was a prince of a guy. Though born in 1929 in Milwaukee, Cooney was raised in New York. He earned an undergraduate history degree in 1952 from Columbia College, the highly selective undergraduate program at Columbia University. It also was the year in which he made thirty-five dollars per week as a functionary in Adlai Stevenson's presidential campaign.

He proved to be something less than the model soldier during his army days at Fort Campbell, Kentucky. Perturbed by America's foreign policy under the stewardship of John Foster Dulles, Corporal Cooney penned a stingingly critical letter to the *Louisville Courier-Journal* about the secretary of state's administration. The commentary reached the desk of Cooney's commanding general, and he was busted back to the rank of private. "Cooney did the thing that most soldiers try to avoid—he made himself conspicuous," the *New York Times* once reported, adding the soldier was "rebuked for registering implicit dissent with his commander in chief, the president of the United States."[4]

The highlight of Cooney's career as an army paratrooper came during a doomed flight onboard a "Flying Boxcar" transport. When the plane crashed en route to Alaska, Cooney and a planeload of others parachuted to safety. The army pinned a commendation medal on his chest, "for saving my own life." Self-deprecating humor was only part of his rogue charm.

After serving in the Korean War, civilian Cooney left America to discover Spain. Assuming the life of a scholar on the Iberian Peninsula, he researched and wrote a scholarly tome, *Ultimate Desires*, published by Philosophical Library in 1958. According to the *Times*, the book explored "man's quest for answers to the fundamental problems of his existence."[5]

When Tim married Joan in the winter of 1964, he was director of public relations for the New York City Department of Labor. In July of the following year, when Cooney was thirty-five, he was appointed executive secretary of the New York Council Against Poverty.

In 1967 Cooney was named interim director of New York's Office of Civil Defense, with the curious mandate to abolish the very department he was chosen to temporarily lead. "I don't want to become a specialist in liquidating offices," Cooney said. The assignment did appeal, however, to his quest to conserve and redistribute taxpayer-funded resources, in the hope that more dollars would be available to assist the poor. It made him feel like an Irish Robin Hood.

So fascinated by African American culture was Cooney that his friends teasingly called him "the blackest man in Harlem." Tim and his bride of two years made for a "powerful one-two punch," recalled Robert A. Hatch, a former Peace Corps executive who became *Sesame Street*'s first public relations director. Hatch viewed the couple as beguiling social activists who found each other at a time of great social foment. They were, for a time, a delightfully unmatched set, a Spencer Tracy and Katharine Hepburn twosome who married despite differences in upbringing, station, and sobriety. They had exchanged vows in the Friars Chapel of the Roman Catholic Church of St. Vincent Ferrer on February 22, 1964.[6]

In the early years of the marriage, Tim's more commendable qualities made up for his less attractive ones. When Tim drank, he could be an ill-tempered lout who'd throw dishes around the apartment. Joan learned to duck.

At their lunch, Tim Cooney spoke ardently to Lloyd Morrisett about Joan, though Morrisett had in fact already concluded that she was the logical person to conduct the study. Morrisett phoned Joan's boss, Lewis Freedman, a few days afterward. "You know who I'd really like on this is Joan," he said, and he meant it. Faced with the Cooney couple's end run and Morrisett's intervention, Freedman had little choice but to acquiesce. To say no would be to risk upsetting a Carnegie vice president and jeopardize possible future funding.

Characteristically certain of what she wanted, Joan Cooney had bested her boss. "I never told Lewis about this because I always felt it was a little tricky," Cooney said, with a smidgen of guilt. "But I'm awfully glad I did it."

It was as if the work of the previous months had provided a brief glimpse into a future beyond documentaries and public affairs programming, a life of greater purpose and a realization that she "could do a thousand documentaries on poverty and poor people that would be watched by a handful of the convinced, but I was never really going to have an influence on my times. I wanted to make a difference."[7]

The plan set, Morrisett instructed Cooney to write a proposal for a feasibility study. By mid-May it landed on the desk of Carnegie president Alan Jay Pifer. Clipped to it was a supporting memo from Barbara Finberg, an executive associate at Carnegie, which read as follows:

TV can reach children before they start nursery school, kindergarten, or Head Start or can be used to enrich the preschool program itself. Large numbers of children, however, will not have the opportunity to attend a preschool program, whether their parents can afford to send them to a private nursery school or whether or not they are eligible for Head Start. This seems to be a chance to find out whether television, a medium that can reach more children than any other method presently available, can offer all children a head start on their education, open their lives to a variety of experiences, and make learning interesting and inviting.[8]

The proposal won quick approval, and Carnegie came up with fifteen thousand dollars to cover Cooney's salary and travel expenses, By June she was off harvesting heaping bales of opinion, working her way down a list of experts provided by Carnegie, with a smattering of additional sources chosen by her.

Over fourteen weeks she swooped down on campuses—not only the nation's elite state and private universities, but a day school in Bloomfield Hills, Michigan, and a Montessori preschool in Phoenix. She dropped in at pediatric research hospitals and consulted with the National Film Board of Canada. She sat with top broadcasting executives at CBS and NBC in New York, and toured a local station in Philadelphia that had success with original programming for children. She conferred with an educational specialist at Head Start and interviewed an animation team and a film-maker. And she also met with game-show creator Mark Goodson, half of the Goodson-Todman production team responsible for giving away truck-loads of washer-dryers and fistfuls of cash on *The Price Is Right*, *I've Got a Secret*, *The Match Game*, and *Tattletales*.

There were twenty-six sessions in all, packed into a summer of sprints to the airport and hikes around college quadrangles. Cooney compiled her careful, detailed notes as a veteran reporter might—on the fly and without benefit of a tape recorder. Given the ever-widening gap in school readiness, the educators and psychologists were surprisingly open to the concept of teaching through TV. "All of them, to a man and woman, were support-ive of [the] idea . . . even though no one knew *if* you could do it. But I knew because as I said in the study, they're singing commercials all over the country. Why can't you teach them something else?"

Harvard cognitive psychologist Jerome Bruner spoke for the majority of those interviewed when he said, "We cannot wait for the right answers before acting. Rather, we should look upon the first year of broadcasting for preschoolers in the nature of an inquiry. There is no substitute for try-ing it and evaluating its effects."

By the time her sojourn was completed in September, she was ready to synthesize her notes, extract the major points, and begin typing like hell. "I remember just laying stuff out on a sofa, each chapter with its backup," Cooney said. "I would call Lloyd every now and then and say, 'Here's where I am,' or read him a paragraph, And he kept saying, 'Fine, that's what we want.' At one point I said, 'Who is the voice?' and he said, 'You! We want *your* opinion. This is an informal report. It's not going to be published. We just want to know what Joan Ganz Cooney thinks, after talking to these people.' I had no credentials for this, except for a BA in education, and hav-ing done one half-hour program on the subject. It was an immense leap of faith for Lloyd to say, 'She's got the brainpower to do it, I'm interested in her opinion.' He just decided that he was going to bet on me, which in a funny way is probably the most significant single personnel decision for *Sesame Street* that was ever made. . . . Everybody else who came on the project from then on was utterly qualified. I was the question mark."

The result of Cooney's travels was a distilled, neatly structured fifty-five-page report entitled "The Potential Uses of Television in Preschool Education."[9] Jettisoning statistics, citations, and psychoeducational jargon, Cooney wrote with authority, clarity, and brevity. In the opening pages she provided background about the long-overdue effort to address the edu-cational needs of children aged three to five, especially those trapped in the underclass. The result of these years of neglect, she explained, was "an academic achievement gap between disadvantaged and middle-class children that manifests itself during the early school years and increases dramatically in the higher grades." The root of the disparity was in the lack of intellectual stimulation for poor kids in the formative preschool years, so critical to brain development. For myriad reasons, some sociological, some economic, and some cultural, children of the underclass were arriving at the school door ill prepared and miles behind their middle-class peers. With little chance to catch up, these students got caught up in cycles of frustration, futility, and failure.

But evolving research in cognitive development suggested that aggressive intervention could compensate for what neglected children were not getting at home. At the University of Illinois, early education researcher Carl Bereiter was reporting dramatic success with an intensive academic program for four-year-olds. Over the course of a school year, his students, broken into small groups, attended daily two-hour sessions of language arts and basic arithmetic. The method, called direct verbal instruction, had all the charm of boot camp, but the results were startling: children who were a year or more behind their middle-class peers essentially caught up in several key areas by the time they were enrolled in school. And that was just one program; there were many others under way.

Although the National Education Association (NEA) had advocated an expansion of classrooms nationwide to include children a year younger than the eligible age for kindergarten, Cooney quoted an estimate in *Time* magazine that it would cost $2.75 billion annually to accommodate the five million four- and five-year-olds in that group, not counting the construction costs of new facilities. It was folly to think elected officials would have gone that far to support education reform, especially given that, at the time, nearly half of America's school districts didn't even offer kindergarten classes.

Emerging research and experimentation had suggested that children four and younger were ready to grasp kindergarten and first-grade concepts much sooner than previously thought, but were effectively being held back by outmoded ideas about their intellectual, social, and emotional capabilities. But a preschool revolution was rumbling, a shift of significance that coincided with the upheaval in civil rights, women's rights, consumer rights, and environmental awareness.

The nursery school model already was in decline by the mid-1960s, a crumbling vestige of the heyday of Dr. Spock. Little was asked of the child in these programs beyond participation in games and songs and remaining quietly attentive during story time. At nursery schools, "self-selection of most activities is considered a sacred precept," the report said, "the child incidentally learning all that is intellectually appropriate to his age and stage."[10]

"Until recently," Cooney wrote,[11] "educators were virtually ignoring the intellect of preschool children. . . . We may have been performing a tragic disservice to young children by not sooner recognizing that their emotional, physical, and intellectual needs are doubtless interdependent from infancy on."

The reformists, adherents of a more cognitive model of preparing young minds, had nothing against fun and games in the proper context. They also recognized the importance of emotional and social growth, given that experiences during the first six years of a child's life were of critical importance to his being able to think and learn. But to fail to offer preschoolers appropriate intellectual stimulus and challenge, they said, would be to squander brainpower and compromise their future. Cooney quoted headmistress Annemarie Roeper of the Roeper City and Country School for gifted children in Bloomfield Hills, Michigan: "Good adjustment is a basic necessity for learning" she said, "but learning also makes for good adjustment."

Cooney's report answered the very question Lloyd Morrisett posed at the dinner party. "Can a television series be designed which would actually realize the general and specific educational aims that have been suggested? I believe the answer is a resounding yes."

Almost as an aside, she added, "I strongly urge that this series be made in color."

Not long after Cooney returned to her job at Thirteen, following completion of the feasibility study, she and Lewis Freedman were summoned to the office of the station's president, John W. "Jack" Kiermaier.

As they took their seats Kiermaier flipped through pages of a fat report on his desk, finally turning to Cooney. "I don't mean to put you down," he said, "but in fact, you are *not* an expert on [preschoolers]. This report is filled with 'I think,' 'I believe,' 'I suggest.' Exactly who are you to be saying this? Why would anyone be interested in *your* opinion?"

For a few moments there was awkward silence. Then Cooney cleared her throat and said, with sincerity, "Jack, I couldn't agree with you more."

There was silence again for a beat as Cooney collected her thoughts. Up until that point, no one in a position of influence had questioned the assertive tone of the study, or its conviction. She had been encouraged by Lloyd

Morrisett not only to synthesize what she had learned during her cross-country interviews, but also to analyze and comment upon it.

Cooney finally spoke. "The Carnegie Corporation of New York is very interested in what I think. I know you find that difficult to believe, but that is the truth."

"I just don't understand it," Kiermaier replied, not exactly a vote of confidence for his producer.

Cooney returned to her desk, thinking about what had gotten her to Channel Thirteen in the first place.

"Someone I was working with on the *U.S. Steel Hour* was leaving to go to Boston to work for an educational station, WGBH," Cooney recalled. "I almost shouted, 'Educational television! What's *that*?' My heart started pounding. I couldn't believe there was such a thing and I knew in a flash that this was something I wanted to be part of. The problem was there wasn't a station in New York at the time. But there was a lawsuit that pitted the Educational Broadcasting Corporation [EBC] against the owners of a commercial station, Channel Thirteen. EBC won the suit. I called everyone I knew in New York saying, 'Get me to that general manager. I *have* to work there.'"

A friend of a friend smoothed the way for Cooney to speak by phone with Channel Thirteen's general manager, Richard D. Heffner. The conversation went like this:

Cooney: Can I be the publicist for Channel Thirteen?
Heffner: I've got a publicist. I need producers.
Cooney: Oh, I could do that.
Heffner: *Everyone* says that.
Cooney (*insistent*): I know all of these people because of the *Partisan Review* and Democratic politics; I know the issues.
Heffner: These shows are going to be about *national* issues.
Cooney (*more insistent*): I know those, too.

Heffner's lack of interest in her did not deter Cooney, and she stayed in touch. "Sure I was bluffing when I said I could produce," Cooney admitted, "but not when I said I knew who was who in public and cultural affairs, and when I said I could get good interviews. And I was such a big reader that I did, in fact, know the issues on foreign and domestic policy, and the civil rights movement, which became the great passion of those years for me."

Heffner finally agreed to schedule a formal interview with Cooney, who, hobbled by a back injury and confined by a brace, nonetheless arrived well ahead of time at the decrepit offices of Channel Thirteen, directly above Lindy's restaurant on Fifty-second Street. Heffner soon appeared, returning from lunch with a female colleague. "When I saw the lovely woman I was about to interview, I blurted, 'I'm going to hire that dame.' The woman I was with got pissed off, but I'll tell you this: it doesn't hurt to be beautiful and brilliant."

It was a brief interview:

Heffner: I've decided to give you a try.
Cooney: Great!
Heffner: But I'm not going to pay you what you're making now.
Cooney (*undeterred*): Any cut's fine.
Heffner (*a bit surprised*): All right, then. I want you to produce a weekly
    show called *Court of Reason*. The idea is two advocates will argue an
    issue before a panel of three expert judges.
Cooney: Great.
Heffner: When can you start?

Cooney quickly devised a plan to weather a three-thousand-dollar pay cut. "I had a thousand dollars in the bank, and I figured I could use a hundred of it every month to make up the shortfall," she said. "And I figured that by the time I ran out of money, I'd get a raise. It never crossed my mind that things wouldn't work out exactly the way I'd envisioned them."

One day early in her tenure at Thirteen, employees were assembled to meet the vice president of programming, Lewis Freedman. "There he sat, handsome as a movie star, with the resonant voice of a trained actor," Cooney recalled. "He did what I had heard no other leader in public television do before: he articulated a thrilling and palpable vision of what public television could be. Where others had spoken in eye-glazing generalities about education and uplift, Lewis stunned us with the picture he created. He made us see what had lured him to that place—a place almost limitless in possibilities for providing illumination and excitement and innovation. It was, at least for me, an epiphany listening to him. I knew in an instant that I had been waiting to work with such a creative and intellectual force, and what a time we had. What days we saw!"[12]

On a pitifully pinched budget, she and her associates had produced a steady stream of half-hour investigations—"Little Grandma Moses documentaries" Cooney called them—that were well received by Channel Thirteen's viewers. *A Chance at the Beginning*, the film about Martin Deutsch's work with Harlem preschoolers, was just one among many, all done on a shoestring.

"The station was really broke," Cooney said. "But Lewis Freedman came up with one brilliant idea after another—one of which was doing teach-ins on major issues on television. Not only potentially riveting as a show concept, it had the added value of being cheap, the sine qua non of all the shows we did in that period. Lewis and I became a platonic, and less criminal, version of Bonnie and Clyde, traveling by car all over New Jersey and New York, trying to beg, borrow, or steal money from local anti-poverty agencies in order to put on shows about their programs. Unlike Bonnie and Clyde, we were notably unsuccessful, probably because, in the spirit of the times, we were nonviolent.

"We finally went ahead without money and put on a three-hour anti-poverty teach-in [entitled *Poverty, Antipoverty and the Poor*]. That show . . . [won] one of eight Emmys awarded to Channel Thirteen that year—amounting to three-quarters of those given in the region—all based on the ideas of Lewis Freedman, who won a special Emmy for presiding over such an unprecedented triumph." Cooney, as producer, was awarded an Emmy for the broadcast.

The audience for the shows might have been comparatively small, by Nielsen ratings standards, but the viewers who did tune in were serious-minded adults who cared about matters of race, injustice, and the imbalance of opportunity in New York and beyond.

That inquisitive, argumentative schoolgirl from Phoenix was tackling topics that made Bud Brown, her rabble-rouser social studies teacher, quite proud. She had gumption.

From her earliest days at Thirteen, Cooney also produced the show she was hired for, *Court of Reason*. For Cooney, it was a trial by fire, for at the time she had no production experience. Yet her fair-mindedness and eagerness to understand all sides of an issue were powerful assets. "They were looking for someone with no ax to grind," she said. "They got her."

The logistics of lining up guests for *Court of Reason* would have made even a veteran producer apoplectic, let alone a rookie. "People love to appear on television, but getting four expert guests on a single subject was not an easy thing. I was in a constant stressful state. And it was *live* television."

Given Cooney's devotion to the station, it was little wonder that she had it in mind as the production center for the proposed preschool show. The feasibility study indicated as much. But that was not to be, at least as long as Jack Kiermaier was in charge.

"Neither Jack nor Lewis Freedman made any moves to get it, and they might have," Cooney said. "Jack did not see the potential at all for Channel Thirteen."

Freedman, who clashed with Kiermaier, was not long for the station. They disagreed over a play's use of a line of dialogue containing a four-letter word. Freedman dug in his heels, insisting that the piece air as written. The impasse ended with his dismissal.

Soon thereafter, Cooney signed a one-year consultancy agreement with the Carnegie Corporation. It called for her to split her time between working on the preschool project with Morrisett, who aggressively recruited her, and working with Carnegie president Alan Jay Pifer on developing a national Citizens Committee for Public Television, which was envisioned as a high-minded lobbying group.

Morrisett and Pifer had urged Cooney to leave Channel Thirteen, and she did so with little regret. Out the door walked a woman who within a few short years would provide public television with its breakthrough program.

Cooney's first task at Carnegie was to begin writing a revised and expanded version of the feasibility study for potential funding sources to review. It was referred to as a sales document and would incorporate projections about the show's content development, costs, and structure. Morrisett gave her three months to complete it, and mindful of his consultant's other responsibilities at Carnegie, encouraged Cooney to hire a professional writer as an assistant.

Cooney convinced her former associate Linda Gottlieb to take the freelance assignment for about twelve hundred dollars. At Channel Thirteen they had adjoining desks, and Cooney knew Linda to be quick, smart, and loads of fun. That Gottlieb was a working mom raising two preschoolers was a big plus. "She and I spent hours on the phone at night and we met for lunch almost every day," Cooney said. After a while, they were finishing each other's sentences and playfully brainstorming. "She'd say, 'I've got an idea,' and I would say, 'I've got an idea.'"

Gottlieb quickly condensed the feasibility study into an opening chapter for the new report. While doing so, she found herself agreeing with the observation that kids could not resist TV commercials. It was true at her home, just as it was for fathers Morrisett and Pifer.

At four years old, Sarah Morrisett had memorized an entire repertoire of TV jingles. The simple melodies, mostly written in bright major keys, were no harder to sing than a nursery rhyme. The more Sarah heard them, the better she was at repeating them, word for word.

It is not too far a stretch to say that Sarah's mastery of jingles led to a central hypothesis of the great experiment that we know as *Sesame Street:* if television could successfully teach the words and music to advertisements, couldn't it teach children more substantive material by co-opting the very elements that made ads so effective? In other words, if the neurotransmitters in their little brains could *snap, crackle, and pop* for a cereal commercial, couldn't similar electrical activity be duplicated by teaching children the concepts of *over, around, under,* and *through* by using a song?

It was understood that young children were at times a captive audience in front of the tube. What led Cooney to a major conclusion in her report to the Carnegie Corporation was the acknowledgment that preschoolers were a *receptive* audience, as well as absorbent and attentive.

Anyone who has small television viewers at home can testify to the fascination that commercials hold for children. Parents report that their children learn to recite all sorts of advertising slogans, read product names on the screen (and, more remarkably, elsewhere) and to sing commercial jingles. . . . If we accept the premise that commercials are effective teachers, it is important to be aware of their characteristics, the most obvious being frequent repetition, clever visual presentation, brevity, and clarity.

Whenever you hear "*Sesame Street* has been brought to you by the letter *T* and the number *8*," think of Sarah Morrisett singing a jingle in her tutu.

Chapter Five

Leland, Mississippi, had a bumper crop of cotton in 1936, the year Paul and Betty Henson welcomed a second son, James Maury, born in a hospital in nearby Greenville.

Paul Henson was a biologist for the U. S. Department of Agriculture, which operated a research station in Leland. Betty was a stay-at-home mother to the new baby and his older brother, Paul Jr. The second-born son was by nature shy and quietly inquisitive, a clever child who enjoyed the adoring attention of his maternal grandmother, known as "Dear," while his mother doted on Paul Jr.[1]

A family photograph, taken when Jim Henson was perhaps ten, shows him kneeling in front of a coiled garden hose. He is wrapped in what appears to be a light blanket or bed sheet, with a makeshift turban atop his head. While tooting on a wooden flute, the boy is casting a hypnotic spell on the hose, convincingly propped off the grass to appear as a cobra. The young Jimmy Henson was already trying his hand at illusion and sight gags.[2]

On sweltering summer days in Leland, Jimmy and a group of boys would meet at the Broad Street Bridge over Deer Creek, dangling their bare feet off the side or playing along the creek bend just beyond Leland Elementary School in a slightly downriver setting straight out of Mark Twain. "I was a Mississippi Tom Sawyer," Henson once said. "I rarely wore shoes. It was an idyllic time. We had a beautiful big barn and we had a creek running in front of the house for fishing. I had a BB gun and I'd shoot at the water moccasins in the swamps just to wake them up."[3]

Every year, like magic, an evening chorus of peeps and croaks along the creek would announce the arrival of spring. At night, the boys would venture out with flashlights to spear bullfrogs with pronged poles, a ritual called frog gigging. After a successful amphibian hunt, someone would skin their slimy legs, dip them in egg yolk, dredge them through flour and bread crumbs, and deep-fry them.

Lelanders are righteously and emphatically certain that these experiences explain why Henson's alter ego took the form of a frog. Like biological life itself, they say, the character rose from the primordial goop along the creek bank. They likewise claim that Henson's boyhood friend, Kermit Scott, one of the bridge kids, provided the inspiration for the name. It's a romanticized tale certainly worthy of Twain, but it is only as true as the citizens of Leland claim it to be, for a dig through the Henson archives reveals no clear confirmation of their contentions. Jim Henson is the only man who would know, and if anyone ever asked him, his best answer might have been *"Hmmmmmm."*

When Jimmy was in fifth grade, he left the swamps of Mississippi for the terra firma of suburban Hyattsville, Maryland, after his father accepted a government job in Washington. It was there, round about 1950, that the thirteen-year-old Jimmy made his international debut as a visual artist when a cartoon panel he illustrated and wrote appeared on a page in the *Christian Science Monitor*, the Boston-based daily newspaper. The primitively drawn gag features two chefs, one quite obese, standing before a pot with a protruding spoon. The openmouthed chef in the foreground, he of the slightly pendulous belly, asks, "Shall we toss it and call it a salad or cook it and call it a stew?"

It was also in that year that "I badgered my parents into buying a [TV] set," Henson recalled. "I absolutely loved television. . . . I loved the idea that what you saw was taking place somewhere else at the same time."[4]

Among the programs Henson enjoyed most was *Kukla, Fran and Ollie*, an unscripted puppet show that originated in Chicago and aired weeknights on NBC. That it was topical and tart enough for adults while amusing enough for kids distinguished it as one of television's first dinner-hour diversions for the entire family.

What the show offered was both old and new. Like a latter-day Americanized Punch and Judy, it played out on a classic mock proscenium stage, and it featured a recurring ensemble of familiar archetypes: a perplexed worrywart (Kukla), a blustery blowhard (Ollie), a haughty grand dame (Mme. Ooglepuss), and a Kentucky-fried Confederate (Colonel Cracky). Together, they constituted the Kuklapolitan Players, a troupe entirely manipulated and voiced by Burr Tillstrom, working unseen behind a scrim. Fran Allison, a winsome, willowy singer-actress, was front and center on the program, trading lines with the puppets. Extemporaneous and quick, she was comic foil and forgiving headmistress to Kukla and the bumptious Ollie, once described by *Time* magazine as "a one-toothed dragon whose preenings and posturings might have been conceived by Molière."[5]

His preoccupation with Kukla, Fran, and television led seventeen-year-old Jim Henson to the pages of the *Washington Post* on the morning of May 13, 1954. Someone had alerted him about a call for talent in that day's paper, an item in Lawrence Laurent's radio and television notes column. WTOP-TV personality Roy Meachum, the *Post* reported, "has started a search for youngsters twelve to fourteen years of age who can manipulate marionettes. Meachum has big plans, he says, and he wants to hear from any puppeteers he may have overlooked."[6]

Henson, who with the assistance of his school friend Russell Wall, had built a couple of cowboy puppets, Longhorn and Shorthorn, and another called Pierre the French Rat, hustled over to WTOP. Both were hired, and to their delight they saw this listing in the Saturday TV Highlights box in the June 19 *Post*:

WTOP-TV. *Junior Morning Show:* Washington youngsters do their version of the CBS-TV network *Morning Show.*

Alas, the joy was short-lived. A note in the Friday, June 25, *Evening Star* by "On the Air" columnist Harry MacArthur reported the imminent demise of *Junior Morning Show.* "Launched last Saturday, [it] will go back into drydock after tomorrow's telecast. Reason: Discovery that the revision of the child labor law permitting children to appear on the stage here applies to [theater] and not televison. Three of the program's participants were under fourteen and consequently could not get work permits. It will resume, says WTOP-TV program manager Tom Tausig, when suitable replacements of proper age, size, and weight can be found."

The cancellation proved to be only a minor setback: in less than a year's time, by the end of his second semester at the University of Maryland, Jim Henson would not only have his own daily television show in Washington, he would also meet his future wife and business partner, establish his own puppet repertory company (like Burr Tillstrom's Kuklapolitans), and dream up his own Charlie McCarthy, a slightly snarky signature character who could say things Jim Henson (or Edgar Bergen) never would. Cut from a section of a discarded spring coat, Kermit became the unbuttoned Henson, a garment that became his altered ego.

One early evening in the spring of 1955, University of Maryland coed Jane Nebel was lingering over dinner with a friend when she caught a glimpse of the time. "Oh, dear," she said. "We're on the air."

Jane was late, and not the kind of late like being delayed for a few extra minutes in traffic. This was late-for-your-own-wake late.

Time had just gotten away from Jane, as it often did. She smiled weakly and tried to reassure herself: "Jim won't be upset or angry. He never is."

Nebel was a senior at the College Park, Maryland, campus during the 1954–55 academic year when she met the man she would one day marry—Jim Henson, a shy, lanky freshman plagued by adolescent acne.

The previous spring, Henson had graduated from Hyattsville's new Northwestern High School, completed in 1952 and located just two miles south of the university campus. Nebel, from New York, had enrolled at Maryland in 1951.

Henson, who aspired to be a stage designer for theater and television, had declared a major in home economics, of all things. A puppetry teacher told him he would not have to take all the math and science required for a fine arts degree, and he'd be able to take more art courses if he switched over. Henson once explained, "The courses in advertising art, costume design, interior design—all of that stuff—were part of home ec." Beyond the desired classes, there was a more primal motivation to switch majors. "I think there were six guys and five hundred girls [in the department]. . . . It was marvelous."[7]

Nebel had chosen the more academically rigorous requirements for a fine arts degree. Her father, Adabert Nebel, was a prominent astrologer who wrote under the pen name Dal Lee. In 1937, he became associate editor of *Astrology Guide*. A year later he was editor of *Your Personal Astrology*, another pulpy horoscope magazine.

After taking a puppetry class together, Henson asked Nebel if she would consider working with him at his after-school job. While other Maryland undergrads toiled at mind-numbing work-study assignments—scrubbing pots in the dining hall or licking envelopes in the bursar's office—Henson was earning his pocket money as a freelance puppeteer at WRC, Washington's NBC affiliate.

The exposure gained from appearing the previous summer on WTOP's *Junior Morning Show* had proved beneficial. "The show only lasted a few weeks, but we were mentioned favorably in a couple of newspaper articles, so I took the puppets over to NBC and they started putting me on these little local shows," Henson later said. "It was interesting and kind of fun to do—but I really wasn't interested in puppetry then. When I was a kid, I never saw a puppet show, I never played with puppets or had any interest in them. It was just a means to an end. I did it to get on television."[8]

Henson was paid as little as five dollar per appearance for his work on Channel 4's daytime shows, including *Circle 4 Ranch* with Cowboy Joe Campbell, and *Inga's Angle*, a fifteen-minute food and fashion program featuring Norwegian-born model and newspaper columnist Inga Rundvold. In 1955, Inga was the lead-in for *Afternoon*, a live variety show with music from the Mel Clement Quartet and singers Jack Maggio and Tippi Stringer. Henson and Nebel worked together for the first time during appearances on *Afternoon*.

The program's master of ceremonies was amiable studio announcer Mac McGarry, who at the time marveled to the local press about the improvisational abilities of his show's nineteen-year-old puppeteer. "He comes up with material just by sitting down and thinking for a few minutes," McGarry said back then. *Afternoon's* producer-director Carl Degen was downright effusive: "The kid is positively a genius . . . absolutely amazing."[9]

McGarry's recollections of working with Henson during the Eisenhower administration are vivid and indelible. "*Afternoon* started in the spring of 1955 and lasted about six months," he said.

"Jim created these little dramas around popular recordings, with the Muppets lip-synching to the songs. The one I remember especially was 'Hey, There,' by Rosemary Clooney, which was a No. 1 hit in 1954. In the bit, Jim had an ingenue kind of character in the foreground. Then, ever so slowly, as you looked to the right, you saw this horrible skull-like creature called Yorick."

Poor Yorick was the size and shape of a good-size coconut. He had sunken hollows for cheeks, a leaden brow, and an expression that could signal menace or morbidity. He was painted a purplish blue, the color of a fresh bruise.

"The ingenue was unaware of Yorick's presence," McGarry said, "but he gradually moved toward her, finally gobbling her up. We had never seen *anything* like that before." Fifty-three years after the fact, McGarry was still laughing about the villain who ate the ingenue. One puppet devouring another—or blowing a character to smithereens—would become Henson's comedy calling card, a signature flourish that was daring and just a shade dark.

"We were college students amusing ourselves," Jane once said. "It had a quality of abandon and nonsense."[10]

"Jim was *Afternoon's* blockbuster element," McGarry said. "It wasn't long before someone at the station got the idea to give him his own show." In all likelihood, that person was WRC program director James Kovach, creator of *Afternoon's* blend of entertainment, talk, and service, a mélange that Oprah's contemporary audience would find familiar and comforting.

Kovach had spotted Henson one Saturday on the set of *Junior Morning Show,* according to WTOP's Roy Meachum. The story goes that Kovach was there to discuss Meachum's possible defection to rival WRC. Kovach eventually passed on him but was duly impressed with Henson, adding him to the *Afternoon* lineup. McGarry, the show's original host, believes it was Kovach who made room on the WRC evening schedule for *Sam and Friends.*

Either way, "it was an incredible break," Jane Henson said. She credited Tillstrom for indirectly paving the way for *Sam and Friends* by proving before 1950 that an intelligently conceived and executed program with puppets could appeal to both children and adults. "*Kukla, Fran and Ollie* really opened the possibility of our career because his show was accepted by a wide audience, a *family* audience," she said.

McGarry concurred. "Washington is a news town, and entertainment takes a backseat here," he said. "But Jim Henson was a phenomenon in Washington, with everyone from kids to great-grandmothers."

Sam and Friends debuted May 9, 1955, a live, twice-nightly comedy spot slotted for the final five minutes of WRC's local evening newscasts at 6:25 and 11:25. At suppertime it provided a giddy lead-in to NBC's two-headed roundup of national and international news, *The Huntley-Brinkley Report*. At bedtime, it warmed up viewers for *The Tonight Show* with Steve Allen.

In a sense, *Sam and Friends* was a stripped-down preview of *The Muppet Show* (1976–81), that deliciously anarchic, pun-filled vaudeville revival that all three major U.S. television networks had rejected before Henson benefactor Sir Lew Grade, later Lord Grade, bankrolled its production in London. At its peak of popularity, *The Muppet Show* was the world's most successful televised comedy, syndicated in more than a hundred countries and dubbed in fifteen foreign languages, including Mandarin, Portuguese, Polish, and Swedish.

Sam and Friends was *The Muppet Show* in cuneiform, 270 primitive seconds of satire and send-ups, parodies and pratfalls, music and mayhem. A live commercial—performed by the puppeteers—was tagged on to the broadcast. The show became a nightly showcase for the eventual dozen or so puppets that populated Henson's original repertory company, characters that were more suggestive than representational. Kermit, for instance, was vaguely amphibian but certainly not a frog in 1955. "All of the characters in those days were abstract. That was part of the principle I was working under. One of the things we've always tried to do with any of our puppets is to try to get them flexible enough so that you can have as wide a range of emotions as possible. The nice thing about Kermit is there's nothing in that head. The whole shape is merely just a cloth pattern, and so it takes the shape of your hand inside. He's so flexible and very responsive," Henson said.[11] "The old-style puppets seemed to me to have a hard, wooden quality. A painted expression on a doll is all right when the audience isn't up close, but on television it's very important that you put life and sensitivity into a puppet's face. I learned early on that the Muppets would have to have a flexibility."[12]

Some of Kermit's early cast mates—notably Sam, the nominal star— were fashioned from hard, smooth materials, including wood. Others were built from foam, felt, and fabric remnants. Some had rods attached to their arms and legs, expanding the possibilities for gesture. Some had exaggerated noses in banana and pear shapes, others had a puff ball affixed at midface. Most had wide flappable mouths, textured derma, and eyes that seemed like white eggs with black yolks.

Sam was an oval-eyed, bald, carved puppet with a bulbous nose, a thick lower lip, and ears like filled-in tea cup handles. Straight on, he had the mouth-agape, wide-eyed cartoonlike look of abject stupefaction. But with a tilt of his head or a shrug of his shoulders, Henson could suggest a limited range of other expressions for Sam. Some people thought that Sam resembled a punch-drunk prizefighter, a pug with a mug.

The character Mushmellon, who could have been Oscar the Grouch's great-grandfather, looked like a birthday balloon wrapped in shag carpeting, with a wide mouth shaped like a wedge of cantaloupe. Icky Gunk was a striped serpent with fangs that hung like apostrophes from above his lips. Professor Madcliffe had a bullet-shaped head and an extravagantly unruly mustache. But Kermit was the scene stealer. "Kermit could be so subtle," Jane Henson said. "Other puppets, not so much."

At one uncertain point, these creations became known as Muppets. Down through the years, Jane Henson has steadfastly held that the name was derived as an amalgam of "marionette" and "puppet." That notion was perpetuated, in part, by Jim Henson himself, who for many years had used it as an easy answer to explain the name's origin. Later, he disavowed that explanation, insisting that Muppet "was just a word we coined." Henson never explained the reversal, other than to say "We've done very few things connected with marionettes."[13]

And yet, consciously or unconsciously, for Henson to christen the ensemble the Muppets was to set them apart from other puppet acts; it created a new and distinctive category and nomenclature. It was the birth of a brand, and to date the most important business decision in Henson's life. Just as the Radio City Rockettes were no mere showgirls, so, too, would the Muppets become figures well beyond the conventional expectation people had when they thought of "puppets."

"When I started out, I didn't know much about puppets, and not having seen that many, I wasn't overly influenced by what had come before," Henson later said. "Puppetry has been around for thousands of years. It's part of theater in which small wooden figures serve to represent people. In theater, people represent things. With puppets, you can deal with subjects in a way that isn't possible with people. I think of puppetry as expressing oneself through charades."[14]

Sam and Friends was to the Muppets what the Cavern Club was to the Beatles. The energy was raw, the atmosphere permissive, the risk level moderately high, and the cash opportunities wherever one could find them. In addition to coming up with fresh sketches five days a week, Henson also wrote and performed commercials for Esskay pork products, Baltimore-based sponsors of *Sam and Friends*.

As the popularity of *Sam and Friends* grew, Jane Nebel went from being just one of Henson's helpers—painting sets, sewing costumes, and performing secondary characters—to being his most valued assistant, even if she occasionally lost track of time. "Jim was very capable of doing five minutes by himself, believe me," she said.

Perhaps because she performed out of camera range and was unseen, Washingtonians were curious about the woman puppeteer they heard about on *Sam and Friends*. She was cheerily profiled in the Sunday *Washington Post and Times Herald* on February 17, 1957. "Jane often turns up in the studio looking fresh from campus life in bright red knee socks, skirt, and sweater, since she spends most of her time on her knees. She's really quite a meticulous dresser and designs and makes many of her own clothes. Three nights a week Jane studies German at an adult education course—'just because it's free.' And on weekends she manages to see the man she's been dating now for two years—a philosophy student at American University."

Henson took on the multiple roles of creator, producer, director, art director, and lead performer for *Sam and Friends*. "I definitely deferred to Jim always," Jane said. "He was the main talent; I was a good assistant." That may be true, but in a Sunday piece that ran in the *Washington Post*'s TV supplement in 1956, Henson described Nebel as his performing partner. Nebel had said that Jim was "the boss" of the team. Henson had countered, "Just a little bit."

Produced without benefit of videotape or multitrack audio equipment, *Sam and Friends* nonetheless explored and exploited the outer limits of television technology, in the experimental, playful, pioneering manner of Ernie Kovacs, who was to the television screen what Charlie Parker was to the sax.

Henson saw no need to erect a puppet theater in the studio as Burr Tillstrom had done with the Kuklapolitans; doing so would have been superfluous. The studio camera's viewfinder defined the physical limits of a virtual puppet stage, Henson believed. Each television set receiving the signal at home, therefore, was its own theater.

Instead of performing from behind a physical barrier, Henson and

Nebel got on their knees and manipulated the puppets from beneath the eye of the camera, seeing their performance in real time. The camera's multiple lenses, mounted on a rotating turret, allowed a director to go in tight with a close-up or, with a wide-angle lens, add spatial layers of depth. "Tillstrom and the Bairds had more to do with the beginning of puppets on television than we did," Henson noted in a 1979 interview. "But they had developed their art and style to a certain extent *before* television. From the beginning, we worked watching a television monitor, which is very different from working in a puppet theater."[15]

In Henson's view, the studio technicians, audio engineers, and camera operators were the sorcerers; he was just an eager apprentice. "In his spare time, he'd be in the control room trying to understand what was going on," Jane Henson said. "And the technicians loved teaching him because he really learned his lessons well. He couldn't wait to try out the things he was learning on *Sam and Friends*. He would tell the technicians he would like to try this or that, and it would become a team thing."[16]

Word soon spread well beyond Washington about the Muppets, and on Friday, November 1, 1957, Jack Paar featured them on *The Tonight Show*. In doing so, Paar, who had succeeded Steve Allen as host, gave Kermit his first national exposure.

Just as Henson had used the Muppets in amusing spots for Esskay bacon, ham, and franks, so, too, did they begin to appear in off-kilter ads for Wilkins coffee, a regional roast. To viewers accustomed to the serious, straightforward commercials of the fifties, product-centric messages that drove home a point with insistent declarations ("Winston tastes good, like a cigarette should") or boasts ("Wonder bread helps build strong bodies 12 ways"), Henson's irreverent coffee ads seemed more like entertainment for its own sake.

The "stars" of these ads were Wilkins, a namesake Muppet who fancied the brand, and Wontkins, a buoy-shaped dolt with a downturned mouth. He never drank the stuff. Time after time, Wontkins paid dearly for it, most often being vaporized by a cannon blast. In one Western-themed, eight-second spot for instant coffee, Wilkins wore a cowboy hat and brandished a pistol.

Wilkins (*to Wontkins*): Howdy, stranger. I hear you don't drink Wilkins coffee.
Wontkins: Yah, so what?
Wilkins (*shooting Wontkins at close range*): Now are there any other strangers in town?

After three fatiguing years on the show, Henson contemplated walking away from the grind. "I decided that what I really wanted to do was go off and paint," he said. "I was an artist, you see, so I was going to take the shows off the air, just quit for a while. The station prevailed upon me, saying, 'Look, we'll pay you—and you can [have] someone else [perform] the show.' And so I brought in a friend of mine to work with Jane."[17] The friend was Bob Payne, an art student at Maryland.

During a yearlong Continental walkabout, Henson took in puppet performances throughout Europe. He returned to Washington impressed at how appreciated the art form was outside the United States. "Until then, I hadn't taken puppetry all that seriously," Henson said. "It just didn't seem to be the sort of thing a grown man works at for a living."

Through the years, both Jim and Jane Henson were reluctant about divulging details of how they went from being coworkers to a married couple. Once, when asked if it had been love at first sight for Jane, she replied, "No, it was admiration at first sight." During most of the years *Sam and Friends* was on the air, they were not romantically linked. In fact, both had been engaged to others, but well before they announced their intention to marry. They exchanged vows in May 1959.

By then, the Hensons were earning a handsome living producing television commercials with the Muppets, a burgeoning business they had started two years earlier. In December of 1959, the *Christian Science Monitor* speculated that the couple had grossed a hundred thousand dollars that year. "Success obviously has not spoiled Mr. and Mrs. James Maury Henson, designers and animators of the television Muppets of *Sam and Friends*," the article said. "Success has been swift . . . but money is not a topic they care to discuss. Jane Henson said, 'Money cannot measure success or happiness.'"[18]

In 1960 the Puppeteers of America annual convention was held in Detroit, to which the Hensons drove in a Rolls-Royce with a sunroof. Along for the ride was eight-week-old daughter Lisa, the first of five Henson children. The highlight of the trip was the chance to meet Burr Tillstrom. He and the Hensons hit it off famously. The story goes that Jim asked Tillstrom to drive the Rolls through the city, enabling him to pop Kermit up through the roof to say "Hi, ho, there" to the Motor City. Among those who witnessed this impromptu, one-car parade were California puppeteers Mike and Frances Oznowicz, whose high-school-age son, Frank, was showing as much aptitude in puppetry as Jim Henson had eight years prior. Henson met Frank at the 1961 Puppeteers convention in Fairmont, California, near Oakland. In a sense, it was the day that Ernie met Bert.

At the Fairmont gathering Henson approached witty writer-performer

Jerry Juhl with an offer to replace Jane Henson on *Sam and Friends*. Jane was pregnant with their second child, daughter Cheryl, and wanted to retire from performing. The idea sat well with Jim.

Juhl, who had worked on a children's show in San Jose, knew of the Muppets only by reputation, and did not know Henson at all. It wasn't until Henson opened a black box from the tailgate of his new station wagon that Juhl became fully intrigued. "The things that he brought out of that box seemed to me to be like magical presences, like totems—but funnier," he once said. "One after the other Jim pulled them out of the box, put them on his hand, and brought them to life. Who *was* this Henson guy? These things weren't even puppets—not as I had ever seen or defined them. This guy was like a sailor who had studied the compass and found that there was a fifth direction in which one could sail. When he offered me a berth on the ship, I signed on."[19]

Sam and Friends signed off in 1961, after winning a local Emmy for outstanding television entertainment. By then, the Muppets were making regular appearances on the *Today* show, and business operations had moved from Washington to New York City, where Henson and Juhl worked in cramped quarters in a three-room office on East fifty-third Street.[20]

The Muppets were by now appearing in commercials for a range of consumer goods that included Wilson Certified Meats, Ivory Snow, Gleem toothpaste, Royal Crown Cola, and Purina Dog Chow. The ads for Purina, the St. Louis–based pet foods giant, featured a flop-eared, self-deprecating, worldly wise mutt named Rowlf. Voiced by Jim Henson as the kind of guy who would listen to your troubles through the slats of the backyard fence, Rowlf was the first Muppet built by puppet designer Don Sahlin. Perhaps more than anyone who would work for the Muppets, Sahlin had an uncanny ability to intuit and decode Henson's wishes. He transformed Henson's rough sketches—virtually napkin scribbles—into fully realized characters. Beyond that, Sahlin was even zanier than the Muppets he worked on.

Six months after Sahlin's arrival, high school grad Frank Oznowicz joined the Muppets. Before the decade was over, Frank Oz—as he would later be known—would become half of one of the greatest duos in comedy history, a master puppeteer, and, most important of all, Bert, Cookie Monster, and Grover, three characters for the ages on *Sesame Street*.

In 1965, Henson began filming commercials for La Choy, purveyors of canned, ready-to-eat Americanized Chinese food. For the campaign, Henson designed a lumbering, life-size dragon fully capable of locomotion. Counting the chef's hat that he wore as a crown, the La Choy Dragon stood considerably taller than the actors hired to play against him. Operating from within the dragon, Frank Oz could swagger, flail its arms, shake its head, crane its neck, and, with the assistance of an aide with a blowtorch, breathe fire. One particularly boisterous commercial featured a Cub Scout and his mother at the supermarket.

Mother (*to herself*): What do you feed twelve hungry Cub Scouts?
Dragon (*rounding a corner*): May I make a suggestion?
Mother (*alarmed and pulling her son close*): Who are you!
Dragon (*knocking cans off the shelf*): I'm the La Choy Dragon!
Cub Scout: Yah! A real dragon!
Dragon: What you need is La Choy chow mein! It's never mushy. It's crisp and crunchy.
Mother (*skeptically*): It is, huh?
Dragon: Yah. La Choy chow mein is cooked by me in real dragon fire. (He exhales flames and sets fire to a La Choy banner.) La Choy chow mein is as crisp and good as the takeout kind. And one more thing.
Mother: What's that?
Dragon: Try La Choy noodles! Serve them with La Choy chow mein for a perfect meal in six minutes. (*Bellowing*) Buy some today!

The blond actress cast as the startled shopper was Jon Stone's girlfriend, Beverley Owen.

Without knowing it, everyone on the set that day took one step closer to *Sesame Street*.

Chapter Six

J on Stone and Tom Whedon remained comrades-in-arms long after the drunken night they told off Bob Keeshan at the steak house.

As newly minted writing partners their first big break came when they met Fred Silverman, a CBS vice president fresh out of Syracuse University. At twenty-six, Silverman had been handed responsibility for children's shows at CBS, under the network's senior vice president for programming, Michael Dann. Still stinging from Newton Minow's complaints about the paucity of quality television for children, Dann and Silverman were hurrying a series into production to placate the FCC. Their new *CBS Children's Film Festival*, sponsored by Xerox, would showcase children's films from around the world. Silverman needed capable hands to arrange for the films to be dubbed and edited and to write scripts and commercials for the hosts of the series. That Stone and Whedon had previously worked with puppets gave them an edge: Burr Tillstrom had already signed to host the series, along with Kukla, Fran, and Ollie.

Stone and Whedon signed on, commuting to Tillstrom's hometown of Chicago, where the show's inserts were produced at WBBM, the city's landmark CBS affiliate. At first, the assignment was a delight. "Burr and Fran took us under their wings at once, showing us Burr's beloved Chicago, dining us at the Pump Room (always at table one, the most visible one just outside the entrance), and telling us countless stories about the old days," Stone said.

It's worth a slight detour to share some of those tales, for they have an indirect bearing on the history of *Sesame Street*.

In 1936, the year Jim Henson was born, a slightly gap-toothed single man attended a Chicago performance of the Ballets Russes de Monte Carlo, featuring Tamara Toumanova. Luminous, dark-haired Toumanova had joined the dance company at puberty and was now one of the internationally known "baby ballerinas" of the Ballets Russes, along with Irina Baronova and Tatiana Riabouchinska. For a spell in the 1930s, the three teens were the toast of Europe.

Toumanova's performance left the Chicago audience members enraptured, none more so than Franklin Burr Tillstrom, the blue-eyed gentleman waiting—more than a bit nervously—to have a word with the dancer. Through luck and pluck, he had been invited to go backstage.

Tillstrom, an ardent bicyclist and swimmer, cut a fine athletic profile. In the parlance of the day, he was a swell guy, a stylishly dressed, neatly groomed, exquisitely polite, mostly happy fella who lived with his parents, Dr. Burt Tillstrom, a chiropodist, and his wife, Alice, in an apartment on Chicago's North Side. Summers were spent at grandparents' homes in Benton Harbor, Michigan, where, as youngsters, Burr and his brother, Dick, were encouraged to hike, sail, and explore. When Dr. Tillstrom joined the family on weekends, he would read classic children's literature to his sons or spin fanciful tales of his own making during their walks in the woods.

Young Burr was precocious and theatrical. "As a child, I always tried to mimic performances and movies I saw with small figures, stuffed teddy bears, dolls, anything I could make move."[1] One day, while home sick, Burr staged a puppet show for the neighborhood children, using the windowsill of their ground-floor apartment as his stage. By fourteen, he had an entire act starring handcrafted marionettes he'd built at home. One of his first professional appearances was at a lawn party; he was paid $8.10 for a puppet performance of "Rip Van Winkle."[2]

After graduation from Chicago's Senn High School, Tillstrom accepted a scholarship to the University of Chicago, from which, to the dismay of his parents, he dropped out after a year to pursue show business. After failing to get work as an actor or radio performer, Tillstrom took a job with the Chicago Park District. The city agency had started a puppet theater, with funding from the Works Progress Administration (WPA), President Roosevelt's massive New Deal relief program to provide income to the unemployed. Along with the construction of some 650,000 miles of roads, 125,000 buildings, and 78,000 bridges, the WPA also allocated 7 percent of its funding to arts projects across the continent, putting writers, painters, and puppeteers back to work. While building characters for the puppet theater, Tillstrom carved a character with rosy cheeks, a red doorknob nose, upholstery-tack eyes, arched brows, and an oval mouth that, depending on the situation, could express astonishment, bewilderment, or bedevilment, or a mixture of the three. The puppet had the startled look of being sprung from a jack-in-the-box.

Until the night of the ballet, the puppet had no name. But then fate stepped in, wearing a tutu. As Tillstrom was ushered in to meet Miss Toumanova, the dancer was facing her dressing-room mirror. Tillstrom, suddenly knock-kneed, needed a drink. But Toumanova, whose mother accompanied her on tour, was chatty and charming around her handsome guest. While Toumanova primped at her dressing-room mirror, Tillstrom reached inside a green paper bag he was holding, dipped down, and, using a seat back as an impromptu stage, revealed the puppet sprite just over the dancer's shoulder. "Ah, kukla," she said, and sighed, with a slight tilt of the head. In Russian, *kukla* means "doll."

Thus was christened the wise, worried, whiny, self-aware, slightly sarcastic, bald, blunt Kukla, a puppet who became a household name in 1940s and 1950s America—and Tillstrom's right-hand man and second self. For laughs, Tillstrom began to take Kukla along to parties, allowing the puppet to sass friends in a way he never could. "Kukla was really smart with people. When I was too young or too ignorant to have an answer, Kukla took over."[3]

The party performances led to bookings at fairs, night clubs, and local theaters. To add an edge of satire and conflict, Tillstrom's puppet repertory company—the Kuklapolitan Players—expanded with the addition of Madame Ophelia Ooglepuss, a delusional diva, and Ollie, the impetuous dragon with a leopard-skin neck.

In 1939, Tillstrom turned down a chance to tour Europe with his puppets, electing instead to take an offer to manage a marionette theater at Chicago's Marshall Field and Company department store. Tillstrom gave Saturday morning performances at the landmark emporium, where the motto was: "Give the lady what she wants."

When General Sarnoff's latest electronic marvel, the television, arrived at Marshall Field's in 1939, Tillstrom begged RCA and store management to add his puppets to a closed-circuit demonstration telecast. With urging from the audio and video engineers, who rather enjoyed Kukla's hectoring, the bigwigs acquiesced, and the televised puppets proved to have surprising dimensionality, immediacy, and rapport with the hosts of the demo, well-known local radio personalities Garry Moore and Durwood Kirby.

The impromptu audition led RCA to invite Tillstrom and his troupe to demonstrate television at the 1939 New York World's Fair. "Kukla and Ollie would be announced by a very straight announcer type," Tillstrom said. "I used to get Kukla up to heckle [him]. . . . There were all sorts of lovely actresses and models, acting as hostesses to explain this new medium of television to the people. Eventually I began to use them [in the act]."[4] Tillstom might have been ready for prime time, but the outbreak of World War II slowed the development of the new medium almost to a halt.

After the war, as TV programming was slowly becoming available in Chicago, Captain Bill Eddy, director of station WBKB, approached Tillstrom to create an hour-long children's TV show. As Max Wilk noted in 1976, there were some three thousand sets in Chicago, but most of them were in taverns and saloons. "They wanted television to be brought into the home and decided that the Kuklapolitans would be just the right choice for that. We were contracted to do thirteen weeks, Tillstrom said."[5] The thought of delivering a daily block of live entertainment made Tillstrom shiver; he had no earthly idea what format the show should take or who should write for it.

"I'll get you all the producers and writers you need," Eddy said.

"What would I do with writers?" Tillstrom asked. "With my hands full of puppets, I couldn't read a script if I had one."

"Well, what *do* you need?" Eddy asked.

It was a good question.

"A girl to work out front," Tillstrom said. "Somebody who could interview guest stars, sing a song now and then. I guess what I really need is a girl who can talk to a dragon." Tillstrom remembered a sweet, sunny vocalist and quick-study comedienne who, months before, had passed an informal audition with him.

"Say," said Tillstrom to Eddy, "do you know how I can get in touch with Fran Allison?"[6]

Tillstrom surmised that dragon charmer might be a perfect role for her; she'd already done something similar once for Tillstrom while chatting between performances at the Great Lakes Naval Training Center. Both were there to entertain wounded servicemen, and when Allison had looked directly into Ollie's soulful sewn-on eyes, she began conversing with the dragon as if it were a sentient being instead of a shirtsleeve extension. It made a lasting impression on Tillstrom, who never, ever referred to his creations as puppets. The Kuklapolitans were "kids" who were born in his home workshop; bachelor Burr was their benefactor and benevolent guardian. In time, Allison would buy in completely to the conceit that Kukla and Ollie were "real," sock puppets with souls. "Fran always believed," said Tillstrom.[7]

Allison was a small-town Iowan with bales and bales of gumption. After graduation from tiny Coe College, she had taught grade-schoolers in the small Iowa towns of Schleswig and Pocahontas. Upon being notified that after four years her hundred-dollar-a-month salary would be increased by only two dollars, she quit teaching to pursue theater. After spotting an advertisement in a Kansas City newspaper for a "wonderful opportunity" awaiting young dramatists, she withdrew fifty dollars from her savings to enroll in a two-week course in play producing.[8] But after a cruel month on the road with a money-losing show, she trudged back home to La Porte City, Iowa, with fifty cents in her pocket.

Still determined to make a go of show business, she sang on local radio shows in Cedar Rapids, Ottumwa, and Waterloo, where one afternoon in 1934 at station WMT, she was startled by Joe DuMond, host of the *Cornhuskers* program. Vamping to fill the final three minutes of the show, DuMond stuck a live microphone in front of Allison. "Well, well, folks," he said. "Guess who just dropped in—Aunt Fanny! Come on up here and tell us what's new." Summoning the voice of a spinster who blabbed small-town secrets, Allison ad libbed fluidly and flawlessly. "Well, Mr. DuMond," she said. "I dropped by to see Daisy Dosselhurst yesterday and her Junior came to the door. I said real nice, 'Junior, is your mother home?' 'No, she ain't,' he said. 'Is your father home?' I asked. 'No, he ain't,' he said. Well, I heard just about enough ain'ts, so I said, 'Where's your grammar?' He answered quick, 'She ain't here, either.'" The impromptu dish of cornpone earned Allison a sponsor (a manufacturer of heavy farm equipment) and a daily comedy spot on WMT.

Impressed with her improvisational comedy, the station manager in Waterloo sent a transcription of an Aunt Fanny routine to Don McNeill, host and toastmaster of *The Breakfast Club*, a daily entertainment hour from Chicago that was quickly becoming a network radio institution for Depression-era listeners. McNeill's upbeat mix of popular music and mild mayhem provided an antidote to the despair of morning newscasts. Allison not only successfully relocated Aunt Fanny to Chicago, she also was chosen as a featured *Breakfast Club* vocalist. *Collier's* noted that "between programs, Fran carried on a rushing business in singing commercials, partly because she could sing in one key and whistle in another, a rare talent which permitted the perpetrators of the commercials to work out a variety of special effects without doubling the payroll."[9]

Tillstrom asked Allison to meet him at a coffee shop to discuss his ideas for *Junior Jamboree*, the new TV show featuring his puppet troupe. As the leggy models at the World's Fair had, Allison would face the camera and freely mix with the puppets. The entire show would hinge on their ad libs; there would be no scripts to memorize and no rehearsal. Before airtime, they would agree to a list of possible topics. Their byplay would be conversational, like neighbors yakking over a fence, and he urged her to summon an air that would be as close to her authentic personality as the situations would allow. This idiosyncratic informality would become a hallmark of the so-called Chicago school of television, the graduates of which included Dave Garroway (*Garroway at Large*) and Studs Terkel (*Studs' Place*).

Junior Jamboree launched October 14, 1947. On October 22, *Variety* cast a cynical eye on the show:

Junior Jamboree, touted as the first 60-minute tele series on a five-day sked, is cued to kids in the 6–16 bracket. RCA-Victor dealers are urging youngsters to visit nabe stores and see the show, idea being that small fry may wheedle mom and pop into buying a receiver. All of which is smart promotion, even though some double-crossing parents may buy another brand.

Kukla, a puppet voiced by Burr Tillstrom, emcees J.J., performing on a stage that simulates the RCA receiver. Continuity includes film shorts, animated cartoons, demonstration of juve hobbies, and interviews by Fran Allison. Mail pull has kids telling why they want a dog, with a barker awarded weekly for best letter. Miss Allison also appears with lost dog for possible recognition by kid viewer.

Dialogue, ad libbed from an outline, ran smoothly. Miss Allison, known to radio fans as Aunt Fanny of the *Breakfast Club*, is a veteran at off-the-cuff repartee, while Tillstrom has been puppet chattering for more than a decade.

Show, which premiered October 14, seems tailor-made for a juve audience.

Renamed *Kukla, Fran and Ollie* when it was aired nationally on NBC in 1949, the show prompted passersby to press their noses against appliance store windows. By 1950, the cyclonic force of the show's popularity prompted toy makers to approach Tillstrom, but the idea of assembly-line replicas of his darlings was anathema to him. "I respected him so much for having turned down a fortune," Allison recalled.[10]

Jon Stone described his time on the *CBS Children's Film Festival* with Tillstrom as "another step in my puppetry education," providing insights that would later inform the Muppets of *Sesame Street*.

"Gus Allegretti [on *Captain Kangaroo*] had given me the introductory course, and, once again, I was in the presence of greatness," Stone said. "Burr was a near genius. The magic that Kukla and Ollie exuded was beyond reason or explanation. It certainly wasn't in the puppets themselves. My kids made better papier-mâché puppets in the third grade. And the magic did not come from the manipulation. Ollie's mouth opened and closed in the most remote relationship to the dialogue he was supposed to be spouting, and with every syllable there was the most disconcerting *clack* whenever the mouth clamp closed. Kukla had no mouth movement at all. What then made these two characters so believable was Burr. He breathed life and humor and depth into his little pals by giving them character. From Burr I learned that the success of the character comes a hundred percent from the puppeteer underneath, not from any externals or cosmetics or tricky gadgetry."

Despite positive reviews and decent ratings, Stone and Whedon were replaced after the film festival's first season. "Fred Silverman's volatility and snap judgments were already legend among colleagues," Stone said. "My association with him taught me other valuable lessons about the television business. [Though] we had set the tone and format of the program and devised an economical and efficient method of operation, the suits apparently had decided that they could find someone cheaper who could carry on our work. We spoke bitterly of our disappointment to Burr, who reassured us that we were his boys, and if we weren't coming back for season two, neither would Kukla, Fran and Ollie. One for all and all for one! But when season two rolled around, Burr was back, and Tom and I were history."

Not long afterward, however, Silverman was back on the phone with Stone and Whedon's agent, dangling a chance to develop a series. After a preliminary meeting at his office to discuss the project, a series built around a classic, albeit well-worn, fairy-tale heroine, Silverman invited Stone and Whedon back to meet one of the creative partners he had in mind for it. "Friday morning we are going to meet with Christ and his dog," he said.

Lean, bearded Jim Henson, whose dog puppet Rowlf had been riffing with that smoothie Jimmy Dean on his popular prime-time show on ABC, listened to the pitch Stone and Whedon had prepared that involved an actress as Snow White who would be surrounded by woodland puppets. "Jim nodded characteristically and *hmmmmmed* as we talked, then gently began to explain to us why realistic animal puppets are not nearly as easy or effective as more abstract puppets. Tom and I glanced at each other. 'He doesn't like it,' we thought. 'We've lost him.' And then, softly, suddenly Jim said he liked the idea. Count him in."

"No sooner had Jim nodded than the door bust open and an army of suits filled the room," Stone said. Among them were Bernie Brillstein, Henson's agent, and Al Gottesman, the puppeteer's business manager. "All were suddenly at the table, machine-gunning demands of a hundred percent of merchandising, percentage of gross revenues, percentages of ownership, residual control, and a hundred other demands. Tom and I watched in amazement. It was my first experience doing business with Jim but far from the last. Over the years, Jim became a close personal friend and we developed a strong mutual professional respect, but none of that ever got in the way of The Deal. Jim was a killer businessman."

The explanation for Silverman's sudden interest in commissioning a pilot script for Snow White turned out to be show business as usual. Bob Keeshan's contract was up for renewal at CBS, and Captain Kangaroo himself had been making noises about leaping to a competing network.

Development on Snow White screeched to a halt once CBS signed a new deal with Keeshan, and Silverman agreed to allow Stone and Whedon's new representative from General Artists Corporation to shop their script elsewhere.[11] "CBS could have cared less now what happened to Snow White. As soon as we secured the rights, we took the idea to ABC. Jim was still willing to participate and the idea was still sound."

An ABC programming chief gave approval for a pilot, with one catch: lose Snow White. "Since it had been CBS's idea to center the story on Snow White, that somehow tarnished the whole concept in the eyes of ABC," Stone said. The network demanded that the lead character come from a different fairy tale. "Tom and I couldn't figure out how the audience in television land would associate Snow White with CBS, but by then we knew better than to try to apply logic when dealing with network suits. Cinderella it was."

Songs for the *Cinderella* pilot were composed by Joe Raposo, that lounge pianist who provided the entr'acte music for the production Stone directed on Cape Cod back in 1955. "We had stayed friends when we moved to New York City," Stone said, "but the *Cinderella* pilot brought us together professionally for the first time." It also marked the first collaboration between *Sesame Street* patriarchs Henson and Raposo. When one considers that the Muppet performers in the project included Frank Oz and Jerry Nelson, who would later give life to the Count, Herry Monster, and Sherlock Hemlock, *Cinderella* was almost a dress rehearsal for *Sesame Street*.

On the final night of taping, a rollicking wrap party also served as a send-off for Oz, who had received his army induction notice. He was due to take his preinduction physical the next morning, and the unspoken concern was that he would be shipped off to Vietnam, like so many men his age. "We all gave him presents and hugs and all the support we could," Stone said. "We partied until the wee hours, and at 6:00 a.m. Frank was to board the military bus to Fort Dix to face his uncertain future."

Oz failed the physical and was reclassified 4-F. He would get no closer to Saigon than Syossett, Long Island.

Everything was progressing splendidly for a fall launch for *Cinderella* on ABC's Saturday schedule when the project was once again denied a happy ending. Roone Arledge, ABC's visionary programming executive for sports, landed a college football Game of the Week package for the network that forced an entire revamping of the late-morning and early-afternoon schedule.

Soon after, Henson approached Stone and Whedon with a plan to expand the pilot into an hour special. Retitled *Hey, Cinderella*, the project was mounted in Canada with the original creative team. Henson served as both producer and director.

When it was finally aired in the United States in 1970, the result was less than the sum of its parts. Though abundant talent was involved, the final edit of *Hey, Cinderella* was bloated, draggy, and all but bereft of laughs. Even Kermit seemed bored by it, and he served as a kind of sardonic Muppet-master of ceremonies.

We'll never know if the half-hour series would have soared, but the hour special sank under its own weight.

In the spring of 1964, a somewhat reluctant Beverley Owen was cast in an oddball pilot for CBS that turned into a monster hit. When *The Munsters* debuted in September of that year, she played the quite normal niece in a household that otherwise included not only the bride of Frankenstein (Lily), but her groom (Herman), her son (Eddie), and a grandpa. Marilyn, a manhunter in the classic coed sense, attended Westbury College. Whenever she would bring a suitor home to 1313 Mockingbird Lane, he would run screaming into the night after meeting the family.

The series was shot in Los Angeles, necessitating long stays out West for Owen, who was under contract to Universal. The absences caused a strain on her relationship with Stone, who had spoken of commitment but had yet to produce an engagement ring. "It was decision time," Stone said, "and we decided that we both wanted to change the bicoastal relationship."

Stone and Owen were unsure how to proceed, but they took the advice of Marvin Josephson, a powerful New York–based agent who suggested they find a way to cost Universal some cash. Stone recalled Josephson saying, "Money is at the core of everything in this business. Not art, not comedy, not fame. If you cost them money, they'll be glad to see the last of you."

A plan emerged. "Beverley made it known how unhappy she was, and this unhappiness began to manifest itself in bouts of physical illness, throwing up in the dressing room, being unable to get to the set on time, interrupting takes with spontaneous bouts of tears."

After thirteen weeks, the part of Marilyn was recast, and Owen was back in New York. She married Stone in June 1966, and the couple moved to an A-frame in Vermont, where Stone split his time between working on the house and developing scripts.

Their daughter, Polly, was born the following November, a child whose little handprints were all over *Sesame Streeet*.

Chapter Seven

C hester and Margaret Spinney spent Christmas Day, 1933, awaiting the birth of their third child. What a blessing it would be for the baby to arrive on that most joyous of all days! But as the hours ticked by, with Margaret abed in the dining room of their home in Waltham, Massachusetts, the baby's trip through the birth canal had stalled. Chester reassured Margaret that everything would be fine, but the delay was terribly unsettling for husband and wife, and for good reason.

In another room slept two Spinney sons: seventeen-month-old Donald and his four-year-old brother, David. On the night David was born in 1929, the doctor who was expected to perform the delivery opted to linger at a party, rather than sit waiting at the bedside of a woman who might take another twenty-four hours to deliver. Instead, he dispatched a midwife. Upon arrival, when the woman saw how far along things were, she tied Margaret's legs together, hoping to hold back delivery until the doctor could appear. Within Margaret's swollen belly, a presumably healthy boy was thrust into distress. The force of the baby's skull ramming the pelvic bone left the child crippled for life with cerebral palsy.

That tragedy was what haunted the Spinneys on the Christmas Eve that Caroll Edwin Spinney—the man who would become the childlike Big Bird—was born.

Chester, a frugal and sometimes obstinate New Englander, made tiny screws at the Waltham watch factory, the town's pride and major employer. His upbringing in Eastport, Maine, had been severe, thanks to a storybook-cruel stepmother and a Scots father with a volatile temper that was forever scarring Chester and his siblings.

Margaret's childhood in Great Britain and Canada was, if anything, even worse. Born desperately poor in Bolton, England, she was taken in at age two by an aunt and uncle in Cornwall, an unkind couple who doted on their misbehaving son while mistreating their niece. Young Margaret was tormented by her rambunctious younger cousin Arthur. Once, while chasing her around the backyard with a stick, he speared her in the cheek with its whittled point. Not only did Margaret's aunt refuse to tend to the puncture wound, she sent the young girl to bed without supper. Her justification for punishing the victim was "Arthur warned you to get out of the way. You didn't listen."

When Margaret was eight, the family boarded a ship bound for Halifax, Nova Scotia. Margaret was never to see her parents again, and she spent the remainder of her childhood as an unpaid scullery maid. She was forbidden to approach neighbors and was taken out of school in the ninth grade. The only Christmas celebration she ever attended was spoiled when her relations departed prematurely after Arthur threw a tantrum at the host's home. Left under a lit Christmas tree was an unopened present for Margaret, but she did manage to grab a tiny pine bough and brought it home, fashioning decorations for it from tinfoil.

At seventeen, after the death of her uncle, Margaret moved to a boardinghouse in Concord, Massachusetts, with her aunt and cousin. She worked the day shift at the watch factory and took art classes at night, longing for the time when she could live independently. It soon came.

One day, while she was bathing at Walden Pond, a young man named Chester Spinney playfully splashed her, much to her annoyance, as it ruined her perm. Family lore has it that the first word Margaret said to her future husband was, "Fresh!"

When she first arrived in Concord, Margaret had signed up for art classes. Later, seeing an ad in the *Boston Globe* announcing an opening for a fashion illustrator at the newspaper, she immediately applied, but heard nothing. A few weeks later, a woman at the boardinghouse cavalierly delivered an old phone message. "By the way," she said to Margaret, "Your boyfriend Roger called, Roger something from the *Boston Globe*." Margaret ran for the telephone and dialed the newspaper.

"I thought you weren't interested," Roger said; the position had been filled. Margaret cursed the fates, and such an employment opportunity never came again. Margaret married Chester in 1925, then Donald and David came along, and a third son completed the family in the predawn hours of December 26, 1933. Caroll Spinney was never late for a Christmas celebration again.

The name choice was his mother's, after she had decided against her initial choice, Douglas. "She cruelly named me Caroll, as in Christmas carol. I like it now, but [growing up] it was like being a boy named Sue."[1]

Spinney's life began at the Depression's nadir, the year 150,000 onlookers at the U.S. Capitol gathered to witness President Roosevelt sworn in as president. When he was six or so, his mother began creating costumes and playthings for nursery school kids at the Green Acres School in Waltham, including a paisley elephant that fit over two children, back and front. It was during a fair at that school in 1940 that Caroll attended his first puppet show.

By second grade Spinney weighed only forty-two pounds and answered to the nickname Peewee. At that early age, he demonstrated artistic talent and was encouraged by his mother to follow his imagination without inhibition. He was a bit of a showman. His first paid gig came while performing under a proscenium-arched doorway at home, mimicking a song-and-dance routine from a Shirley Temple movie. "My cousin Caroll, who I was named after, applauded and gave me fifty cents," Spinney said. "A fifty-cent piece looks *this* big when you are only four or five. It was the most money I'd ever seen in my life. It would have taken me to the movies five weeks in a row when I was a little older."

In 1940, the Spinneys moved from industrial Waltham to a nine-room house on Main Street in Acton, purchased for sixteen hundred dollars. "It was a lovely country town with horse wagons pulling hay and a Baker electric automobile running around," Spinney recalls. His father commuted the fifteen miles to the watch factory, even during the gas-rationing days of World War II. "Watches were considered crucial by the government, so he got more coupons than he needed," Spinney said. "He sold them on the black market, as many people did in those days. Someone would say, 'I have no way to get gas' and my father would reply, 'Here's two coupons. Give me a dollar.'"

When Spinney was eight, he bought a monkey puppet for a nickel at a rummage sale in Acton. Then, as a Christmas gift, his mother fashioned a snake puppet for him from a length of green flannel stuffed with batting. With that, Spinney set about building a theater in his family's barn from orange crates, boards, and logs. His first audience in the barn theater— a mix of adults and children—paid an admission of two cents. "I can't imagine what I did with only the monkey and the snake to keep people entertained for half an hour. But as I recall, everyone left with smiles on their faces."

For the following Christmas, his mother spent long hours in the local library researching the raucous, irreverent history of Punch and Judy. As a child, Margaret had seen a version of Punch and Judy performed in Blackpool, England, and she had introduced her youngest son to their violent slapstick. As a combination Christmas-birthday gift, Margaret built eight handmade replicas of the characters for Caroll, and, with the assistance of his older brother, Donald, a collapsible puppet stage. "Having that Punch and Judy show was the beginning of finally having a repertoire of shows," Spinney said. "My mother wrote them all." Like the radio actors he so admired, Spinney worked on comic voices, a talent that would expand as he matured. Naturally, his characters all had tinges of a Boston accent. If he was doing a ghost, it would sound like a ghoul from Gloucester.

When Spinney was in seventh grade, his English teacher paid him two dollars to bring his puppets to a child's birthday party in Concord. The teacher agreed to turn script pages for him, but afterward chastised him for being unprofessional, telling him, "Don't you ever give that show again without memorizing it." It would not be the last time Spinney would be criticized for relying on a script. Other bookings followed, and by sixteen he was appearing regularly at churches, fraternal lodges, and private parties. "I had this desire to perform," Spinney said. "The great thing about puppets is that you can be several characters at the same time, and they interact. When I'd hear the response from the audience, I'd say, 'This is for me.' I used to be accused of being a showoff on occasion, but I was very insecure. I never had any serious desire to be an actor, to be seen by the audience."

One afternoon in 1947 Spinney sped through the streets of Acton on his bicycle. It was nearing 5:00 p.m. and he did not want to arrive late for the gathering at Dr. Forbes's house. In his mind, he was breaking the sound barrier, thunderous booms trailing in his wake.

Spinney never lacked for imagination, due in part to his devotion to the theater-of-the-mind that was radio. He'd sit cross-legged on the floor and listen to Edgar Bergen and his wisecracking dummy, Charlie McCarthy; to George Burns and his daffy spouse, Gracie Allen; to *Blondie* and *Henry Aldrich*. Radio provided daily stimuli. "All [a character] would have to do is say, 'Gee, Billy, look at that castle. *Whooo.* Why, it goes right up into the clouds,' and I would see that castle," Spinney said. "Later, when TV started, they couldn't afford to build a castle that went up in the clouds. It would look crappy." But in postwar Boston, a new era in home entertainment was dawning. "TV became big all of a sudden and radio was over," Spinney said, with the tone of regret one might use to describe the loss of a best friend.

Spinney was twelve on that afternoon in '47, a glorious time to be a pre-teen. The lean years were over, America was on the upswing, and there seemed to be an explosion of new things to see and think about in the Boston area, not the least of which was television. Back in 1940, Spinney had seen a demonstration of the technology at the New York World's Fair, then in its extended second year. "There was a lady singing on this gray picture on a twelve-inch screen," he recalled. "The box for the screen was huge, and I couldn't quite understand it at first. 'How come she's in there and I'm seeing it right now?'" It seemed miraculous.

Seven years later, Dr. Forbes invited Spinney and some neighborhood friends to see a local television show on the physician's newly purchased set, the first one in town. Spinney arrived just in time to see a few minutes of a children's show on WBZ, Channel 4. "There was a guy with a swan puppet," he recalled. "Swans are big in Boston, like the swan boats on Boston Common. But [the puppet] was like an oven mitt, and it was just flapping along. The guy did not know how to lip-synch." The performance was underwhelming, and as Spinney rode home, he told himself that he could already do better than that guy, muttering, "If *he* could get a show . . . "

"I decided right then. That's it, I'm going to be on television when I grow up," Spinney said. "Even before that, I had thought that TV would be great for puppets, because puppet theaters were a lot like TV screens. I went home and said to my mom, 'I saw television today.' And she said, 'What did you think?' I said, 'Well, it was great, but I've decided that someday I'm going to be on the *best* kids' TV show.'"

The Spinneys became the second family in town to have TV, a shocking purchase for "the biggest tightwad in the world," as Spinney described his father. "He always bragged about being Scotch and then went about proving it.

"The television had a seven-inch screen with a big bubble magnifier in front of it," he said. "People would drive for miles around to see it. Sometimes there would be as many as thirty people trying to see that seven-inch screen. So we all had to sit in a triangle within the range of that bubble. People sat behind the couch, looking over people's shoulders. But we had to watch what my father decided to watch. We could not change the station unless he wasn't watching."

Chester's alpha-male lording over of the TV dial proved to be both obstinate and ignorant, Spinney recalled. "In 1950, when *I Love Lucy* came to TV, I said, 'The kids are all talking about [this show]. We've got to watch it!' My father said, '*I Love Lucy*? I don't want a love movie. I wouldn't like it with a name like that.'

"I said, 'No, I *know* you'd like it, Dad. I know what you like and it's funny.' He said, 'No, I wouldn't!'"

Chester the grouch, the wary watchmaker, eventually welcomed the Ricardos into his living room when "finally the guys at work said, 'Boy, is that show funny.' Then he would tune in," Spinney said.

Chester Spinney vowed that he would not contribute a single penny toward an art school education for his youngest son. "He didn't want me to go to college," Caroll Spinney said. "He wanted me to work in the watch factory." As a high school student, Spinney had demonstrated a fine aptitude for drawing, as his mother had. But his father was unimpressed.

Spinney needed to raise $250 to cover tuition at the School of Practical Art. Coming up with it was difficult, he recalled. "If you got a job, you only made fifty-five cents an hour—if you were lucky." So, with help from his father's connections, he landed a position at the Waltham clock factory manufacturing axels for gears. As a machinist, he was a fine artist. "I remember running the lathe right through my thumb," he said, an excruciating mishap. But he bandaged it up and returned to his post within a half hour, as nothing was going to get in the way of his determination to attend art school. "I managed to come up with the money," he said.

"I studied all the way from figure drawing to calligraphy, lettering, advertising layout, and product illustration," Spinney said. "I remember drawing a Milky Way [candy bar] whose wrapper was ripped a little bit. I was really good at drawing oozing caramel."

Commercial art was enjoyable, but whatever praise might follow was always delayed, Spinney said. With puppetry, the gratification of applause was immediate. He pursued both until the middle of his second year in the School of Practical Art's three-year program. "The Korean War was raging and I began to worry about being drafted," he said.

A tiff with Chester over use of the family car pushed Spinney out the door. "I never seemed to put enough gasoline in it for him," Spinney said, "even though I brought it back with more gas than when I left. He always said it was full and that I had not left it full." So one morning, totally fed up, Spinney impulsively turned to an art school buddy. "Wanna join the air force?" he asked. They enlisted that day.

"Somebody gave me great advice," Spinney said. "He said that when you go to basic training, if you're good at something, take some samples of what you can do. So I brought all of my best samples of [what I'd done] in art school." Spinney had admired the air force recruitment posters he had seen in Massachusetts and was overjoyed to discover that the art studio where they had been created was right where he was stationed: Sampson Air Force Base, near Waterloo, New York. "I took my art to the department but they said all of the positions were filled. I said, 'Curses! I've got to get in there.'" Spinney petitioned to take a specialist's test to qualify as a draftsman. "You had to get an eighty-five on the exam and I got an eighty-six. It was multiple choice, and just by using logic I passed. But an officer said, 'I'm sorry. I'm afraid you didn't make it. They'd like you to have at least a ninety.'"

Crestfallen, Spinney walked back to the barracks, test results in hand. On his way, he encountered a major he knew. "Well, did you pass?" he asked.

"No, sir," Spinney said.

"Let me see," the major said, looking over the results. "Yes, you did pass. You've got an eighty-six. You're a draftsman."

With that, "Everybody had to go off for five months of training but me," Spinney said. "I went off to a real job, stationed in Las Vegas. The first day I got there was 117 degrees, then it was 119, the third day 122. The base was just broiling. When I was being assigned, I learned there were a lot of draftsmen. So I said to the captain, 'I'm not really a draftsman. I'm an artist.' He said, 'What?' Seconds of silence felt like minutes.

"I showed him my work from art school and he said, 'Oh, there is a God. I've been asking headquarters for an artist, not just draftsmen, and they keep saying there aren't any.'" After a pause, the captain looked directly at Spinney. "All right," he said. "You're an artist."

Among the projects that came his way, Spinney helped design a poster entitled "How to Bomb and Strafe." He said he worked for days to make the bombs appear shiny.

Spinney's run of good fortune took an unexpected turn when the wife of a marine captain convinced local television station KLAS to audition the puppeteer. "I had given a show for her PTA group," Spinney said. The day of the audition he arrived at the station with the title card for what he called the *Rascal Rabbit Show*. So I came in with all my puppets. The [director I saw] was quite unimpressed."

"We already have a kid show," he said. "But who did this artwork?"

"I did," Spinney replied.

The director brightened. "Okay," he said. "We'll hire you as an artist."

Because of the desert heat, Spinney's workday on the base began in the cooler hours before dawn. By 2:00 p.m., "our life was our own." That favorable schedule allowed him to work afternoons at Channel 8, for two dollars an illustration. He never lost hope that he might one day be on camera, and when he returned from Christmas leave, the station offered him a chance at a weekly show.

"What will I get paid?" Spinney asked.

"Five dollars per sponsor," they replied.

"I got two, but I would have done it for free," Spinney said. Using a white rabbit puppet his mother had long ago built for a staging of *Alice in Wonderland*, Spinney used up twelve years of material after only three episodes of *Rascal Rabbit*. "I didn't have any material to go on the air with, and I didn't know what to do."

Once again, fate marched in. "Morton Langstaff was in the air force with me. One day, he said, 'How are you doing with your television show?'"

"It's fine, except I've run out of material," Spinney said.

"I've always wanted to write a kid's show," Langstaff said. "Could I write it for you?"

Fifteen minutes before airtime, Langstaff's script arrived, well written but wordy. Spinney, working without a monitor, struggled, but the show went on.

Rascal Rabbit might have lasted longer than its three-month run had Spinney not received orders to be transferred to Germany. He learned to speak the language during his tour there and appeared on German television. "I almost got my own TV show there, and probably would have, had I reenlisted. But four years was enough."

Spinney returned to Massachusetts in late March of 1957. That summer, he and a friend made a thirty-state, eighty-day tour of the United States in a 1954 Chevy station wagon. Another friend had provided the phone number of Clarence Nash, the cartoon voice of Donald Duck, and Nash arranged an interview for Spinney at The Walt Disney Company during his tour stop in California. Spinney had brought a portfolio of drawings along.

"They said, 'We like your stuff. We'll hire you.' Then, and all of a sudden, Walt appeared in the doorway. He didn't speak to me, but I thought, *Wow. That's getting close.* I remember at six years old I decided that I was going to be a cartoonist for Walt Disney."

Spinney was told the job would not begin for a year, after the studio had completed *Sleeping Beauty*. He was fine with that. Then they said he'd be paid fifty-six dollars a week.

"Fifty-six dollars?" he said. "I knew I could do better than that. So I returned to Boston, went back to art school. A year later I was making a hundred five dollars a week for Trans Radio, a little film company in Boston." One of his first projects for television was an animated commercial for Narragansett Beer ("Hi, neighbor! Have a 'Gansett"). It was hand drawn on cells, just like *Sleeping Beauty*.[1]

In 1958, Boston's WHDH, Channel 5, held auditions for children's performers. It was a sunny April day and Spinney arrived with his puppets. He left disappointed. "It was one of those things where they said, 'Don't call us. We'll call you.'" Spinney didn't have his own phone, so he left the number of a lakeside pay phone in Connecticut he often used, and he put the audition out of his mind.

Two years later, while he was visiting that lake, the pay phone rang. He picked it up.

"Person-to-person call for Ed Spinney," the operator said. Spinney was more amused than stunned at the one-in-a-million occurrence.

"This is Ed," Spinney said. (During his time in the air force, he had begun using his middle name. "I decided not to go through [the service] being known as Caroll," he explained. "I've got enough troubles.")

The voice that then came on the line belonged to the very man who had auditioned Spinney in '58. WHDH was looking for a summer replacement for its popular children's show *Captain Bob*, on which its star, bewhiskered actor and artist Bob Cottle, portrayed a sea captain. He'd asked for a month off. Would Spinney be interested in filling in for him?

Spinney jumped at the offer and, along with singer Judy Valentine, worked six days a week that summer. The station provided a set meant to suggest a rocket ship headed for the moon. One of the puppet stars was Goggle, a large yellow-beaked bird "with goggle eyes," Spinney recalled. The show performed nicely in the local Nielsen ratings, doubling Captain Bob's ratings, but when Cottle returned to work, Spinney was, once again, out of television—but this time not for long.

A month later, he joined the cast of Boston's *Bozo's Circus* on WHDH, whose producers had admired Spinney's versatility during his replacement stint. On *Bozo's*, he played costumed character Mr. Lion. In one episode, without benefit of rehearsal, Mr. Lion created in less than thirty seconds a drawing from the name of a child in the audience. The gimmick became a fixture of the show, but Spinney remained a puppeteer at heart.

In 1962, performing at a puppet festival in Sturbridge, Massachusetts, one act in particular fascinated him, a performing duo who managed to do eight riotous routines in fifty-five minutes. One involved a platoon of wooden soldiers and their drill sergeant. "Sarge would march them in and they'd get tired, then he'd get them up for target practice," Spinney said. "They were all carrying little guns. Sarge then puts up this little target and steps back. And they're all aiming at the target, but then they do a 180—all the guns are facing [the sergeant], and, *boom*, they blow him away. It was really incredible." It was Jim Henson, Jerry Juhl, and the Muppets.

Spinney's turn on stage came soon after, and Henson watched as he performed with Goggle, a bird who could be obnoxious. When Goggle refused to get off the stage—"It's time to leave!" Spinney pleaded from out of sight—a human hand appeared and began to strangle the bird. "Jim loved that," Spinney recalled.

Later, when the two met backstage, Henson said to Spinney, "I kinda liked your show. Why don't you come down to New York and talk about the Muppets?"

Spinney said, "Gee, that would be good," thinking Henson's casual remark was an invitation to talk shop someday, like one hobbyist to another.

But Henson meant otherwise. He had been impressed enough with Spinney's skills to invite him to Manhattan to discuss possible employment—he just hadn't made that invitation clear to Spinney. So the two men shook hands and parted. That exchange fell into the category of "understandable understanding," given the indirect and sometimes obtuse manner in which Henson spoke, even while conducting business.

It would be seven long years before the chance to join the Muppets again presented itself to Spinney, just months before the debut of *Sesame Street*.

Chapter Eight

There are risk takers and risky risk takers. Some are calculated, others impulsive. Some are reasoned, others reckless. Lloyd Morrisett is an example of the former.

In the late spring of '67, after doing considerable research, Morrisett was ready to bet that television could teach children something more substantive than "Mr. Clean gets rid of dirt and grime and grease in just a minute / Mr. Clean will clean your whole house and everything that's in it."

The question was Would anyone else lay money on that bet?

The odds were only fifty-fifty that Carnegie, the foundation that paid his salary, would participate, even though the philanthropy had bankrolled the feasibility study and in May had taken on Joan Ganz Cooney as a consultant to develop the project.

"Television was not thought well of at Carnegie," Morrisett recalled. "It had the perception of being a black hole in terms of using up money, and there were doubts that what you produced would have any value, [that] it was ephemeral. So my job became how to convince my colleagues to take a chance and do something like this, when we hadn't done anything in television. Zero."

Morrisett had to follow the same procedures in procuring a grant for the preschool series as he did for any other project at Carnegie. That he was vice president provided certain clout, but not a golden ticket. The preschool series was just another idea up for consideration, and Morrisett would have to defend it, promote it, and, ultimately, sell it to his boss, Alan Pifer. Morrisett believed that if Carnegie could show good faith and guarantee the first million dollars for the effort, it would "likely be the key to releasing funds from other interested agencies."

Fund-raising at this stage became Morrisett's highest priority and foremost responsibility. "We didn't know whether we would have the money to produce the series, and we didn't know if we did produce it how we would get it broadcast," Morrisett said. But the self-described "true believer" made a plan. Rather than cast a wide net, he would cherry-pick, targeting only major corporate and philanthropic entities and the federal government.

Cooney encouraged Morrisett to aim high. "We had decided from the first that we wouldn't go around begging for pennies," she said. "Either we could get full funding to do the show right or we would drop it." If it was to be a bold endeavor, she reasoned, they should assume an air of confidence. After all, they were intending to enter the arena of big-time, big-budget television, where the size and scope of an audience determines success or failure. Cooney said, "We'd have to compete with the loud noise, mad music, and strong wine the kids were getting on commercial shows."[1]

And so, with no funding commitments, hard or soft, the hunt was on, with Washington the first stop.

You can't discuss what transpired at the United States Office of Education (USOE) on the final day of June 1967 without using that vivid, if slightly impolite, noun, *balls*.

The USOE's commisioner, Harold Howe II, had them.

A civil servant known from childhood as Doc, Howe slew a roomful of bureaucratic dragons that day. He had called the meeting only weeks after receiving a bulky parcel from his old friend Lloyd Morrisett that contained Cooney's feasibility study, which Howe devoured. He was so intrigued by its argument and aims that he phoned Morrisett right away to ask that he come to Washington—with "that Cooney dame." Cooney recalled that Howe said to Morrisett, "We don't have the money to do this, I don't think, but come on down and we'll sit around the table with the department people, the research people, the preschool education people."

Doc Howe was a man of action, conviction, and concern for his fellow man, traits seemingly passed genetically. Born in Hartford, Connecticut, in 1918, he was the son of the Reverend Arthur Howe, a Dartmouth College professor who became president of Hampton Institute in Virginia, now Hampton University. Reverend Howe's father-in-law, Samuel Chapman Armstrong, had been a Union general who commanded black troops in the Civil War. He later founded Hampton as a trade school for freed slaves. Doc spent a part of his upbringing as a young white man on that traditionally black campus, the rest of it near Dartmouth's campus in Hanover, New Hampshire.

A northern New Englander by transplantation, he hiked in New Hampshire's mountains, fished for trout, and skated on local ponds. At just a shade taller than six feet, with a sinewy build and springy legs, he never stood still for too long in one place. A blur on the ice rink, the left-handed winger skated with the varsity at Yale. He left New Haven in 1940 with a history degree and briefly taught at a private school. During and after World War II he skippered a minesweeper in the Pacific.

Back in the States, Howe earned a master's degree in history from Columbia University. Upon graduation, he joined the faculty of the then boys-only elite boarding school Phillips Academy in Andover, Massachusetts, better known as Andover.[2]

Howe taught history and coached hockey, then later completed postgraduate work at Harvard and the University of Cincinnati. Education administration jobs beckoned thereafter, and Howe served as principal at schools in Andover, Cincinnati, and Newton, Massachusetts, before being named school superintendent in Scarsdale, New York, a wealthy enclave in Westchester County. It was there that Carnegie president John Gardner, whose children attended Scarsdale schools, came to know the superintendent and his wife, Priscilla Lamb Howe, known as "Sibby."

But it was Morrisett who recommended Howe for the directorship of the Learning Institute of North Carolina, an integrated men's boarding academy for promising high school students in that state. Howe's next move catapulted him onto the national stage in Washington.

Gardner was a key figure in President Lyndon Johnson's Great Society programs, that wave of social change intended to reduce poverty, enhance educational opportunities, promote equality, safeguard the environment, and rebuild cities. On January 27, 1965, Johnson swore in Gardner as secretary of Health, Education and Welfare. In 1966 Gardner convinced LBJ that Howe was ready to fill the role of USOE commissioner, even though he had no experience as a political appointee. Such was the respect between the president and his HEW secretary that LBJ gave his blessing.

"What the president didn't know at the start was how seriously my father viewed *Brown v. Board of Education*," said Howe's daughter, Cathy Short. "After all, my father was around black people all his young life at Hampton." Indeed, during Howe's term of service, he became Johnson's steely champion of school desegregation—and a target for the wrath of southern legislators, who alternately referred to him as the "commissar of education" and the "U.S. commissioner of integration." Under the provisions of the Civil Rights Act of 1964, Howe withheld billions in aid to local school districts where minimum integration goals had not been achieved. In response, a House Resolution, HR 382, dated March 13, 1967, resolved that Howe should "resign or be replaced." Howe barely blinked.

On June 30, 1967, Howe had summoned representatives from the Children's Bureau, the Bureau of Research, and the Bureau of Elementary and Secondary Education to discuss the merits of the preschool television proposal. Jule Sugarman, then associate director of Head Start, was unable to attend, but sent a favorable note about the proposal to Howe.

This visit to Washington was the first major presentation before a potential funder by the team of Morrisett, Cooney, and Carnegie staff member Barbara Finberg, who was on hand to elaborate on the proposal and take questions. They encountered frost from the moment they crossed the threshold.

"I'd have to say that the attitude around the table was highly negative, and you could understand why," Morrisett said years later. "All of these people had *their* own programs; *their* money was going to things *they* were interested in. Here were essentially a couple of outsiders coming in with an expensive idea. Furthermore, it was *television,* and they weren't doing anything in television."

It was, to say the least, discouraging to encounter a roomful of men with their arms folded, the body language favored by the peeved, not the persuaded. But Morrisett, Cooney, and Finberg calmly and confidently carried on, with an occasional glance toward the commissioner. "We were true believers," Morrisett said. "We talked about the research background and the need."

When it came time for questions, the attendees were sour and surly, until Howe stepped up. "I want to know where each man stands on this proposal," he demanded, narrowing his eyes. He canvassed the room, and the refrain was consistent: "We don't have the money for this."

Howe went silent, slowly scanning the table.

"Well, then, the ayes have it!" he said. "We'll do it," he said. "The end!" He paid no heed to the incredulous stares he faced from the naysayers. As commissioner, Howe outranked them, and they knew it.

Howe leaned slightly forward, hands on hips, head slightly turned. "I've got some money squirreled away and I know each one of you has, too," he said. "We are going to classify this preschool TV idea as a research project, using departmental research funds. Find the money."

He then turned to his assistant, former television executive Louis Hausman. '*You* are to go from department to department getting them to cough up money.'"

Hausman, like Howe, was new to Washington, drawn to public service after retirement from a career at CBS and NBC. He immediately viewed the Carnegie report with a skepticism that bordered on cynicism. "I didn't have too much confidence in it, and I had no knowledge of whether you could take a program like this and teach kids anything," he acknowledged. "No one knew that."[3]

This is not to say Hausman was opposed to the use of television as a teaching tool. He was actually eager to draw upon the resources of the Office of Education to test its potential, but doubted that Morrisett, a seemingly square social scientist, and Cooney, a former producer of public affairs for a channel shunned by the masses, could pull off a show that any child would ever watch. He seemed disdainful of educational television in general, which many at the time viewed as mind-numbing, arch, and amateurish.

After the room had cleared, Hausman told Howe point-blank that the Carnegie idea, as proposed, was wrongheaded. He effectively said that people from educational TV know only one color, gray, and only one speed, deadly. He characterized the proposed budget for the show—then at $1 million—as laughably inadequate, given the scope of what was being considered. "I think they had their program priced out at twelve thousand dollars an hour. I said that this is ridiculous!" Hausman said, adding that The Walt Disney Company budgeted *ten times* that much for a similar hour of television. Hausman estimated it would take a million dollars just to research the show, another two to three million to produce it, and at least a million to promote and advertise it. He threw in another million "for the unexpected."

Hausman told Howe, "I see a budget of around six million dollars."

"This is a *terrible* figure," Howe said, blanching.

"Yes," Hausman replied, tamping down his hand in that way when people mean to say, *Hold on, wait a minute.* "All we have to do is guarantee 50 percent of the six million dollars," he continued, reasoning that a government commitment of $3 million could be stretched over two fiscal years. The project would get $1.5 million in its development year, with another $1.5 million for its first year on the air. "We've thrown *that* away on a lot of other things. . . . Let's once and for all see if a [television] program can be built to gain the attention of a significant number of youngsters, and after their attention is engaged, can they learn anything? Let's give it all the money that can reasonably be asked for."

Howe nodded, thinking about that lonely graveyard on the outskirts of the District of Columbia, where many a misguided project rotted until eternity.

Hausman walked around a bit, digging into his pants pockets. His years in Manhattan had provided plenty of training in projecting realistic production budgets and launch schedules, and plenty of exposure to top-drawer producers. What had he learned? That network-quality television devours money—and time—like few creative endeavors can. Studio time alone is like having a five-minute parking meter that gets fed hundred-dollar bills.

"Unless you are willing to do it [at $3 million], I really don't want anything to do with it," Hausman told his boss. "Otherwise, turn it over to the research department."

Howe nodded again and leaned back in his chair. He'd have to give it all some thought.

A few days later, Hausman launched a torpedo. In a memo to Howe meant to disparage involvement in such a project by ETV, he wrote, "I am seriously concerned about how Carnegie proposes to get a broad-appeal, educationally acceptable program to compete successfully with other offerings on television." He suggested an end run, asking Howe to encourage Carnegie to order pilots from "four or five" film or television production studios in Los Angeles, the suppliers of shows for commercial television. "Each of these producers would be given a budget of, say, a hundred thousand dollars . . . [and] guidelines of what should or should not be in the program. They would then be told to produce a pilot and furnish a script outline for twelve additional hours of programming. That's how mass-appeal entertainment is produced . . . [and] there is no reason that a similar method shouldn't be employed in this project."[4]

"Lou wrote us a memo about this pilot plan that absolutely put me in cardiac arrest," Cooney said. But instead of panicking, Lloyd just remarked, "I think I have an idea how to handle this."

Collegiate rivals Harvard and Yale can each claim a measure of paternity for *Sesame Street.* During the show's three-year gestation period, from 1966 to 1969, researchers, faculty leaders, and graduates of both Ivy institutions touched nearly every phase of its development.

Chief among the contributors with Yale backgrounds was Morrisett, who received his doctorate there in experimental psychology. In 1967 he functioned more as an applied psychologist when he began to reach out to friends, colleagues, and competitors in philanthropy, government, and education, many of whom emanated from that Harvard-Yale nexus. With their interest and largesse, Morrisett laid the financial foundation for *Sesame Street.*

In the early stages of fund-raising, Morrisett delivered a copy of the series proposal to F. Champion "Champ" Ward, the Ford Foundation's director of education projects. Ward had earned his doctorate in philosophy at Yale in 1937 and went on to become undergraduate dean at the University of Chicago before joining Ford in New York. Like Morrisett, Ward was a high-level gatekeeper for grant applications. He was expected to identify and back projects worthy of Ford's time and money.

Approaching Ford made sense, given the foundation's history of supporting educational television. The foundation's advocacy began in 1952, the year the FCC set aside 242 channels across the nation for noncommercial use. As an enticement to prompt communities to sponsor educational stations, Ford issued matching grants for construction that provided a dollar for every two dollars raised locally. Additionally, Ford had awarded $1.35 million to the newly incorporated Educational Television and Radio Center, a program-exchange service based in Ann Arbor, Michigan, that distributed locally produced educational programs to far-distant stations. By 1963, the Ann Arbor group had moved to New York and morphed into National Educational Television (NET), a confederation of educational stations that shipped programs back and forth via U.S. mail.

NET was hardly a "fourth network," as has been claimed. Its stations were not interconnected by long-distance telephone lines, the transmission method that predated satellites. Though NET had some worthy programs, they aired on a schedule determined by local program managers. The early years of *Mister Rogers' Neighborhood*, which began in 1967, were "bicycled" from station to station, airing on different days and in different time slots. In brief, NET was to PBS what the Pony Express was to FedEx; it accomplished a similar goal but without the timeliness, precision, or reliability.

Ford's first foray into commercial television programming came in 1953, with *Omnibus*, a Sunday afternoon cultural cavalcade on CBS that brought theater, dance, and symphonic music into the American home, along with ruminative segments on history and art. Its host and narrator was Alistair Cooke, a U.S.-based correspondent for the BBC who would gain wider fame on these shores as host of PBS's *Masterpiece Theatre* (and as the basis for a character on *Sesame Street*'s *Monsterpiece Theatre*, that delicious parody featuring a scenery-chewing Alistair Cookie).[5]

By the mid-1960s, noncommercial television was desperately in need of a makeover and a rebranding. Educational TV, too tweedy and chalk dusted for its own good, had slim appeal. But there was a palpable and undeniable desire for cultural and public affairs programming among viewers who wanted more from television than shoot-'em-ups in Dodge City, caper-and-cop shows shot on the mean streets of a studio lot, fish-out-of-water sitcoms, and the song stylings of the Lennon Sisters on *The Lawrence Welk Show*. A more demanding audience craved stage plays adapted for the small screen, the music of Beethoven and Brubeck, discourse and debate on the issues of the day, nonviolent children's programming, and, perhaps without knowing it, *Monty Python*. In response to this hunger came a vision of "public television," a new label the Ford Foundation promoted and hoped would stick. It suggested something broader and more populist, something more democratic and representative, something protected and unsullied, something to which Thomas Jefferson and his Constitution-framing contemporaries would pledge allegiance, "pledge" being the operative word.

In 1966 President Johnson used the bully pulpit of the State of the Union address to ask for increased support for noncommercial television. With Johnson's blessing, a Carnegie-sponsored commission took up the task of investigating what it would take to vitalize the system. Ford awarded a ten-million-dollar stimulus grant at the end of the year to develop programming that would be shared by educational stations connected by long-line telephone cable, "a two-year demonstration of the power of interconnection."

Out of that grant came the Public Broadcasting Laboratory (PBL), a costly experiment to test what would happen if a rich pool of television talent was set free to create bold, ambitious, and unconventional programs, the likes of which would never appear on commercial television.

PBL's champion was Fred W. Friendly, a broadcast innovator-agitator who got his start on radio producing *Hear It Now* with Edward R. Murrow, a news magazine of the air. Its television successor, *See It Now*, set the standard for aggressive, probing—and often puncturing—documentary television. It was on *See It Now*, on the evening of March 9, 1954, that Murrow and his unseen editor Friendly stood up to a politician as no television newsmen had dared to do before. The footage aired that night, accompanied by Murrow's commentary, exposed Wisconsin senator Joseph R. McCarthy for what he was: a scheming, power-mad demagogue who trampled and twisted the constitutionally guaranteed rights of innocent citizens. That night, *See It Now* threw up a blockade to the mad march of McCarthyism.

Friendly, born Ferdinand Friendly Wachenheimer in New York, was once described as "a big, imposing man who hurled ideas and opinions around like Olympian thunderbolts."[6] From the ranks of producers he rose to the presidency of CBS News in 1964, unleashing reporters like barking hounds to attach their jaws to the pant legs of the powerful. In doing so, he established the network's reputation for unfettered, unblinking news gathering. But Friendly, who had fractious moments with his overlords at the network, resigned from his post in 1966 after CBS refused to preempt its daytime lineup of sitcom reruns, game shows, and soaps to make way for the long-awaited Senate Foreign Relations Committee hearings on the Vietnam War, which came to be known as the Fulbright hearings. Friendly no longer wished to be associated with a network that would choose a time-worn *I Love Lucy* episode over coverage of historic testimony.

Friendly found a soft place to land at the Ford Foundation, where he played a critical advisory role in the passage of the Public Broadcasting Act of 1967, which led to the formation of the Corporation for Public Broadcasting and PBS. "TV is bigger than any story it reports," he said in 1966. "It's the greatest teaching tool since the printing press. It will determine nothing less than what kind of people we are. So if TV exists now only for the sake of a buck, somebody's going to have to change that."

In joining Ford, Friendly had a formidable new boss in McGeorge "Mac" Bundy, a thinking man's thinking man who had been a foreign policy adviser to presidents Kennedy and Johnson. Once described by Harvard historian Arthur Schlesinger Jr. as "a man of notable brilliance, integrity, and patriotic purpose,"[7] Bundy would also be damned by David Halberstam in *The Best and the Brightest* for his role in plunging the nation into the quagmire of Vietnam and the resultant loss of fifty-five thousand American lives.

After graduating Phi Beta Kappa from Yale with a mathematics degree, Bundy was appointed to Harvard's Society of Fellows, a program reserved for only the most promising of scholars. In 1953, at the age of thirty-four, he became Harvard's dean of the faculty of arts and sciences.

Lloyd Morrisett understood that any hope of assistance from Ford ultimately would require validation and support from Bundy and his television adviser, Friendly. Complicating matters was the news that Ford was contemplating support for a children's television project of its own, a program to teach reading to the underprivileged.

Like the always-civil rivals from Harvard and Yale, so, too, did the gentlemen from the Ford Foundation and the Carnegie Corporation compete for dominance and regard in the 1960s. On paper, there was no comparison. Ford had been established as a family foundation in 1936 with assets of $164,000. By 1942, its coffers had risen astonishingly to $30.7 million. Within a year, the assets had shot up by nearly a factor of seven when Edsel Bryant Ford, the only son of Detroit industrialist Henry Ford, died at age forty-nine and named the foundation as chief beneficiary of his estate. When Henry Ford died in 1947, the foundation expanded to the point that its assets exceeded the combined balances of all other foundations within the then forty-eight states.

Carnegie was a muscular institution in the 1960s, but Ford was the world's wealthiest. Carrying on compatible missions, the foundations roamed

in realms of their own choosing, crossing paths occasionally with respectful nods.

It was not always a certainty that *Sesame Street* would end up on public television, at least in the eyes of Lloyd Morrisett. He was open to the idea that
it could air as a commercial venture, with advertisements bracketing—but
not interrupting—the program. There were precedents for such an arrangement in corporate underwriting of network specials and event coverage.

Morrisett called on top television executives to measure their interest
in committing funding or airtime or both to the show. But after a month
of consideration, neither Julian Goodman, president at NBC, nor John A.
"Jack" Schneider, Goodman's counterpart at CBS, offered much beyond
their best wishes for success. Two television ownership groups, Time-Life
Broadcasting and Group W (Westinghouse), likewise politely passed on
the proposal.

So let the record show that two years before *Sesame Street* would debut,
NBC and CBS, the networks of Sarnoff and Paley, rejected a project that
would ultimately reshape children's television and make Big Bird as recognizable as Mickey Mouse. Given the revenue generated by *Sesame Street*
licensing and merchandising through the decades, and the global reach of
the franchise, turning down *Sesame Street* was a billion-dollar blunder.

What is more, the networks missed a chance to alter perceptions of
commercial television itself, long regarded as a great thief of time. All the
applause, all the gratitude from parents, all the awards and recognition, all
the praise from critics, could have been theirs. It was an opportunity that
Newton Minow himself might have described as vastly wasted.

The lode of goodwill generated by the arrival of *Sesame Street* in 1969
was accordingly lavished upon public television, which would be perceived
thereafter by viewers at all income levels as a safe haven for children.

On September 21, 1967, Lloyd Morrisett met with another quintet of TV
executives. This time he wasn't trying to sell anything.

In what was essentially *Sesame Street*'s first focus group, five experienced men from the business and programming sides of television, commercial and noncommercial, were briefed on the preschool project. They
were then asked to assess its viability and estimate its cost. In attendance
were George Heinemann, executive producer of children's programs for
NBC; Oscar Katz, a former vice president of programming at CBS; Mark
Goodson of the Goodson-Todman production company; Lewis Freedman
and Stuart Sucherman of the nascent PBL; and George Dessart, director of

community services at WCBS-TV. Gerald Lesser, the Harvard Ed School researcher who had advised *Exploring*, sat in alongside Morrisett, Cooney, Finberg, Hausman, and freelance writer Linda Gottlieb.

In a calculated move, Morrisett also invited Lou Hausman, who was still advocating his pick-a-pilot plan to steer production of the series to a Hollywood studio. Hausman agreed to attend the meeting and abide by whatever his former CBS colleague, Oscar Katz, deemed the smartest course. He anticipated that Katz would see things his way.

Their viability verdict from the TV pros was swift, clear, and unanimous: a show for preschoolers that taught as it entertained, or vice versa, was an idea whose time had come. Lewis Freedman, who attended the dinner party in 1966, took charge of the conversation. "You cannot possibly do this without setting up an organization," he said. "There's no production company in the United States that can do this, so you have to create that animal." That sentiment echoed around the room, and a call arose for the creation of a new, autonomous, hybrid organization that in Morrisett's words, would "be given the task of fusing education and entertainment." "It was said right away that L.A. was not the right climate for this kind of project, that it was a New York project, where you can get the right kinds of people," Cooney recalled. You could almost hear Hausman's balloon burst.

"Lloyd was so shrewd," Cooney said. "One of the reasons he had that meeting was to have Hausman in attendance. Lou respected the producers, and when everyone was in favor of creating a new entity, that was the end of the [showbiz pilot] discussion. It was a turning point. Lou left knowing it wasn't going to go his way, but he came around. And to his credit, he never looked back."

Heinemann, Katz, Goodson, Sucherman, and Dessart called for an aggressive rollout of the series, with a sufficient number of episodes spread across a long enough time period to build a substantial audience. Their ambitious suggestion was a daily one-hour program to be seen over either a twenty-six- or thirty-nine-week schedule, with perhaps as many as 130 episodes in its debut season. Each episode would air twice daily, presumably morning and afternoon, to reach as many children as possible.

No one was sure what it would cost, but Sucherman agreed to help Cooney craft a more realistic budget, one that would be much closer to Hausman's $6 million projection than the first stab at $2 million.

As the meeting broke up, WCBS's Dessart caught up with Cooney on her way out to share a thought that had occurred to him during the discussion. Excitedly he said, "You're going to teach numbers and letters, right?

And your hunch is that kids learn from catchy commercials, right? Then why not make commercials to teach letters and numbers?"

In one brilliant flash, the first streetlight on *Sesame Street* was illuminated. "I had noted the attraction of commercials for young children in my report, but I hadn't put it together myself how commercials could be used, or if they could," Cooney said. "We knew we were going to teach letters and numbers and we knew we wanted commercials in some form. I don't know how I missed that connection, but [George] brought it together."

Dessart, pleased by Cooney's response, added a flourish. "I'll bet you could get a string of advertising agencies to donate enough commercials to get you started."

How right he was.

Cooney retreated to her apartment to work on rewriting and expanding the feasibility study into something that more resembled a plan for season one. In November, Morrisett was at the typewriter as well, drafting a well-considered memo to his boss, Alan Pifer, in which he said that a $1 million commitment from Carnegie "would be enough money to get the project organized and to finance the core staff over a period of approximately two years. It would not be nearly enough money to ensure production and distribution of the program, but this core support would allow the recruitment of key personnel and would tide the project over until the other agencies act."[8] Pifer was inclined to agree; a grant of that magnitude would represent Carnegie's largest of the decade.

In a moment of candor long after *Sesame Street* was a reality, Pifer said that as he deliberated, he took "wry amusement at the thought that all this enormous effort—and the substantial funds involved—[might] be frustrated by the determined little four- or five-year-old who, the minute his mother's back is turned, slips up to the TV and switches it to the cartoons."

Chapter Nine

I n the fall of 1967, shortly after Lloyd Morrisett had convened the meeting of television experts, he arranged for a panel of educators to travel to New York to discuss how the television series might be researched and evaluated.[1] While that marked the first gathering of academic advisers to *Sesame Street*, its significance was greater than that.

Once again Gerald Lesser, the Harvard professor who had advised NBC's *Exploring* during its four-season run, was in attendance. At the time, Lesser was one of the few academics of note who was conducting serious research on children and television. Another was Dr. Edward Palmer of the Oregon state education system, who was developing tests to measure children's attention to television.

Lesser's manner was informal, unpretentious, and collaborative. "I remember when I first met him in his office at Larson Hall at the Harvard Graduate School of Education," said Milton Chen, executive director of the George Lucas Educational Foundation and a former director of research at the Children's Television Workshop. "I was maybe eighteen, a college sophomore. And here's a Harvard professor with an endowed chair whose standard uniform was tennis sneakers, corduroy slacks, and an open shirt. He was as casual with students as he was with distinguished psychologists and educators from around the country." Lesser's hallmark was his ability to extract information in a nonthreatening manner. "Gerry's style was to listen, observe, and make suggestions, but in a way that did not turn people off. Whether it was his personality, his clinical training, or his work in the School of Education, I can't say. He just wanted to know where you were coming from, and then he would make suggestions that you'd clearly understand, and not impose something on you. He wanted to help you do your work."

With Lesser's gentle prodding, three guiding principles emerged at the Carnegie gathering that proved essential to *Sesame Street's* success:

- A team of in-house researchers should consult with producers and writers as scripts were being developed, providing a healthy give-and-take about what preschoolers could and should learn.
- Prior to broadcast, field researchers should test content being considered for the show—at a day-care center or Head Start classroom. This formative research would help shape the direction of the series, providing

clues to what worked and what didn't by observing the reactions of the
target audience.

- Researchers should go back into the field to evaluate programs after
  they had aired, in order to measure the effectiveness of the show's
  educational goals.

If one were to look upon this project as a true experiment, the participants argued, fair and effective measurements would need to be in place to
prove or disprove the major hypothesis. The question that Morrisett posed
at the dinner party in 1966 could be adequately answered only if the show
had specific educational standards, goals, and rigorous pre- and posttest-
ing. The project would establish its credibility, they predicted, based on its
backbone of scientifically valid research. *Sesame Street*, then, would be the
first children's television series with a bona fide curriculum and evaluation
mechanism.

In the 1950s matronly Miss Frances may have taught children effectively on *Ding Dong School*, but not by following a pedagogical master plan.
The Captain and Mr. Green Jeans imparted plentiful information in the
'50s and '60s on *Captain Kangaroo*, but never with a systematic program
of instruction and appraisal. The same was true for *Romper Room*, a live-
action show for preschoolers that mimicked a kindergarten class. Stations
purchased rights to the program's franchised name and format, launching
their own versions with a female teacher-host. *Romper Room* no doubt educated and entertained children, but educational research played no role in
its development or long-range planning.

Sesame Street came along and rewrote the book. Never before had anyone assembled an A-list of advisers to develop a series with stated educational norms and objectives. Never before had anyone viewed a children's
show as a living laboratory, where results would be vigorously and continually tested. Never before in television had anyone thought to commingle
writers and social science researchers, a forced marriage that, with surprising ease and good humor, endured and thrived.

After the meeting, Lesser privately admitted to Morrisett that he wasn't
sure he wanted to continue with the project. But Morrisett was certain the
educator was the perfect choice to be *Sesame Street*'s founding educational
director. "He took some convincing," Morrisett admitted. "I remember
going up to Cambridge and visiting with Gerry and his wife, Stella, one
night, trying to convince him that he should take this on. He was the skeptic in the group. He wasn't sure television could teach."

Lesser also expressed concerns about Cooney, whose credentials he found lacking, even as he found her an engaging, intelligent contributor. He would not be the only one to raise doubts about Cooney's lack of experience and academic training, as the time grew near to choose a formal project director. Qualifications aside, there also was the matter of gender. Lesser contributed to an undercurrent of doubt about whether any woman could command enough respect to steer the project, an attitude that nearly eliminated from consideration the very person who had developed the idea.

On Tuesday, November 7, 1967, President Johnson was in great good spirits as a marine band played triumphant marches in the marble foyer outside the East Room.[2] It was slightly before noon, two days after the debut of something called the Public Broadcasting Laboratory, the pet project of Fred Friendly.

The November 5 broadcast of *PBL*, the Sunday night television program the laboratory named after itself, was as notable for who didn't watch as for who did. The opening-night topic was race relations in America, an inflammatory and polarizing issue, to be sure. Sight unseen, ten stations in Georgia, seven in Alabama, and five in South Carolina refused to air the premiere. In Tallahassee, Florida, station officials cited "financial reasons" for pulling PBL. In Cleveland, WVIZ delayed its broadcast of the program until after a mayoral election, fearful that its content might agitate voters. In Athens, Ohio, one broadcaster sent a one-sentence telegram to PBL's executive director and PBL's executive producer, Avram (Av) Westin: GOD HELP PBL AND ETV.[3] Altogether, some twenty-nine noncommercial stations refused to air the program. Friendly's vow to "mobilize the hearts and minds of the nation" had backfired badly. Westin later gave the two-and-a-half-hour broadcast a middling grade of C+, as it fizzled rather than sizzled on the topic of racial divide.[4]

Hyped as a dramatic departure from previous attempts at public service broadcasting, *PBL* offered 150 minutes of live television that missed the mark by miles and drove disappointed viewers away. What was billed as new seemed tired and stretched out. *New York Times* critic Jack Gould slammed the premiere as a "blight of awkward confusion and dullness . . . a sorry affair in all respects":[5]

> The gee-whiz bias of the opening presentation and the disregard of hard pursuit of information in favor of surface emotion could, if continued, give the cause of public broadcasting an unnecessarily hard time in the years ahead in Washington. If the premiere should be regarded as representative of what lies ahead, congressmen could scarcely be blamed for

wondering if a huge permanent investment in noncommercial video is warranted. By contrast, the normal workings of National Education Television and the commercial TV chains look good.

Nevertheless, some three hundred dignitaries had already been invited to the White House to witness the signing of the Public Broadcasting Act of 1967, and there was optimism that the bill institutionalizing the Corporation for Public Broadcasting (CPB), a nonprofit body charged with invigorating and strengthening noncommercial television, was a milestone in television history. After all, it marked the first time the federal government had authorized funds—$9 million for fiscal 1968—for, among other things, the creation of culturally enriching content for public stations. Though the funds had not yet been appropriated by Congress, Mr. Johnson confidently stated his hope that the money would be made available soon. Then, in praising the quick passage of the bill, the president singled out Douglass Cater, an administration aide who almost single-handedly steered the legislation through Congress.

After LBJ's remarks, Carnegie Corporation president Alan Pifer rose to pledge $1 million from his organization to the CPB. Its public-private charter allowed for foundation money to supplement the government's subsidy.

Hands were pumped, backs were slapped, and LBJ enjoyed a brief moment of release before returning to the Oval Office and the weight of a war in Southeast Asia that seemed without end.

Over at HEW, Doc Howe persistently battled with school districts in noncompliance with federal desegregation mandates. It was an ongoing struggle, his own little civil war. But amid that confusion, he still managed to make good on his pledge to Morrisett and Cooney, rounding up money from other government agencies to support the preschool TV project. In a memo, Howe appealed to representatives of the Office of Economic Opportunity, the Children's Bureau, the National Institutes of Health, and the National Institute of Children's Health and Human Development. "It strikes me that this project represents a fine opportunity for government-foundation cooperation to solve a major human problem," he wrote. "My current thinking is that . . . federal agencies should be prepared to fund at least half . . . with Carnegie and other interested foundations funding the balance."[6]

"Howe took upon himself the job of spokesman and convener and negotiator," said Carnegie's Barbara Finberg.[7]

The pieces were starting to fall in place. At a meeting of Carnegie Corporation's board of trustees held during the second week of January in 1968, approximately two years after the Cooney dinner party, a resolution passed to allocate a million dollars toward a project that was now budgeted at seven million dollars. Lloyd Morrisett had persuaded Carnegie to ante up; it only remained to be seen whether other funders would follow, as he dearly hoped.

Howe, meanwhile, had heard that the Ford Foundation had been considering support for an unrelated children's television project, a show to teach reading skills expressly to inner-city viewers. Word of it had also reached Morrisett and Cooney, who were both baffled by the notion of limiting the audience for such a show to the underprivileged. "What are they going to call it, *The Poor Children's Hour*?" Cooney asked, only half facetiously.

Howe, the Yankee pragmatist, phoned McGeorge Bundy, the Boston Brahmin, urging him to drop the reading show and back the Carnegie project instead. Howe argued for one concerted effort to assist all economic classes of children, with the indigent as a target audience but with concentric circles of more privileged viewers gaining from it, as well. "Why should we be going in two directions when we should be going in one?" he asked.

Unbeknownst to Howe, Bundy had made quite a study of the Carnegie idea, but only after Champ Ward, the officer charged with bringing forward education initiatives at Ford, had rejected it. A copy of the discarded feasibility study had found its way to Howard Dressner, a quiet and unassuming administrator at Ford. But after reading the document that had been set adrift, he sailed it over to Bundy's office. "Mac," he said, "you've just got to read this!"

Bundy told Howe he might consider support for the Carnegie study if it was more explicit about using television to address the needy. The foundation was less interested in the experimental aspects of the project, he said, than in its remedial possibilities. If Cooney's proposal rewrite could demonstrate how the project might benefit the underprivileged, and could clarify how word of it would reach its intended target audience, Ford would likely join the consortium. "Ford wanted it made clear that the disadvantaged child was the bull's-eye," Cooney said. "We all agreed totally."

It sounded good to Howe, who for the third time had exerted his influence on behalf of the preschool television project. His person-to-person plea to Bundy ultimately fused a three-way partnership among the U.S. Office of Education, Carnegie, and Ford.

On January 31, two weeks after Carnegie appropriated the first $1 million, Morrisett received a letter from Ed Meade, informing him that a check for $250,000 would be arriving from Ford within two weeks. The letter also indicated that Ford would consider awarding an additional $1 million if a series of planned curriculum seminars the following summer proved "satisfactory."

In a marriage of convenience, Morrisett arranged for NET to provide financial management and legal and administrative assistance to the fledgling Children's Television Workshop. "They needed a home for this project," said John F. White, then president of NET. "We devised a letter of agreement . . . that said we would provide the legal tent and the fiscal tent under which this could operate. The government and the Ford Foundation had to have a place to which they could give the money. We had it. For our part, the board of NET and I would be helpful in any and every way we could by providing whatever advice and assistance we deemed wise or Joan requested. We would handle and assume responsibility for the expenditure of dollars, but we would not interfere with the development of the program. The CTW was to be a self-enclosed entity under the direction of Joan Cooney and it was so established. One of the reasons it worked so well is because [we learned] from some of the mistakes at PBL."[8]

Fresh in everyone's mind was the fractious mess that Fred Friendly's PBL had become. Despite an all-star team of production and on-air talent, suffocating interference from two boards of advisers—and a strangulating management structure—doomed the project from the start. In his smart, concise history of public television, author James Day described the dilemma faced by Westin, the respected CBS News producer who was PBL's executive director and executive producer: "Responsible to not one but two committees—and with an actively kibitzing Ford Foundation bankroller on the sidelines—Westin found himself atop a hydra-headed structure that produced confusion, frustration, and anger and promoted organizational malaise from which PBL never fully recovered."[9]

"We learned so much from PBL," Cooney said. "Everything they did we did differently. Jack White wanted the project at NET, and it could not have been easier. We were independent but we always called [ourselves] semiautonomous. We didn't want to have NET unhappy."

Tom Kennedy and Stuart Sucherman finalized details of the arrangement. Kennedy, a finance whiz who had toiled for CBS during the tumultuous reign of Fred Friendly, had been the chief number cruncher for PBL. "I used to control the budgets for the space program and for the elections, among other things," he said. "I was into very heavy-duty pressure. I remember Fred Friendly calling me into his office one day. He had all of the vice presidents there . . . and was complaining about the pressure I was putting on them on the budgets. He said, 'You don't understand, my people are out there in the snow and the rain and they're trying to get a story, and you and your accountants are home with your loved ones, snuggled up in a warm bed.' I thought, 'I have to say something,' because Fred was a very overbearing kind of guy. I reached into my pocket and took out a piece of paper and pencil. I don't know where I got the idea, why it jumped into my head, but I wrote my telephone number down, leaned over, and handed it to him. 'Fred, tell them if they get confused about spending any time of the day or night, give me a call.' He was speechless."

Both Sucherman and Kennedy had "fought hard and long to get a concept, at least, of independence within NET, sort of a wholly owned subsidiary concept," Kennedy recalled. "The NET way of doing things . . . wasn't necessarily the shrewdest or sharpest. . . . They didn't manage well and they were a little too political in some areas. [But] Jack White was so anxious to get CTW as part of NET, and so anxious to prove that he was *not* going to interfere, that he gave more independence to the Workshop than he had to PBL. He didn't want to look like he was being political after PBL."

"It was a stunningly bad deal for NET," Cooney said. "They administered the project without getting any money at all, except their actual costs. The deal made no sense to me then and it makes no sense [to me] now. It was one of the things that gave us a lot more money.

"The project reported to the board of NET through Jack White, and the board was ultimately responsible. I went and addressed that board, and in attendance was [board member] Pete Peterson, the head of Bell & Howell. It was the first time I had ever met him, and he was, by far, the most interested person in that room on this project. He asked me a hundred questions and came up afterward and said, 'This is the most exciting thing I've ever heard.'"

In the late winter of 1968, Joan Ganz Cooney's knack for easily landing jobs without the requisite qualifications was about to betray her.

At stake was the opportunity to steer the preschool television project to completion. As an organizational structure for it began to emerge, it was Cooney who had expressed the importance of identifying someone to be, in her words, "a central figure . . . a person in whose mind the whole project exists . . . someone functioning to see that the mix of programming, information, and research worked." That person, she said, would carry the title of executive director and would be someone "terribly important to the morale and functioning of an organization; a central, on-premises figure who stands or falls with you and to whom you have access on a continuing basis, somebody you know keeps his eye on the ball and has a vision."[10]

That person, she said, must also be indomitable in the face of compromise, turning away any idea that would dilute or distort the original vision. And, she said, the role of executive director must be at the apex of the management pyramid. Direct reports would include an executive producer, a director of research, a financial director, an outreach director, and a public relations director. The executive director would report to a board of advisers, but those advisers would be prohibited from tampering with any of the content creators or researchers. In short, she eliminated the bureaucratic entanglements that undid PBL.

Because Cooney had guided the project's content development from inception as both researcher and writer, she might have been viewed as the natural choice for executive director. But representatives from two of the emerging financial backers for the project, the Ford Foundation and the U.S. Office of Education, like the project's leading academic consultant, Gerry Lesser, expressed serious reservations about Cooney's lack of high-level managerial experience and leadership: How could someone with untested financial management skills be expected to oversee a multi-million-dollar budget? How could someone with no experience in children's television be expected to launch the highest-profile show ever mounted for young audiences? How could a producer from ratings-challenged Channel Thirteen be expected to helm a project aimed at a national audience? How could Cooney be expected to hold her own against renowned educational researchers, with only a Bachelor of Arts in Education and a short student-teaching stint to her name?

Doubters also questioned whether a woman could gain the full confidence of a quorum of men from the federal government and two elite philanthropies, institutions whose wealth exceeded the gross national product of entire countries. Ironically, a woman was among the most adamant of these naysayers. Marjorie Martus, Ford Foundation's education and research director, "did not think a project headed by a woman could be taken seriously," Cooney said. "Ford thought more of having a scholar as the executive director, with producers working for him. Lou Hausman of the USOE had major reservations about anyone from public television becoming executive director, and indeed, the show being on public television at all."

To make matters worse, the same people who found Cooney wanting had expected her to submit a list of candidates for executive producer. Only after Cooney did come up with five prominent names was her own added to the list, and perhaps only as a courtesy to Morrisett, who assumed an air of professional neutrality in the early stages of the candidate search. Cooney

Back in 1966, Sarah Morrisett and her baby sister were hooked on television. Her father, Lloyd, took notice and wondered aloud whether television could teach.

Lloyd Morrisett and daughter Sarah stood for a picture in October 1965.

In February 1964, civil rights activists Joan Ganz and Tim Cooney were married at the Roman Catholic Church of St. Vincent Ferrer in New York. The bride was a public affairs producer at Channel Thirteen, the groom the public relations director for the New York Department of Labor.

BELOW: Ten-year-old Joan Ganz, far left, joined her sister, Sylvia; brother, Paul; mother, Pauline; and father, Sylvan for a portrait taken in Prescott, Arizona.

Mr. Moose, performed by puppeteer Cosmo "Gus" Allegretti, visits with Captain Kangaroo (Bob Keeshan) at the back door of the Treasure House.

Kermit was only vaguely amphibian in 1957, when Jim Henson and Jane Nebel performed twice nightly at WRC studios in Washington. Sam, the title character of *Sam and Friends*, is at far left.

Dr. Edward Palmer, the founding research director of Children's Television Workshop, was one of the first social scientists to measure television's ability to hold the attention of children.

Piano prodigy Joe Raposo's promise was evident at age seven.

Harvard undergraduate Joe Raposo let a cigarette dangle from his lips—"to appear older," says his wife, Pat Collins—during a summer-stock rehearsal at the Hyannis Playhouse on Cape Cod.

BELOW: Author-illustrator Maurice Sendak's doodles provided sharp commentary on educational television—and the proceedings at the curriculum seminars held at Harvard University and a hotel in Manhattan—in the summer of 1968.

Bob McGrath performed as a child at the LaSalle County Fairgrounds in north-central Illinois.

In the first decade of *Sesame Street*, nothing could come between David (Northern Calloway) and Maria (Sonia Manzano), but that didn't stop Oscar from trying.

BELOW: After test audiences yawned, Jim Henson brought on Caroll Spinney to give more life to the street. Big Bird and Oscar became a sweet-and-sour combo for the ages.

Big Bird was ungainly—and a bit of a dodo—in Jim Henson's early imaginings.

Though undeniably a star, Kermit took direction well from Jon Stone, who was never without his editing pencil.

BELOW: The big guns were summoned for an appearance by Lena Horne, standing between Joe Raposo and Jon Stone. Jim Henson cradled the puppet known as Fat Blue.

Actress Linda Bove toured with The Little Theater of the Deaf in 1970. When she joined the *Sesame Street* cast she received strong support from writer Emily Kingsley.

The idea for Oscar— the comedic contrarian— sprang from the curriculum seminars in 1968. Psychologists suggested that a character who reveled in nondestructive deviance might click with kids.

Actress Sonia Manzano, here with Jeff Moss, became a writer for *Sesame Street*.

RIGHT: Cookie Monster owes part of his existence to Jeff Moss, head writer when the character was introduced. The most memorable of Muppets have obsessions, as Cookie does.

To Jeffie, Me love you.

Big Bird got a lesson on breast feeding from Buffy Sainte-Marie and her son, Cody. The scene took less than a minute of screen time and was a first for children's TV.

RIGHT: Jerry Nelson, who got his start in puppetry with Bil Baird, joined the Muppets in the 1960s. In 1972 he gave life to the vampiric Count Von Count on *Sesame Street*.

LEFT: From beneath the camera, Jim Henson and Frank Oz, as Ernie and Bert, made for one of the greatest comedy duos in the history of television. They were like brothers.

Puppeteer Richard Hunt's milieu was the studio, where he was a force of nature. Hunt was the creative force behind Don Music, Forgetful Jones, and the bovine diva Gladys.

Colleagues Richard Hunt and Jerry Nelson collaborated on the feuding Two-Headed Monster and the comical construction workers Sully and Biff.

From season one, Frank Oz, far right, imbued lovable Grover with energy, imagination, and healthy self-esteem. Kids think he's super.

Before he was Bob on *Sesame Street*, "Bobu" McGrath was a singing sensation in Japan. The young tenor rose to fame in Asia thanks to the American TV show *Sing Along with Mitch*.

Student and teacher reunited on *Sesame Street* when stage and film star James Earl Jones appeared in an episode with his former drama instructor, Will Lee.

ABOVE: Just by being himself, Jason Kingsley helped *Sesame Street* become a more tolerant and diverse neighborhood. Jason, born with Down syndrome, appeared in fifty-five episodes.

In season seventeen, Gordon (Roscoe Orman) and Susan (Loretta Long) adopted Miles, played by Orman's real-life son of the same name. The family was given the surname Robinson to honor Matt Robinson, the original Gordon.

Kevin Clash got his break on network television right out of high school, performing on *Captain Kangaroo* with puppets he made at home in Baltimore.

LEFT: Over time, Kevin Clash (working alongside Jim Henson and Kermit) emulated his mentor by excelling in performing, directing, and producing. He now also recruits puppeteers for international coproductions of *Sesame Street*.

Joining Big Bird at the White House Christmas party in 1978 were, from left, Jim Henson, Walter Cronkite, First Lady Rosalynn Carter, and bandleader Joe Raposo.

Al Hirschfeld sketched the *Sesame Street* cast to promote season fifteen.

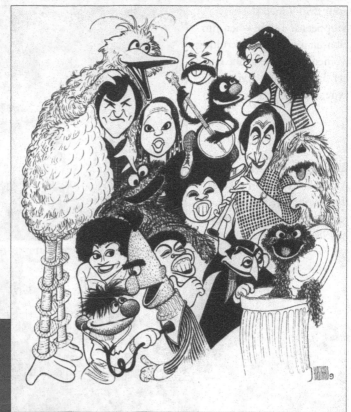

Kevin Clash has a helium-high falsetto for Elmo, a character that literally fell into his arms. Clash also performs Hoots, the owl who plays sax and sings like Satchmo.

Executive producer Dulcy Singer was the matchmaker who decided that Luis (Emilio Delgado) and Maria (Sonia Manzano) should marry. They exchanged vows in an operetta-style segment composed by Jeff Moss that aired in May 1988.

Fran Brill joined the Muppets at a time when Jim Henson was actively recruiting women puppeteers. She had her hands full satisfying expectations for Zoe.

Eighteen-month-old Alexandra Peterson visited the *Sesame Street* set with her grandmother Joan Cooney in 1987.

When executive producer Dulcy Singer left the show, she took a Muppet doppelgänger with her as a going-away gift. They see the same hairstylist.

At his studio in Connecticut, Caroll Spinney draws and paints fanciful scenes involving Big Bird.

Rather than bow to tradition, Jon Stone, far left, wore a dashiki to the Emmys. From left, in tuxes, were Joe Bailey, Norman Stiles, and Jeff Moss. A beaming Emily Kingsley took home a statuette, as well.

The cast for the thirty-fifth-anniversary season appeared in a well-received special on PBS, "*Sesame Street* Presents: The Street We Live On."

In awarding her the Presidential Medal of Freedom, the nation's highest civilian honor, in 1995, President Clinton said, "Joan Ganz Cooney has proven in living color that the powerful medium of television can be a tool to build reason, not reaction, for growth, not stifling, to help build young lives up rather than tear them down."

likewise did nothing to promote her own cause. "I wasn't even considering myself," she said. "It just wasn't the sort of thing I thought women could seek even though I realized I was the most qualified."[11] The search committee, such as it was, discussed the possibility of Cooney's being named deputy director. "The idea was that as deputy director, I would succeed whoever took the top job," Cooney explained.

Her disinclination to fight for the executive director position did not go down well at home with her husband, the New York City political hand. Tim was appalled by the objections raised regarding his wife's candidacy. It seemed incredible to him that anyone familiar with the evolution of the project would question her command of the material or organizational competence. That gender was an issue provoked him even further and he pushed Joan to pursue the top job. "I just wouldn't have asked for the job if Tim hadn't persuaded me," Cooney once said.[12] "I was considered an 'inexperienced woman.' All I had been was a producer, which I suppose didn't count for much, and of course I did the study that was the basis for the whole program. But I was still considered to be totally inexperienced in terms of running anything."[13]

Cooney knew enough about television to understand how ill suited she would have been producing a series for preschoolers, having never worked a day in children's television. "Everyone talked about me being executive producer. . . . But I am not creative in this way," Cooney said. "I had never worked on the kind of techniques we were talking about. I would not have known where to begin."[14]

Tim Cooney was not about to see anyone else named executive director, and so he devised a strategy: one night he turned to his wife and said matter-of-factly, "If they offer you the deputy position, the answer is, *No*, you are not going to be with the project at all. Just tell them you are not available for the second spot." Such a tactic would force the deliberators to consider the consequences of moving forward without her involvement. If she walked, he reasoned, the project would lose its eyes and ears.

"Being number two didn't seem all that odd to me as a woman in that period," Cooney admitted. "And Tim said, 'That's just nuts. There's no project without you. They'll have to put you in as number one.'"

Joan agreed. She promptly informed Morrisett of her unavailability for the No. 2 job, if offered, confident that the decision would quickly become known to the players at Ford, Carnegie, and the USOE. "That focused their minds rather quickly on the fact that the project was not actually on paper yet. It was in my head," Cooney said.[15] "I don't think a threat was necessary, but by then I had made up my mind I would leave.

"Lloyd, who was nervous that I would leave, said, 'How can you be married and take this kind of job?' I said, 'Lloyd, I was born to do this job!' And I knew it. I knew that I was going to do the job and I knew that it would be successful. All that crazy confidence."

The Ford Foundation's Edward Meade, a product of the Harvard Graduate School of Education, was among those charged with identifying the best candidate for executive director. "I didn't know Joan too well. . . . And I said, 'Gee, can't we get someone who has more educational experience?'" Meade said. "So some people, including myself, went out looking for somebody who doesn't exist. As we looked around, we could offer no alternatives that seemed to make any sense at all. Not just alternatives to Joan, but alternatives per se. I think it was Lloyd Morrisett who said, 'Why don't we just turn to someone who started the whole thing?'"[16]

Cooney understood that Morrisett was solidly in her corner, even if his blank expression gave no clue of it to others. "Lloyd had worked with me so long and so closely that he had no doubts," Cooney said. "So he was both at an advantage and a disadvantage in suggesting me."[17] As deliberations narrowed, Cooney urged Morrisett to temper his support of her candidacy a bit. "Make sure you don't ram me through," she said. "The project can't succeed if you will not appoint an executive director you trust and say, 'We'll leave that person alone.' That must be built in. You can't negotiate it after you have the money."[18]

Meade's apprehension about Cooney eventually abated. "The more I talked to Joan, the more I saw what a foolish question I had raised. She had done a good feasibility study and was anxious to get the show on the air. She *never* once promoted herself. There is no question about that. If anything, she was far too humble. We suddenly realized we had the diamond right in our hands."[19]

On February 15, Cooney was selected as executive director. "They realized that it would have been impossible to move on without me," Cooney said, with a slight smile. "They were stuck with me!"[20]

Doc Howe's assistant, Lou Hausman, may have seemed to some an annoying contrarian at first, but his contributions to *Sesame Street* were not insubstantial. He was the first to realize that the feasibility study did not come close to projecting what the show would actually cost. That reality check helped to boost the budget to $6.7 million by January 1968. Included in that sum were funds to cover the prebroadcast months and the first twenty-six weeks of shows.

As substantial as that figure was, Hausman, the commercial television veteran, was not convinced that even it would do. One day, with an eyebrow cocked, he asked Cooney, "How do you know you won't need a million dollars more [for animation]?"

"We don't," she flatly said.

Hausman's question triggered one final now-or-never review of the financial plan. When the dust settled, the budget had taken a last leap, to just under $8 million, a staggering sum.

Undaunted, the Office of Education agreed to put up half, leaving something less than $4 million to be made up from Carnegie, Ford, and whoever else might drop by with a checkbook. "We were short by $1.5 million," Cooney said, just before another stroke of good fortune—and well-lubricated networking—fell upon *Sesame Street*.

The good news came hand delivered from John W. Macy, the newly installed president of the Corporation for Public Broadcasting. He had heard about the shortfall for the preschool project and wanted to help. "John was another person out of those times who believed in getting things done, a real no-nonsense guy in many ways like Doc Howe, and easy to deal with," said Morrisett. "He had been a very good friend of Jim Perkins, who was vice president when I was first at Carnegie. And I knew John well. That combination of people and friendship was enormously important. I'm not exactly sure how the conversation came about, and how the amount of money was arrived at, but it was certainly eased by the personal relationships."

On behalf of CPB, Macy came forth with the final $1.5 million.

With that, the project had a home at NET, a fat bank account, the beginnings of a leadership team, and a name. "We were going to call it the Children's Television Laboratory until someone said, 'No, that sounds too much like PBL,' Cooney said. "That's how it became Children's Television Workshop."[21]

On March 20, 1968, the first day of spring, a gaggle of well-wishers at the Waldorf-Astoria Hotel formed a semicircle around McGeorge Bundy, president of the Ford Foundation; Alan Pifer, president of Carnegie Corporation; and Harold "Doc" Howe, commissioner of the U.S. Office of Education. There representing the three major funding institutions, each man had been given a short opportunity to speak to the assembled multitudes at a press conference to announce the formation of Children's Television Workshop. Protocol dictated as much.

But as the room began to empty and the microphones and cameras were packed away, it was the speaker whom no one had recognized at first who had caught everyone's attention. There, off to the side, was Joan Ganz Cooney, the newly introduced executive director of CTW.

In his taxi ride back from the event to the *New York Times*, Jack Gould must have been already crafting what his lead should be for the following day's article, the pithy paragraph that would open a multidimensional story about the event he had left only minutes earlier:

> The heads of the Carnegie Corporation, the Ford Foundation, and the United States Office of Education, at a meeting yesterday at the Waldorf-Astoria Hotel, announced plans to see whether a child's avid interest in TV can be excitingly channeled into preparation "for the educational journey so vital to their lives and the well-being of the nation."
>
> If a spot commercial can arouse interest in an item of merchandise, the plan suggests, why can't a spot engender interest in the letter "A," the numeral "1" or the scientific phenomenon of a snowball?
>
> One of the primary aims of the plan, sponsors said, "is to stimulate the intellectual and cultural growth of young children from disadvantaged backgrounds." They cited Federal statistics showing that an academic achievement gap between disadvantaged and middle-class children shows up very early in the school years.
>
> A detailed outline of the venture, which is to be called Children's Television Workshop, cited statistics taken from the Nielsen Television Index showing that children under the age of six spend upwards of 54.1 hours a week watching TV. The workshop hopes to capitalize on the medium's potential by teaching numbers, classic stories, the alphabet, language, and the art of reasoning.

In fact Gould had had more than just that morning to prepare his story, as on the day before the press conference, Cooney and Morrisett had taken the *Times*'s television writer to lunch, providing an exclusive briefing about the preschool television project, with the proviso that the newsman honor an embargo not to publish details until the Thursday edition. This was done not entirely to curry favor but rather to give Gould information that he, in turn, could share with the top editors of the *Times*, their hope being that the newspaper might give the story decent play on its news pages.

Gould surpassed their expectations, convincing his bosses that the announcement was one of the most important television developments of the decade. It made page one, along with a "Woman in the News" profile of Joan Ganz Cooney. The appointment, the paper said, "automatically thrusts her into the forefront of women executives in broadcasting."

Mike Dann, the brash and brilliant potentate of entertainment programming at CBS Television, snapped open his morning-fresh copy of the *Times*, read the CTW announcement story, and drew a sheet of stationery from his desk. Two days later, the congratulatory note reached Cooney. Expressing his enthusiasm for the idea of a children's show that educated as it entertained, Dann offered "any support you desire."

Chapter Ten

At the *Times* the next day, Jack Gould followed his coverage of the CTW press conference with a newsy column of television notes that included media reaction to the preschool show: "Michael Dann, vice president of the Columbia Broadcasting System, hailed the workshop as conceivably one of the most important breakthroughs in the evolution of the mass medium."[1]

Gould also slyly noted that life had changed virtually overnight for the Workshop's executive director. "Mrs. Joan Ganz Cooney . . . encountered yesterday the immediate problems of the head of a new agency. Before breakfast, the job applicants were on her phone."[2]

He didn't know what others might make of Gould's story, but that morning all Dave Connell could do was shake his head. *This isn't any way to do a television program that's going to appeal to kids,* Connell thought. *It's a lovely idea, but they are going to blow eight million bucks.* He all but gagged over the mention in the *Times* about the show having a panel of academic advisers. "It's going to be debated to death," he predicted. No way could producers be expected to churn out 130 episodes and have the time—or patience—to deal with a cap-and-gown committee looking over their shoulders.[3]

Life had improved immeasurably for Connell after bailing from Robert Keeshan Associates to join Ken Snyder Enterprises, a Santa Barbara, California–based independent film and animation company that had just established an office in Manhattan.[4]

In his new position, Connell split his time between New York and Los Angeles, occasionally flying out in a twin-engine private aircraft he owned and piloted. "I was extremely happy for the first time in ten years," he recalled later.[5] Connell's income rose and his stress level dropped. "Bob Keeshan had been a difficult man to work with, and my dad got pushed around a lot," said Connell's son, Alan, a former CBS News employee who lives now in New Hampshire. "But Keeshan was pretty upset when Dad left."

Connell didn't spend much time with his wife and three children at their suburban New Jersey home. In those days he was never one to place family over work. "We didn't see him as much when we were kids," Alan Connell said. "I remember him being around on weekends." Dave Connell's daughter Jan, a therapist based in Warwick, New York, has childhood memories of a rigid and regimented father. "He was obsessive-compulsive," she said. "He had to make sure everything was in its place and working, that everything was exactly the way it was supposed to be. It served him, but [also] tortured him."

Connell's demeanor at work was at variance with what it was at home, especially when he was around his new California pal Jim Thurman, a comedy writer who also provided voices for cartoon characters. "They were thick as thieves," Jan Connell said. "They had a marriage after twenty-five years of working together."

When Connell departed *Captain Kangaroo*, he took Carol Jorjorian, who was only weeks away from marrying a man from the *Kangaroo* bullpen of writer-producers, with him as his secretary. Just as Connell had indirectly brought Jon Stone and Beverley Owen together, so, too, did he have a hand in the romance between Carol Jorjorian and Sam Gibbon, a love affair that was kept secret from Keeshan.

"Keeshan was a terrible tease," Gibbon said. "If it became known that two members of his staff were dating, he would've been on an unmerciful tear."

Upon arriving back at his office one midafternoon, Connell was surprised to find a pink "while you were out" message to call Mike Dann at CBS. *What on earth could this be about?* he wondered.

Connell's name and phone number were in fact at the top of a list of names on Dann's desk, a ranking prepared by one of the fourteen vice presidents who served under him. In fact, Connell had been the topic of conversation that very afternoon at the Ground Floor, the elegant, street-level restaurant at Black Rock, CBS's headquarters at Sixth Avenue and Fifty-second Street.[6]

Upon arriving at the restaurant, Joan Cooney greeted Dann, who led her to their table and introduced Fred Silverman, the thirty-year-old CBS vice president for daytime and children's programming. Cooney sensed right away that Silverman "couldn't have cared less" about her project.[7] He was there only because Dann insisted on it.

Silverman was a young man on the make, but in those days his domain was limited. To be charitable, his interest in young viewers was clinical, detached, and pragmatic. To him, children were the unseen pajama demographic, the cereal-eating number clusters that he was paid to lure to the screen. Of course, Silverman was hardly the only children's programming executive in the 1960s and '70s to place matters of commerce above matters of content. Nevertheless, he did create the *CBS Children's Film Festival*, which indirectly linked *Kukla, Fran and Ollie* to *Sesame Street*, and he did use his knowledge of *Captain Kangaroo* to lead executive director Cooney to her first big hire.[8]

Dann had run a background check of sorts on Cooney after she had taken him up on his offer to help. "I got her dossier," Dann recalled. "I found out she was a real proper lady, a well-bred girl from Arizona. But I also realized that she had no background whatsoever in programming. What she had was a *concept*," he said, one that happened to appeal to him in a powerful and profound way.

At the time, the forty-seven-year-old programming executive was undergoing a crisis of conscience, nagging bouts of self-doubt that robbed him of sleep and churned acid in his gut. While he had been responsible for much of the quality programming that had once distinguished CBS as the "Tiffany network," he also populated its prime-time schedule with the likes of *The Beverly Hillbillies*—popular but weightless shows that in his estimation deflated the television medium. He was especially pained that children's television on all three networks had devolved into nothing more than a Saturday morning marketplace to peddle plastic toys, super-sweetened cereals, and marshmallow-domed cupcakes zapped with preservatives and entombed in shrink-wrap.

"I wrote the note to Joan and picked up the phone when she called almost out of a sense of guilt," Dann said. "I had three young children of my own at home, and I knew the networks, mine included, were putting on such awful programming for them."

After twenty years in network television programming, the appeal for it had begun to wane. Dann, who had once aspired to write comedy, began his career at NBC in 1948 around the time of the debut of *Howdy Doody*. He worked on the classic musical adaptation of *Peter Pan* with Mary Martin, Dave Garroway's *Wide Wide World*, and on the launches of the *Today* and *Tonight* shows. As programming chief at CBS, he championed *The Defenders* (1961–65), the Reginald Rose–written courtroom drama featuring the father-son legal team of E. G. Marshall and Robert Reed, and the much-acclaimed *East Side, West Side* (1961), with George C. Scott as a New York social worker. Dann brought Leonard Bernstein's Young People's Concerts to the home screen, along with *A Charlie Brown Christmas*, and the 1966 staging of *Death of a Salesman* with Lee J. Cobb as Willy Loman.

But Dann felt these achievements were overlooked amid the prime-time mix for which he was also responsible, the derivative sitcoms (*My Living Doll*) and the formulaic cowboy (*Cimarron Strip*), medical (*The Doctors and the Nurses*), and detective programs (*Mannix*).

The ego absurdities of show business had taken its toll, as well. With no small amount of sarcasm, he once said, "For twenty years, in the action world of the networks, I had been involved in many critical, turbulent problems that shook the nation to its very roots. Such issues as how to repair Jackie Gleason's golf cart or how to build Danny Kaye's dressing room on the top of Television City."[9]

By the spring of 1968, Dann was in a downward spiral. "The only thing I knew for sure was ratings, which I was addicted to," he said. "The A. C. Nielsen Company was my lord and master."

He was aware of all this, which may be why Cooney's quest to test the prosocial potential of television proved so alluring. "After her call, I had a staff meeting to talk about how we could help her find an executive producer, saying, 'I want you to give me a list of names of value to this project in descending order.' That's when Fred Silverman said, 'Why not Dave Connell?'"

Connell had departed *Captain Kangaroo* and CBS on the best of terms, leaving a legacy of solid and dependable work.

During the lunch at the Ground Floor, candid and to the point, Dann told Cooney that the greatest obstacle facing her was "you don't know what you don't know." And of all the unknowns, the most important was that she needed to find an executive producer familiar with "volume producing," if she hoped to shoot 130 episodes of a show without keeling over. "It's running a sausage factory, as Dave used to say," Joan remembered. "You need to find someone who knows how to make the sausage."

Cooney was attentive. She had already missed her first choice as number two, having offered the executive producer slot to George Dessart, the clever chap who had first made the inspired suggestion of using the same approach Madison Avenue used to sell soap to sell the alphabet to little kids. To his credit, Dessart felt he was not the right candidate and told her as much. She was surprised—not the least because she had no second choice.

But Dann and Silverman did.

Dann went on to explain that only volume producers had the superior organizational skills and temperament to keep one eye on that day's shooting schedule and the other on tomorrow's, next week's, and next month's. The volume producer is to the studio what a plant manager is to the widget factory. The smoother and more efficient the assembly line, the better the product and the happier the workforce.

Dann then suggested Dave Connell as a "proper, well-educated man" who had all of the requisite skills of a volume producer and a sterling track record in children's television. He offered to call him as soon as he got back to the office, and Cooney gratefully accepted.

When Dann reached him, Connell expressed satisfaction with his new life and an unwillingness to return to daily television. Added to that, he said he wanted no part of a children's show that seemed to him doomed from the start. In full sales mode, Dann responded with a fabrication of parade-balloon proportions. "Bill Paley and Frank Stanton would like you to consider this," he said, dropping two ten-megaton names.

Did Connell really believe that two titans of broadcasting rose from their thrones and pointed to a fairly anonymous guy in black-framed glasses sitting at a tidy desk? It seems unlikely. But at the close of the conversation, Connell did agree to meet with Dann's new friend, Joan Cooney.

"I was instantly enchanted by her," Connell said. "We had four rather lengthy conversations and we discussed all my reservations about the project. I was so concerned as to whether I could function in an organization with this huge academic advisory board and felt a little arrogant about it because I didn't need a job. I wasn't going to take this unless it was on terms I felt comfortable with and, in fact, I wasn't even sure I'd take it then because I had obligations to my business partner. I had gotten a three-year lease on an office, a secretary, and an assistant. To walk out on all that nine months into the thing was a fairly important problem."[10]

For her part, Cooney said, "I convinced him that he would have a lot of artistic freedom, that I would not be breathing down his neck. But I said there were certain nonnegotiables, one of which was that there would be commercials to teach letters and numbers, there would be four or five hosts who were men and women, black and white. That the show was never going to be 'owned' by a single talent. And that of course, it would be an educational program. The education and entertainment would not be separate. Every piece of education would be entertaining, and every piece of entertainment would be educational."

Connell said, "In time, we discussed all my reservations, and I came to find that she agreed totally with me that the staff should be largely, if not exclusively, first-rate successful commercial television people and the ultimate decisions about what goes on the air has to remain with the producers. If it had to be run by an academic advisory board, there was the risk of disaster. If we were going to err, it must be on the side of entertainment, not education."[11]

While Connell deliberated, a chain reaction of events complicated matters.

It started one night when Lou Hausman of the USOE phoned Cooney at home. She remembers Hausman saying, "My friend Tom Whedon tells me the most creative guy in children's television is Jon Stone." Cooney, pleased to have another lead on a candidate, tracked down Stone at the

A-frame in Vermont. Infant Polly was asleep in a tiny room off the kitchen when Beverley picked up the phone and handed it to Jon.

Cooney's call found Stone at a time of marital and parental bliss. He was joyously bound to his wife of two years and equally infatuated with his sweet-faced daughter. By day, he was strapping on a tool belt and adding cabinetry and wood accents to the house. By night, he was developing an action-adventure series based on the exploits of Ethan Allen and the Green Mountain Boys—after abandoning a plan in early 1968 to adapt Laura Ingalls Wilder's *Little House* books for television when an executive at Harper & Row informed him that Michael Landon had only weeks earlier secured rights to the series.

Jon, Beverley, and Polly were splitting their time between an apartment they kept in New York and the house in Sandgate. "I was bringing in a pittance here and a trifle there with sundry jobs," Stone said. "We were somehow making ends meet and spending a lot of time in Vermont, skiing, gardening, happily hanging out, happily driving the Porsche down to the city for [New York] Giants games with Polly stuffed into the little shelf behind the seats. Financially and professionally Beverley and I were in total darkness with no dawn in sight, and we were happy as clams."

Stone greeted a possible return to children's television with indifference, but he agreed to discuss the matter with Cooney in New York. His insouciance "disappeared within moments of my entering Joan's office," he said. "Her enthusiasm for her subject was contagious and I was immediately captivated by this gentle dynamo of a woman. I had never heard of anyone involved with children's television speak of it with such fire, not even Bob Keeshan, whose commitment to the betterment of the medium was famous. Joan spoke earnestly of the good this program might do in righting some of the inequities in our society, in closing some of the grievous gaps that existed in the education system."

Stone returned to Vermont intrigued with the possibility of applying his years of experience in television toward an effort to assist the less fortunate. And after years of hustling for work in television, it was satisfying to be the pursued instead of the pursuer.

The second event involved Stone's former roommate Sam Gibbon, that dashing Princeton grad, song stylist, and lady killer. Cooney had indentified Gibbon as a target for hire after meeting him through an introduction from writer Linda Gottlieb. Cooney sensed that Gibbon was not suited to the role of executive producer, but she was equally certain that his seriousness of purpose, good humor, and intelligence was just what CTW needed as a producer. But after meeting with him, it did not seem in the cards. "I had asked Sam to come aboard and he had turned me down flat," Cooney said.[12]

"I'd had enough with children's television," Gibbon said. "I'd been with Bob Keeshan for almost seven years and had quit and gone to work with Norton Wright to get a movie produced. I thought I had graduated into grown-up media, and that was a happy issue for me because I had sort of burned out on *Captain Kangaroo*." In addition, he was about to be married and looking for more pay than what children's television typically offered.

In the weeks that followed, Cooney remained in contact, using Gibbon as a sounding board. "He was the only person I could call on who knew [both Dave Connell and Jon Stone]. I called him, in agony, and we probably had two hour-long conversations while I was seeing those two guys. [Sam] was immensely helpful."

From Gibbon she learned of the bad blood between Dave and Jon, dating back to the drunken night when the Keeshan table at Christ Cella's steak house suddenly went from a party of five to a party of three. Connell, executive director of *Captain Kangaroo*, had backed Bob Keeshan, and Stone took it as a slight that Connell, a married man with children, didn't jump off the cliff with him.

Gibbon praised Connell's management skills and television savvy, his character and reliability. "There was nobody in the business then who had more experience with children's television, nobody who had worked on a show with the concern for kids that *Kangaroo* had, nobody who was more in sync with the spirit of CTW than Dave," Gibbon said. "Also I hoped that if he got hired and I couldn't get this movie produced he might hire me. So I had a slightly ulterior motive in that suggestion."

Gibbon described Stone, his roommate of seven-plus years, as a gifted writer-producer whose milieu was the studio. "Jon is very, very talented . . . but he is not an executive producer," Gibbon said, well aware of Stone's stubborn resistance to authority. Gibbon could not imagine Stone navigating the tricky waters of higher management, even at a relatively intimate start-up like CTW. However, it *was* easy to see how effective Stone would be in the mix with actors, writers, and directors, not to mention cranky carpenters, cameramen, electricians, and grown men with sock puppets running up their arms.

Taking Gibbon's and others' recommendations into account, Cooney concluded she had two outstanding talents in her sights. "At some point I had decided that it had to be Dave [as executive producer] and I *had* to get Jon on board, as well," she said. "How was I going to tell Jon he was not a contender for the top job?" Connell only complicated matters by warning, "I don't think Jon will work for me."

Stone asked Cooney to lunch, unaware that she had already decided on Connell for the chief position. "When Joan outlined the plan for the structure of the production staff, I saw immediately that the executive producer's job would be a step removed from the day-to-day production tasks," he said. "I interrupted Joan's explanation to tell her that I really had no interest in the top job, that I would be much happier and more useful at the producer level. My turning it down without her having offered it was certainly presumptuous on my part, but if it was, Joan fielded my gaffe with characteristic grace and proposed that I take one of the producer positions."

Cooney said, "Fine, the executive producer is going to be Dave Connell, in that case."

Stone cleared his throat. "I wouldn't want to work for Dave," he said, "and I would only consider it if I could report directly to you."

"Jon, that's the road to chaos," she said. "You've been in this business long enough to know that. Why don't you two guys talk? Often these old quarrels go away when it is years later and you're focused on something new."

Connell and Stone agreed to talk. Whether their meeting took place in a drawing room at high tea or a boxing ring at high noon, they walked away from it having reached détente. They would never be bowling partners, but they did agree to work together. Over time and true to form, Connell was more successful at burying past differences than Stone.

Tim Cooney was working in Harlem on the evening of April 4, 1968. He was a coordinator for Fight Back, an advocacy group working to end discriminatory hiring practices in the construction trades.

When the news broke that Dr. Martin Luther King Jr. had been assassinated while standing on the balcony of a motel room in Memphis, rioting broke out in black neighborhoods in New York and other cities. "It was not safe to be a white man in Harlem that night," Joan Cooney recalled. "The black construction workers on whose behalf Tim was working made him lie down in a car that one of them had," she said, "and they drove him home."

Together in their apartment, the Cooneys sat alongside each other in disbelief watching the news. "We were devastated," Joan Cooney said. "Dr. King was *the* American hero of my lifetime."

On Palm Sunday, three days after Dr. King's murder, Sam Gibbon and his fiancée, Carol, joined a throng estimated to be between ten thousand and twenty thousand people assembled in Central Park for a massive public outpouring of grief. Similar gatherings were being held in San Francisco, Newark, Houston, and Salt Lake City, as well as in smaller towns throughout the nation. At Forty-fifth Street and Seventh Avenue in New York, a few hundred mourners began a solemn march to Central Park at 1:30 p.m. By the time they reached the park's northern gate, their ranks had swelled to between 3,500 and 5,000 men, women, and children, white and black, marching twenty abreast, arm-in-arm. In a front line, Governor Nelson Rockefeller linked his left arm through the right arm of black militant Charles 37X Kenyatta, the onetime bodyguard of Malcolm X and leader of Harlem's Mau Mau Society. Impaled on a machete Kenyatta carried were an open Bible and a presidential report on civil rights rioting.[13]

No permit had been issued for the eighty-block procession that ended with a stream of humanity pooling at the park's band shell at 3:30 p.m. A pale sun lit the scene with soft, diffuse light.

Rockefeller and New York mayor John Lindsay eulogized Dr. King, along with spiritual leaders from throughout the city. "He lived as God's kind of king," said the Reverend Wyatt Walker, pastor of Harlem's New Canaan Baptist Church. "Just as a cross could not kill Jesus, a bullet cannot kill King. His work will live on."[14]

Led by Leopold Stokowski, the American Symphony Orchestra, 100 members strong, joined the 250-voice Westminster Choir and the Camerata Singers in selections from Beethoven, Bach, and Verdi. The musicians and singers performed for free. "Everybody is giving their services," Stokowski said. "Nothing is too great for such a great person as Martin Luther King."[15]

At the conclusion of the fifty-five-minute service, all in attendance sang two verses of the civil rights anthem "We Shall Overcome."

Gibbon said, "These crowds of people in tears, black and white, holding hands together . . . it was an astonishing outpouring of feeling. I guess it felt to most of us as though the country was in real danger of crumbling, as though the center would not hold." After the service, at Carol's urging, Gibbon acted on an impulse to honor the spirit and vision of the civil rights martyr. "The notion that maybe it was time to do something useful was pretty overpowering," he said. "And it did seem as though CTW was a place to put your energies, a place to do what we had learned."

Cooney recalled that soon after the memorial, "Sam Gibbon called me and said, 'I'm aboard.'"

On a warm June day in 1968, a critical day in the development of *Sesame Street*, thirty participants and observers chosen to take part in the first of five extraordinary seminars arranged by CTW were packed into a room a stone's throw from the Harvard Graduate School of Education. There would be two such gatherings held that summer on the Cambridge campus and three in Manhattan, bringing together renowned scholars, educators, authors, filmmakers, illustrators, wits, and sages from all corners. The goal was threefold: to extract expert opinion on what *Sesame Street* should attempt to teach in its first year, to expose the production team to those experts, and to engage an elite corps of academic advisers in the process of creating the show. It was hoped that in doing so, participants would gain a sense of ownership and be less likely to criticize the show once it began.

It fell to Gerry Lesser, chairman of the CTW advisory board, to keep the sessions productive and on point, relying on the charm of a ringmaster and the whip-crack alertness of a lion tamer.

Great pains had been taken to keep the guest list free of grandstanders, blowhards, and show-offs. Lesser sought participants who could show "eagerness—(or at least willingness)—to think hard about television for children, a topic that many academics might dismiss as trivial." A sense of humor helped, as did "the inclination to avoid converting meetings into debates where points are won and lost, but the job does not get done."[16]

Despite these precautions, there were moments on that first day when the room filled with hot air, and organizers worried that the whole affair would amount to a fifty-thousand-dollar filibuster.

"There was little reason to expect that the seminars would be productive," said Daniel M. Ogilvie, a Harvard research associate who was working under Lesser at the time. "One could envision the invited specialists, especially academics, wasting time, space, and money in boring jargon-laden meetings that would result in impractical suggestions. Practically none of the specialists would have any experience in television, so how could they be helpful?"[17]

The new team of executive producer Dave Connell, producer–head writer Jon Stone, and producer Sam Gibbon approached the seminars with varying degrees of skepticism. But in Lesser they found an accessible, congenial researcher who had experience and interest in television. That he spoke their language helped to forge a bond of mutual respect, even before the seminars began. Once they did, that skepticism dissipated.

"Gerry would come into these meetings of gray beards from all over the country, [academics] who were accustomed to defending their turf and fighting with each other," Gibbon said. "He'd take off his coat, loosen his tie, and roll his sleeves up. He would introduce everybody and say something about

their work. There would be sixty people in the room and he would introduce every single one, calling them by their first name. It was an amazing
feat of memory. [Professional] titles were out the window, and he'd say, 'Any
good idea is as good as any other good idea, and it doesn't matter where it
comes from.' What that did was get *everybody* intellectually excited in the
curriculum. *We* got as involved in the curriculum as the outside advisers, and
they got as interested in the show development as we were. So it really made
people cross that barrier between the blood of show business and the brain of
the curriculum and they meshed nicely."

This is not to say there weren't dead spots, detours, diversions, and disagreements along the way. "The artists and performers, those professionals
who must rely upon and trust their intuitions—often vehemently protested
the imposing of objective, abstract analysis upon the creative act of inventing television for children," Lesser said. "They contended that any book,
film, music, or television program—indeed all creative products—can only
be conceived intuitively and lovingly, with the creator drawing freely upon
his own fantasies, feelings, and experiences; the dissection of deliberate
thought and methodical planned analysis destroys the naturalness that
must be inherent in the product.

"The timing of these protests . . . was unpredictable, but they often
occurred when it appeared the academics were dissecting not only the creative
product but the child himself, dividing and classifying his mind and heart
into 'symbolic representation,' 'cognitive processes,' and 'self concept.' "[18]

Lesser recalled "temporary armistices" that lowered participants' blood
pressure: "Academics and educators—presumably the thinkers and analyz-
ers—acknowledged the necessity of intuition in designing creative materials, but argued that adding some elements of analysis in deliberate planning
need not smother that necessary intuition. The protesters were skeptical
of this compromise, but they also were eager to avoid a stalemate. They
agreed that since we were meeting to exchange thoughts about the goals of
a children's television series, we should proceed in the unlikely hope that
thought and intuition were not inevitably incompatible."[19]

There was no seating plan for the seminars, so Jon Stone arrived early to
each session to sit near Maurice Sendak, the daring author-illustrator of
Where the Wild Things Are, a book that contained only 338 words but that
had spawned a million opinions. Published in 1963, Sendak's phantasma-
gorical tale of Max, a rambunctious boy whose mother sends him to bed
without his supper, was hailed by some as a bold and fanciful exploration
of how a parent can get angry at a child and vice versa. Others fumed that

a child's rage at his mother—upon being punished, Max threatened to eat her—was inappropriate subject matter for a storybook. Child psychologist Bruno Bettelheim, writing in *Ladies' Home Journal*, criticized Sendak for illuminating the "destructive fantasies in the child."

"Sendak's patience with some of the long-winded debates was minimal," Stone recalled, "and to vent his boredom he drew dozens of X-rated cartoons expressing his opinion of the proceedings. I could watch over his shoulder as he doodled. For the most part his cartoons dealt with basic sex and violence, much as his published writings often do. The drawings were incisive, the perfect scalpel to cut right at the heart of the sometimes unbearably stuffy discussions. My favorite, I guess, he titled 'One Minute of Educational TV.' It showed a normal-looking child watching television, then yawning, then sticking his tongue out at the screen. The child grew more and more ferocious, hitting the set with his fist, then attacking it with a hatchet, reducing it to a smoldering pile of wires and plastic, and finally taking out his tiny penis and peeing on the whole thing."

Sendak's portfolio of drawings from the seminars included a classic rivalry-inspired sketch of a child pointing a drawn pistol at his mother and baby sibling. A discussion of television's effects on children yielded a sketch of an agitated child doing a war dance in front of a hideous, grinning woman on TV. The boy's cat is hanging from the ceiling by its collar. "I have been doodling with ink and watercolor and paper all my life," Sendak once said. "I recommend doodling as an excellent exercise in stirring up the subconscious, just as you would stir up some mysterious soup, all the while hoping it would taste good."[20]

In Gerry Lesser's book about the developmental years of *Sesame Street*, he wrote that the stresses of the seminars caused many of the participants to have little "nervous breakdowns," moments when it all got to be too much. Sam Gibbon was among them.

"I remember we were meeting in Boston to talk about kids' social and affective development, and Chester Pierce, who was a psychiatrist and professor at Harvard, and an absolutely wonderful man who was very important in the education of the staff, unloaded himself one day about what it was like to be a kid in the inner city, what kinds of horrors they lived with and the dangers of life and the dim prospects of ever emerging from it. He was saying the show would have to reflect this reality. It couldn't be white bread. It had to reflect the reality of these children's lives.

"I listened to this all morning and the image of the show that was building in my mind was absolutely horrible. I couldn't imagine how this

children's show could reflect the reality that he was describing and do anything other than destroy the viewer. It just seemed so hopeless and awful,
and I said as much. I exploded in this meeting.

"Gerry instantly said, 'I think we should break for lunch.' And as we
left the meeting room and headed for the elevators I was surrounded by
Chet, Gerry Lesser, and a couple of others who sort of were stroking me
and saying, 'There, there. Let's go get a cup of coffee.'

"I recovered," Gibbon said.

Seminar III, devoted to mathematical and numerical concepts and held
at the Waldorf, was well under way when Joan Cooney panicked. "This
bearded, prophetic figure in sandals walks in and sits way at the back, ram-
rod straight, staring straight ahead with no expression on his face," Cooney
recalled. A shiver ran up her spine because she feared that the intruder
might be a member of the radical Weathermen, a splinter group of former
members of SDS [Students for a Democratic Society]. "The Weathermen
were blowing up buildings," Cooney said, "and some radical kids were trying to make bombs and had recently blown themselves up in a Greenwich
Village brownstone basement. Here we are sitting at the Waldorf in a conference room . . . and in comes someone with long hair and wearing an
outfit dripping in leather. I remember whispering to Dave Connell, 'How
do we know that man back there isn't going to throw a bomb up here or
toss a hand grenade?'"

Connell, always one to keep a cool head, assessed the situation with
care. He discreetly turned his head toward the back and realized he recognized the tall, angular man carrying a small purse under his arm. A slight
smile curled as he assured Cooney the hippie back there posed no threat.

"Not likely, that's Jim Henson," he said.

Chet Pierce got everyone's attention at one seminar when he said, "What
I want the show to do is prepare my three-year-old daughter to react properly the first time somebody calls her a nigger."

"We were all shocked and didn't know quite how to react," Dave Connell said. "It was a real confrontation. Chet is such a brilliant man, he was
doing it to get the issue on the table, to discuss it."

From the ensuing discussion came the decision that the show would
lead by example. There would be an integrated cast, but nothing would
be done artificially to draw attention to their diversity and harmony. The
actors would regard each other with kindness, respect, and tolerance.

When the seminars ended in August, Connell, Stone, and Gibbon had received a crash course in child development, psychology, and preschool education. "It was a horrendous strain, physically and mentally," said Connell. "I can still remember, at the end of those things, feeling as though I had just played linebacker for the Chicago Bears. I ached after three days of those meetings. But it was terribly exciting."[21]

Of this he was certain: "Three days locked up in a hotel with fifty people, you come out knowing those you want to drink with and those you never want to see again."[22]

Gibbon described the seminars as a "wonderful mixture of excitements. We worked our asses off getting ready for the meetings, going through the meetings, and digesting them afterward. For me, it was an enormous high."

Stone recalled it this way: "Weekend after weekend . . . the ideas and convictions filled the room in dizzying confusion. Often I was left behind when the academicians began arguing in their own arcane language. Sometimes I was near falling asleep when the talk droned on in the afternoon July heat. But I tried to learn and absorb and take notes and make sense out of the overwhelming barrage of information that went down," he said.

"It was a summer of opportunity few in my position are ever afforded. And, I was to find out, it was only the beginning."

In attendance at two of the seminars was Edward L. Palmer, the man who took the longest trip of all to get to *Sesame Street*.

"When the Children's Television Workshop was announced, I was finishing my first year in Oregon working with the state system of higher education in a full-time research lab," he said. "I was an associate professor there . . . and I thought I was going to do theoretically based research on children and their thinking and learning, and publish, and that was going to be my life."[23]

By a quirk of fate, he had taken over a USOE grant to study what holds a child's attention to the television screen. "[The original researcher] was an alcoholic, and he'd spent half the money and hadn't started the research. The Oregon people [got] him some health care he needed, and they needed to have somebody take this study over. I was happy to take it, but I had to start from scratch because I didn't like his proposal. At that time there were a lot of locally produced children's programs, [like] *Jack the Engineer* or *Tilly the Teacher*, or whatever. He was going to do a comparison, pitting two programs against each other, running them at the same time.

"I said, 'We need just *one* program and we need to find out if we can pull the kids away from it. That'll be the test.'" Palmer devised a diabolical apparatus he called "the distractor." No one has ever described the architecture of Palmer's experiment—and the distractor—better than Jim Day, the founding father of San Francisco's jewel of a public station, KQED: "The distractor was a portable movie screen, set at an angle off to the side of the television receiver, which showed a series of slides with random images appealing to children.

"Using this device, Palmer could determine from moment to moment the young viewers' attention to the program on the tube. By changing the slide every seven and one-half seconds and observing whether the eye movements of the youngsters were on the screen or the tube, Palmer developed an attention profile of each episode that resembled nothing so much as the chart of stock-market prices in a highly unstable economy—instant evidence of what held the children's attention and what didn't."[24]

Around the time Palmer delivered his findings to the USOE, a colleague who knew Joan Cooney arranged to have a copy of the series proposal sent to Oregon.

"I had all the credentials that would have been needed by someone who wanted to find out how much a television series could influence children," Palmer said. "There was a real natural affinity. I had a background in research and a PhD in measurement and research design."

A program officer at the USOE recommended Palmer to Cooney, Morrisett, and Lesser, who were in search of a research director for CTW. "They were going to come out and visit my lab in Oregon. Then the Workshop began the series of summer planning seminars, and instead of them coming out, I went to New York City. I met Sam Gibbon and Dave Connell at the first seminar I attended and was impressed that they had been with *Captain Kangaroo*. I had children who watched [it]."

On a second trip to New York, Cooney all but gave Palmer the job, but he still needed to pass muster with Lesser, the advisory board chairman.

"Ed Palmer was the only social scientist in the United States, other than Gerry, who had studied children and television, and he was the right age, in the right stage in his life," Cooney said. Lesser emerged beaming from an informal interview with Palmer, a session Cooney said lasted five minutes. "You don't have to look any further," Lesser said to Cooney. "Trust me, this guy is it."

Cooney worked out the details. "Joan Cooney was always utterly, utterly forthcoming," Palmer said. "I took the job on the basis that we'd have to see if the research was going to work. . . . We would have a good faith agreement that if it wasn't working on either side we would give ample notice and take care of things properly. That was the basis for an academic to jump up with a family, two children, and come from Oregon to New York. I took a two-year leave of absence from my job and it never occurred to me, not even a glimmer, that CTW would become an institution, forevermore and all that. I was sure that an eight-million-dollar grant for children's television was an anomaly, and I thought, *This is a wonderful once-in-a-lifetime opportunity.*"

Chapter Eleven

I n the amazing summer of '68, two items with special relevance to the story of *Sesame Street* appeared in the *New York Times*.

Item No. 1: Writing in the Sunday, July 14, *Times Magazine*, critic John Leonard cast a cynical eye toward the Children's Television Workshop and its supporters. "Any project seducing the philanthropies of two private foundations and a government agency is suspect," he warned. "Government agencies are permitted to exist . . . only so long as they use hair sprays to attack our various social Medusas."

Item No. 2: In the July 31 *Times*, television beat reporter-critic Jack Gould covered a press conference at the *Captain Kangaroo* studio at 229 West Fifty-third Street. There, CBS senior vice president Mike Dann announced that the Bank Street College of Education, a graduate school for teachers and guidance counselors, had been enlisted to create a series of ten-minute educational segments for *Kangaroo*. The new "structured" elements, Gould wrote, would "encourage youngsters to learn more about themselves, the outside world, living, eating, and clothing habits, improvement of vocabulary and speech patterns, elementary use of numbers, and the job obligations of family members, policemen, firemen, and doctors."

Gould continued, "Mr. Dann said that CBS hoped tests might be given to groups of preschool children who had and had not followed *Captain Kangaroo* to determine in what ways the TV hour had contributed to preparation for formal education."

Bank Street president Dr. John H. Neimeyer and Bob Keeshan were asked if "the innovations for *Captain Kangaroo* did not bear a marked resemblance to the aspirations of the recently announced Children's Television Workshop. Dr. Neimeyer indicated his discussions with CBS had preceded announcement of the Workshop plans. Mr. Keeshan noted that several members of his production group had joined the Workshop staff. He said if time conflicts could be avoided, he doubted if there could be too much TV programming expressly intended for preschoolers."

Whenever the subject turned to the remarkable way things just seemed to work out in the formative years of *Sesame Street*, Joan Cooney liked to quote E. B. White. "White said, 'If you're going to be in New York, be prepared to be lucky,' and we were always prepared," Cooney said. "We took advantage of it when it came over the transom and we did careful planning so that we could use the luck when it happened. We were always prepared to be lucky."

That she was able to lure Connell, Gibbon, and Stone back into the fold of children's television was probably more attributable to her recruiting abilities than to karma, but it was her good fortune that they were open to her pitch and available. "Had I come to them before or after that golden moment, they might not have been," Cooney said. "CTW has been a place where miracles have happened over and over again, and I count these hires among them."

The three colleagues were wildly unalike, constitutionally and attitudinally. But they shared the essential quality of a hungry inquisitiveness, and each was humble enough to admit that he actually knew little about children, beyond what his better instincts told him. During their days working on *Captain Kangaroo,* they had relied on intuition, common sense, and the dictates of Bob Keeshan. Much more would be expected of them—required, in fact—as they shaped *Sesame Street* in the extraordinary fifteen months leading to its launch, a generous research and development period that no other children's show had ever enjoyed.

"Quite by accident, we each drifted into our particular areas of interest," said Stone, who assumed responsibility for the show's writing, casting, and format, while Connell took charge of animation—in part because of his familiarity with that end of the entertainment industry in New York and California. Gibbon became the chief liaison between the production group and the educational community, largely because of his affinity for translating the arcane language of education research into plain English.

In concert with Cooney, research director Ed Palmer, advisory board chairman Gerry Lesser, and the production team all zeroed in on a simplified list of teaching goals for a show targeted at three- to five-year-olds. Reducing the number to only a handful came as a suggestion from Frank Pace, the CPB's chairman of the board: "I'm going to give you a piece of advice. Select five things that you know you can teach and teach them. Don't try to do more than that. Show you can do *something* before you try to do *everything.*"

Lesser agreed. "Let's bet our asterisks on the most important things to teach," he said, suggesting that the show should attempt to get children to learn how to recognize the twenty-six letters in the alphabet by their sound and shape and train them to recite the ABCs. The curriculum would also strive to teach viewers how to count from one to ten and likewise recognize each of those numbers by its sound and shape. "If anything, we undershot our goals in the first year," Cooney recalled, "but Frank Pace's advice was just what we needed to hear."

Cooney's mantra to the production team during the summer of '68 was to create television that would be hip, fast, funny, and, whenever possible, tuneful in a way that reflected the times. "Music was relevant to the whole period," Cooney said. She recalled thinking, *We can't get the inner-city kids if we can't reflect what's going on.*[1]

Cooney's frequent reference point for hip, fast, and funny television that summer was a wildly popular prime-time comedy hour that viewers in the age group two to six had been watching in droves since its series debut in January. "They were viewing it because their parents were," Cooney said. "They didn't get all the humor, but they got something."

Rowan and Martin's Laugh-In first appeared as an NBC special on September 9, 1967. Slotted in the hour leading in to the Miss America finals from Atlantic City, *Laugh-In* was a long-shot attempt to draw a younger audience to watch TV on a Saturday night. In the mid-1960s, as the quake of counterculture rumbled underfoot, the Saturday prime-time lineup on all three networks was almost hopelessly square. The creaky schedules were geared to wives in flannel robes and husbands with pot bellies, each tipped back in the Barcalounger with the blue-gray flicker of *The Lawrence Welk Show* and *The Hollywood Palace* somewhere south of their feet.

Laugh-In featured some of the oldest comedy conventions known to man—pratfalls, puns, blackouts, recurring gags, even *knock-knock* jokes. But it spun them around in such a dizzying satirical swirl that it made it all seem new again. *Laugh-In* loosened granny's dentures with its rapid pace, cheeky satire, and pulsating beat. It made Grandpa's eyes snap open at the sight of gyrating go-go girls, not the least of whom was a giggling blonde in a bikini and body paint whose biggest gig before this one had been working as a dancer at a family-style theater-in-the-round called Melodyland, just across the street from Disneyland. On the Sunday morning after the *Laugh-In* special aired, worshipers on church steps and the less devout in doughnut shops were talking more about Miss Goldie Hawn than Miss America.

NBC moved quickly to schedule *Laugh-In* as a midseason replacement, where it just as quickly became a white-hot hit, and where its rapid-fire pace and freshness proved to be a model for how *Sesame Street* would be directed and edited.

Second to *Laugh-In* in buzz that TV season was ABC's *Batman*, a goofy, spoofy take on the Caped Crusader that draped the once shadowy crime fighter from Detective Comics in the exaggerated Pop Art funny-papers hues of the 1960s. *Batman*'s irreverence appealed to the *Sesame Street* production team, as did its ability to please two audiences simultaneously. Children saw it as a comic book come to life, complete with thought-balloon punctuation (*Pow!*). Adults enjoyed its camp sensibility, its visual references to the art of Roy Lichtenstein and Andy Warhol, and its slinky villainesses. More than one adolescent boy caught cat-scratch fever from watching Julie Newmar as Catwoman, the feline femme fatale.

Both shows caused TV executives to reconsider what they thought they knew about the medium. For her part, Cooney understood the risk of trying to go head-to-head against big-budget network programs. She told columnist Sidney Fields of the New York *Daily News* that mounting a show for kids that could compete with the youthful programming suddenly appearing on commercial TV would be tricky. Combining the two, she said, was a possibility, "but the wedding was going to be big and expensive. We'd have to compete with the loud noise, mad music, and strong wine the kids were getting on commercial shows." Plus, she added, "A half hour of *Batman* costs ninety thousand dollars."[2]

Nevertheless, she said, "I want [*Sesame Street*] to jump and move fast and feel and sound like 1969, because kids are turned on visually."

She knew it was pointless to ignore the visual language of *Laugh-In* and *Batman* and other shows because, in that unique way television has of insinuating itself into the private worlds of its viewers, the programs had already struck a chord and become part of the lives of millions. As Cooney told a reporter from *Saturday Review*, "TV has become the new reality. Kids know more about *Batman* than they know about what is going on in their own homes."[3]

Jon Stone figured the odds of success for the preschool show would rise geometrically if he could hook adults into watching it with their children, as with *Batman* and *Laugh-In*. He could think of no better way to build that two-tiered audience than to enlist the aid of his bohemian buddy, Jim Henson. Whenever the Muppets appeared on *The Ed Sullivan Show* they simultaneously delighted kids and fractured adults.

In his memoir, Jon Stone wrote this about the efforts made by the production team to guarantee that Jim Henson was on board:

Ever the businessman, Jim made sure up front that his interests would be protected and drove a hard bargain with the Workshop's lawyers regarding ownership of his characters. During the negotiations, the CTW lawyers periodically came to me and asked, "How badly do we need this guy? He's killing us with demands." And I answered that we needed him. There were no degrees of need. Not a little bit or a lot. We needed him. The lawyers were somehow outraged that Jim wanted to retain ownership of the Muppets he had so carefully invented and nurtured over the years. The rest of us, after all, had docilely come on board without demanding participation in any characters or other elements we might create.

Henson's comedy was once described by Muppet writer-performer Jerry Juhl as "affectionate anarchy," a term that also could have been applied to the radio work of Edgar Bergen, Jack Benny, Bob and Ray, and Stan Freberg. Because Henson and Stone were children of radio's golden age, in adulthood they both sought ways to provide contemporary families with a reason to sit around and be entertained, just as many once had in front of a full-throated Philco floor model.

As keepers of the flame, Stone and Henson drew upon countless radio conventions and vestiges of vaudeville in the show's early years. Bert and Ernie—straight man and comic, target and provocateur—were descendants of Burns and Allen, Abbott and Costello, Martin and Lewis. And, as we shall see, the hilarious team of Chet O'Brien and his brother Snooks— identical-twin stage managers for *Sesame Street*—were a living link to vaudeville and the radio kings of comedy who conquered early television.

Connell, Gibbon, and Stone were so set on signing Jim Henson for their new show that they made a pact: "If we can't get Henson," they swore, "then we just won't have puppets."

"The name Jim Henson probably passed Jon's lips first," Cooney said. "I hadn't remembered the name at first. I'd blanked it out, but then a lightbulb went on. When I was doing the study for Carnegie, my friend Edith Zornow called me and said, 'Joan, I want you to come with me to the Johnny Victor theater to see a screening of the commercials done by a guy named Jim Henson.' I went to the . . . theater and was on the floor. I couldn't believe puppets could be so hip and funny."

"When I realized who Jon was talking about—the puppeteer whose commercials made me fall over laughing—I was thrilled."

It was Cooney who negotiated the first deal Henson made with CTW. His compensation request was modest by show-business standards, perhaps an accommodation made to a fledgling nonprofit enterprise. But Henson not only made sure that the trademark for any Muppets created for the show would remain with his company, he also insisted that any future revenues generated by the licensing and merchandising of those characters would be split between him and CTW.

By any reckoning, it was a win-win arrangement. The character revenues would fill Henson's coffers for twenty years, providing a renewable and dependable flow of cash that proved essential to the stability of his entrepreneurial, unconventional company. For CTW, signing Henson was not only the single most important decision in *Sesame Street* history, it was also the keystone to success for the entire Workshop.

Not surprisingly, Cooney, the former network publicist, had definite ideas about whom she wanted handing CTW public relations. "It was hard to find substantive PR people in those days, but Bob Hatch, who had done great work for the Peace Corps, *was* substantive," she said. "The heaviest-duty courtship I did for *Sesame Street* was of Bob Hatch."

Hatch first learned about CTW from Terry Turner, a former colleague in the public information office of the Peace Corps. Hatch recalled that Turner said, "'I've got an interesting proposition for you,' and he started telling me about the Workshop. I said, 'That sounds like a really interesting idea, except for one thing. It'll never fly.' And he said, 'Why?' I said, 'Because nobody has ever heard of National Educational Television. They are going to have one helluva big job trying to get an audience, particularly of poor people . . . most of whom can't even dial the station.'"

It was a valid point. For many viewers with old-model TV sets, tuning in to the weaker UHF frequencies—broadcast channels numbered above thirteen—required an additional antenna and considerable fuss. "Many of those stations were so small they were designated 'BMS' by A. C. Nielsen, which meant their viewership fell 'below a minimum standard' to be counted within the ratings," Hatch said.

"[Terry] called me back about a week or so later and said, 'Would you be interested in taking on the job?' I said, 'Oh, I don't know that I would. I don't even know what I'll be doing next year.' I had had a two-year leave of absence from Carl Byoir [a public relations agency], and I had spent an extra year at the Peace Corps. I was supposed to go back to Byoir the year before. They had offered me a couple of accounts . . . [but] both of them kind of left me cold, so I managed to finesse those and stay that one last year at the Peace Corps. But the Johnson administration was coming to a close and I really didn't want to be around for what looked to be a Nixon administration. So I had . . . mentally packed my bags to leave at the end of the year.

"The next person I heard from . . . was Joan Cooney . . . [who] was down seeing the Office of Education in May or June of '68. I remembered seeing the announcement of the Workshop in the *New York Times* a month or two before, and I was impressed by the kind of ink that she got right off the bat. It was obvious she knew where the levers were and how to pull them, and it was fun talking to her because she knew exactly what she wanted . . . I don't think I have ever run into a would-be employer or client or anybody else who had a better sense of just exactly what was . . . needed. She had a unique notion for the Workshop. I think it may have been partly because of Tim's experience working in the inner city, but also her own interest in reaching people in the inner city. She described something to me that I thought was going to be darn difficult, trying to put together an organization that could be sustained over a period of time in order to build an audience in the inner city.

"I particularly remember another meeting with Joan in New York City at her place [near] Gramercy Park, where she and Tim had me up for dinner. They were very, very gracious. I walked into the place and Tim said, 'Well, congratulations. I understand you've accepted.' I said, 'I have?' Tim was always trying to rush the season. I had never met him before, but I liked him. I was drinking a lot then and so was he. We got along just fine.

"I finally said, 'There's a chance at the end of a year's time that you won't be refunded, and then you're going to have to lay off a whole bunch of people, including me. Why don't you hire an agency, like Byoir, the people I used to work for, then you've only hired for a year. People expect to be laid off, it's no big deal. And besides, you're going to need a lot of people in a hurry to make this happen, many, many more people than you could afford to hire or than you would have time to hire, so the agency makes sense. But I said, 'You ought to feel safe about this. Why don't we ask a couple of other PR agencies if they would also be interested?' "

Cooney contacted four agencies, with mixed success. "They were either going to give [the Workshop] their second team, or, in a couple of cases, they thought the Workshop would not pay its bills," recalled Hatch. "That was even a concern at Byoir, 'Can we collect on this?' That was how wary anybody was of a project in public broadcasting. It was such an anonymous service at that point.

"I had had a lot of conversations with Joan that really didn't focus on me. . . . I think she was just probing my interests to see if I could talk myself into it, which is ultimately what I did. By the time I decided to go to CTW, I *really* wanted to go there. And I had come to one of those advisory seminars, just looked in. I was very silent. I didn't feel that I had any expertise that would add to what was happening, but I was fascinated by the people who were there and the kind of thought that was going into the preparation for this. . . . What Joan had in mind was really ideal."

Hatch was seen at Byoir as something of a hero. "It isn't often that you can come back to an organization like Byoir and bring your own account, so that worked out perfectly," Hatch said. "The stars, the moon, and what have you were in alignment that year."

Cooney had signed with Byoir in January 1969, getting the milk without owning the cow. "The fix was in," she said. "I knew Hatch would be our man, based on the fact that [the agency] proposed a full-time person and I knew who the full-time person was going to be."

Cooney was less certain who she wanted to hire to build awareness of the show in the inner city, but she knew she needed an outreach director who could quickly and effectively reach the target audience. For help, she called Jimmy Booker, a well-known and well-regarded black publicist. He, in turn, phoned Evelyn Payne Davis, the director of fund development for the New York Urban League.

"Jimmy said there was someone he wanted me to meet," Davis said. "He didn't say who or why, and I assumed it was a contact to raise money. He called for me . . . with a limousine, and I was thinking, *I wonder how much money I should ask for?*"

The car pulled up to the Bible Building at Sixty-first and Broadway. "Jimmy walked me inside, introduced me to Joan Cooney, and left. I had never heard about the Children's Television Workshop, and Joan never mentioned anything about a job. We just talked about what I did, and I was thinking, 'Okay, I have to assess this and then see what I'm going to hook them for.' I didn't know what she thought *I* thought we were talking about, and I didn't know what she was talking about. We just had a nice conversation. We had a second meeting about two weeks later and that's when she offered me a job. I was stunned; I wasn't looking for one."

Cooney explained the importance of a black audience. "My job," said Davis, "would be to make sure we had black people watching. I remember [Cooney] said, 'It's a utilization job.' And I said, 'What is *utilization*?' She used it in the context of television, and since I didn't know anything about that, I didn't know what she meant."

"You mean getting the community involved and organizing it?" Davis asked.

"Yes," Cooney said.

"Well, I know how to do *that*," Davis said.

A week passed. "I called and said I thought I'd like to try it," Davis said.

With that, the inner-city show had its first inner-city ambassador. She proved remarkable, unsinkable, and indispensable.

One of Jon Stone's first assignments with Jim Henson was to prepare a "sales film," a preview for a show that had yet to be developed. Joan Cooney's intention was to hit the road with CTW's new assistant director, Robert Davidson, visiting the top markets in the country to urge programming managers at public stations to pick up the show.[4] "I asked Jon and Jim to create something that had the Muppets talking about what we were going to do," Cooney said. "I needed something representative and convincing, something that would move them to schedule the show at nine a.m. They wanted to put it on at eight because almost all of them were paid by local school boards to air educational programming from nine on. I went out to say to them, 'You can't put it on against *Captain Kangaroo*. We are not going to try to harm the only other decent, constructive show on the air for kids!'"

Because little content for the show had been completed by the time the sales piece was taped in January 1969—save for a few preliminary animation pieces—Stone's task was the equivalent of producing a baby picture from an embryo. Complicating matters was that the show at that point had no name, no format, no setting. Still, Stone was certain of one thing: he wanted to move as far away from children's show conventions as possible. There would be no Treasure House, no toymaker's workshop, no enchanted castle, no dude ranch, no circus. To the underprivileged, the target audience, these settings seemed as foreign as the dark side of the moon.

A breakthrough idea eluded Stone until one night in late winter 1968, when a televised public service announcement provided a jolt of inspiration. The PSA opened with a printed message: "Send your kid to a ghetto this summer." It then cut to a street scene in Harlem, where a black actor named Lincoln Kilpatrick narrated a mock travelogue of an inner-city neighborhood, touting its supposed amenities. "We have all kinds of facilities here," he said, pointing out "pools" (fire hydrants gushing into gutters) and "ball fields" (a car-lined street where children played stickball), not to mention "field trips" (to fetid, trash-strewn lots), and "cozy camp cabins" (where black children slept three or four to a bed).

The actor pointedly asked, "You don't want your kids to play *here* this summer? Then don't expect *ours* to."

The spot was shot in the spring of 1968 as part of a fifty-city campaign to provide opportunities for urban youngsters. Its final seconds included the lines "Give jobs. Give money. Give a damn."[5]

The ad's unflinching realism provided "the answer," Stone said. "For a preschool child in Harlem, the street is where the action is," he said. "As often as not she is housebound all day while her mother works, and from the vantage point of her apartment, the sidewalk outside must look like Utopia. Outside there are kids hollering, jumping double Dutch, running through the open hydrants, playing stickball. Our set had to be an inner-city street, and more particularly it had to be a brownstone so the cast and kids could 'stoop' in the age-old New York tradition, sitting on the front steps and watching the world go by."

As it happened, Stone was to meet the following day with his friend, set designer Charles Rosen, who took him on a studio tour of a feature film on which he was working. Stone marveled at the detail lavished on a part of the set meant to suggest a backstage room at a run-down jazz club. Scenic artists had created the illusion of decades of decay on wood that had only weeks before come off the lumberyard. Old phone numbers had been scratched into a wall next to a pay phone, and a light-switch plate had been rubbed up to appear so smudged by dirty hands, it could have been carbon-dated.

Stone decided—on the spot—that a movie-quality set was needed for the preschool show, "not a television set of canvas and cardboard." Turing to Rosen he said, "I want it to be as real as this room, and I want *you* to design and build it."

Within days, Rosen was scouting locations in and around Harlem, drawing and photographing details of neighborhoods not unlike the one depicted in the "give a damn" campaign ad. And so, the happy home where Bert and Ernie pop up from window ledges grew out of a stinging public service message that was anything but funny. And that iconic brownstone at 123 Sesame Street, the faux dwelling where untold thousands of scenes have been shot? That may well have been inspired by an apartment building Rosen sketched on Columbus Avenue.

Joan Cooney recalled the day Stone presented his vision of the gritty urban set. "Jon said I turned several shades paler than usual when he first talked to me about it."

"I made an appointment to see her," Stone recalled, "and I didn't need to work up any enthusiasm. I was so sure that this was the right set, the right characters, the right situation that my thoughts just bubbled out. When I finished my pitch and sat there waiting for a response, Joan, God bless her, remained true to her laissez-faire approach to leadership. I recall she said something to the effect that we were the people she chose to create this program, and if this is how I saw it, so be it."[6]

The choice to build the show around a brownstone on an inner-city street was unprecedented, but an equally important decision remained unresolved through the winter of 1969 and into the early spring: As a date for a press conference neared—one in which the show's premiere date would be announced—selecting an acceptable title for a show set in the inner city became a matter of urgency.

"We were just frantic for a title," said Cooney. "Our press and publicity people were going nuts. How were they going to promote a show that had no name? Finally we said, 'There is no more time.'"

In Stone's characterization, "The name was set at the "eleventh hour and fifty-ninth minute."

It fell to executive producer Dave Connell to pressure the production staff—and other CTW employees—to resolve the issue. He asked each member of the CTW team to generate a list of twenty names. Using the brownstone as inspiration, Stone came up with a title that, with the benefit of hindsight, now seems pitch-perfect: *123 Avenue B*. That made the rounds for a few days, and it had its supporters among those who liked that it rhymed and referenced two of the show's top goals, learning the alphabet and counting to ten.

But just as many argued that the title was precious and provincial. It sounded too much like a show tailored to New York viewers rather than to a national audience. *123 Avenue B* was discarded.

Among the remaining contenders was *Sesame Street*, a title that some found fanciful and alliterative. Others thought it missed the mark.

The contributor who threw *Sesame Street* into the mix was Virginia Schone, a CTW consultant who worked in a West Side day-care center in Manhattan. One day she turned the dilemma of finding a title over to the children at the center, explaining little more to them than that the show was going to be set on a neighborhood street. "Whether it was she or one of the kids who came up with it, I don't know," said Connell, "but she had a list of six or eight names, and one of them was *Sesame Street*."

Connell, who had two sons and a daughter, immediately worried that some children would have difficulty pronouncing *Sesame*. "I remember an argument erupting," he said. "Someone said a child losing his baby teeth might have trouble saying '*Theth-a-me Threet*.' It seemed charming enough to me. Anyway, I put a memo out to the staff saying that if nobody came up with a better idea, as of Monday we were going to call the show *Sesame*

Street. Everyone on the staff, I think, came in with the memo and said, '*Sesame Street?* Yuk!'"

Even beyond the walls of CTW the title was unpopular. Bob Davidson said, "I had calls from our advertising and PR agency saying, 'You're going to have a terrible time with that. Nobody is going to remember it. It's got too many esses.'"

"I was very much against it," said Stone. "I thought it was too cute and that it looked like it should be pronounced '*see-same*.' It was an obscure word and the meaning was so far out, of 'opening sesame' and 'opening doors.'"

Though there were protests and howls, no one managed to trump Virginia Schone's title suggestion.

"Somehow we decided that *Sesame Street* was the least bad," Cooney said.

Sam Gibbon, the Rhodes Scholar, once offered this profoundly apt observation about the origins of *Sesame Street*: "Alcohol probably was as responsible for its success as anything else."

Indeed, the patriarchs of *Sesame Street* regularly and enthusiastically drank together after hours, sometimes at a tavern, other times at someone's apartment. One regular haunt was the welcoming domicile of Tom Whedon, a gathering place for thirsty writers, musicians, and actors. "We would drift in sometime between six or seven and midnight, and it seems there were always eight or ten or fifteen of us exchanging views and jokes and ideas and sipping vodka and laughing till all hours," Jon Stone said. "You could come early and leave late or come late and stay all night. People joined the group after the theater, whether performers or audience, and the constitution of the salon assemblage was constantly changing."

Joe Raposo, a friend of Whedon's from his undergraduate days at Harvard, would frequently drop in. At the time, Raposo and his diminutive drummer friend, Danny Epstein, were part of the house band for a daily show on Channel 5 in New York, hosted by Skitch Henderson.[7]

Whedon was a senior at Harvard working on the student-written and performed Hasty Pudding Theatricals when he met freshman Raposo. "We learned right away he was an extraordinary musician, and we used him in the show under an assumed name," as freshmen were then ineligible to participate in the annual burlesque. "Eventually we became friends, and when I got out of the army and was living in New York, I'd visit him in Boston. He was married—with a child—and doing three jobs at once to make a living, maybe netting two hundred fifty dollars a week. Once when he was totally out of work, he listed his occupation as 'conductor.' Unemployment people offered him a job on the trolley cars.

"I finally said to him, 'A piano player always works in New York. They're needed at auditions and dance rehearsals. There are so many clubs and you could play lounge piano and sing. We have some extra rooms in our apartment, why don't you stay with us and [look] around? Bring the family down."

Raposo accepted the offer, and fortune soon smiled. "A talented composer friend named Sam Pottle had just taken what he thought would be a one-month thing as musical director of a theater production called *The Mad Show*, a revue based on *Mad* magazine. He thought it was going to fall flat on its ass because it was a disaster in previews. But it got fixed in the final week of previews and became a huge hit. Sam, however, wanted out, and he gave the job to Joe, who had only been in town for two weeks. Suddenly he was making seven hundred dollars a week, and from then on he just sailed."

Raposo quickly gained a reputation in Manhattan as a kind of ambidextrous showman-virtuoso. On the one hand, he was a classically trained pianist who never failed to point out that he had studied with Nadia Boulanger in Paris, the influential composer-conductor whose pupils included Philip Glass, Virgil Thomson, and Quincy Jones. On the other hand, Raposo was an unabashed populist who reveled in Tin Pan Alley, ragtime, Broadway, and standards from the American songbook. He was an exuberant blend of Chopin and showbiz. "Joe was many things," Stone said. "He was a singularly gifted composer and songwriter, and a remarkably facile pianist."

But Raposo was a curious, complex specimen. Gregariously entering a room with a flourish, he'd embrace friends and colleagues, even the ones who seemed unhuggable. He could entertain like nobody's business, dropping down onto the piano stool at a party and filling the room with music that was sumptuous and sophisticated. At his best moments, he was irresistible.

Whenever people praised his gifts, though, they inevitably followed their assessment of him with a "but," almost to balance out his foibles, quirks, and irritating habits. "He was a lazy last-minute worker who often would be scribbling arrangements on scraps of old envelopes as he taxied to a recording session," Stone said. "Joe hated editing. If he didn't get it right the first time, it would stay unright. I often pleaded with him that with just the slightest additional effort, significant improvements could be made, but Joe was always in a rush to get on to the next challenge. Redoubtable

Joe was the most talented, infuriating, charming, lazy, prolific, unpredictable genius I had the happy fortune to work with."

Raposo, who had a quicksilver temper, could be petty and egocentric, cutting and conceited, withering and caustic, greedy and ungracious. To underlings he could be domineering; to the famous, obsequious. "Somebody said to me that when you're with Joe, you are his very best and only friend in the world, until he meets somebody else," Whedon said.

Raposo's bombast and braggadocio bespoke insecurity and fears of being unworthy. "He could never get over the fact that a poor kid from New Bedford, Massachusetts, could grow up to rub elbows with the rich and famous," Stone said. Friends and coworkers alternately forgave, mocked, accepted, or abhorred his name-dropping, an unnecessary effort to impress. Joan Cooney, who had abundant fondness for Raposo, described his juvenile desire to be stroked and adored as "pathetic."

Though Raposo's talent and fire were undeniable, Dave Connell and Sam Gibbon wanted him to audition for the job as *Sesame Street*'s music director, after Jon Stone had all but handed it to him. "Raposo said, 'I audition for no one,'" Gibbon recalled. Raposo had marked his turf.

To Stone's relief, Connell and Gibbon backed off, and Raposo was reunited with his *Hey, Cinderella* colleagues Stone, Henson, Frank Oz, puppeteer Jerry Nelson, and set designer Charles Rosen. "I was both astounded and deliriously happy at his commitment," Stone said.

For those keeping track of names beginning with *J*, *Sesame Street* now had a Joan, a Jon, a Jim, a Jerry, and a Joe.

The jaunty, deceptively simple *Sesame Street* theme song has a complicated, contentious backstory, one that brings to mind more visions of stormy temperaments than sunny days.

At issue in 1969, however, was not Raposo's composition in F, but the song's lyrics, which fell flat.

"Joe's music was just plain brilliant," said Jon Stone. "It was melodic and simple enough for a child to recognize and even sing along to, but still had a musical sophistication. It gave the whole show a sound and an attitude, and it underscored the footage of joyful children running to the recurring line, 'Can you tell me how to get to Sesame Street?' There was no other sound like it on television, and once the child learned to identify it with *Sesame Street*, the first few notes would bring her running from wherever she might be at the moment."

As much as Stone embraced the melody and orchestration, he derided the rhyming lines that had inspired it. In his memoir, Stone explained that he turned to Bruce Hart to fashion the lyrics, but before he sent Hart off to work on them, he provided a list of "musts" to weave in. "An integral part of Charlie Rosen's set was a wall of doors, much like the ones construction crews used to put up to seal a building site," Stone said. "I wanted to use those doors as transition gateways from the reality of the street to our puppet or animation pieces. I told Bruce to include 'Every door will open wide.' This was also an oblique reference to the title of the program, embodying the idea of 'Open Sesame,' or the opening of the minds. More important, I insisted that the recurring theme in the lyric be 'Can you tell me how to get to Sesame Street?' The opening I envisioned was one of children—real peer-group children—running happily, tumbling, playing along the way, but always intent on getting to Sesame Street, perhaps occasionally pausing to ask an adult this recurring question.

"The result was a musical masterpiece and a lyrical embarrassment," Stone said. "Trite and thoughtless" was how he described Hart's work on the assignment, resulting in "platitudinous kiddie-show lyrics." While Stone acknowledged that Hart had followed his basic instructions, he bitterly complained the writer "surrounded those elements with happy little clichés." Stone especially disliked the phrases "sweeping the clouds away," "where the air is sweet," and "everything's A-OK," which he described as "astronaut slang [that] would become obsolete."

Stone said, "I kept thinking that in a week or so I'd get around to getting rid of such hackneyed phrases as 'It's a magic carpet ride,' but I never did, and once it aired there was no way to go back and make repairs."

At some point in the song's gestation, Stone added his own name below Hart's on Raposo's original music composition paper. It may be that upon reflection, Stone concluded the best lines of the lyric were his, and that he should share in any royalties generated by the song. In the arcane algebra known only to the accountants at ASCAP (American Society of Composers, Authors and Publishers), revenues from song royalties are split between the composer (or composers) and the lyricist (or lyricists). Raposo complicated things further by adding *his* name to the lyric credit line, after making a slight adjustment in a musical phrase, thus diverting another slice of the royalty pie to himself.

Sesame Street's signature sound grew out of sessions with a seven-piece band that Raposo wrangled for the occasion. On most of the recordings there was a keyboardist, drummer, electric bass player, guitarist, trumpeter, a winds instrumentalist on flute or piccolo, and a percussionist on vibraphone, xylophone, or bells. Some arrangements called for an old-timey tack piano, the kind someone in a bowler hat played during saloon scenes in Westerns.

On the day the ensemble recorded the opening and closing themes, Raposo asked percussionist Epstein, a product of the Juilliard conservatory and the newly installed music coordinator of *Sesame Street*, to find a harmonica player to add a "strolling" dimension to the closing. Epstein lined up Jean-Baptiste Frédéric Isidor "Toots" Thielemans, a Belgian-born jazzman then living in Yonkers, New York. Thielemans, who had emigrated to the United States in 1952, was an internationally regarded guitarist and chromatic harmonicist who had toured Europe with Benny Goodman and performed with Charlie Parker's All Stars. But when Epstein called, he was grateful for the session work, even at thirty-seven dollars an hour. "In those days, I was just a guy in New York you could hire for scale, doing anything and everything, including jingles and anonymous club dates.[8] I'd play a bar mitzvah on a Saturday and fly off on Sunday to play the Montreux Jazz Festival."

The session lasted less than ninety minutes, from rehearsal to completed tracks. "A recording session with Joe was an on-the-fly, off-the-cuff experience," Jon Stone said. "He would circle the room addressing each of the musicians in turn, saying to Bobby Cranshaw, the bass player, 'Give me a kind of *boom-ticky-sha, boom-ticky-sha . . .*' Then, to Jimmy Mitchell on guitar, 'Why don't you try it on banjo this time? It's so crazy it might work.' There was always a plan in mind, and nearly always the result was just what he wanted."

This is especially true of *Sesame*'s opening theme. The frolicsome sound of the first two measures came from an Epstein experiment, striking the vibraphone bars not with standard fabric mallets but instead with ones made for xylophone or bells, with harder plastic heads. Raposo loved it, and he added his own touches of mirth and modernity by choosing an electric keyboard—the then revolutionary Fender Rhodes—over acoustic piano.

A mixed choir of children singing in unison joined in on the first beat of the third measure. "They were called the Wee Willie Winter Singers," Epstein said, "just a group of kids—six, seven, eight years old—rounded up by the Lois Winter Agency." They, too, worked for scale.

Through the years, the theme became a siren song for preschoolers and a source of high amusement for Thielemans, who, at the age of eighty-six, still plays to packed houses throughout Europe, Asia, and the Americas. "When I play the United States I often will include the *Sesame Street* theme in my concerts," he said. "People are surprised. They say, 'That was *you*, Toots?'" I laugh and say, 'That was me, back when I was a session musician.'"

In 2001, King Albert II of Belgium ennobled Thielemans with the title of baron. "I may be quite famous now, but I don't let it get to my head," he said during a phone interview from Belgium in 2008.

"My playing on the *Sesame Street* theme has always been an important little reward on my lapel."

Raposo was so inspired by the goals of *Sesame Street* that he composed a stack of curriculum-inspired songs and soundtracks in the weeks leading to launch. He worked in a creative frenzy, vast in its scope and range.

His new forte became songs about the alphabet. "You name the letter, he had a song in five minutes," said Epstein. For Big Bird, Raposo wrote a bouncy tune in 6/8 time that turned all twenty-six consonants and vowels into one multisyllabic, perplexing word. Collaborating with Stone, who provided lyrics, Raposo also set to music one of the concepts first mentioned in Cooney's series proposal. Entitled "One of These Things," it asked children to assess a group of items (a banana, an orange, an apple, and a shoe, for instance) and identify which did not fit, a classification task. It went like this:

> *One of these things is not like the others;*
> *one of these things just doesn't belong.*
> *Can you tell which thing is not like the others*
> *By the time I finish my song?*

Viewers were given an eight-measure interlude to answer the musical question. The song would then resume.

> *Did you guess which thing is not like the others?*
> *Did you guess real hard with all of your might?*
> *If you guessed this thing (pointing) is not like the others*
> *Then you're absolutely right!*

In the early days of production, nobody "got" the gestalt of *Sesame Street* faster or better than Raposo. For a good long while, he might have been America's most educational entertainer.

Jim Henson earned his stripes as an entertaining educator as well, venturing well beyond puppetry. "From the moment he signed on, Jim channeled his huge creative input into our project," said Stone.

Henson produced a series of short live-action and animated films to "sell" numbers, a catalogue of work that producers used as mortar to connect and reinforce the live-action content. As had Raposo, Henson rose to the challenge of translating sometimes arcane academic goals into effective and pleasurable viewing, "He would work an entire weekend and come in with a film on Monday," recalled Henson's oldest son, Brian, now co-chief executive officer of the Jim Henson Company in Los Angeles. "He would do all of the soundtracks on them with a Moog synthesizer that he set up in the back of his workshop. It was one of the first privately owned Moogs available and was the size of a Ford Econoline van."

From a small animation studio built within the workshop, Henson, Frank Oz, and designer Don Sahlin adapted stop-action techniques—using an array of media, including cut paper, pastels, and clay—for the number commercials. Perhaps best remembered are the combination live-action and animation pieces. They began with counting from one to ten, then counting down back to one, and built to a slapstick finale. A stunt man dressed as a baker and carrying a proscribed number of desserts would sing out, "Five chocolate cream pies!" before tumbling down a flight of stairs. Henson provided the voice of the pratfall-prone pastry chef.

More subtle and contemplative was a film in which two young boys played in a sandbox, scooping and piling with their hands. Intercut with those scenes was footage of men at construction sites, digging, hauling, and dumping with backhoes and earthmovers. Done without narration, the soundtrack featured the heaving groans of the heavy machinery. It was abstract and understated, traits not always associated with a performer who reveled in chicken tossing and toy-cannon explosions.

The sand epic proved to be young Brian's first *Sesame Street* cameo.[9] "I worked two full days on that, and throughout, my dad explained to me what it meant to be professional during a shoot. The following week he came to me in the kitchen as I was eating breakfast and said, 'Here's your paycheck for the work you just did. It's fifty dollars.' To a six-year-old, that was like ten thousand dollars. Then he took me to a bank in Greenwich, Connecticut, opened an account, had me deposit the check, and then handed me the bank book. In that moment he taught me how people earn a living and how the world works. I probably learned more from that experience than anything else in my life."

Starting with Henson's moonlighting days at the University of Maryland, there were always "monster" puppets on hand, goofy grotesqueries from the black lagoon region of the puppeteer's brain. These obsessive and often omnivorous creatures tended to eat victims and, sometimes, everything else in sight. A prime example was the baggy sack puppet with googly eyes and shark's teeth that performed on *The Ed Sullivan Show* on October 8, 1967. Component by component, it devoured a "modular system console," a marvel of space-age engineering that the inquisitive creature with meaty paws thought good enough to eat. It was as if the audience that night was seeing a beta test of Cookie Monster.

Henson and his team fashioned a multihued taxonomy of creatures that emerged in *Sesame Street*'s first season. Inserted mostly for comic effect, these off-kilter puppets were generally more mirthful than menacing. While not under-the-bed monsters, they were far from benign. "From Day One, *Sesame Street* was destined to break as many rules as possible," Jon Stone said. Jim's monsters were *monsters*. They wrestled and bonked and body slammed and slugged and occasionally ate each other. I wrote a sketch for the first show wherein Kermit, sitting on a wall next to a large Styrofoam *W*, is lecturing on that letter. As he speaks, a monster enters and eats one arm of the *W*, rendering it into an *N*. Kermit nervously continues as the monster eats another section, turning the *N* into a *V*, and simultaneously inching closer to the frog. Kermit continues. The monster eats the *V* into an *I*. As the piece ends, Kermit is valiantly trying to continue his lecture and fend off the voracious monster, who has one of Kermit's legs in his mouth right up to the thigh."

Perhaps to no one's surprise, given the gently irreverent and completely compatible style of humor preferred by Stone and Henson, their "sales film"—which was updated for a closed-circuit televised press conference held in May—made fine sport of CTW's inability to find a title for the show.

In a multipart Muppet skit, a gathering of network "suits" are summoning what little executive brainpower they can muster.

> First Muppet: All right! All right! How about this for a title: *The Two and Two Are Five Show*!
> Conference Leader Muppet (*amid protests*): Are you crazy? This is supposed to be an educational show. Two plus two don't make five!
> First Muppet: They don't? Then how about *The Two and Two Ain't Five Show*?
> Second Muppet: This is a show for kids, right? How's about we call it the *Little Kiddie Show*?
> All: Sounds all right! We like it!
> Third Muppet: But we ought to say something about the show telling it like it is. Maybe the *Nitty-Gritty, Little Kiddie Show*?

All: Not bad! Yeah! We like that!

Fourth Muppet: Yeah, but "Little Kiddie" can mean any child up to the age of seven and eight. I think we should aim the show right at the preschooler.

First Muppet: Well then, how about the *Itty-Bitty, Nitty-Gritty, Little Kiddie Show*?

Fifth Muppet: But we shouldn't aim at either just the city kids, or just the country kids, so we call it the *Itty-Bitty, Farm and City, Witty-Ditty, Nitty-Gritty, Dog and Kitty, Pretty Little Kiddie Show.*

It all ended with the first Muppet noting, "Hey. These kids can't read or write, can they? Then how's about we call the show . . . 'Hey, Stupid!'"

Some eighty public stations around the country were hooked into the press conference to announce the title *Sesame Street* and provide a sneak peek at its content. Reaction was almost breathlessly exuberant, with a few exceptions.

In a May 7 news story headlined RICH TV PROGRAM SEEKS YOUNGEST, the *New York Times* explained, "*Sesame Street* is named to reflect the balance between fantasy and the real-life educational open-a-new-window need of preschool youngsters—particularly members of minority groups in the inner cores of big cities—that the show hopes to achieve."

On the same day, the *Chicago Daily News* reported "A group of Muppets—puppets created by Jim Henson—will be springboards for much of the action on *Sesame Street*, a city street where the candy store and a building targeted for demolition are chief landmarks. The colorful fence of old doors surrounding the demolition site will be the symbolic gateway to many of the new worlds *Sesame Street* hopes to open to preschoolers."

San Francisco Chronicle TV critic Terrence O' Flaherty spoke for the minority when he rejected what he saw of *Sesame Street* in a column dated August 28, 1970. "Twelve million youngsters are in jeopardy from foolish grotesqueries deeply larded with ungrammatical Madison Avenue jargon. If children learn from jargon, we are all in trouble." He claimed the letter *J* stood for "junk, jargon, and jabberwocky."

Chapter Twelve

B ert and Ernie were lying mute and prone in a mirrored rehearsal room when Jim Henson and Frank Oz picked them up for the first time. It would have been great if Ernie had immediately said, "Hey, Bert," but it didn't happen that way.

What did occur? What usually happens when the Muppet masters encounter a new arrival: they try it on and goof with it in front of a mirror, playing with different voices and attitudes. Muppets most often evolve in an organic way, in fits and starts. In some cases, it takes a year or more for the fully formed personality to bloom. And sometimes the puppets are test-driven, passed around from one Henson troupe member to another, in the hope of finding the perfect human-Muppet match.

For a few minutes on that rehearsal day in 1969, Jim Henson was performing Bert while Frank Oz was working Ernie. It was as if Bert Lahr (Cowardly Lion) and Jack Haley (Tin Woodsman) had swapped costumes on the MGM lot during the filming of *The Wizard of Oz*. It was, in other words, unthinkable.

As some point, the universe righted itself and Henson began ad libbing with Ernie. Around the room Jon Stone and his writers kibitzed and called out suggestions about what the characters might say or do. Oz turned the upright oblong yellow puppet with the unibrow into what CTW film coordinator Arlene Sherman once described as "everyone's idea of a blind date": a pigeon fancier and paperclip collector who marches around his apartment to John Philip Sousa recordings.

"Gradually a relationship emerged which reflected the real-life Jim-Frank relationship," Stone said. "Jim was the instigator, the teaser, the cutup. Frank was the conservative, careful victim. But essential to the rapport was the affection and respect which these two men held for each other. Ernie and Bert are best friends; so it was with Jim and Frank."

Ultramarine blue Grover was born looking at himself in a mirror, as was fitting for an exuberant, wiry, self-aware projection of four-year-old energy. Self-referential and prone to calling himself a "cute, furry little monster," Grover was *Sesame Street*'s equivalent of a second-born child, the more carefree, confident, assertive sibling who aims to please. He recovers easily from stumbles, makes the best of situations, explores without inhibition, and plays well with others.

Grover's personality sprang to life fully formed in that rehearsal room. "I recall Frank Oz holding the puppet that was to become Grover in front of the mirror," Stone said. "The high, raspy voice fit immediately. The carefully precise diction fell into place. Then we played games with the names. I asked, 'What do you think your name is?' Grover would study himself in the mirror and try a few out. 'Armand? Hector? Perhaps my name is Grover.' "

Grover felt right, and Grover it became. His personality gave Frank a release from the uptight Bert, and Frank reveled in the opportunity to have him rush up behind Kermit, wallop him on the back, and shout, "Hey, Froggy Babeeeee!"

Jon Stone had a penchant for procrastination and a tendency to take on too much. As a juggler of time, Stone occasionally took his eye off matters and got bopped on the head by a ball in motion.

Stone served as both a producer and head writer during the fifteen developmental months of *Sesame Street*, a massive task, to be sure. But he put off the critically important job of finding a cast until late spring, 1969, mere weeks before five test shows were going to be shot over a ten-day span. He hurriedly scheduled audition time in a studio, where a succession of actors was videotaped doing a comedy sketch, singing a song, and "selling" a curriculum point to the camera. Research director Ed Palmer would then take the videotaped auditions into the field, testing children's reactions to the performers.

In even the best of situations, casting is fraught with challenges. "Picking cast members is a frightening thing," Dave Connell once said. "It's like picking a wife."[1] Stone made the process all the more difficult by simple avoidance.

In his memoir, he wrote, "I have no rational explanation for this flagrantly uncharacteristic deviance from our careful and precise management of every aspect of the show, but the fact is the casting was just completely haphazard. I didn't employ a casting director to bring in the available talent to audition. I relied on the fact that I knew a lot of actors. And I could find the right people without help. The shows were cast in a ridiculously nepotistic manner." Of course, "ridiculously nepotistic" would just as aptly describe the decisions that led to Stone's hiring cronies Joe Raposo (music), Jim Henson (puppetry), and Charles Rosen (set design), all of whom found their way to *Sesame Street* through personal contacts and friendship.

Joan Cooney steered clear of the casting process, asking only that the four hosts be a mix of male and female, white and black, and that no character assume a lead role. So as auditioning began, Stone had a fairly specific set of characters in mind:

- There would be a black male character who would hold a job of responsibility in the community, a teacher perhaps. His character name would be Gordon, after the photographer-filmmaker Gordon Parks, an artist Stone revered.
- There would be an older proprietor of a neighborhood variety store, the type that had a soda fountain with pedestal stools. At that time in Bronx sociological history, the owner of such a business would likely have been male, Caucasian, and Jewish. Stone asked Rosen to build into the set what ultimately became Hooper's Store. "It gave us a wonderful location both for comedy and curriculum-driven bits," Stone said.

  Slightly cranky but good-hearted Mr. Hooper—given the first name Harold in a 1976 episode when the character earned his GED—was a bow to an old friend. "I insisted on casting someone from an older generation, someone the age of Bob Keeshan's character on *Captain Kangaroo*," Stone said. "The Captain was still [then] one of my strongest influences. When the time came to have a hand in creating my own dream program, its content and style were directly the result of the best and worst of my experience. Much of the best came from the Captain."
- Stone also wanted a male singer-actor—of either race—to carry the load of curriculum-based music. He had the character name Bobby in mind, among others.
- Finally, there would be Susan, a singing actress of either race. She would be named after Stone's actress friend Susan Watson, baby Polly's godmother.

On a Saturday afternoon in mid-June 1948, nine-year-old Loretta Mae Moore was waving to passing cars from her family's roadside stand outside Paw Paw, Michigan. Farmers in that town of thirty-five hundred not only grew the berries to slice atop Kellogg's Corn Flakes, manufactured thirty-five miles away in Battle Creek, they also grew the Concord grapes that were trucked to a Welch's juice plant in Lawton, the next town over.

The farm where Loretta and her two siblings were raised was unremarkable, except for the fact that their father, the proprietor, was black and held a day job to supplement the farm income. Verle Moore would tend the land by night, stringing lights at intervals on his property to provide enough illumination to run his tractor. "We were from the city and people thought we didn't know what we were doing; they would come from miles around to watch this crazy black man driving around in the middle of the night farming," said Loretta, who found her way to *Sesame Street* by way of Highway M-40 in southwestern Michigan.

Everyone in the family worked on the farm, including Loretta's mother, who sold Mary Kay cosmetics as a side business. During World War II, Verle had been trained as an aircraft repairman, welding bombers. After the war, he took a welding job with Consumer Power, a local utility company while farming under the stars. The Moores hoped Loretta would attend college and get a teaching degree, but as a child she set her sights on show business. "Out in the field, I used to say, 'Mama, I feel special,' and my mother would say, 'Oh, you're special to us.' And I'd say, 'Mama, I feel like a *star*.' And she'd look at me and say, 'Star on that row of strawberries right over there. And then—when you put them in the bushel basket—you can be up at the farmer's stand in front of the house, getting the cars to stop.'"

And so, with hummingbirds darting overhead, Loretta would head up to the stand and belt out show tunes. "I used to be out there singing 'Another Opening, Another Show,' and the people passing by would say, 'Oh, look at that little colored girl singing. Let's stop and see what she's selling.'"

She was, in many ways, hard to ignore. "The Moores were one of only three black families in Paw Paw," said town historian Susan Erion. "The races didn't mix much here back in the early 1950s, sad to say."

While other children spent their free time fishing for walleye and perch at Maple Lake, Loretta went to the library. One summer, she read a set of encyclopedias, A to Z. "Nobody ever had to say get on the school bus," she said. "I was the first one in line." As a teen, Loretta worked summers as a mother's helper, babysitter, and day camp counselor. The harvest couldn't come soon enough. "I liked the fall because that meant everything that grew up out of the ground we had already sold, put out in a basket or jar, peeled or fed to the hogs," she said.

Though Loretta demonstrated ample talent in dance during tryouts for cheerleading at Paw Paw High, she was never chosen. Once, when she auditioned for drum majorette, a judge told her she lacked a sense of rhythm. It was, she said, a preposterous decision, and to this day, she ruefully recalls the adjudicator's response when she questioned his eye for talent. "Next," he said.

After graduation from Western Michigan University with an education degree, Loretta gave herself six months to make it in New York City. Half a year would pass, and then another. "It seemed like every time it was just about time to go back to Michigan, something would happen to encourage me enough to stay for six more months." By day, she was substitute teaching at junior high schools in Harlem and the South Bronx, tough duty for a young teacher with little experience. "Junior high sub jobs were always available," she said. "The kids tend to burn out subs pretty fast." Loretta used her skills as an entertainer to tame unruly teens. Her classroom was always the noisiest, but it was filled with positive energy and excitement. "I was always an actor-singer who happened to be teaching," she said. "We had a lot of screaming teachers around, but I was not about to leave my high notes up in the classroom. I saved them for the audition at 4:15. I didn't have a last-period class, so I would sneak out at 1:30 as some of the kids were sneaking out."

Loretta married Pete Long, the landmark Apollo Theatre's assistant manager. She may be one of the few actresses ever to admit turning down a Broadway musical directed by Bob Fosse to sing in a supermarket. "I got chosen for a role in the chorus of *Sweet Charity*," she recalled, "and it was a hard audition because Fosse was as tough on his singers as he was on his dancers. You had to be able to sing and move. He wanted somebody to replace a singer and needed me to start in two days. But I had already been rehearsing for a lead role in a Roundabout Theatre production," a 1930s-vintage revue called *Pins and Needles*. Back then the Roundabout was housed in the ground floor of the Chelsea Consumers Co-Op Supermarket on West Twenty-sixth Street. *Pins and Needles* was the amateur company's fourth production, and patrons entered through the same electric-eye door as grocery shoppers. Tickets were priced at two fifty for the two-act musical.

Loretta had a dilemma. "These are the career decisions you sometimes have to make as an actor," she said. "Do I take a part in the chorus on Broadway or a leading role off-Broadway?" She chose the latter. "When I walked away from *Sweet Charity*, Fosse couldn't believe it," Loretta said, dismissing her with "Good luck in the basement of the supermarket."

But in a shining review of *Pins and Needles* in the *New York Times*, reviewer Dan Sullivan wrote, "Miss Long enjoys being alive so much that an evening with her is a spring tonic."

Loretta may have missed *Sweet Charity*, but that ink in the *Times* was sweet redemption.

Loretta Mae Long, that resourceful farm girl from Paw Paw, arrived at the auditions for "Susan" ready to belt out a show tune or two. By 1969, the singer-actress had a great gig as cohost of *Soul!*, a weekly variety showcase on WNET that provided television exposure to top talent appearing at the Apollo, in Harlem.[2]

During a lull one day while taping, Loretta noticed that *Soul's* set designer, Charles Rosen, had brought in to work a scale model of another project he had undertaken. The mock-up was a miniaturization of an inner-city block, with brownstones, a playground, and little stores. "Charles had twin three-year-old boys at the time, and I thought he was making them a present," Long said. Rosen explained that Jon Stone, a classmate at Yale's drama school and a colleague on *Hey, Cinderella*, had enlisted him to build the set for an experimental children's show.

"You're a teacher, right?" Rosen said to Long. "This show is going to be about teaching preschoolers. You need to know about it."

Long shook her head.

"Why are you taking that attitude?" Rosen asked.

Long explained that she abhorred television targeted at younger children, especially *Romper Room*. "Let's all be good do-bees," she said, sing-song style. "That ain't me."

"That ain't us either. Don't worry, it's not going to be like that," Rosen said, sharing some of what Stone had described. "There are going to be four human hosts that will be like educational guides for the children. You should audition."

Long had good reason to trust Rosen, who had collaborated with her husband on a number of projects and was considered a family friend. When Rosen was single, he and Pete Long would frequent the city's jazz clubs. "All right," she said. "I'll look into it."

On the day of her audition, Loretta Long gazed at the other women up for a role on *Sesame Street*. Everywhere the eye could see were white folk-singers with long straight hair and Gibson six-strings strapped across their shoulders. "This was 1969, and here I was with my big hair, my flaming red fingernails, my short skirt, and my show tunes," Long said. "I looked like Angela Davis, I did *not* look like Joan Baez."

Checking a clipboard, a production coordinator approached Long. "Can I help you?" he asked.

"I'm here to audition," Long said.

"But where's your guitar?"

Long said, "Oh, I don't play guitar."

The coordinator pointed toward the back of the room. "Stand over there, please."

One after the other, the folksingers strummed. After each performance, Jon Stone, a folk-music aficiando, said, "We'll be in touch. Thank you."

Long took it all in, noticing that many of the performers did not know enough to look straight into the television lens as they sang, connecting with an unseen viewer who would be watching later on videotape. A few of the folkies allowed their head to actually sink while they sang, a faceless mop of hair filling the viewfinder.

The crew was about ready to call it a day when a voice shouted out that there was one more woman left to audition.

"Everyone was getting ready to leave and I said, 'Wait a minute! I sneaked off from my teaching job in the Bronx to sing for you.' I was going to put a cross-body check on anyone who got in my way."

"Aw, jeez," a cameraman said to no one in particular.

Long walked forward with sheet music and asked, "May I talk to the piano player?"

"We didn't hire one," the production coordinator said. "Everybody plays guitar but you."

"But I came to sing," she said.

Then, in a less than encouraging way, he said, "Okay, sing."

The cameraman framed Long in the viewfinder and said, "Oh, gawd."

"And so," Long recalled, "I laid my little show tunes down and I started clapping my hands, in the best Baptist tradition."

Long began to sing. "I'm a little teapot short and stout. Here is my handle, here is my spout." The cameraman mocked her by placing a crooked arm on his hip and wagging his backside.

She said, "Come on, kids! Everybody sing! Tip me over and pour me out."

Drawing on her babysitting and camp-counselor experience, Teapot Lady exuded confidence, ebullience, and instant likability. When Ed Palmer tested the performance before an audience of preschoolers, the kids clapped along.

Robert Emmett McGrath was five years old in 1937, when his mother taught him the lyrics and melody to "In the Good Old Summertime," a sheet-music serenade favorite of parlor pianists since its Broadway debut in 1902. Self-taught pianist Flora McGrath was no exception. She roamed the keys of a bulky upright piano that had once belonged to her mother, and it dominated a room in the farmhouse where young Bobby was raised with his two brothers and two sisters.

Because Flora's husband, Edmund, couldn't carry a tune, he was pleased beyond measure when he came in from the fields for lunch that afternoon to hear his son Bobby singing on key, with his mother providing accompaniment. It was the first recital for a cheerful Irish tenor who followed his musical muse all the way to *Sesame Street*.

Bobby, later known to countless millions as Bob, was born on a farm that straddled the north-central Illinois towns of Ottawa and Grand Ridge, deep in the bosom of corn, oats, and soybean country, near the confluence of the Fox and Illinois rivers. The McGrath farm was without electricity until around the time Bobby entered first grade. He attended a one-room schoolhouse with his older brother Edmund. "We went to school in a horse and buggy," McGrath said. "When I tell this to my grandchildren now, it sounds like *Little House on the Prairie*. They can't believe it."

When the rural school was shuttered by the time Bobby was ready for third grade, he enrolled at St. Columba school in Ottawa, the town made historic by staging the first of the Lincoln-Douglass debates of 1858. Word quickly spread around Ottawa about the McGrath boy's talent, and by the age of seven—with private training—Bobby was winning singing competitions in Chicago. By the time he reached high school, the farm kid now known as Bob had his own half-hour radio show on a small downstate station and was winning singing competitions in other states. As the time neared for college, he was considering engineering at the University of Illinois, following the path of brother Edmund. "Out of the blue, a local music club gave me a three-week scholarship to a music camp outside Chicago," McGrath said. While there, faculty members encouraged him to rethink his college plans. "I did an about-face," McGrath said, "and ended up going to the University of Michigan as a voice major." He excelled in his studies, joined the glee club, dabbled in barbershop quartet, and soaked up the classical song literature of the Italian, French, and German repertoire. He blossomed vocally and drank in all that was Ann Arbor, Michigan, in the early 1950s.

To stay afloat financially, he and a fraternity brother worked dinner duty at the Alpha Phi sorority house on Hill Street, mere steps away from the Phi Gamma Delta house where the boys lived.

Bob McGrath washed dishes; Dave Connell waited tables.

After graduation from Michigan in 1954 and basic training in Arkansas, Pvt. Bob McGrath prepared to be shipped overseas. "Half the class went to Korea, the other half to Germany." he said. "I got lucky and went to Germany."

"I was trained to be a clerk-typist, but I was squirming to get myself attached to the Seventh Army Symphony in Stuttgart, begging on my knees with the guy interviewing me. 'Sorry,' he said, 'we don't have permanent slots for vocalists. Instrumentalists, yes.'"

McGrath sighed.

But then the corporal looked up from the young private's service records. "So you went to the University of Michigan, huh? I met a girl in Rome last year from Michigan." You wouldn't know Cynthia Boyes, would you?" the corporal asked.

McGrath half smiled, recalling his sorority-house dishwashing duty. "As a matter of fact, I do," he said. "She pledged Alpha Phi. Nice girl."

The corporal raised one eyebrow and rummaged through McGrath's orders. "Now, where did you say you wanted to go?"

McGrath all but broke into a chorus of "The Victors."

His revised, oxymoronic orders placed him on "permanent temporary duty" at Seventh Army headquarters in Stuttgart, where he led a local church choir and sang in an army quartet that toured France.

After a two-year army stint, McGrath decided to pursue a master's degree at the Manhattan School of Music. "I had a wonderful first day in New York," McGrath recalled. A chaplain friend had given him the name and phone number of a former roommate, with instructions to look him up and ask for a drink. "I knocked on his door and he said, 'So what are you up to?' I explained that I'd come to New York to go back to school, but I needed a place to live and a job. He sent me across the street to St. Thomas More Catholic church on East Eighty-ninth Street, where Bishop Philip J. Furlong gave me a job in a quartet that sang at Sunday services. He thought I looked pathetic, like I didn't know where my next meal would come from. The bishop said, 'I'll pay you double what I'm paying the other lads.'

"I said, 'I'm looking for a place to stay, Bishop. Do you know anyone in the parish who might have an empty room?'

"The bishop said, 'St. David's Boys' School is just a half block away. I think the Latin teacher there just got married, and he had lived on the top floor of the school.'"

McGrath recalled, "I walked over and sort of stumbled through an interview with the headmaster, David Hume. He listened, then finally said, in a get-to-the-point kind of way, 'What you're looking for is a free sack, right?'

"I said, 'Well . . . something like that.'

"So we made an arrangement," McGrath said. "I taught there for a couple of years, leading the choir and teaching music appreciation and theory. I ate lunch in the faculty dining area, and David Hume suggested that if I sweet-talked the cook, I'd get all I could eat later in the day. She used to set aside something for me every night for dinner.

"So on my first day in New York I got a drink, a job, a place to live, and all I could eat. I called my friends and said, 'You know, New York's not so tough.'"

But the story does not end there. "When I had walked into the school office at St. David's, I spied this lovely twenty-one-year-old, Anne Sperry, who was there with her mother."

In 2008, Bob and Anne celebrated their fiftieth wedding anniversary.

In almost no time, more freelance work came McGrath's way than he could handle: he did backup singing for recording artists and concert performers, jingles, Gregorian chant requiems, even the occasional TV appearance at the NBC studios, at Avenue M and Fourteenth Street in Brooklyn. It was there that he sang a supporting role (as a chauffeur) with Patrice Munsel. "I remember thinking, *Someday I'd really like to be standing here doing this by myself.* And a year later, I was doing solos right on that stage."

McGrath got a shot at a prime-time show on NBC by virtue of his hustle and likability; it proved to be the break of his life. "When you first come to New York as a singer, the trick is to become known by auditioning for as many vocal contractors as you can. Mike Stewart was one of the best." It was through Stewart—who took a shine to the small-statured Illinoisan—that McGrath learned a search was under way to replace a tenor on a music-variety hour entitled *Sing Along with Mitch.*

Launched first as a series of specials, the show immediately connected with American viewers who found Elvis Presley anathema. *Sing Along with Mitch* landed on NBC's Thursday night schedule at 10:00 p.m. It featured a chorale of twenty-five men with matching sweaters and demeanors who looked as if they had been bused in from a Rotary meeting in Kokomo, Indiana.

During the show's final segment—a community sing during which conductor Mitch Miller would prompt the home viewer to join in on chestnuts like "By the Light of the Silvery Moon"—superimposed lyrics ran across the bottom of the screen, and a bouncing ball highlighted each word in time to the music—a kind of proto-karaoke.

Miller, a classically trained oboist from Rochester, New York, took a degree from the Eastman School of Music and parlayed it into jaw-dropping success as an A&R man for Mercury and Columbia records. He signed or produced a stable of Eisenhower-era recording stars—including Tony Bennett, Rosemary Clooney, Johnny Mathis, Frankie Laine, and Johnnie Ray. Miller also popularized the homogenized sounds of Ray Coniff and Percy Faith, the Haydn and Mozart of elevator music. With his Vandyke and peculiar charm, Miller has often been regarded by purists as the Rasputin of Easy Listening.

McGrath signed on for a production schedule that cranked out a show every ten days, with four days in a recording studio, four days of rehearsal, and two full days of taping. After one day off, the cycle repeated. As spring approached, Miller turned to McGrath one day in rehearsal. "Bob, how would you like to sing 'Mother McCree' on the St. Patrick's Day show?"

"No problem," McGrath said. "I've been singing *that* since I was six."

On the day the track was recorded, Miller came over to the booth where the soloist performed and conducted. "I decided I was going to sing better than I'd ever sung in my whole life, since this was the first Mitch had ever heard me solo. I poured my heart out."

At first Mitch said nothing as the track ended, but then raised his arm and pointed to the tiny hairs. "You son of a bitch," he said. "Where did you learn to sing like that?"

McGrath, taken aback, said, "You know, my mom, whatever."

Fan mail poured in from listeners, and Miller doubled McGrath's salary and appointed him featured tenor. The show's popularity climbed so high that Miller booked his Sing-Along Gang for a couple of weeks at the Desert Inn in Las Vegas during hiatus. "The local paper said we'd probably be finished in a week," McGrath said. "It was sold out every night, and the tour was extended by two weeks."

The road shows expanded, the money flowed, and then, out of nowhere, the *Sing Along with Mitch* phenomena crossed the Pacific. Japanese viewers couldn't get enough of the television show, which had been picked up by NHK, the nation's public broadcaster. Concert halls filled from Fukuoka in the south to Sapporo in the mountainous north during a thirty-night, thirty-city tour. "We had anticipated having the same over-forty crowd in Japan that we had in the United States," McGrath said, "but we had four thousand to five thousand *teenagers* at every stop. We were quite amazed that they wanted to hear these old songs, but it turns out they were learning English by listening to us. Because we sang clearly on television—and they could see the bouncing-ball lyrics—it was a fun, fast way to learn the language."

McGrath was prompted to learn a few Japanese songs for the tour. "Every time I came out to do a solo, the teenagers were screaming 'Bobu! Bobu!' They hadn't heard many Americans with my particular quality voice, a lyric tenor. And then all of a sudden there were Bobu fan clubs springing up all over Japan. Our booker in Japan asked me if I would like to come back as a single act to open the two top clubs in Tokyo, the Latin Quarter and the Copacabana. I thought it would be a lark, but I worked hard to learn half a dozen more Japanese songs."

It was the era of the Rat Pack, even in Japan. "All of the clubs had Sinatra-style big bands," McGrath said. "I had eighteen musicians behind me and I gave it all I had, thinking it was a one-time venture. But it spun off into a total of nine trips over a three-year period. I was going back three times a year for six to seven weeks at a time. I did commercials, TV specials for NHK, recorded thirty or forty singles and seven or eight LPs, one of them completely in Japanese. It was really bizarre, an Irish singer from rural Illinois singing Japanese folk songs with a guy playing a bamboo flute for the prime minister."

"'There's an old expression,'" said Bob McGrath. "'If you want to hear God laugh, tell Him your plans.' That was the story of my life. I always ended up going in the wrong direction from where I *thought* I was going. I'd just returned from my ninth Japan tour and realized I'd been doing the same things over and over. The money was good, but I was away from home, and my poor wife was taking care of our four children by herself. So I turned down the next invitation to Japan and decided instead to take acting lessons in New York and look for freelance work singing. I wanted to get the kind of career going here that I had in Japan. I could be the next Andy Williams or Perry Como. I was copying everything they did. Then one day, right out in front of Carnegie Hall, I bumped into a fraternity brother, Dave Connell."

Connell said he was working on a new children's show and that they'd be auditioning people soon. "Do you think you'd be interested?" Connell asked.

"No," McGrath said. "Not in the least."

"Okay," Connell said. "Just thought I'd mention it."

A few months later, McGrath was formally asked to audition for the role of Bobby and shook off his reluctance long enough to sit through a screening of early animation pieces. It took mere minutes for him to realize he was watching no "silly kiddie show," as he had wrongly assumed. "This is not like anything I've ever seen before," he said to Connell, who simply nodded. "I suddenly want to do this more than anything."

McGrath's audition tape delighted the preschool focus group. He was cast as Bobby (later shortened to Bob, at McGrath's request) and chosen to sing the opening musical theme for the five test shows.

Character actor Will Lee came to Stone's attention thanks to the husband-wife writing team of Bruce and Carole Hart. Stone had hired the Harts to write scripts for the new show, but both had experience in writing song lyrics, as well. The Harts knew Lee from their neighborhood. To them, the Brooklyn-born actor looked the part of a slightly cranky Jewish shop owner, the kind of guy who might wear a white apron smudged with ink, from selling newspapers piled outside the store.

By 1969, Lee had amassed a long list of theater credits on and off Broadway and was a well-regarded acting teacher. (Among his more notable pupils was James Earl Jones, who would famously follow his mentor to *Sesame Street* in the summer of '69.) Back in the 1930s, Lee was an ensemble member of the Group Theater, the consortium of acting and directing idealists who strove to bring to the New York stage drama that not only would reflect the travails of the common man but also trigger social reform. *New York Times* critic Brooks Atkinson called it the "school of revolutionary theater."[3] During World War II, Lee staged shows for troops overseas as a member of Army Special Services. But a decade later, former friends and colleagues from the Group Theater implicated him in the McCarthy anti-Communist witch hunt. Lee appeared as an unfriendly witness before the House Un-American Activities Committee in 1950 and was blacklisted from film and television for five years. Elia Kazan and Clifford Odets had named names.

Lee's acting career was slowly restored in the early 1960s, when he began playing character roles onstage and film. He also began to teach at Boston University, the American Theater Wing, and the Herbert Berghof Studio. During those years, he made scant mention of the blacklist years. But Bob McGrath, who shared a dressing room with Lee, recalled a day when the actor arrived at the studio ashen and shaking. He was crossing a street in Manhattan when he spied Elia Kazan coming toward him. "Will said he was so full of revulsion and rage, he had to turn around and walk up to the next corner."

In 1970, Lee told *Time* magazine, "I was delighted to take the role of Mr. Hooper, the gruff grocer with the warm heart. It's a big part, and it allows a lot of latitude. But the show has something extra—that sense you sometimes get from great theater, the feeling that its influence never stops."

A revolving door of candidates auditioned for the part of Gordon. "We auditioned player after player and no one fit our image of the part," Stone said. "Time passed and auditions fizzled and our deadline grew closer. Panic was working itself in. At the last moment we cast an actor with whom no one was completely happy, but time had run out on us."

And so, on July 9, 1969, the small universe of *Sesame Street* began to reveal itself, as ten days of taping began.

Chet O'Brien reported in to the production manager at Reeves Studio one morning in the summer of 1969, expecting "just another day's work." His assignment that day was to stage manage some test video for a children's program he knew nothing about. The previous December, however, he had worked with Jim Henson and Frank Oz on *The Pied Piper of Astroworld*, a Saturday morning special on ABC hosted by Soupy Sales and shot at the Houston amusement park.[4]

Jon Stone liked O'Brien's work. Within weeks, after the test shows were shot, he was offered the job as stage manager for the planned one hundred and thirty episodes. He accepted immediately, excited by the possibility of working on a noncommercial project. *What a breeze*, he thought. *Just a bunch of Muppets and no agency people with their stupid commercials. So far, everyone connected with the operation seems pleasant and intelligent.*

At the time, O'Brien's pack-a-bag existence of stage managing remote assignments for television specials—everything from the Miss America Pageant in Atlantic City to Bob Hope specials in Los Angeles—was taking a physical toll. "I told my wife, Betty, about [the children's TV offer], and she, too, thought it would be a good assignment.[5] It might run for several months and we could stop driving all over the map doing remotes. I would just be the stage manager—no directing or producing, no staging of musical numbers." He sheepishly added, "That's what I thought."[6]

O'Brien was the rarest of birds, a show-business journeyman who could claim experience in vaudeville, Tin Pan Alley, network radio and television, musical theater, and feature films. In the 1920s, he and Mortimer "Snooks" O'Brien, his identical twin, played the small-theater circuit as the dancing O'Brien Twins. As a chorus boy in the 1934 Broadway revue *As Thousands Cheer*, he romanced the show's glamorous star, the Ziegfeld girl Marilyn Miller, and the pair soon ran off to be married in Harrison, New York.

O'Brien went on to work as both performer and production stage manager for Irving Berlin's two wartime stage and movie extravaganzas, *This Is the Army* and *Winged Victory*. O'Brien's nephew, writer Brian Garfield, said that following a performance of *This Is the Army*, President Franklin D. Roosevelt approached O'Brien to express his condolences over Miller's death. It would not be the only time an O'Brien twin would come into contact with a commander in chief. "They directed or stage directed quite a few White House galas for Truman, Eisenhower, Kennedy, and Johnson," Garfield said. "And they continued to do so for Nixon, Ford, and Carter. They also managed dozens of TV variety shows for Bob Hope and Frank Sinatra."

Even with such a remarkable résumé, the summer of '69 was a turning point for Chet, as the stars aligned in ways unimaginable.

During the summer of 1969—the summer of Apollo 11 and Woodstock—a sound truck with speakers bolted to its roof began crisscrossing the poorer neighborhoods in Brooklyn and the Bronx. CTW's outreach director, Evelyn Davis, had dispatched what was essentially a carnival barker on wheels to alert the populace that something wonderful was about to come their way. Davis was building awareness for *Sesame Street* with a street-level, drum-beating strategy targeted to parents and grand-parents. She distributed pamphlets at churches and day-care centers, staged nighttime community meetings, enlisted a corps of volunteers, knocked on corporate doors for donations, and, in general, made a lot of noise. It was an effort akin to a political campaign.

In the parlance of the time, Davis had it *together.* "There's a belief in the white community that the black community is chaotic and disorganized," she once said. "That's totally untrue. It's probably more highly organized than any community you can think of. . . . There are all kinds of groups to go to to get information to them, which they will disseminate."

It was important that Davis's message was clear: "We had to help par-ents understand that their home is the first school and they're the first teachers," she said. Experience had taught Davis that "the way to get to people is to appeal to their self-interest. All parents are concerned about their children and want them to be educated, and I was out there telling them there were ways they could help. They know a lot. They're not stupid and ignorant simply because they are black or poor."

She arranged meetings at public school auditoriums, and made sure that child care was provided in classrooms. "[It's a matter of recognizing that] you have to do it within the context of the realities of people's lives, in con-text," Davis said. "If they are poor, they can't afford babysitters. So we pro-vided them, and we packed the auditorium night after night after night."

Davis's bookmobile-style buses were donated by Con Edison, New York's electric power provider. Inside, tape-replay equipment screened ani-mated and filmed previews of *Sesame Street* in a continuous loop. Volun-teers from the National Association of Jewish Women and the National Association of Negro Women welcomed families onto the buses, touted the benefits of the show, and sent family members home with flyers. Simi-lar buses were used in other localities across America.

Davis tapped corporations to purchase or replace television sets for day-care centers, where so many of the children in the target audience spent the day. RCA was first to respond, donating 150 color sets to centers around the country. "Each RCA dealer would have an event and give sets to cen-ters in their viewing area," Davis said. In New York, WNET viewers were asked to donate color TVs, new or used. "A lot of them needed repair, so we made arrangements with TV repair schools to have their students repair them at no cost," Davis said. "They had to be delivered to the centers, so we had to get other companies who would do that on a donor basis. We got involved with all kinds of organizations and associations, and that's what makes a project like this work," she said. "You have to link up and tie with people to help them achieve their objectives."

Ed Palmer had good news and bad to report from the audience research conducted after the five one-hour dry-run shows were tested before small groups in Philadelphia and New York. The good news was that there was strong evidence to show children learned while they watched. Post-test analysis demonstrated that preschoolers had grasped material that was unfamiliar to them before the screening. Animated segments, the Muppets, and films about animals scored high during Palmer's distracter tests. The brisk format, with its mélange of topics and techniques, was an overall success, but there were dead spots. Some scripted live-action segments fared poorly, including a spy spoof starring Gary Owens (the announcer on *Laugh-In*) as *The Man from Alphabet*.

"I'm sure we did all five of these shows with somewhere around twenty kids individually watching the program," recalled Palmer. "We worked with fairly small numbers because we wanted to cover a lot of issues and we had to get just a suggestion. We also wanted to test for comprehension. Even kids with very little verbal ability were able to indicate that they were following, or they weren't. We played around with testing methods, doll play, re-creating scenes. Sometimes we'd bring a kid into the room and say, 'You just saw a story about such-and-such, and so-and-so didn't have a chance to see that. Would you tell so-and-so what it was about?'"

The children also rejected the stiff, stumbling actor chosen at the last minute to play Gordon. He came off as a person in the neighborhood that children would run away from, not to. A change was necessary.

In recasting Gordon, Jon Stone knew precisely what he wanted—someone like Matt Robinson, the producer-coordinator of live-action films for *Sesame Street*. Robinson joined Stone on the studio floor during auditions, prepping actors with writers' notes about Gordon's motivation, attitude, voice, and demeanor. "Matt would quietly give them hints by saying, 'No, that's not the way to do it. Try it this way,'" said Dolores Robinson, Matt's then wife. "He was by nature shy, and he knew that they were having a difficult time casting Gordon. And the people overseeing the taping up in the booth, peering at the monitors, kept saying, 'Matt knows what to do. *He* should be Gordon.'"

The camera loved Robinson's naturalness and affability. With his Walt Frazier–style muttonchop sideburns and soft, crowning Afro, he was a near-perfect blend of urban cool and downtown sophistication. "Ultimately the production staff decided, 'He's the one,' " Dolores Robinson said, "the only problem is Matt didn't want to be 'the one.' He wanted to be a writer."

Robinson's genial exterior belied his politics. "The private Matt was militant," Dolores said. "He grew up in a racially stirred household. His mother was very middle class and bourgeois, a schoolteacher. His father, who had been a writer for the *Philadelphia Tribune*, was a Martin Luther King before his time. He belonged to a group of poets and black renaissance people who were revolutionary in their thoughts. They had so much pride in their blackness. In Philadelphia, his father was involved in a network of Socialists, who believed as he believed.

"When Joseph Stalin died, he wrote, 'Stalin is dead, peace be to his ashes.' The *Tribune* sent him a telegram that said, RETRACT YOUR STATEMENT OR ELSE. He sent them back a telegram that said ELSE. That was the end of his job at the newspaper. Matt's father went to work in the post office after that and was never a happy man. Matt was embittered by what happened to his father, and he, too, was never a happy man."

A family tragedy may account for some of his torment. "Matt had a sister who basically died of racism," Dolores said. "She caught scarlet fever when she was five or six, and her parents took her to several Philadelphia hospitals, where they were turned away because they were black. In all the traveling around to hospitals, she got pneumonia and died. If they had admitted her, she'd be alive today. And that affected Matt's father for the rest of his life. His father was just furious with the hospitals, with the system, with racism in America. And it affected his life and it affected his children's lives. Matt carried that stuff around with him."

Stone prevailed upon Robinson to take on the role of Gordon, a science teacher who owned a brownstone with his wife, Susan. Robinson reluctantly accepted, originating the role in a manner that established Gordon as a dutiful husband and steady provider, a well-liked and respected figure in the neighborhood. In episode 1, scene 1, Gordon is the first character introduced.

"When Matt was on the set, I think he rather liked being Gordon," Dolores Robinson said. "But when he left that studio, he never was comfortable with the attention. Some people love the recognition; he never did. I remember going in public with him and women and children running up to him. He just didn't seem to know how to handle it."

Caroll Spinney was drenched in flop sweat, a scorching beam of white light outlining his form at the edge of the stage. Squinting and shielding his eyes, Spinney asked, "Would you please turn off that big spot?"[7]

Out of the darkness from the sound booth in the back of the theater came the unsteady response of a student volunteer. Like a lament echoing down a canyon, the voice admitted, "We don't know how!"

This was to be Spinney's big moment at the Puppeteers of America convention in Salt Lake City, the unveiling of a mechanically complex multimedia extravaganza. Using a rear-projection screen, filmed animation, and an array of switches and levers he would operate while on his knees, Spinney had fashioned a contraption Rube Goldberg not only would have admired but trademarked.

It called for a 16-millimeter film projector and a slide projector, a sound system, ladders, a seven-foot wide screen, black velour drapery. In an elaborately timed illusion for the finale, Spinney would roll an animation of birds in flight, only to incorporate handcrafted bird puppets into the scene. The birds would then seem to fly off the screen and into the three-dimensional world of the theater.

"Not only would the puppets have movement, but the backgrounds themselves would move in time with the action," Spinney said. "I thought combining of the media of film and live puppetry could bring a new dimension to puppet theater."[8]

Instead, due to glaring technical difficulties, Spinney had been thrust into that area known to performers on the brink of bombing onstage as *The Twilight Zone*.[9]

Jim Henson shifted slightly in his audience seat. As one who had designed and executed many an experimental routine, often on live television, he could relate on an almost visceral level with the struggling puppeteer onstage. Who more than Henson knew the perils of attempting something new and risky?

In the quiet hour before the show began, Spinney had checked and double-checked his equipment and the theater's light and sound. He had made sure to train the spotlights in a way that would illuminate the puppets but not wash out the movie screen behind them. Everything was aces, and he went off to grab a quick dinner. How and why it came to pass that one intense spotlight blasted Spinney just after he hit the stage, throwing the movement, music, and animation completely out of sync, only the theater gods know.

Normally, puppeteers think with their hands. Now, Spinney landed on his feet. He began to improvise, using the cone of light to turn himself into a shadow puppet—pulling out his hair in mock frustration—while the student tech team struggled to turn off the spot. As Spinney, walking away from the spotlight, mimed his torment and exasperation, a voice cried "Stop!" from the wings. Mere footsteps away was a twenty-foot pit, a man-made cliff created after a section of the stage had inadvertently been lowered. Spinney nearly concluded his act with a Wile E. Coyote–style dive into oblivion.

Mercifully, the students eventually regained control of the lights, leaving Spinney just enough time for the flying-bird finale. The audience, made up almost exclusively of empathetic fellow puppeteers and their families, gave Spinney a big hand. He all but slunk off stage, so disappointed that puppet-palooza had crashed into a steaming heap.

It was then that he heard Jim Henson's soft, reassuring voice say, "Hello." Henson had loped backstage to catch up with Spinney, the chap who had made him laugh years before with that confounded puppet Goggle. "I saw your show . . . I liked what you were trying to do."

In Massachusetts seven years earlier Spinney had misinterpreted what Henson had meant when he had said, "Why don't you come down to New York to talk about the Muppets?" It didn't sound like a job interview then, and it still didn't when, amazingly, Henson uttered the exact same words. This time, however, Spinney asked for clarification, "What do you mean by 'talk about the Muppets?'"

"I mean, would you like to come work for me?" Henson said. Henson had walked Spinney to a nearby couch, so at least Spinney was sitting down.

Unbeknownst to Spinney, Henson was on a recruiting mission, looking for someone to provide voice and movement to two new characters for *Sesame Street*. One would be a grouchy contrarian. The other would be a sunnier sort, a dimwit bird of man-size proportions.

The idea for the character had its genesis in the summer seminars, according to research director Ed Palmer. "I remember Harvard professor Sheldon White said, 'You need a Mr. Bumbler on your program. Somebody who makes mistakes, who gets flustered and is like a four-year-old, but picks himself up and dusts himself off and keeps going. He provides other people with a whole lot of opportunities to be helpful because he needs a lot of help. Four-year-olds can identify with that.' That idea got merged into Big Bird's character." The puppeteers agreed to meet in New York. Spinney arrived for his job interview both excited and apprehensive. Joining the ranks of the Muppets seemed almost too good to be true, but the prospects of working in New York—a city he found dirty, crowded, and overpriced—was of no small concern. He already held two mortgages on his property in New England and had an easy hour's commute to Boston.

He drew in a deep breath when he arrived at 227 East Sixty-seventh

Street, a former carriage house that housed the Henson Workshop, identified only by a small, hand-painted sign. To nearly every visitor who passed over the threshold, the place seemed magical.

Henson explained that the bird puppet and the trash grouch were created to add a fantasy element to the street scenes, which had tested so flat following the test shows. He added that the production team had overridden the objections of researchers who had advised against mixing the Muppets with humans on the street. The scientists preferred there be a line between fantasy and reality.[10]

Spinney said Henson described the bird as a yokel, "just a big dumb guy who would bang his head on a door frame and say, 'Stupid door!' He imagined the grouch would live under a tall pile of litter."

According to research director Ed Palmer, in some early sketches of street scenes laid across Jon Stone's draftsman-style desk, all of the Muppets lived under the pavement in an environment separate and distinct from where the humans did, "like the Teenage [Mutant] Ninja Turtles. There was going to be a whole world of puppets that you could go into—and a world of humans—and there would only be occasional transactions between the two." It may be that Henson filed away this notion for *Fraggle Rock*, the allegorical HBO series of the 1980s that many Henson admirers consider his finest and proudest achievement.

One of the reasons Henson was looking outside his circle of puppeteers for someone to step into the role of Big Bird was that Frank Oz had had quite enough of working within the confining, sweaty apparatus that was the La Choy Dragon. Being inside Big Bird would be restrictive and physically challenging in that the puppeteer would need to work with one arm stretched out above him to operate the character's head. In addition, Oz—who was already committed to doing Bert—was at the time as much a visual artist as a performing artist and wanted to preserve time away from the television studio to sculpt.

Over lunch Henson elaborated further on how the characters grew out of a need to inject the street scenes with vitality, humor, and fantasy.

At one point during the meal, Henson said, "We have a tradition at our company."

"Oh, what is that?" Spinney replied.

"You won't get paid very much," Henson said.

Spinney, who was more than a bit crestfallen and still filled with anxiety about relocating to New York, said, "Oh, I'm sorry to hear that."

On the ride home to Connecticut, Spinney was even more burdened with worry than he was on the way down to the interview.

Like so many performing artists before him and after, he would have to take several steps back financially for a shot at success in New York. He could remain in New England with his bird-in-hand gig on local television, or he could take a considerable cut in net income and become *the* Bird.

"Jim said I wouldn't make much money, and then he went out and proved it," said Spinney.

Sometimes in New York, the taxi driver hands the passenger a tip.

That's what happened on the morning Spinney formally met Oscar the Grouch. A cab had picked him up for the ride over to an old RKO theater at Eighty-first Street and Broadway, a movie palace converted into a television studio. The first thing the cabbie said to him was, "Where to, Mac?" in a coarse, road-weary voice that sounded like he had gargled with Ajax. In the back seat, Spinney smiled and thought, *That's it!*

"On the way over to the studio I was asking myself, *What am I going to use for a voice for Oscar?* And then this driver, who was talking with a cigar out the side of his mouth and was wearing an old newsboy cap, starts complaining about Mayor Lindsay, who he says is ruining New York. I'll leave out the colorful words, but as he was talking, I was taking it in. When I got out, I kept repeating 'Where to, Mac?' just as he said it. It was nothing like I had in my repertoire of voices. 'Where to, Mac?' "

Entering the studio, Spinney sized up the Oscar puppet, a ghastly orange shag carpet of a character with a wide mouth shaped like a melon slice. It was a vintage Muppet, with no teeth or ears but with wooly caterpillar eyebrows. Oscar easily could have been yanked out of a trunk containing assorted oddities from Henson's *Sam and Friends* years.

According to Stone, the original Oscar was envisioned as being considerably creepier. "The garbage can was a compromise," he said. "We wanted Oscar in a manhole. Every once in a while, the cover would lift up and you'd see these little eyes looking at you. The camera would push in and the picture would dissolve through some vertical dripping tunnel. Tilting down into semidarkness, you'd see these scruffy things and water flowing by in the foreground. Something would come by and grab one of the scruffy things out of the water. The more Jim and I talked about it, the funnier we thought it was. But when we presented the idea, everyone went 'What?' So we compromised and settled for a puppet in a garbage can, which they weren't wild about, either, but since we started with a wild idea, they bought it."

Master puppet designer Don Sahlin built Oscar, but for reasons unknown, it appeared to be made for a left-handed puppeteer. It had a work glove sewn into it, and Spinney struggled to get Oscar on his right hand. "The thumb was on the wrong side," he said, so Spinney reluctantly switched hands. "Left hands are much stupider than your right if you are right-handed," he said. It was a bit of an awkward how-do-you-do.

Spinney walked over to the trash-can home and maneuvered himself into position under it. Jim Henson, awaiting the grouch's coming-out party, gave Spinney a few extra moments to get settled, then knocked on Oscar's galvanized home.

Out popped this annoyed, wide-eyed puppet, chastising the intruder who dared to disturb him. "Get away from my trash can!" Oscar warned, in the cab driver's cadence and pitch.

"That'll do nicely," Henson said.

The trilateral production partnership of Dave Connell, Jon Stone, and Sam Gibbon served as Joan Cooney's cabinet. Executive producer Connell was her buttoned-down, dry-witted Secretary of Planning and Coordination. Producer–head writer Stone, the passionate, theatrical high-creative, was Secretary of Series Development. Producer Sam Gibbon, the warmhearted, sometimes wary, intellectual, was Secretary of Education. Gibbon, in concert with Ed Palmer and Gerry Lesser, fused content and curriculum. Along with Stone, Gibbon was also available to studio-produce some shows.

Script development depended on continuous back-and-forth among the cabinet members. "A lot of it evolved out of Jon and me spending time pacing back and forth," said Connell. "We would say, 'What if we did this? What if we did that?' It's very hard to concretize what is a messy situation. You write something and it doesn't work. You write something and it does. We certainly had curriculum to deal with. We had some sense of the characters, Mr. Hooper in the store . . . Big Bird as the child surrogate . . . live characters on the street. So Big Bird doesn't know how to count to twenty. You can do a sketch about it. You had Oscar as the big kid's grouch surrogate, who could dump on stuff. . . . Jon, as head writer, would look at a piece that someone had written, or even he had written, and know in his head what he would do in the studio to make it work. But when Sam Gibbon was studio-producing, he'd look at a piece of material and say, 'This doesn't work' or 'This could be better.'

"There would be conflicts. Sam would be constantly calling me, saying 'Have you seen next week's scripts?'

"I'd say, 'Yes.'

"He'd say, 'We've got real trouble here.' And he was partly right. Sam would pound on the table and say, 'We can make this better!'

"Jon would say, 'Fine.'

"The way we ultimately ended up settling conflict, Sam and I would meet at night with the next week's scripts. We would go through and edit them, with Sam paying attention to the curriculum and me paying attention to 'Was it funny and does it work?' It sounds more unpleasant than it was. I don't recall Jon ever coming to me saying, 'Why did that get changed?'

"One of the things we agonized over was how to do the first show. We really couldn't figure out how to do it because it was going to be seen as a first show and reviewed as a first show. But it was only one of 130, and how much introducing can you do? Jon came back from Vermont one Monday with a brilliant idea, which was that Gordon would introduce a little girl who had just moved into the neighborhood. That way, you could introduce everything by means of this girl.

"It was absolutely perfect."

The first taping of Muppet segments, referred to as inserts because they were to be slotted at various points into the show, occurred on Monday, September 29, at the Reeves Studio at Sixty-seventh Street and Columbus Avenue. Working from a Jon Stone script, Henson and Frank Oz—as Ernie and Bert—set up what would be a motif for episode 1: the letter *W* and the word *wash*. The scene also established Ernie's compulsion for hygiene and fondness for bathing, with or without a rubber duckie.

From this moment forward and forevermore, Bert would be the straighter-than-straight man, Ernie the comic. It opened with Ernie rub-a-dub-dubbing in the tub:

> Ernie (*calling out*): Hey, Bert. Can I have a bar of soap?
> Bert (*entering*): Yah.
> Ernie: Just toss it into Rosie here.
> Bert: Who's Rosie?
> Ernie: My bathtub. I call my bathtub Rosie.
> Bert: Ernie, why do you call your bathtub Rosie?
> Ernie: What's that?
> Bert (*slightly annoyed*): I said why do you call your bathtub Rosie?
> Ernie: Because every time I take a bath I leave a ring around Rosie.
>   (He-he-he-he)

Having put one over for the first time on ole buddy Bert, Ernie introduced his signature laugh, a slightly saliva-bathed *hee-hee-hee* that is reminiscent of the sound expectant parents practice at Lamaze class. That *hee-hee-hee* would become a comic calling card for a character that would reflect the sunnier aspects of Henson's personality—the aspects that weren't already projected onto Kermit.

Bert and Ernie actually made their national television debut on NBC, appearing on the Saturday night before the Monday-morning PBS premiere in a thirty-minute preview entitled *This Way to Sesame Street*. Underwritten by a fifty-thousand-dollar grant from Xerox, the sneak peek was written by Jon Stone and produced by CTW publicist Bob Hatch. "No one else had time to do it," Hatch said.

The program, taped the day before it aired, began with an acknowledgment of the corporate sponsor. As Hatch recalled, "A little door opened and a Muppet came out and said, 'This is brought to you from the folks at Xerox.' That seemed harmless enough."

But into the studio barged Gene Aleinikoff, a lawyer for NET, who shouted, "You can't do that!" Aleinikoff, explained Hatch, "had been used to the limiting funding credits public television allowed in those days." But there was no time for changes.

They were so up against the clock that they nearly forgot the show had to clear NBC's Standards and Practices unit before it could air. "Censors for a *preschool show*?" Hatch asked in astonishment. When Hatch's phone rang at eight on Friday night, the NBC censor said, "Loved it."

The special aired on some one hundred NBC stations. On October 17, 1969, *Newsday* deemed it "a unique display of cooperation between commercial and noncommercial broadcasters. . . . Competitive considerations are being put aside momentarily at least to get the program designed to teach the Three R's to twelve million preschoolers, to as many tots as possible."[11]

The newspaper reported that in New York, *Sesame Street* would get a first airing each weekday on commercial station WPIX at 9:00 a.m. Channel Thirteen would air the same show at 11:30 a.m.

It seems Joan Cooney's former boss, Jack Kiermeier, had struck again. "I had been unsuccessful in my efforts to persuade Jack to run the program earlier than 11:30 a.m.," Cooney said. "He did not want to interrupt the station's bloc of in-classroom programming, which ran from 9:00 a.m. until 2:00 p.m. and which brought the channel much-needed revenue from the school board."

When Kiermeier held firm to his decision, Cooney convinced the union leadership of several New York locals to grant an exemption, allowing her nonunion show to air on WPIX.[12]

Despite what she described as a "howl of protest from public TV people," Cooney said the waiver "proved to be a godsend. WPIX had a much bigger audience than Thirteen, and it got the show into the inner city in New York immediately and at the right time of day."

On the Sunday night before the *Sesame Street* premiere, Tim and Joan Cooney took in the movie *Funny Girl* at the Ziegfeld Theater, just to kill some time until the early edition of the *New York Times* rolled off the presses. "Watching Barbra Streisand bite her nails over Omar Sharif's caddishness seemed better than staying home and biting my own nails while we waited for the *Times* review," Cooney said.

A few days earlier, editors and reporters from New York's daily newspapers and the newswire services had been invited to Sardi's, the legendary celebrity watering hole, to screen the first episode of *Sesame Street*. A similar session for magazine journalists had been held two weeks prior.

The Cooneys walked to the Times building on West Forty-third Street and asked a delivery driver if the bulldog edition was already loaded in his truck. "No," he said, and they went off to dinner. At 11:00 p.m. Tim bought the paper at a newsstand and hurried home with it.

George Gent's review began as follows:

American parents have long complained about the paucity of good television programs for children, particularly for preschoolers. Well, starting today and continuing weekdays for the next twenty-six weeks, they will have to look no further than channel 13. . . . Based on a preview of today's opening program, children should love the series.

Adults might reasonably question another adult's judgment on a children's television program, but the workshop assures us that each hour-long program has been thoroughly researched and tested many times before audiences of children. The success of the program as an educational tool will have to be evaluated later. But right now it provides an exciting and potentially revolutionary new instructional technique within the context of television.

"I called Dave Connell and read him the piece," Cooney said. "Then I called Bob Hatch and gave him the news. We all did the equivalent of high fives."

For those who worked on its development, that *Sesame Street* had made it to air was a pinch-me experience. Never had the participants worked so hard—for so long—on a project, abandoning all other pursuits and placing personal considerations on hold. Never had so many disparate voices blended with such harmony, led by a woman who described herself as having no special talents beyond the ability to conduct. Never had so much cash been earmarked for an experiment that had no guarantee of success. Never had the inert box of tubes and wires that was television been tested in such a way. Never had the fortunes of indigent preschool children mattered so much.

Chapter Thirteen

Intermission

Monday, November 10, on PBS: *Sesame Street*, sponsored by the letters *W, S,* and *E* and the numbers *2* and *3*.

To see that first episode today—and the four succeeding ones in *Sesame*'s first week—is to be transported back to 1969.[1] The minute Matt Robinson as Gordon, with his muttonchop sideburns and his dandelion-soft Afro, steps onstage you can practically hear Sly and the Family Stone singing "You Can Make It If You Try" or watch Clarence Williams III, the laconic Linc from the groovy ABC cop show *The Mod Squad*.

Robinson is front and center during debut week, the cast member who seems most at ease addressing children in the home audience and children on the set. He was a smooth and confident tour guide, exuding both streetwise cool and parental warmth.

His welcoming lines in episode 1 are to a pigtailed girl in a purple striped dress and red socks. Sally is holding his hand as they stroll Sesame Street, with Toots Thielemans's harmonica rendition as accompaniment. The scene is benignly familiar, a kind of everykid's version of an urban block, where taking the hand of a friendly stranger doesn't seem at all unusual.

"Sally, you've never seen a street like Sesame Street," Gordon assures the new-to-the-neighborhood child. "*Everything* happens here. You're going to love it." The immediate message is clear: *everything* and *anything* can happen on Sesame Street—except bad stuff.

It's a statement meant as much to convince the first-time viewers of *Sesame Street*, adults, children—even the young actress in front of the camera.

But to at least one preschool child in Philadelphia, the scene caused consternation, confusion, and tears. For weeks, Holly Robinson had been missing her father. Matt had been working long hours on the show in New York, catching quick weekend visits when he could. Seeing him with another child was almost more than Holly could bear. "She thought Sally was taking her daddy," said Matt's then wife, Dolores.

Things only became more traumatic minutes later when Holly saw her daddy kiss a woman who wasn't her mother. "That *really* threw her," said Dolores Robinson, "even more than when Matt said, 'Hi! My name is Gordon.'"

Holly said, "His name's not Gordon, his name is Daddy."

In time, it would all make sense to Holly, who in the early 1970s would make one of her own first acting appearances on *Sesame Street*, long before she played police officer Judy Hoffs on *21 Jump Street*. In the pop culture nexus that is *Sesame Street*, connections are often established in less than six degrees.

In episode 1, Gordon is dressed in an ash-gray suit and totes a leather portfolio. These are his work threads, for Gordon is a teacher at a secondary school located beyond the sound of honking car horns that play as audio backdrop. Thanks to a canceled faculty meeting, Gordon is home early and available to take his walk with Sally. Together they meet cheerful Bob in his blue cardigan, then Mr. Hooper, who says, "Welcome, new Sally," and then Gordon's wife, Susan. Joan Cooney's mandate that Gordon and Susan be married is carried out, almost to an extreme. Loretta Long plays Susan as an obedient bride, who happily takes Gordon's briefcase from him through an open window in their brownstone. "Will you come back and see me later and have some milk and cookies?" she asks Sally. One gets the sense they were fresh-baked, and not sliced from a tube purchased at the supermarket.

For the first few minutes of the opening segment, things appear quite copacetic and calm on Sesame Street, a place that is considerably better cared for than the neighborhood depicted in the send-your-kid-to-the-ghetto-this-summer public service message that jolted Jon Stone.

But suddenly the normalcy is interrupted by Big Bird's *crash-bang* entrance. He is a stuttering, fearful, ungainly bird with a tiny head and an even tinier brain. With the benefit of hindsight, the first appearance of Big Bird brings to mind the introduction of Mickey Mouse in *Steamboat Willie*: he's so primitive and unrealized, so first draft and foreign. Just as was the case with Mickey in 1928, Big Bird was, on first appearance, a work in progress.

Gordon then introduces us to Caroll Spinney's other character, the toxic-orange, rude, antisocial, positively misanthropic Oscar. With his elongated neck and arch attitude, Oscar seems like the kind of neighbor who would keep your baseball if it landed in his yard. He pops up far more frequently during the first week than Big Bird.

In one episode, Oscar threatens to leave Sesame Street and goes missing. Though his departure is like a toothache that suddenly subsides, Gordon is concerned by his absence and goes in search of Oscar, who sends himself home to Sesame Street, gift wrapped in a cardboard box within a cardboard box within a cardboard box.

Far more intriguing and charming are the animated and live-action films produced by Jim Henson. With his Moog synthesizer pumping out electronica and his pinball-style graphics, Henson's number films fairly explode with creative joy.

Seen several times during the opening week is an irresistible jingle for the number 3, sung by a gaggle of children ("Three! Three! Three! / Let's sing a song of three! / How many is three?"). Henson himself juggles three balls, as the numbers (*"1-2-3 Booooiiing!"*) are superimposed on a frozen image of him. His son, with gloriously uncombed hair, counts three peas on a plate. Then, as a finale, the clumsy pastry chef sends three birthday cakes flying, a pratfall right out of *The Three Stooges*.

Later comes a lesson that grew out of the summer seminars of '68: a film of children playing follow the leader that covers the concepts of "up," "down," "over," "under," and "through." That lesson is reinforced during a live-action scene that sends Bob over to Gordon and Susan's apartment to assist in hanging a painting, and as he searches for the most pleasing spot on the wall.

Next comes the slapstick comedy team of Buddy and Jim, two dim bulbs who attempt to hang a picture using a spike and a balloon instead of a hammer. Stone, with the enthusiastic support of Dave Connell, had a notion that lessons in logic might be best taught by bumblers like Buddy and Jim. In test screenings, children were alternately squealing and screaming in response to the segment, calling out instructions to the duo about how to bring an ironing board through the kitchen door. (Buddy and Jim sawed it in half, vertically. When that didn't work, they bashed gouges in the door frame to make room for the board.)

Susan then pleasantly took up the mantle of teaching classification, singing Joe Raposo's guessing-game song "One of These Things." (A felt board had three cutouts of the numeral 2 and a cutout of the letter *W*.)

Though there were some dead spots in the first five episodes, the series covered considerable ground in its first week, its pace brisk, its mood cheery (except for Oscar), and its feel contemporary. Those shows provided a foundation for the production staff to build upon, and because the series was funded for a full 130 episodes, there was no specter of cancellation hanging overhead. Still, nearly everyone associated with the project thought it might last only a season or two. They understood it was just a little television show on PBS, that network you had to hunt to find on the dial. They also knew that the same founders who had come up with eight million dollars might not be able to pull another rabbit like that out of their hats.

So they decided to have fun while it lasted and gave it everything they had. Not one of them was making the kind of top salary available at the commercial networks. But, then again, the pressures and pains of a job on the networks tended to take years off lives.

Working on the start-up that was *Sesame Street* provided abundant freedom and license to create, which for some was golden compensation of its own.

Chapter Fourteen

On November 10, 1969, *Sesame Street* finally debuted, a triumph of brain chemistry and electromagnetic physics. Every thought that had contributed to its creation—all of that synaptic activity over forty-five months, starting with the after-dinner discussion at the Cooney dinner party—was processed, analyzed, modified, and finally transmitted back to children like Sarah Morrisett, the preschooler who got it all started with a click of the On-Off switch in 1965.

At 4:00 p.m. on debut day, a celebratory VIP screening of the first show was held in a private room at the Essex House in Manhattan. Fred Friendly of the Ford Foundation attended, as did CPB chairman Frank Pace and Mike Dann of CBS. During the screening, Dann kept glancing at his watch. A suburban commuter, he was merely keeping an eye on the time so as not to miss the 5:31 to Greenwich, but the gesture distressed Cooney.

While the end credits rolled, Pace raced up to her. "Congratulations!" he said. "This is the most important thing since the discovery of the atom bomb."

Dann bolted for Grand Central as the rest of the group repaired to the lounge. "When the bartender handed us our drinks, Lloyd Morrisett and I locked eyes," Cooney said.

" 'Joan,' he said, 'we did it.'

"And I said, 'Yes, we did it.' I felt as though I could exhale for the first time in months."

Afterward, FCC chairman Dean Burch, Joan's close classmate and onetime beau from her University of Arizona days, joined the Cooneys for dinner and drinks.

Finally, the big day was over. "I got home, exhausted and happy with the slightly surreal awareness that somehow we had pulled off something much bigger than just a nice children's show," she said. "But later that night, Tim went out on a bender, and after I realized he was gone, I never went back to sleep. He came home at 8:30 in the morning and went to bed. Two weeks later I turned forty, and Tim gave me a surprise birthday party at a nearby Japanese restaurant. I was happy that night, but it marked the moment when Tim's downward spiral began."

Hosannas for *Sesame Street* echoed from Maui to Maine, and it quickly became the rare children's show stamped with parental approval. The switchboard at Boston's public station, WGBH, fielded more than seventy-six hundred calls commending *Sesame Street*, and more than two thousand letters of appreciation reached the station. "I didn't know what a succès fou meant, but I knew we had it," Cooney said.

Newsday recounted that "scores of glowing newspaper and magazine stories fluttered down on Mrs. Cooney and her workshop like confetti onto the heads of conquering heroes."[1]

After only two weeks on the air, *New York Times* critic Jack Gould predicted, "When the Educational Testing Service of Princeton, New Jersey, completes its analysis in the months to come, *Sesame Street* may prove to be far more than an unusual television program. On a large scale, the country's reward may be a social document of infinite value in education."[2]

Variety canonized CTW's executive director as "St. Joan" under the hyperbolic headline: SESAME STREET: WUNDERKIND. Les Brown, *Variety's* television industry reporter, hailed *Sesame Street* as "One of the few shows in memory that has lived up to its advance ballyhoo. It is the apotheosis of education through show business, and anyone who thinks it is only for small fry ought to give it an hour. The show moves, seduces, diverts, dazzles, amuses, and infects, and in the captivating course of things it teaches the very young basic human values, the meaning of numbers, the alphabet, and solutions to simple problems."[3]

Brown reported the show rang up a 3.3 national rating in its second week, translating into 1.9 million households. It was a remarkable Nielsen number, given that *Sesame Street* reached only 67.6 percent of the nation at the time and that viewers in some key metropolitan areas—including Los Angeles and Washington, D.C.—had to watch it on UHF stations. Brown concluded, "If commercial television may be likened to Broadway and noncommercial TV to off-Broadway, *Sesame Street* is a clear-cut off-Broadway hit."

Los Angeles Times television critic Cecil Smith recounted how he attended an advance screening of *Sesame Street* seated behind three children. "A boy about six stuck his thumb in his mouth and seemed completely absorbed in everything he saw; a girl, maybe five, was thoroughly attentive, but her little sister, possibly three, soon got restless, more interested in the people around her than those on the screen. That's a Nielsen rating of 66.6, which ain't bad."[4]

The chorus of praise continued for a year, reaching a crescendo in the November 23, 1970, issue of *Time*, the weekly yardstick of the zeitgeist. On its cover was Big Bird, who had gotten a makeover for season two, returning after hiatus with a shorter beak, wider eyes, and a dandelion bloom crowning his head. To viewers watching new episodes in the fall of 1970, it was as if Big Bird had shed his ugly duckling gawkiness over the summer.

Time devoted nine pages to assessing the show's impact and importance, asking, "[With] a profusion of aims, a confusion of techniques, how could such a show possibly succeed? Answer: spectacularly well."

Writer Stefan Kanfer provided a tick list of reasons to support his contention that *Sesame Street* "is not only the best children's show in TV history, it is one of the best parents' shows as well."

Highlights from his story read like critics' blurbs on a marquee:

- "As meticulously planned as a semester at medical school."
- "Backed like a government bond, nurtured like a Broadway musical."
- "Catches the preschooler almost before his society does. Thus [it] is as popular with well-to-do-kids as it is with the slum dweller."
- "Learning seems almost a byproduct of fun."
- "The switched-on school reaches its audience at a cost of about a penny per child, 'A bargain,' says Dr. Benjamin Spock, 'if I ever saw one.' "[5]

Quoted elsewhere, Spock predicted that such "well-conceived" television would result in "better-trained citizens, fewer unemployables in the next generation, fewer people on welfare, and smaller jail populations." This was high praise indeed from the man who, at the time, was revered as the nation's baby doctor.

The show was not just a boon to kids and parents, but also a cultural triumph. For the programs aired in its inaugural season, *Sesame Street* won a Peabody Award, three Emmys, and the top honor from the Prix Jeunesse Foundation, an international body formed in 1964 to promote excellence in children's television.

Even the president sent a fan letter.[6]

January 28, 1970
Dear Mrs. Cooney:
    The many children and families now benefitting from *Sesame Street* are participants in one of the most promising experiments in the history of that medium. The Children's Television Workshop certainly deserves the high praise it has been getting from young and old alike in every corner of the nation. This administration is enthusiastically committed to opening up opportunities for every youngster, particularly during his first

five years of life, and is pleased to be among the sponsors of your distin-
guished program.
Sincerely,
Richard Nixon

Cooney was inundated with attention. "The press requests were end-
less," she said. "We were going into 1970 and the women's movement was
becoming a very big thing in America. There were very few women to
make a fuss about. . . . No one said, 'Why are they making so much of
her?' Even here, the men who resented each other getting press had less
resentment of me getting press. I begged Bob Hatch to get the press to
interview anybody but me, and the press wouldn't. So I frequently insisted
that David Connell sit with me, so that he would be quoted in the article,
even if it was a profile of me. But there was no way to get Gerry [Lesser]
involved, no reporter cared about the academic adviser. It was simpler to
focus on 'Saint Joan,' and that became a way of doing the story. We had
Look magazine trailing me around, going to hearings with me."

Working his Washington connections, Bob Hatch had arranged for
Cooney to testify before Congressional hearings on children and televi-
sion even before *Sesame Street* debuted. "We were a Washington presence,"
Cooney said.

At one education conference held in D.C., Cooney shared a platform
with Bob Keeshan. He exhorted the audience to "back her one hundred
percent," but he couldn't resist getting in a little dig. "I know she has the
best possible staff to do the job," he said. "She stole them all from me."

"Keeshan used to drive me crazy," Cooney recalled. "He greatly resented
Sesame Street. And it was because of him I was determined to have multiple
hosts on the show. I never wanted anyone to own it or be able to blackmail
me for higher wages. That whole concept of how we ran things must have
outraged him."

Though *Sesame Street* was almost universally greeted with huzzahs, even
before Thanksgiving feasts were served that November certain educators
who were upholders of traditional classroom methods were finding aspects
of the series objectionable or even threatening. Kindergarten teachers began
to wonder of what use their time-tested lesson plans would be if students
arrived in the fall having already mastered the alphabet, counting, sorting,
identifying geometric shapes, and knowing the difference between near
and far, around and over, under and through.

In 1970, Loretta Long told a reporter about an encounter she'd had while addressing a group at a Massachusetts university. "Loretta described one man, presumably an educator, who asked her what he was supposed to do with his lesson plans if children started coming to school already knowing letters and numbers. [She] told him, 'If you feel threatened, I think you need more creative schools of education. I would hate to see a teacher view *Sesame Street* as a threat or an enemy rather than an ally.' "[7]

Thoughtful criticism of *Sesame Street* also began to bubble up from that segment of media theorists and cultural critics that was renowned for its narrow-eyed wariness of television. *Sesame Street's* rapid pace and high entertainment quotient were roundly scrutinized. In his landmark 1985 book *Amusing Ourselves to Death,* Neil Postman argued that parents embraced *Sesame Street* because it "relieved them of their responsibility to teach their children to read." The series, in his eyes, provided children a questionable introduction to an amusement-obsessed culture and undermined American education.

That *Sesame Street* was subject to such serious review indicated that the project had ascended to a level of importance not usually associated with children's television. It made *Sesame Street* a topic worthy of debate— something that could not be said for, say, *Huckleberry Hound.*

"I thought there would be mixed reaction," Cooney said. "While I felt that the TV critics would understand what we were trying to do, I was very concerned that teachers and educators would not. The conservative early-childhood people didn't like what we're doing at all."[8]

Preschool authority Carl Bereiter of the Ontario Institute for Studies in Education, in Toronto, whom Joan Cooney had consulted while researching the original feasibility study, weighed in on the pages of the *Wall Street Journal* the morning after the premiere. He complained that what he had seen of *Sesame Street* was too removed from "structured" teaching and warned that the show could flop because "it's based entirely on audience appeal and is not really teaching anything in particular."[9]

There were other dissenting voices:

- Urie Bronfenbrenner, an esteemed professor of psychology at Cornell University and a cofounder of Head Start, questioned the show's geniality. "The children [on the show] are charming, soft-spoken, cooperative, clean, and well-behaved. Among the adults there are no cross words, no conflicts, no difficulties, nor, for that matter, any obligations or visible attachments. The old, the ugly, or the unwanted is simply made to disappear through a manhole."[10]

- Frank Garfunkel, a professor of education at Boston University and director of the Head Start Evaluation and Research Center, attacked the series in the university's alumni magazine, claiming that it relied on rote memorization and "puts a noose around" the ability of children to "engage in sustained and developed thought." Any claim that *Sesame Street* "is a major educational or media innovation is preposterous. The values implicit in the form and content—strictly three Rs with a mixed bag of dressing—are traditional. . . . The image of *Sesame Street* as a unique vanguard of educational experience is a mirage."
- Maria Piers, dean of Chicago's Erikson Institute for Early Education, concluded that *Sesame Street* "force-feeds facts. It doesn't give the child a chance to conjecture, to solve problems, to be creative."[11]
- Leading education writer Arnold Arnold was among the first to suggest that watching *Sesame Street* might actually be detrimental to its target audience. "[It] has created unfounded hopes for improving the education of poverty children and may be harmful to them."[12]
- In *Childhood Education* magazine, Minnie P. Berson, director of an experimental program for young children at New York's State University College of Fredonia, objected to any claim that the show could teach. "Why debase the art form of teaching with phony pedagogy, vulgar sideshows, bad acting, and layers of smoke and fog to clog the eager minds of small children?" Her suggestion: "Tap some of the marvelous artist-teachers in nursery schools and kindergartens" to teach on TV.[13]
- *Chicago Sun-Times* television critic Ron Powers, a wry, penetrating observer, viewed the range of response to *Sesame Street* with high amusement. "If *Sesame Street* is the most successful show on television, it is also the most analyzed, criticized, evaluated, debated, debunked, championed, viewed with alarm, pointed to with pride, interpreted, misinterpreted, and overinterpreted media event since William Randolph Hearst declared war on Spain."[14]

CTW corporate response to such criticism was measured and non-confrontational, a reflection of a style preferred by Cooney and her public relations adviser, Hatch. For pragmatic purposes, it was best to be reasonable. "First, you can't be saintly all of the time and maintain the interest of the press," Hatch said. "Second, if somebody has something legitimate to say—or something semilegitimate . . . that may be contrary—it gives you and others something to chew on and rebut."

More complicated was how to respond to an outright broadcast ban of

Sesame Street in Mississippi, where members of the newly convened State Commission for Educational Television were opposed to the show's integrated cast. During the first week in May 1970, word leaked out of the state capitol in Jackson that the five-member commission had voted 3 to 2 to block the show from airing on the state's educational TV system. One commissioner, granted anonymity by the *New York Times*, said, "Mississippi was not yet ready" for a program in which black, Latino, and white children played together.[15] A second commissioner, quoted anonymously in the *Chicago Sun-Times*,[16] said the state "had enough problems to face up to without adding to them."

Speaking on the record, Joan Ganz Cooney called the ban "a tragedy for both the white and black children of Mississippi."[17]

The Mississippi commission ultimately reversed its decision, but only after the initial ban had made national news.

As the waves of attention washed over *Sesame Street*, a CBS media relations team attempted to pump up some publicity for Bob Keeshan's venerable morning program, which had begun to seem stodgy and tortoise-slow compared to the new show that followed it at nine in many markets. In May, publicists scheduled an hour-long closed-circuit event for TV critics and network affiliates during which Keeshan reaffirmed *Captain Kangaroo*'s philosophy and took questions from Peggy Hudson, television editor of *Scholastic* magazine. When asked whether the success of *Sesame Street* had affected his show, Keeshan said it had not and that the shows were not in competition. He was quick to reiterate, however, that its cast notwithstanding, almost all of *Sesame Street*'s creative talent had trained under him. "We like to say there's over fifteen years of *Captain Kangaroo* behind *Sesame Street*."[18]

Writing in the *Indianapolis News*, critic Richard K. Shull responded with a sympathetic column on May 7. "It's no secret [Keeshan's] feelings have been hurt . . . by the adulation and gushing over *Sesame Street*," he wrote, adding, "this year the nation has tended to forget who pioneered the field of intelligent programming for children."

Sesame Street, Shull continued, "operates out of a privileged, sheltered position, with multi-million-dollar grants to assure that it isn't tainted by advertising. The Captain made his mark the hard way, working within the hard-sell work of commercialism."

On August 21, 1970, Clarence Petersen of the *Chicago Tribune* offered his take on the virtues of *Captain Kangaroo*, in which Keeshan was quoted in a put-down of the competition. "When someone writes a history of television, there should be a chapter on *Sesame Street* as the classic case of how to promote and publicize a television show."

Joan Cooney used to quote a saying credited to Sophie Tucker: " 'I've been rich and I've been poor, and rich is better.' I eventually formulated an aphorism of my own a couple of years after we'd been on the air: 'I've known success and I've know failure, but success is better . . . *in some respects.*'

"I said *'some* respects' because your telephone never stops ringing. Every toy manufacturer in the world is after you. All the power people in the commercial world are trying to figure out how to cash in. 'How do we take this over and squeeze it to death for all the money that's in it now? And then, throw them out [because] they don't know what they're doing.' The nonprofit world, public television, had never known this kind of success, with this kind of potential for moneymaking. That's what the commercial world saw."

And yet, getting *Sesame Street* on the air was no guarantee it would *stay* on the air. For there to be sufficient funding for a season two, and for the core staff of CTW to remain employed, cofounders Cooney and Morrisett would need to move swiftly. "As soon as we got on the air, we had to think about survival," Cooney said.

Morrisett was quick to remind Cooney that foundations like Ford and Carnegie exist to seed projects, not sustain them. Grants are like sun showers nurturing tiny shoots. As soon as projects take root and bloom, philanthropies move on to water someone else's idea.

CTW needed a revenue stream, and within weeks of *Sesame Street*'s debut there was no shortage of opportunities to capitalize on its rising popularity. Cooney began fielding cold calls from marketers eager to attach the likenesses of Muppet characters onto products, in exchange for a licensing fee. In commercial television, such entreaties would be looked upon as manna. But in the nascent world of public television, no one was quite prepared for come-ons from toy companies. Complicating things further, not-for-profit CTW was the oddest of contraptions, a television production operation with one power cord plugged into the federal government, another into megafoundations, and a speaker wire hooked into NET.

And then there was the not insignificant factor that Big Bird, Oscar, Bert, and Ernie were trademarked characters controlled by CTW but owned by Jim Henson. No deal to license and market them would happen without Henson's buy-in.

For potential partners, precious little about dealing with CTW and

Henson would be business as usual. CTW was a semipublicly endowed content provider. Its administration and staff were a patchwork quilt of highly educated elites, untested in the rough-and-tumble of commerce. While more experienced in business matters, Henson was but a service contractor to CTW, an essential but independent vendor. Their joint mission was to build and sustain an experimental television program targeted primarily to impoverished preschoolers but available to all. Its success hinged on whether an audience that couldn't tie its shoes would tune in to a channel identified on the dial by a number beyond the target audience's range of understanding.

Cooney, Morrisett, and their advisers wrestled with the legalities and proprieties of reaching out to business partners, concluding that any introductory product line would need to be transparently educational in nature and priced affordably. "Business goes where the money is—and our purpose is to go where it isn't," Cooney told *Variety* in the summer of 1970. "The multi-million-dollar companies know that their targets are in the great economic center of society, and they'll grab what they can at either end of the consumer scale. They aim for the middle class. We've made *Sesame Street* for the poor people and the ghetto communities, although we wouldn't discourage the more privileged from watching. . . . It's not our purpose to make any child whose family wouldn't buy [a book or record] for him to feel more deprived than he might be. . . . We want it to be at a price people in the ghetto can afford."[19]

CTW also vowed that tie-in products would not be advertised on *Sesame Street* or marketed directly to children. Cooney stressed restraint, prudence, and caution.

Some advisers were adamantly against any efforts toward licensing and merchandising. Among them was Gene Aleinikoff, general counsel for NET and a legal consultant to CTW. "Aleinikoff had a fit," Cooney recalled. "He said, 'It will never make over a million dollars and you will have commercialized yourself. It's a whore's way of doing things.'"

Producer Sam Gibbon feared that the pursuit of deals would be corrupting, a stain on an organization that was more a public trust.

Even Jim Henson initially seemed to resist plans to capitalize on the popularity of his creations. Bernie Brillstein recalled a tide-turning meeting in 1970. "Jim and Jane came to my house on a hot summer's day. I was trying to convince them to merchandise the *Sesame Street* puppets, and it was like a knock-down, drag-out fight. Jim actually thought it was undignified to merchandise. But once I told him he would have complete creative control, and that the money would make his company financially independent, that's all I had to do. Maybe some of the people around him didn't want him to do it. But in my mind I think Jim really wanted to. I just had to give him the *reason*."

Upon returning from Los Angeles, Henson asked to meet with Joan Cooney.

As Cooney recalled, "Jim Henson brought Jay Emmett with him. Jay was head of the Licensing Corporation of America. He was doing some licensing for the Muppets. Jim sat down and said, 'You know nothing about this, and it is wrong for you to try to do it. Jay Emmett will handle the licensing of *Sesame Street*.' And I said, 'Jay Emmett is *not* going to go *near* it. This is one thing *Sesame Street* is going to control totally. What we will do and not do is going to be decided product by product, and we are going to approve everything. This is not a commercial enterprise as you understand commercial enterprises.' I remember Jim saying, 'But you don't know anything about it, Joan.' And I said, 'But we'll learn, Jim.'

"The first thing I did was call Jason Epstein at Random House. I wasn't sure that he would remember me, but he picked up the telephone right away. I forgot that by then I was a famous person. After the *Sesame Street* publicity, who in New York publishing would not know who Joan Ganz Cooney was? *Sesame Street* represented a huge potential account for Random House.

"I said to him, 'We have to start a nonbroadcast materials division, and I need someone like Jason Epstein to run it.'

"He said, 'Well, I'm not your man, but let me come help you organize it, and we'll talk about who might do it.'"

The first extension of the *Sesame Street* brand involved deals to publish series-related books that underscored and amplified the curriculum. Epstein recommended Christopher Cerf, the infectiously high-spirited, abundantly talented, merrily mischievous, idiosyncratic son of Bennett Cerf, cofounder of Random House, and his wife, Phyllis, an editor at the children's imprint Beginner Books. Phyllis had famously edited the comic canon of author-illustrator Theodor Seuss Geisel, the wubbulous Dr. Seuss.

In word and deed, Geisel proved not only that laughter was the best medicine, but that in the right hands it could also provide pathways to learning. "Shortly after the Russians launched Sputnik, there was an article in *Life* magazine by John Hersey," Cerf said. "That was about the time when everyone was asking why Ivan can read but Johnny can't. Hersey suggested that one of the reasons was that reading primers used in the schools were so dull. And so he actually asked in print, why can't someone like Dr. Seuss write a primer?"

That nudge led Geisel to write *The Cat in the Hat*, the vocabulary for which was suggested by Dr. Jeanne Stemlicht Chall, a tenacious Harvard School of Education researcher and phonics advocate. Christopher Cerf said Geisel's collaboration with Chall "provided a model before *Sesame Street* of how top-notch educators and creative people can work together. "And," he noted, "*The Cat in the Hat* is very much like *Sesame Street* in spirit. To me, Hersey asked a similar question to the one that led to *Sesame Street*: why does educational television have to have no creativity? Or, turned around, why does creative television have no education?"

Cooney was surprised that Random House would allow one of its talented young editors to leave the family so easily, considering how steeped he was in the company's culture.

But Cerf, coeditor of the *Harvard Lampoon* during his days in Cambridge, had a splendid first year on the job, building a $900,000 business from nothing. As the business expanded to include toys, however, his lack of experience in management and brand building began to show. He asked to be reassigned from the business side to the creative side, and his request was granted before CTW had a firm idea of who should replace him.

CTW's business inexperience was becomingly increasingly evident, too. "We needed a body, and Jim Drake walked in at the right time," Cooney said. "I don't know why we hired him; he hadn't any experience. We went from plus $800,000 to minus $200,000 in a year. When he told me about the loss I called him in the next day and told him it wasn't working out."

Nineteen seventy wasn't shaping up to be a great year for Emily Perl Kaplin. Divorced, childless, and out of work, she was a behind-the-scenes, TV industry gal Friday who had rarely faced unemployment before. Her experience ranged from the brilliantly wrought drama (doing research for George C. Scott's *East Side, West Side*) to the hyperventilated game show *Supermarket Sweep*.

"I spent my weekends in the freezer counting pork chops and arranging fish on platters for *Supermarket Sweep*," she recalled. "I'd poke their little eyes back in and put parsley around them. I'd line up sausages and whatever else the contestants were going to be bidding on. I did all kinds of crazy stuff, but I had never done a kid's show."

With time on her hands, she tuned in to *Sesame Street* one day to see for herself whether the breathless praise the series was receiving among her friends was justified. "They said how innovative it was, *blah, blah, blah*. So

I turned it on . . . and immediately thought, *This is where I belong.* I just knew. I began watching it twice a day, admiring its edge, sophistication, and humor. Plus, its mandate to get to underprivileged kids . . . everything appealed to me socially and politically."

Kaplin took a freelance assignment as talent coordinator for the Emmy Awards. "I was the person who was booking the people who say, 'May I have the envelope, please.' That was right around the time when I found out that the technicians on the studio floor for *Sesame Street* were the same guys that I'd worked with on *Supermarket Sweep,* including the camera guy, Frankie Biondo.

"So I wrangled an introduction to Lutrelle Horne,[20] floor producer at that time, and I offered to do anything they needed. He thought I was bright, smart and had good experience, and sent me over to meet Jon Stone, who said 'Bright . . . good experience, *da, da, da, da,* but we don't need you. We're fully staffed.' So he sent me over to Ed Palmer because I had done research for *The Dick Cavett Show* and *East Side, West Side.* Lovely interview, but again, it was bright, experienced, fully staffed. So I went over to Editing because I had done some editing on a game show in California. Same result. I must have had about fourteen interviews.

"Simultaneously I was doing this job for the Emmys and *Sesame Street* was nominated up the gazoo for its first season. So half the time I was talking to Jon Stone saying, 'Please, please hire me. Do you need someone to sweep the floors?' with him saying, 'Gee, we just don't need anybody.' The other half of the time I was talking to him about where he was going to sit and what he should wear and who's going to give the acceptance speech if *Sesame Street* wins an Emmy. I was talking to him a couple of times a week over a nine-month period.

"I literally would have done anything, and finally I heard the Muppets needed somebody to sew puppets. So I went over to interview wearing a dress that I had made, carrying a patchwork quilt I had sewn, and some little dolls I'd made." The job was filled, but the interviewer picked up on how much Kaplin wanted to work on the show. "Look," she said, trying to be helpful. "The only thing they can't find is writers. They're desperate. It's a very specific kind of writing: curriculum plus humor."

She told Kaplin that Stone was holding a workshop to train writers. "So I called and asked Jon if I could attend and be taught how to write for *Sesame Street.* By this time we were on a first-name basis.

"He said, 'Look, Em. You can't afford to do this; you've been in the business for years. I'm taking students out of school, paying them three peanut butter and jelly sandwiches a week.'

"I said, 'Put me on your writers workshop a couple of days a week, and then let me do production stuff the rest of the time. I don't care what I make. Just teach me to do this.'"

Stone said, "All right. Write me an Ernie and Bert bit, and a Kermit one, too."

Kaplin poured a surge of elation onto a short sheaf of typed pages. "I had never written anything before beyond an occasional letter to my mother. *Never* anything for television. But I was so motivated. And one hour later I was in front of Jon with the two bits. He was surprised to see me so fast, and said, 'All right, I'll call you tomorrow.'"

After an anxious night and morning, the phone finally rang. "Em, we read your two pieces with great care and we've decided we don't want to put you on the writers workshop," Stone said, pausing.

Kaplin recalled how her heart sank. "I thought, *Shit! What do I have to do to get on this show?*"

That's when Stone said, "Your bits can go on just as they are. They don't need a word changed. We want to put you on as a full-time writer immediately."

Persistence had paid off. "A couple of weeks later I had the incredible, life-changing thrill of going into the studio and watching Jim Henson and Frank Oz performing my words."

Kaplin remarried in 1972 and changed her name to Emily Perl Kingsley. She got the hang of writing for Kermit, the wry observer of foible and calamity. Throughout the '70s, she and others on the writing staff capitalized on the frog's ability to somehow rise above madness—while stationed squarely in the midst of it—by creating a journalistic guise for him. Donning a trench coat and fedora, Kermit, the intrepid correspondent for *Sesame Street News*, was dispatched to cover breaking stories involving fictional characters (the Invisible Man, wearing a straw hat), historical figures (Christopher Columbus pulling away from the dock in Spain, with the dock in tow), and classic fairy-tale protagonists, villains, and victims. He was on hand to cover emergency reconstructive surgery on Humpty Dumpty, hurricane-force winds puffed up by the Big, Bad Wolf, and a stalled uphill summit by a Jack without a Jill. (At the top of the bit, Kermit is caught by an open microphone confessing, "I've never understood why he goes *up* the hill to fetch a pail of water. Logically, water would be down at the bottom. . . .")

The colossal wrestling match that was taking place between Mike Dann and his conscience ended on a Saturday in mid-June 1970 when the top

CBS programming executive resigned to join a nonprofit corporation, leaving behind stock options and base pay estimated at $125,000 annually. He was poised to take a salary cut of nearly 75 percent. Writing in *Newsday*, Long Island's literate morning tab, TV critic Marvin Kitman described the development as "the old riches-to-rags story."[21]

Dann's departure from commercial TV was not completely unexpected. He had spoken often of "getting out and doing something for the betterment of the human race."[22] But on the Thursday before he quit—on Page One of *Variety*—he had denied any intention to leave CBS. *Variety* had it that "Mike Dann put the official quietus on reports he was giving up his post as program veepee at CBS by stating, 'I'm safe and sound and not looking around.'"[23]

But he was looking. Unbeknownst to all but a handful of board members and executives at Children's Television Workshop, Dann had been discussing the possibility of joining the nonprofit as a vice president and assistant to Joan Cooney, the woman he had once offered "any assistance you desire." Over the weekend, word got out that CTW envisioned an ambassadorial role for Dann, establishing *Sesame Street* adaptations and coproductions internationally. This prompted Kitman to quip, "After he sells [*Sesame Street*] in Russia and Czechoslovakia, he might try Mississippi, where it is considered too controversial for educational TV."

And so, the man who had a hand in developing *Ding Dong School* at NBC at the dawn of television, would, at age forty-eight—after twenty-one years in commercial network television—bring his native intelligence and promotional instincts to CTW. Within weeks, Dann was on the road exporting *Sesame Street*.

The global conquest began in the summer of 1970, with the announcement that thirty-eight stations affiliated with the Canadian Broadcasting Corporation would broadcast the series to English-dominant provinces. A representative of the CBC had actually made an inquiry about acquiring rights to *Sesame Street*.

Under an agreement with the Armed Forces Radio and Television Network, the first one hundred thirty episodes of *Sesame Street* were made available to children of servicemen and -women in sixteen additional countries, including Iceland, Greece, Ethiopia, and South Korea.

Dann then lined up the Caribbean nations of Bermuda, Trinidad and Tobago, Antigua, Martinique, Curaçao, Jamaica, Barbados, and Aruba. "Representatives from the various countries met in Kingston, Jamaica," Dann recalled, "school superintendants who couldn't agree on a thing, even which country should take care of sending the tapes around.

Finally, everyone agreed on Tobago. In the first years, the tapes often got lost or mutilated. Eventually, it worked out, but not without a lot of headaches."

A Mexican foothold came about after Dann negotiated a coproduction deal with Emilio Azcarraga Milmo, the principal owner of the Spanish-language entertainment colossus Televisa. This was before Azcarraga, known as "El Tigre" (the tiger), became the Rupert Murdoch of Latin America and the popularizer of the cleavage-bearing, Kleenex-honking telenovela.

"I was aggressive and I knew people around the world," Dann said. "I called someone I knew at the ABC network of Australia and made a quick sale. Then I called Benny Yoshida, a friend at NHK in Japan. At the time, they had four networks, one of them devoted to educational programming. I explained to him that *Sesame Street* was an experiment that might be copied in Japan. But I also suggested it might be used there as a way to teach English, and that I'd give it to him at a very good price. He gave me two hundred fifty thousand dollars to run the series on Japanese holidays, to fill in for regular programming. That was pretty good."

Dann tangled with representatives of Imelda Marcos over a plan to air the show in the Philippines ("She demanded a cut," he said) and insulted the French when he suggested they use a version of *Sesame Street* created in Ottawa. "What are you talking about, Mr. Dann?" a French television executive sniffed. "When we use a news clip in French from the Canadians, we use subtitles."

Dann made a pilgrimage to the Holy Land, as well. "The Israelis knew how to do *Sesame Street* better than we did," he said with a half grin. "We got into the worst fracas ever there. The religious educators said, 'Oh, you're going to make the series in Jerusalem, right? And the children are going to be wearing yarmulkes, right? And you aren't going to be shooting on the High Holidays, right?' The people in Tel Aviv? They didn't insist on yarmulkes, but they insisted we shoot the program there. Ultimately, Charles Revson put up the money to make it in Tel Aviv."

Dann conquered Germany with a coproduction titled *Sesamestrasse*. The arrangement with the NDR network was not without its culture shock, said Norton Wright, the former *Captain Kangaroo* production team member who joined CTW to work on the international productions. "Over in Germany, I kid you not, they wanted to include sex education on *Sesamestrasse*, which raised our eyebrows," Wright said. "So did their desire to include street vernacular. If there was a surprise moment in a script, the German character would say, '*Scheiss!*' which means 'shit.' Of course, we would never say 'shit' on *Sesame Street* domestic, but we had to bite our tongues with the Germans. And we never would have included sex education, either. When we used the Burt Bacharach tune 'What the World Needs Now' in an American segment, we used momma bears and bear cubs. When they did it in Germany, it was men and women embracing. Some of the trial things they did in Germany were even more specific, with body parts.

"One day at a meeting in Germany we were joined by five attractive female child development specialists, all with their doctorates . . . and all braless. This came as something of a surprise to Gerry Lesser and Ed Palmer. One said, 'Vell, Dr. Lesser, there's much to talk about with your curriculum and ours. But could you first give us your opinion about *focking*?'

"Gerry didn't miss a beat. 'I'm all for it,' he said."

On September 8, 1971, the London bureau of the Associated Press reported that Monica Sims, children's program chief for the British Broadcasting Corp., had turned thumbs-down on airing *Sesame Street* in Great Britain.[24] Describing the series as "indoctrination," Sims condemned *Sesame Street* as "a dangerous extension of the use of television." Criticizing what she characterized as the show's "authoritarian aims," Sims said, "Right answers are demanded and praised, and a research report refers to the program makers' aim to change children's behavior." At the same meeting with the British press, Sims said the BBC was purchasing two American shows: *The Further Adventures of Dr. Doolittle* and *The Harlem Globetrotters*.

ITV, Britain's other TV service, announced it would air *Sesame Street* on a London station as a thirteen-week experiment. An ITV station in Wales had screened ten episodes of *Sesame Street* in the spring of 1971 to test its suitability for children. Adult reaction was mixed. Some found it wholesome and humorous, others found it vulgar.

Eighteen months after *Hey, Cinderella* was filmed in Canada, Jim Henson's musical adaptation of the fairy tale—starring Kermit the frog and a cast of unknown actors—finally aired on a U.S. network. The success of *Sesame Street* had likely led ABC to pick up and broadcast the special.

New York Times critic Jack Gould slammed the production the morning after it ran, diminishing it as a "grotesque" modernization of a classic. He also accused Kermit of breaking faith with his PBS audience—and CTW of "cashing in" on *Sesame Street*'s success. Gould incorrectly assumed that the nonprofit had had a hand in the production. Though the creative team for *Hey, Cinderella* included Jon Stone (cowriter with Tom Whedon), Joe

Raposo (original score), Charles Rosen (set design), and puppeteers Frank Oz and Jerry Nelson, the production had wrapped in 1968, well before the team was reunited to work on *Sesame Street*.

The wise-guy Kermit of *Hey, Cinderella*—a persona significantly more sardonic than his familiar one on *Sesame Street*—provided the lead-in to commercials for the special. This set off Gould, who accused the frog's handlers of compromising the character's integrity. He was speaking for the home viewer when he raised objections about one of the most visible stars of public television suddenly surfacing as an amphibious pitchman for cigarettes on the home screen. As Kermit, himself, might have said, what the hey?

Two days after the review appeared, Henson defended CTW—and his puppet—in a letter to Gould.

April 13, 1970
Dear Mr. Gould:

In your April 11 review of our special, *Hey, Cinderella*, you made an erroneous assumption, which I believe it is important to correct.

Because there were several people from the *Sesame Street* staff involved in the production of this special, you inferred that they, and Kermit, the frog, who is very close to my heart, were capitalizing on the success of *Sesame Street* and had sold out to commercialism.

Kermit, the frog, is a Muppet I made over ten years ago and have used on many network shows and commercials. For the past ten or twelve years, approximately half my income has been derived from producing Muppet commercials. These have most often been for adult products, as most of my work has historically been adult.

However, since the advent of *Sesame Street*, and my own interest and concern for children's television (I am an enthusiastic member of Action for Children's Television), I have become a great deal more selective, and have turned down many lucrative offers that seemed to be trying to capitalize on *Sesame Street*. R. J. Reynolds, the sponsor of *Hey, Cinderella*, and its agency were quite respectful of my feelings on this and agreed that Kermit, the frog, and Rufus, a dog puppet who has also appeared on *Sesame Street*, would not be promoted or merchandised in any way that would link them to a commercial product.

The Children's Television Workshop is a very dedicated group of people who function with the highest sense of integrity. To mistakenly attribute a motive of exploitation to these people is not only insulting but potentially quite damaging to the job they are doing.

As for myself, I don't intend to leave commercial television. This is where the Muppets and I have worked for many years, and it is the income from commercial TV that makes my participation in educational TV possible.

What I will try to do is what I have tried to do on *Sesame Street* this season, that is, to work with a degree of integrity and responsibility to the children of the country.

Yours truly,

Jim Henson

As these controversies swirled, Joan Cooney gave her creative team extraordinary latitude and support, only once summarily reversing a decision. After learning during the test-show period that Gordon and Susan were to be unmarried romantic partners, she called in Dave Connell, Jon Stone, and Sam Gibbon and demanded change. "I said, 'Good Lord, marry them!'" Cooney recalled. "They're clearly mommy and daddy on the show. Why not model a sound marriage for our target viewers?"

Stone scribbled furiously on a pad. Gibbon nodded. Connell remained outwardly placid but his gut churned. Cooney had violated her promise to always approach him first with a complaint, and never to undermine his authority. He didn't speak to her for a week afterward.

"I certainly was involved in the decision that Susan was going to be a housewife," Cooney said. "We wanted to model two evolved adults who behaved like parents, and were involved in the community even though they did not have a child at the time. Gordon was a teacher and involved in the community. Susan was a homemaker." Little was made of the fact that they were co-owners of the brownstone, landlords to Bert and Ernie.

A small but vocal chorus of white feminists was rankled by the portrayal of Susan, whom they saw as a subservient, powerless dispenser of milk and cookies. At first, their displeasure was privately shared, in barbed letters to Cooney and her producers. But then members of the National Organization for Women took their dispute public after season one, threatening a boycott of General Foods, which had pledged corporate support to outreach programs for *Sesame Street*.

The antagonism came to a head in April 1972, when Cooney wrote to NOW president Wilma Scott Heide.[25] Though dipped in the honey of business-etiquette prose, it was a bee's nest of a rebuttal. Here are some highlights:

- "Happy as I am to hear from you and other members of NOW about the importance of the feminist movement and the portrayal of females on TV, I can't help but be reminded of the story about Clare Boothe Luce visiting the pope and his being overheard to say, 'But Mrs. Luce, I already am a Catholic.' To summarize, I am with you.

"However, Ms. Anne Grant West's threatening letter to General Foods last year and her recent threatening and offensive letter to Jon Stone and me really set the feminist cause back in this organization. . . Such threats and the recent letter-writing campaign only cause a counterreaction that I must work very hard to dispel, and it seems a waste of energy."

- "I don't know how useful it is to look at *Sesame Street* solely through feminist eyes when clearly it is trying to do a number of things for young children. . . . We consider our primary aim of reaching and teaching the disadvantaged child a life and death matter, for education determines whether these disadvantaged youngsters enter the economic mainstream of American life or not.

"While I certainly don't object to having our faults pointed out to us (and God knows, everyone is doing it), I wonder if NOW is really performing a service by concentrating so much public attention and energy on one of the few really decent programs for young children on television. Perhaps you are not aware that preschool children watch up to eight hours a day and that the number of badly sexist commercials and situation comedies they are exposed to during that time is not to be believed. Further, I don't know of a single cartoon that is popular with children that portrays females as other than dopey, meddling, and objects of ridicule. Shouldn't NOW begin to address itself to the male-dominated media of commercial TV and advertising that have created this situation on TV and which brainwashes children day in and day out, year in and year out?"

- "I continue to be disturbed by the strong belief held by some prominent whites, as well as blacks, that the feminist movement, and NOW in particular, is displaying anti-black attitudes. In a recent letter to me, Ms. Anne C. Hall said: 'The majority of NOW members that I have discussed *Sesame Street* with feel that change has not occurred as fast as they would like to see, and the program has shown greater responsiveness to the needs of blacks than women . . .'"

- "Perhaps Ms. Hall is not aware that *Sesame Street* was funded to serve the needs of disadvantaged children in this country, with particular emphasis in the inner city poor. Naturally, then, their needs come first, though I see no conflict between their needs and feminist goals on *Sesame Street*. We acknowledge that we can and should change our portrayal of women and girls on *Sesame Street,* but we don't like to see the issue cast in racial terms nor compared with the nightmare of racism and poverty. And, certainly, our Black staff—men and women—harbor resentments against the feminist movement when it speaks in such terms, making it more difficult for us to achieve our mutual aims."

It wasn't just angry feminists that were challenging CTW. Evelyn Davis was ambushed by enraged Hispanic activists one morning in San Antonio, where the outreach director had hardly expected such a welcome when she and her staff arranged to meet with Hispanic leaders from across the country. Texas seemed a logical midpoint for the gathering, though the majority of participants were West Coast residents. "I kept asking the person who was working on it for me, 'Are you sure there are no problems? What's their agenda?'"

CTW had received a grant from the Department of Education to produce translations of *Sesame Street* in Spanish. As a provision of the award, the Workshop had to formally evaluate the program with the Hispanic community and plan for the following television season.

After being assured the meeting would pose no unforeseen challenges, Davis rounded up a large contingent of representatives from production, research, and outreach. All went cordially during an opening-night reception. "The CTW people said, 'Oh, this is wonderful,'" Davis recalled. "But when we got to the meeting site the next morning at nine, the doors were locked! Someone came out and told me that they wanted to delay the meeting. They were going to caucus first, saying, 'We don't know each other very well. So we'd like to meet. We'll call you when we're ready.'

"I thought, *Okay, that seemed logical.* They were caucusing to get a common agenda among themselves. In those days, Puerto Ricans and Chicanos and all the different groups didn't talk to each other that much. So in order to face the enemy, they needed a common voice. They had to straighten out a lot of stuff among themselves, which took all day. They wouldn't let us in, all evening and all the next day. By the end of the second day they called me to say they wanted to speak to Joan Ganz Cooney.

"'I'm representing her,' I said.

"'We're not going to talk to you. We will only talk with her.'

"I said, 'You'll have to tell me what this is about.'

"Then they started making demands. They would not listen [and] they would not talk with me.

"'You might as well go home,' they said. 'We're not going to talk with anybody here.'

"They called the press in and I called Joan and Bob Hatch and told them what was developing. Hatch's recommendation was that Joan shouldn't talk to them. It became very incendiary, and the phone calls were flying back and forth. I would transmit their demands to Joan, and I'd get responses back from them, unacceptable, totally. It ended up in their demanding a meeting in New York at CTW's expense to talk about their demands. Joan agreed to that.

"I told those making the demands that there wouldn't have been a meeting if it hadn't been for me. I was angry because they did not recognize that.

"'What are you doing?' I asked them. 'I am trying to bring you in, and you're shutting me out, acting like I'm the enemy.'"

The New York meeting in Cooney's office was "a virtual sit-in," she said. "They screamed and yelled a lot."

The protests were not only legitimate—*Sesame Street* had made no initial effort to include an Hispanic character, human or otherwise—but they were timely.

"No agency in the government was focusing then on the needs of the bilingual community," Davis said. "This was after the [civil rights movement] riots, so the question was 'How are we going to keep the black folks quiet?' The Latinos were saying, 'Well, we didn't riot and we have even less. We're being totally left out and we are not going to be left out anymore.' *Sesame Street* was seen as something dear to all children. All segments of the population thought they needed to be represented, and that their children had needs that should be addressed. And since the money was initially federal, they thought they had a right to insist upon inclusion.

"CTW did become sensitive to those needs as a company after that, and try to adjust to them. The amount of noise made a difference. Sometimes that's the only way to get someone's attention."

Within a few months after the launch of *Sesame Street*, Lloyd Morrisett called Joan Cooney. "Start talking about developing a reading program. You've got to do a second show."

"I wanted to say, 'Give me a break,'" Cooney recalled, "but Lloyd was right. We had to get going on something new while we had momentum." Ever politically astute and savvy about the ebb and flow of federal funding, Morrisett took dead aim at a surefire topic: First Lady Patricia Nixon's pet project, the Right to Read program. Morrisett lined up his contacts and connections, just as he had for *Sesame Street*.

"Sid Marland was by then Commissioner of Education, and then became undersecretary of HEW for education," Cooney said. "Sid was a friend of Lloyd's and became a friend of mine. So the government, via Sid Marland, said, 'Fine, more money.'"

Some seven million dollars was ultimately raised for CTW's reading project, bankrolled once again by the Carnegie and Ford foundations and the USOE. Under the guidance of top reading experts, a curriculum was researched and tested, and a content team, led by executive producer Dave Connell, producer Sam Gibbon, and associate producer Naomi Foner was convened.[26] Foner worked alongside head writer Tom Whedon, whose son Joss later created television's delectably demonic *Buffy the Vampire Slayer*.

Fierce debate attended the curriculum seminars for the series, as academic advisers—including Harvard's Jeanne Chall—argued the merits of using phonics to teach reading over the whole-word method. "We avoided a buzz saw of ideology by saying it was a *remedial* program, not a show to teach reading from the beginning. It was for viewers age seven to nine who were having trouble," Cooney said. "That gave us maximum freedom."

Lightning struck twice. *The Electric Company*, with a cast that included Bill Cosby, Rita Moreno, and Morgan Freeman, was an instant hit. "We were so scared the press would say, 'It's fine, but it's not *Sesame Street*,'" recalled Cooney. "But nobody said that."

Critics hailed the new show's conceit of using sketch comedy to explore the rudiments of reading, with such recurring characters as Easy Reader (a rail-thin Freeman as a hipster who can't resist reading), Otto the director (Moreno as a Hollywood tyrant who enjoyed punctuating things on the set with a riding crop), and Fargo North, Decoder (Skip Hinnant as a slightly dense detective who unscrambles text).

The soap opera parody, *Love of Chair*, always ended with the question, "And what about Naomi?" an oblique reference to the show's associate producer.

"At the time, I found the show kind of tasteless," Cooney said. "Some of the sketches worked and some were, as we say, kind of eggy. You sat there during a sketch and waited for the payoff, but the payoff wasn't very good. I was used to sweet little *Sesame Street*, and not at all used to the sensibility of seven- to nine-year-olds. But Dave, Sam, and Naomi understood who it was for."

So did Whedon. "Dave Connell was at first reluctant, but I convinced him that nothing is funnier to a nine-year-old boy than a guy in a gorilla suit," Whedon said. Enter Paul the Gorilla, a student of language and an upright citizen. Paul provided ample evidence that Darwinism sometimes goes backward.

In time, Cooney came around to appreciate the ape shtick. "I now think *Electric Company* was more brilliant than *Sesame Street* in its way," she says.

"By 1972, we had plenty of money for *Sesame Street* and then plenty of money for *Electric Company*," Cooney said. "Sid Marland couldn't have been more supportive. I remember calling his office one day. Their grant wasn't due for a few weeks, and I left word that we would have to borrow a million dollars to make it through. There was a check the next day for one million dollars. He said to his people, 'Why should they be paying interest on a loan? Let's advance it.' We were the darling of the federal government for a brief period of two or three years.

"But then the Nixon administration moved against public television. They wanted public television not to do public affairs. They were really trying to put it almost out of business. They wanted it to become local only. So PBS was in a chronic fight with the Nixon administration. I remember one of the Nixon hatchet men said to me, and I'll never forget how he said it, '*This* president does not want any federally funded programming of any kind.' They weren't anti–*Sesame Street*. They were anti the principle.

"We were largely federally funded, which was very dangerous. You get into government spending deadlines, how much you can spend per night in a hotel, and so forth, if you are a hundred percent funded. I remember fourteen-hour days. I went home exhausted every night. I was sometimes woozy walking out. It wasn't clear how we would make it through. We had almost no problems getting CTW started and getting *Sesame Street* and *Electric Company* on the air. Then, suddenly, we had enemies, all these powerful forces were against us and wanted to see us curbed. I couldn't believe it. It disoriented me. The argument was, 'Why don't you put your shows into repeat? Your audience graduates.' Unassailable. But we knew that every show that goes into repeats dies.

"On the other hand, by then we were a powerhouse in this country, and I had become an assault weapon. The potential of my having a press conference and explaining that the government would not support *Sesame Street* was always hanging over the government. Bob Hatch understood that. He had decided early to let the press build me up, saying, 'If that's what the press wants, we'll make her strong enough so it's very hard for the government to take her on.' I did become a singular weapon in the 1970s, when we were under assault by the Corporation for Public Broadcasting and the government was trying to pull their funding out.

"You couldn't understand what was going on and what the motives were. So Lloyd and I went to see Caspar Weinberger, who was secretary of HEW. He was not very forthcoming, and I think he was probably caught up in politics.

"So I went to see Barry Goldwater. He had known my family in Arizona. I told him that we would phase out federal funding, that we would do a six-year program where at some point *Electric Company* would go into repeats. CTW's costs would slowly descend, and product income would rise. So that by 1980 or 1981 we would be free and clear. He did not take a note, and he did not have an aide in the room. He then wrote a letter to Weinberger saying exactly what I'd told him. He wrote:

> Dear Cappy,
>   Joan Ganz Cooney has explained to me what she wants, her father being one of my oldest friends and constituents . . .

"My father had been dead many years, but Goldwater did it ambiguously so you could think that he was still alive," Cooney said. He said, in effect, 'Give little Joanie Ganz anything she wants.'

"In addition to Barry's letter, Caroline Charles, one of the really major women board members of PBS, got wind of what was happening and contacted Weinberger. At HEW they said, 'Some old lady in San Francisco got in touch with Cap and that's all there was to it.' So Cappy then took Barry's letter and our request and said, 'We will do it their way.' "

CTW got its own line item in the federal budget, which enraged some supporters in Washington at the Office of Education and the hierarchy of PBS, but relieved tensions in New York for Cooney and Morrisett.

Chapter Fifteen

The first season of *Sesame Street* raised the curtain on a new kind of television program for kids, and by the mid-1970s, the show was in full flower, with a huge cast of creative, dedicated people working to continually tweak, adjust, and experiment. Over the course of the next ten years, the series became much more than its originators had ever hoped it could be. *Sesame Street* became an American institution.

In any city or town in America, you could see children with Ernie dolls riding along in their strollers. At local parks, toddlers wearing Bert T-shirts were shooting down the aluminum slide. Record stores featured the cast album. Turn on a prime-time special, and damn if it wasn't Caroll Spinney as Big Bird, riffing with Bob Hope.

The show had critics aplenty, but the American people had spoken, and what they said was, "Me like Cookie!"

Followed, of course, by *"Umm num-num-num-num."*

The Production Team

The man who did the navigation through those early years was Jon Stone.

The show's puppeteers, cameramen, and Teamsters thought of him as one of their own because his manner and work ethic were right out of Brooklyn. But when the situation required it, he could ditch his blue collar for a starched one and emerge as polished and well-mannered as any other graduate of Williams and Yale. Celebrities in the studio for guest appearances found him a welcoming and warm host, who invariably brought out the best in them.

Stone was to CTW what Orson Welles was to the Mercury Theatre on the Air in the 1930s. The future film auteur might have been surrounded by studio talent, including Mercury cofounder John Houseman, during his radio days, but it was Welles's presence and bearing, his vision and vitality, that elevated the radio theater company's performance to the level of art. So it was with Stone, who gave *Sesame Street* its soul.

Stone realized that in Jim Henson and Joe Raposo he had two grand masters as collaborators, men who were much celebrated—and handsomely compensated—for their contributions to *Sesame Street*. Stone, entirely unknown to the press and viewing public, was every bit their equal creatively. His influence on their work was as generous as it was anonymous. "Jon was the father of *Sesame Street*, the key for everything," said Frank Oz. "He was the one in the control room laughing and guiding us along during all the playing around and rehearsing. Once in a while someone would say, 'What are we teaching?' And Jon would say, 'Who cares? We're having fun.' What he meant was that imagination and fun is as valuable as anything else. Fucking around [in the studio] was the key to *Sesame Street*. It allowed for that affectionate anarchy that Jim reveled in."

As a producer, Stone was a fair-minded judge of talent. In an age when top production jobs were denied women, Stone evinced gender bias of a different sort. He actively sought ways to hire and promote capable women, sometimes even at the expense of capable men. The product of his enlightened policies provided *Sesame Street* with a seamless succession of top-flight women in the studio and elsewhere behind the scenes in production, many of whom went on to become the architects of the boom in children's programming at Nickelodeon, the Disney Channel, and PBS in the 1990s and 2000s.

The grand marshal of this parade of progress was Dulcy Singer, who ultimately rose to become the first female executive producer of *Sesame Street* and a magnificent mentor of her own. "I never found a glass ceiling at the Workshop," Singer said. "Jon encouraged me, forever told me that I underrated myself. And I was not the only person he did that with. One thing that helped was I certainly was never competitive with him, and I never wanted to top him. I was only too happy to assist him. It's why we got along so well. Jon instilled it. He hired great people who took pride in their work."

Singer came to *Sesame Street* at the age of thirty-five, following the series of promotions and transfers that were triggered by the development of *The Electric Company* in 1971. When Dave Connell and Sam Gibbon went off to work on the new show, Stone moved up to executive producer at *Sesame Street*, the position he had backed away from in 1969.

A 1955 graduate of Mount Holyoke College, Singer grew up in a theatrical household. Her father, producer Louis J. Singer, introduced Tennessee Williams's *Glass Menagerie* to New York audiences in 1945, followed by many more Broadway successes produced with his partner, Eddie Dowling.

Singer spent three of her college summers working at the Westport Country Playhouse, the storied red-barn theater in suburban Connecticut. "The first summer I was an apprentice. The second I worked in the box office. The third I was the assistant stage manager."

Soon after earning her degree in English, Singer applied for work at CBS in Manhattan. Just as Stone's first job in television was answering *Captain Kangaroo's* mail, part of Dulcy Singer's initial responsibilities at CBS was to answer fans of *The Garry Moore Show*, a daytime variety program starring the congenial entertainer and game-show host. "We had these printed cards to send that would include a personal note from Garry . . . that I wrote," she said. "It would be like, 'Thanks so much for the nifty argyles.' I used to go home at night and practice his handwriting."

Singer said, "I just wanted a job that was fun and paid the rent. I had no ambition back then, and I never for a minute thought I'd even become a producer."

When the show jumped to a Tuesday night prime-time spot in 1958, she was assigned to coordinate research for *That Wonderful Year*, a long segment that celebrated the highlights of a year in comedy and song. When Moore's show was canceled in 1964, Singer signed on as a production assistant for the venerable daytime drama *The Secret Storm*.

In 1966, a revamped *Garry Moore Show* returned to prime time, and Singer became the host's personal secretary. "He was a lovely, easy man, and a mentor to many performers who went on to become stars," she said. "It was through Garry that I got into public television. He wanted to be the host of PBL and asked me to go with him to the studio to be his secretary. Garry didn't get the job, but the producer later called me to ask if I'd like to work at PBL." She rose there to the level of associate producer.

When PBL folded after two years, Singer was doing production assistant work when Tom Kennedy gauged Singer's interest in working for CTW.

"I said '*Ugh*.' I really wasn't interested in working on a children's show," she recalled, "but when I came back from [a trip to] Europe I spoke with someone at a party about *Sesame Street*, and called Tom to say I was interested."

What she saw convinced her more than what was said. "During my interview, Dave Connell and Sam Gibbon showed me the pilot, and what appealed to me was that it was essentially a comedy-variety show that children could understand. That, and the fact that it was double-level entertainment, that adults could enjoy it. I saw that it was so much more than a children's show."

Connell and Gibbon hired Singer as an assistant to the producer. "It was just a title," Singer said. "I was a PA in the studio." But from her very first few days, Stone picked up on her quiet competence and ability to anticipate and ward off problems. Stone later told her that he'd noticed that whenever she was around, "the right props and other things would appear miraculously, even before he would ask for them."

That began a relationship that lasted for twenty years, with Stone and Singer forging an extraordinary professional bond based on trust and mutual respect.

Of all the cutups from the annals of the *Sesame Street* crew, and they are legion, the O'Brien brothers were tops. How many productions could boast that their stage managers had danced on the vaudeville stage with female Siamese twins? Or claimed to have romanced the same woman in a hotel room one night, switching on and off by means of a pass-through? Or who worked with Abbott and Costello, Howard Cosell, a bevy of Miss America titleholders, and Mr. Aloysius Snuffleupagus?

But more than merely being spinners of show-business tales, Chet and Snooks were among the best backstage pros in show business. Chet, *Sesame*'s longtime stage manager, played a critically important role in the first seasons of the series, when cast and crew were pumping out the live-action elements for two sixty-minute shows every three days. It was Chet who broke down every episode into component parts, arranging them in an order for maximum efficiency and lowest cost.

"I remember the storyboard panels Chet prepared at home," said Brian Garfield, a nephew. "First, he'd list all the scenes in weeks to come. They were taped out of sequence, as the Muppets were only available for a certain number of days each month. All of their segments had to be taped at once. Guest stars sometimes were scheduled to appear on various shows, all of which had to be taped on the same day. Chet brought home the scripts for an entire arc, which was a season or a significant part of a season. He used them to draw boards showing virtually every shot and setup. He appended lists of all required props and personnel for each one. They were done in various colors. He then figured out the arrangement in which the setups needed to be shot, so as to make the most efficient use of (and to avoid wasting the time of) everybody concerned. He'd arrive at work amazingly prepared. I have the feeling that his system cut the time and complications by somewhere between fifty and ninety percent before they even started taping." Jon Stone, who prized efficiency as a director and producer, was well served by O'Brien methods and manner.

"Chet genuinely liked people," Garfield added. "He had good things to say about nearly everyone, and he was genuinely kind to people. He loved his work and wasn't ambitious to move up in the world. Quite often, a former subordinate would become his boss. He didn't step on anyone on the way up. And therefore few people felt they had reason to step on him."

O'Brien, a patient and encouraging mentor, took a shine to Lisa Simon, a Hunter College night student who by day looked after the children who were brought in to appear on *Sesame Street*. "Chet—and later, Snooks—were incredibly knowledgeable about the craft and skill of putting on a show," Simon said. "They knew how to run a studio, how to organize, how to treat people. They were just masters at making people feel welcome and involved. They not only knew how to do things the right way, they talked about it and taught you how to do it. The pervading atmosphere was, 'Stick around. You can watch and then try it.'"

Simon, who became a protégée of not only the O'Briens but also Jon Stone and Dulcy Singer, would become one of *Sesame Street*'s first home-grown masters of the craft of kid entertainment, starting at the babysitter bottom and rising to become one of the premiere directors of children's television.

"It was a remarkable group of people to learn from," she said.

If laughter is the universal lubricant, the O'Briens provided it by the gallon.

"Sometimes when they appeared onstage they did a routine where Snooks played the piano and Chet danced," said Garfield. "The routine usually began with Snooks sitting down at the piano and moving his head slowly side to side, while he searched the keyboard.

Eventually Chet said. "What are you doing?"

Snooks replied, "I've never played this piano before. I'm searching for middle C."

If Joan Ganz Cooney was queen of CTW's domain, Chris Cerf was its minister of mirth and high priest of the practical joke. Son of a famous wit and pals with the *National Lampoon* set, Cerf approached a joke the way Michelangelo approached marble.

Cerf's most memorable stunt was developed over long weeks of painstaking work, all toward the goal of convincing Cooney that her worst corporate nightmare was about to come true.

With coconspirators Frank Oz, Joe Raposo, and Danny Epstein, Cerf planned an elaborate ruse that would supposedly herald the launch of a new product bearing the likeness of Cookie Monster and the *Sesame Street* logo. This would be no book, record, or toy, nothing of educational value, as policy dictated. Rather, this product would represent a striking departure from those dictates.

The forked-tailed boy inside Cerf's head prompted him to imagine Joan Cooney's reaction when she was presented with a steaming platter of *Sesame Street* kielbasa, served in her own office by waiters who would arrive with an oompah band dressed in lederhosen and Tyrolean hats with feathers.

The first step in the ruse came after Cerf had Raposo write and record a jingle for the sausage, with Oz chiming in as Cookie Monster. A tape was sent to Cooney's office. "Somebody played it for me," she said. "There was the voice of Cookie Monster advertising a kielbasa place out on Long Island. It was definitely a local commercial, and I couldn't understand how our people got involved in this commercial business. I was going crazy trying to get to the bottom of it. Who were these people out on the Island?"

Cerf paid for custom-designed shrink-wrap labels for some sausages, packaging that had a likeness of everyone's favorite ravenous Muppet, saying, "It better than cookie!" He arranged for a delivery. "These people sent crates of kielbasa!" Cooney said. "I was so upset."

To add to the mystery, Cerf had a fake print-ad campaign worked up, complete with mock-ups for billboards. Word of this began to circulate among horrified CTW executives, especially the humorless suits in legal affairs and accounting, Cerf's favorite targets.

And, finally, it was time for product launch. "Into my office came Joe Raposo leading a five-piece Polish band," Cooney said. Cerf had also arranged for the completely bogus owner-operator of the Polish Imperial Kielbasa Factory to phone in, just to thank Cooney for the grand opportunity to bring to market a kielbasa that would make kids beg for more.

The legend of the kielbasa caper grows with each passing year. In some versions, Cooney was fooled right up until the last minute, enraged that the imbeciles she hired had failed to protect the *Sesame Street* brand. "She was ripped," insists oompah drummer Epstein, who arranged for the faux radio commercial recording session. "When she was let in on the joke she said, 'Get out! I ought to fire every last one of you!'"

Another, perhaps more credible version goes like this: Fearing that her boss would succumb to stress, Cooney's assistant clued her in to the joke on the day of the reveal. "All she said was, 'I'm afraid you're going to have a heart attack if you don't understand this is a joke.' No one told me any details. I didn't know that they were going to burst into my office with this band. I just remember that it was the most well-executed, detailed practical joke imaginable," she said.

The Cast

Sonia Manzano recalled riding on the Third Avenue elevated train as a child in the 1950s, gazing at the posted advertisements overhead. "I asked my older sister what the ads said, and she encouraged me to figure it out, saying, 'Why don't you just try reading it?' It had never occurred to me that reading is everywhere, that it's something everyone does. I found that I could read the ads, and I learned how smoking was good for you and how wonderful it was to be in a Maidenform bra."

Manzano's laughter spills out from a small office at Sesame Workshop, her creative home for all but five years of her adult life. Clearly, time has been her ally. As she approaches age sixty, her skin is smooth, her body fit, and her vibe joyously youthful. Often in television, an actor's stage persona is at odds with his or her off-camera personality, at times even diametrically opposed.

But Manzano, the actress, and Maria, the character she has portrayed for so long, are hardly distinguishable. That Manzano grew up in a Puerto Rican neighborhood not unlike the one Charles Rosen had in mind when he designed the *Sesame Street* set suggests that she may have been born to the part.

"The Bronx is where I learned about life," she said. "My mother was a seamstress and my father was a day laborer who put tar on roofs. They met in this country, having come to New York in the 1940s when the first group of Puerto Rican immigrants came from the island. My mother told me that she used to learn sewing terms phonetically so she could go to work the next day and ask for thread or seam binding or scissors. That's how she learned English. My parents were poor and in the odd position of being American citizens that didn't speak the language. They weren't welcome in the United States, in the mainland, anyway, but they prevailed, like most immigrants."

Over time, she said, the Manzanos became bilingual, thanks, in part, to television. "TV was a big influence on my life. I saw this black-and-white world and I used to wonder where I would fit in. It was all Dick and Jane, and you never saw the inner city or immigrants, which was all I knew. I remember one teacher would tell her fourth grade class of Puerto Rican kids, 'There are white people, there are black people, and there are yellow people.' One kid said, 'Well, what about brown people?' And she said 'There is no such thing as brown people.' I remember thinking later, *How can we be expected to contribute to a world that doesn't even see us?*

"My parents used to take us to the beach with our neighbors. We were just so *different* from everybody else. My mother would make huge amounts of rice and beans and chicken and coffee. Everybody else at the beach was having a peanut butter and jelly sandwich. And you'd watch the other people and then you'd see what your parents were doing and want to fit in. I learned the difference between race and culture on one of these trips. We used to go with this Puerto Rican woman who was black. Once, when I came out of the water, I went up to a person who I thought was this neighbor, asking for a towel in Spanish. The woman turned around and said to me in an African American southern accent, 'Child, I don't know what you saying!' It dawned on me that day that there's a difference between race and culture."

Manzano's performing talent evidenced itself in junior high, around the time she wrote an adaptation of *Oliver Twist* for the drama club. "This particular teacher said, 'If you stay in this neighborhood, you'll go to the local high school and you won't reach your potential.'

"And, of course, I didn't know what he was talking about. He then said, 'You should try to go to the High School of Performing Arts in Manhattan. You'll meet people and broaden your horizons.' He picked the monologue for me, helped me memorize it, and took me to the audition. I went from being an A student in the ghetto to a failing student in a middle-class school. Very little is expected of ghetto kids; I used to paint my nails and do my makeup in school. So when I went to Performing Arts, I had to compete with kids who knew what a noun was. I plummeted, but I recognized that my only way to get into college was on acting, something that had nothing to do with grades. So once again I studied monologues and got into Carnegie Mellon University. Society was on my side; it was the Kennedy years, a time when universities wanted to diversify. I was going to college in '68, a great time to come of age."

One morning, as she passed a television in the student union tuned to *Sesame Street*, she simultaneously glimpsed her past and future. "I saw Susan and Gordon on the stoop and I said, 'Hey! That's my street! That's my stoop! That's my construction doors! I know that place!' "

That she was momentarily stopped in her tracks adds a note of irony to the story of how a multitalented Latina got to *Sesame Street*. The door opened for her only after fellow Hispanic Americans banged and pushed on it.

At Carnegie Mellon, Manzano joined the original cast of *Godspell*, which began as a student production on that campus. When the musical, based on the gospel according to Saint Matthew, moved to New York for a two-week, ten-performance run at the La MaMa Experimental

Theater Club in Greenwich Village (also known as Café La Mama), Manzano took a leave from the university, then dropped out, to continue on as
the character Sonia, the sassy, sexy, cynical urbanite.

"I was with the show for a year and a half when it was off-Broadway.
Then two years later I went into the show again when it was on Broadway.
I still dream about being in *Godspell*, of having to do it with a new company. It was a great time in my life. I now know the euphoric feeling of
being in a creative role, when you just can't think of anything else but what
you're doing. *Godspell* was the first time it had happened to me."

In 1971, an agent encouraged Manzano to audition for *Sesame Street*.
She immediately recalled how impressed she was that James Earl Jones had
appeared in early episodes. "I walked by the student union [television] one
day and he was reciting the alphabet. It was around the time he had done
The Great White Hope on Broadway. He was thin and very bald and so
compelling, and the letters were flashing on the screen as he said the ABCs.
It was so in-your-face, it just grabbed me by the neck.

"Then I saw Susan and Gordon on the stoop. At that time there were
no people of color on television, and if there were, they certainly weren't
nice. Susan and Gordon were so friendly and cheerful and there was Mr.
Hooper, you know, nice Jewish candy store guy just like the guy in my
old neighborhood. I was just thrilled by this show, and I thought it was
hilarious."

Manzano auditioned in Jon Stone's office. "I walked in wearing a simple little dress and some cheap Indian sandals. Jon showed me a set of
circles, and he asked me to explain why two things were the same and one
was not, just like that song on the show 'One of these things is not like the
others, / one of these things just doesn't belong.' Then he asked me to tell
a scary story, like somebody was following me. And then I left. Today, it
could not happen that way. You would have a casting committee to audition an actress. But Jon had such vision; he knew what the show was, he
didn't have to ask anybody what they thought. He didn't have to have data,
he didn't have to have a chart that said this is what kids want to watch. It
was one guy."

Stone, who had seen Manzano in the Broadway version of *Godspell*,
gave her the part with little guidance on how to play Maria. "I wanted to
know what kind of character she was, and Jon kept saying, 'We want you
to be yourself. We want the kid on the Lower East Side to look at you and
say, "That's me." '

"One time the costume designer put me in a pleated skirt and knee
socks and a little vest; I looked like a coed. And I had makeup. Jon, who

was a passionate, short-tempered man, came on the set and was furious. He grabbed me, we went into the makeup room and I sat down in the makeup chair. He said to the makeup artist, 'God damn it! I go through all this trouble to cast real people and you make her look like a Kewpie doll.' Well, the makeup artist was very nervous and she starts taking off my makeup. And I'm looking in the mirror and I'm realizing that, this is my position on the show, to be myself, to be real, to talk the way I talk, to dress the way I dress. This is why I got cast. It was like, '*Ding!* Got it.'"

Perhaps the most telling statement one could make about Northern Calloway is that early in his acting career he appeared in a play entitled *The Me Nobody Knows.*

The piece was a stage adaptation of a book compiled by an inner-city schoolteacher in New York, who turned samples of student prose into a powerful anthology of anguish. At age twenty-one, Calloway was the oldest cast member of the racially and ethnically mixed cast, doing six performances a week at the off-Broadway Orpheum Theatre in 1970. Calloway, who grew up on 151st Street in Harlem, beat the odds, purely on the basis of talent. He demonstrated so much promise at Fiorello H. LaGuardia High School of Music & Arts and Performing Arts, where he was Sonia Manzano's classmate, that he was working with the Lincoln Center Repertory Company within two days of graduation in 1966. His work in *The Me Nobody Knows* provided a brief moment to look back to the conditions of his youth while he was ascending into what he hoped would be a better life and stardom.

No one seemed better destined for the bright lights than Calloway, who was the understudy to Ben Vereen in the stage musical *Pippin.* "He was ballsy," Manzano said. "Northern was not a trained dancer, but he was a showman. I remember him saying to me, 'The only thing that I can't do that Ben Vereen does is three twirls at once. I can only do two.' That took a lot of chutzpah."

Puppeteer Marty Robinson caught a performance of *Pippin* when Calloway was playing the lead role. "This guy was flying out there, just floating on the stage with no relationship with gravity whatsoever," Robinson said. "He was just stunning."

After seeing him perform in *The Me Nobody Knows,* Jon Stone hired Calloway in 1971 to take on the new role of David, a kid from the neighborhood who helps out Mr. Hooper. To castmates and crew, the new arrival gave off mostly warm and positive vibes. The camera loved him.

Within weeks of working together on the show, Manzano and Calloway, as Maria and David, began gravitating to each other, as two attractive young people might. Soon, subtle signals indicated that the Latina and black characters were an item. Anyone watching at the time would have concluded that romance was blooming on *Sesame Street*.

"The producers took some heat for that, but they stuck to their guns," said Loretta Long, "just as they did with the viewers who objected to Matt and I wearing Afros." Long found Calloway to be brimming with talent and more than once danced "The Hustle" with him at social gatherings in the early days. "He was a positive young black image that little kids related to very well," she said. "He was like a teenager, and little kids want to stick to teenagers like gum on a shoe."

Over time, Long said she noticed Calloway was prone to mood swings and was warned to steer clear of him. "Apparently, he had issues with black women, stemming back to problems with his sister. But performers can be nuts, all right. Our cast was like family, but when you live with people long enough you know who to leave alone and who to tease. When you walk in the makeup room you can see by the look on their face whether to mess with them or leave them alone. So, basically, I left Northern alone. And I tried never to be around him when he started in on his thing about if he was white he'd be a major star. That's the way he felt."

Emilio Delgado was down to his final unemployment check, adding gasoline to the tank twenty-five cents at a time, on the summer day in 1971 when he was to meet Jon Stone at the Beverly Wilshire Hotel.

"My former wife was working, but I wasn't," he said, "and we had a son who was a year-and-a-half old." Delgado had already met with Dave Connell a few weeks prior about a new Hispanic character that would be added to *Sesame Street* for the upcoming season. Meeting with Stone in Beverly Hills was a callback, of sorts. Delgado has said that he was uncertain how Connell and Stone had come to be aware of him, speculating that they may have seen a tape of him on *Angie's Garage*, a weekly children's show in Los Angeles.

"It was a homegrown show on the local ABC affiliate," Delagado said. "I was its cohost and I'd play a little guitar and sing. I'd started acting professionally in 1968, but for nine years before that I had been trying to knock doors down in Los Angeles to get in," Delgado said. "In the sixties, there weren't that many opportunities for Chicanos and Latinos in film and television, other than playing banditos, gang members, low-life characters, and sleepy Mexicans under a cactus. But I was a part of several groups of Chicanos and Latinos that came together to protest that. We were meeting with producers and directors and big honchos in Hollywood, telling them, 'You've got to look at us as people. There are doctors and teachers in our community, but we are not being represented that way.'"

When Delgado sat down with Stone, a surprising interview ensued. "I didn't sing for him or act or do anything but answer questions and be myself. He interviewed me for about twenty minutes and said, 'If you want to work for us, be in New York on October eleventh.' I said to myself, *Oh my God! They want me! I have a job! I cannot believe it!* There's no other way to describe it, other than to say it was an ecstatic day. It was from the laps of the gods.

"Jon saw something in me. He knew that I would fit in and that I would be perfect for that show, which I was. I showed up the first day and hit the ground running with everybody that was involved in the show."

Stone provided few clues as to what he was looking for in the new character. "Therefore, there's a lot of Emilio in Luis," Delgado said. "What happened is that I just went with what felt natural and right. They wanted reality, and that's what they got from the cast. We all came in at the same time to do the same thing, and it was a perfect union of people playing up the humanity of everything."

Delgado followed Stone's lead. "Jon was a perfectionist in the best sense of the word," Delgado said. "When he showed up on the set to direct, he had done his homework, with every camera angle written down on that script for that day. It was not like he made it up as he went along. He already knew what everything was going to look like, where he wanted to place the cameras, exactly what he wanted from the actors. He was completely at the helm, and he could be a very serious professional who knew exactly what he wanted. If you didn't give it to him, he'd get frustrated. But he was respected because he had been an actor, a writer, a producer, and a director.

"Jon used to say to the actors, 'When you are working with the Muppets, you really are the ones directing the scene.' He guided us, but it was up to us to make the scene go. We often gave him something that wasn't planned for the scene, and that's what he was hoping for by setting everything up so precisely it allowed us to safely go a bit beyond, relying on the wit and creative genius of the Muppets."

In 1972, Jon Stone dispatched Emily Kingsley to Great Neck, Long Island, to see a small ensemble that billed itself The Little Theater of the Deaf. "Check out this group and tell me if you think they should go on the show," he told her.

"I drove out and was entranced," Kingsley said. "They did a wonderful variation of *The House That Jack Built* called *This Is the Key to the City*. It went something like this: 'In the city there is a road, and on the road there is a house, and in the house there was a room, and in the room there was a bed, and on the bed was a basket, and in the basket there are flowers.' It was just so beautiful, so lyrical. You could almost see the room.

"I came back and said they had to be on the show, and I started writing bits for the troupe. I thought if I'm going to become friends with them, I'll need to communicate with them. My new husband, Charles, and I discovered that one of the members of the company was dean of students at a school for the deaf near us in White Plains. He agreed to teach us sign language, and we met with him every Wednesday night for a year, along with my colleague Sharon Lerner. Then Charles and I began volunteering at the school, running dances and basketball games. We donated a couple of pinball machines to them and got to know a bunch of the kids. And then we started thinking about having a family of our own, thinking, *Maybe we would have a kid and then if we wanted a second adopt a kid who was deaf.* We were already beginning to be politicized about disability issues. And in the middle of all this I get pregnant. The kids at the school were all hoping for a deaf baby.

"Jason was born late at night in June 1974. In the morning we got the news that we have this baby who, in the eyes of the doctors, was essentially garbage. Jason had Down syndrome, and they told us he'd never be able to sit or stand or walk or talk or read or write, never be able to distinguish us from any other adults, never have any concept of his own situation, never have a sense of humor, never have an imagination. They recommended that we institutionalize him immediately, before a bond was established. We should go home and tell our friends and family that he had died in childbirth. That's what we were told. I remember being in my hospital bed when this hit me in a very visceral way: I didn't exist anymore in that world of perfection that existed on television and on the pages of *McCall's* magazine.

"I didn't stop crying for three days because I had this vision of the world's smartest, most endowed, most brilliant, most talented child. I had been saving things like a first edition of Lewis Carroll and I had all my Gilbert and Sullivan stuff and all the things that I was going to do with this child. I had been preparing for months. They pulled all the props out from under me, with nothing to replace them.

"But a social worker came in and said there was an experimental, controversial program of early intervention being offered. Would my husband

and I consider giving it a try? It made sense that you don't send your flesh and blood away without even trying. And if we tried it—and if it turned out to be as much of a heartbreaker and disappointment as they said—we could always send him away later. But at least we'd be able to sleep at night knowing that we gave it our best shot. So with trepidation, not having any idea what was in store, we took this baby home. But we didn't know what we were getting ourselves into.

"When Jason was ten days old, we met with the head of the early intervention program. She held him up in her arms and he was like a noodle; those kids have no muscle tone. She said, 'We are going to work with him and to teach you and he's going to be wonderful.' Charles and I looked at each other like, *Oh my God. This lady is crazy.*

"She suggested we surround him with color, music, and movement. So we tore down the bland pale wallpaper we had put up in his room and put up these big, blinding red and purple flowers. We hung things from the ceiling on springs so there was stuff going up and down all the time. We put three mobiles over his crib instead of one. The intervention director advised us to keep talking to Jason. I said, 'What do you talk to a two-week-old baby about?' I had no idea what she was talking about. But when he was on the changing table I would point and say, 'See this red thing? It's a flower.' Finally one day when he was four months old, as I was pumping his legs and moving his arms, he looked at me and pointed right in the middle of this red flower. It could've been stretching, or gas, or totally random. But it was as if he was saying to me 'Okay, I've got it. Can we move on to something else, please, Mom? At that moment I kind of went nuts, saying, 'Hey, there's a brain in there. He can learn and make connections. He's not a vegetable, he's a person.' For tactile stimulation, we dumped him into tubs of Styrofoam and boxes full of rice. I made this huge pan full of Jell-O and we dumped him into that, too. He got it all over himself, and it was absolutely fabulous."

Kingsley had gone from skeptic to true believer by the time Jason started running around the house, fully engaged in the world.

"It became vitally important to me to let people know that kids like Jason had potential to learn, and that they need not be invisible," she said. "We got a letter at the Workshop around the time Jason was three from a mom who had two kids, a five-year-old and a two-and-a-half-year-old with Down syndrome. She put them in front of the television assuming that the older one would be educated and the little one would be entertained. Imagine her surprise when she walked in one day and the little one with Down's looked up and recited the alphabet.

"That letter was a starter's pistol for me as an advocate. I became a real nuisance to a lot of people, a broken record on disabilities. Once, in the middle of a meeting at the Workshop, the publishing division proudly held up a new book called *We're All the Same, We're All Different.* I took a look at this book and burst into tears in front of 200 people. There were 492 people in this book and one teeny little wheelchair way on the next-to-the-last page. Here was this book about inclusiveness, about how we're basically all the same even though we have individual differences, and they all but left out what I later found out was America's largest minority.

"I wrote a six-page letter to the head of the book department, to Gerry Lesser, to Joan Cooney, to whoever the suits were at that time. I just let it all pour out, how this hurts and how unfair this is for the kids out there who need to see themselves, all the people who feel this sense of strangeness and separateness, who need to have that strangeness eradicated."

"I got on the book lady's shit list," Kingsley said, years after *Sesame Street* wrote the book on how to portray the disabled on television. Just like *Sesame Street* itself, it all started with a preschooler. For in the early-to-mid-1970s, Jason Kingsley blended with the other kids on the set, appearing in fifty-five episodes as his charming, exuberant self. He not only counted to ten on *Sesame*, he did it English *and* Spanish.

Linda Bove first came to Jon Stone's attention in 1969, when she was just a year out of Gallaudet University. Instead of pursuing work with her library science degree, she auditioned for a spot with the Connecticut-based National Theater of the Deaf. Formed in 1967, the company of players mounted productions using American Sign Language. Stone had attended a performance by the five-actor touring group, The Little Theater of the Deaf, a group spun off from the main company that would do shows in schools.

After appearing sporadically on *Sesame Street* in the 1970s, as a recurring character who used ASL to communicate, she was added to the cast in 1979. In time, romance bloomed between bachelor Bob, the music teacher, and the saucy brunette who knew her way around the Dewey Decimal System. "I said to Jon, in my scenes I always look like a loner on *Sesame Street*," Bove said, "even when there are other cast members around. They have relationships, families, and partners on the show. I think that planted the seed. It was like, 'Who could we pair up with Linda?' Bob seemed like the most comfortable fit."

Writing for a deaf character came more easily to some writers. Bove tried to assist the more reluctant or unsure of them with a workshop she arranged. "I wanted to explain things to them about my language and culture," she said. "It was sort of an everything-you-wanted-to-know-but-were-afraid-to-ask session. One by one, they began asking questions. And I used that opportunity to suggest some obstacles that might arise, some things that we could figure out in advance. Then, as I was learning who the writers were, and where they got their information for stories, I became aware of the research department and concluded that I'd have to approach *them* about language and culture. Sometimes I would think to myself, *I'm an actor. This is not my job.* But Jon would say, 'Linda, we can't help it. *You* are the one who is knowledgeable. *You* know best.'"

Stone encouraged the actress to be outspoken and demanding, through an interpreter on the set. "I wanted to make sure that I could put my two cents in about how best they could use me," she said. "I came to see I had a function to show children all over America what my life looked like."

Bove had a natural ally in writer Kingsley, who first imagined situations for the character and then later applied whatever adaptations were needed. "She wrote Linda as a person first, *then* she worried about the other stuff," Bove said.

Toward the end of Richard Nixon's first term, raven-haired folksinger-activist Buffy Sainte-Marie was touring European clubs and concert halls and Indian reservations in Canada, where her haunting ballads and protest anthems ("Universal Soldier" and "My Country 'Tis of Thy People You're Dying") had not fallen from favor. For reasons she did not understand at the time, concert dates in the United States had dried up and airplay of her catalogue was limited to low-watt college stations.

It was surprising, then, when a call came from Dulcy Singer, inviting her to appear on *Sesame Street*. "She wanted me to come on like other singers had and recite the alphabet stuff or count," Sainte-Marie said. "By that point I had already founded the Nihewan Foundation for American Indian Education and was awarding scholarships. But I wanted to expand my outreach to little kids and their caregivers, to reach children before they ever ran into stereotyping or racism against Native America. Before I was a singer I was an elementary grades teacher, and I'd completed a double major in Oriental philosophy and education at the University of Massachusetts. As a teacher I saw right away that *Sesame Street*'s format, diversity, and caring about young children was revolutionary—and right on. So I was interested in doing something more significant than a onetime appearance."

Sainte-Marie accordingly countered with a proposal to assist in developing a curriculum about modern-day Native American culture. That offer, tendered by a distinctive artist born on a Cree reservation in Saskatchewan and raised by adoptive parents in Maine and Massachusetts, proved to be gently groundbreaking over Saint-Marie's five seasons on the *Street*.

"After doing my first few episodes I discovered that my husband, Sheldon Wolfchild, and I were expecting a baby," Sainte-Marie said. "I let Dulcy know, figuring she would wish me well and say good-bye." Instead, Singer and Jon Stone incorporated the pregnancy into the show, adding Wolfchild to the list of regularly occurring characters. Upon the birth of Dakota Starblanket Wolfchild, known as Cody, the writers developed a story line for Big Bird, who acted out when the baby appeared on *Sesame Street*. "It was brilliant in portraying sibling rivalry the way it really is for a poor little kid who is supposed to be thrilled about a new baby. Before the arrival, I had been set up as Big Bird's best friend. So Big Bird was clearly not thrilled at the fuss. In his opinion, Cody was no fun at all. *Sesame Street* really rose to the challenge of dealing with reality as experienced by Big Bird, the universal, all-races six-year-old."

Later, Sainte-Marie approached Stone and Singer with a suggestion for a segment on breast feeding. "I expected that it might be too much for television, but they were keen to do it," she said. The result was an understated scene using 150 words and lasting 56 seconds. With Sainte-Marie seated in the foreground nursing Cody in her arms, Big Bird watches with appropriate childlike interest over her shoulder.

> Big Bird: Whatcha' doin' Buffy?
> Buffy: I'm feeding the baby. See, he's drinking milk from my breast.
> Big Bird: *Hmmmm*. That's a funny way to feed a baby.
> Buffy: Lots of mothers feed their babies this way. Not all mothers, but lots of mothers do.
> Big Bird: Oh.
> Buffy: He likes it because it's nice and warm and sweet and natural. And it's good for him. And I get to hug him while I do it, see?
> Big Bird: Oh. Well, is that all he ever needs to eat?
> Buffy: Well, at first when he was just born and very tiny, this is all that he wanted and that he needed. But now that he's getting bigger, see, I mash up fruit and vegetables and sometimes a little bit of meat. As he gets older he'll need more and more different kinds of food to eat. But for right now this is just fine. He's drinking his milk.
> Big Bird: Y'know, that's nice.

"The scene was discreet and made sense to children," Sainte-Marie said. "Most kids' shows look wooden and phony. But *Sesame Street* was both magic and real. And I'm so proud to have been part of it. It not only presented characters that were all different shades of people-color, they also created characters whose diversity was of an emotional-behavioral nature. Sometimes in our family or circle of friends we have to deal with alcoholics, drug addicts, or emotional characters like Oscar," she said, "and I spent *plenty* of time near the trash can with him. The show has always taught us that we can love and respect Oscar without becoming like him or letting his grouchiness control us or our own moods. Similarly we can love and respect the difficult people in our circle without giving them the keys to the car or the keys to our lives. For me it's a huge metaphor and typical of the gestalt and wise synergies that permeated and underlay Jon Stone and Dulcy Singer's work.

"The quality of the writing—and listening—was remarkable. They asked me for ideas, and they came up with quick, to-the-point vignettes that still mean a lot to Native American viewers because they reflected the reality of our communities. They appreciated, like I did, that as a cast member I wasn't only written into 'Indian' parts. I got to sing and dance on the show to Joe Raposo tunes that had nothing to do with Native American life, even some Broadway-style numbers, which to someone who lived in New York was fantastic. Plus, I wrote a lot of songs for *Sesame Street*, some even for babies. It came naturally to me when Cody was an infant to sing to him and make up little play games and poems. These were songs I've never recorded and for which there's never been any demand, but that's what writers do. We write about what's really happening. And they were perfect for *Sesame Street*."

It wasn't until decades later that Sainte-Marie became aware that during her years on *Sesame Street*, her name had been listed on White House stationery as someone whose music "deserved to be suppressed."

On the day in 1975 that Judy Collins recorded "The Fishermen Song" for *Sesame Street*, a gaggle of Anything Muppets formed an old-salt chorus, some bedecked in yellow oilskin slickers. It was a scene right out of Gloucester harbor, with nets and lobster traps strewn about and a lighthouse in the distance. Strumming an autoharp at a tempo that recalled a sea chantey, Collins poured out the melody clear and true as the Muppets harmonized and danced about. The puppeteers were Jane Henson, Frank Oz, Richard Hunt, and Jerry Nelson, invisible to the eye of the camera but palpable in presence.

It was an enchantment of a performance, directed and made entirely possible by Jon Stone, first a fan and later a dear friend of Collins, the classically trained pianist and storyteller in song.

"Jon called me shortly after I had recorded my album *Judith*, which was released in 1975," Collins recalled. From an invitation for a single guest shot grew a series of appearances for Collins on *Sesame Street*, coinciding with an unstable, often difficult period in the performer's personal life.

"I was drinking heavily in those years," she said. "I was very controlled, but the truth was I was really teetering. Being able to appear on the show gave me a spark, a will to live. It was the only playful thing in my life at that point, and I want to tell you, I was not a playful person in my regular life. I was just trying to get by, to get through this physical issue that I was genetically programmed to be in. In part, my relationship with Jon was especially important to me because of the physical trauma that I was going through. He gave me reasons to stay alert and clearheaded."

Collins said that Jim Henson recognized that she was an alcoholic, and that being around his Muppets provided a cocoon of support for her. To an outsider, it might seem inconceivable that puppets could enhance a troubled person's well-being. But to be within touching distance of the Muppets is to be drawn into a safe zone, where teasing occurs but never ridicule, where praise is public and criticism private, where colleagues lend a helping hand, literally, figuratively, and continuously.

"For me, the appearances on *Sesame Street* were like this little light that kept flickering on and off, a beacon that seemed to be saying, 'Come to the party. We're having fun; you can have fun, too.' Everybody was very much about the same purpose, which was to have a good time and to let the characters shine," she said.

"It was Jon who set the tone. He'd always be so concerned about whether everything was set up properly for me and how comfortable I was. Jon loved the characters, and he'd encourage me to interact with them, saying, 'Go ahead. It's all right to hug Kermit.' It was like a pet owner encouraging you to pet to establish a connection with the cat. He understood that was part of the magic, and he encouraged play. The Muppets were totally convincing to me and I was absolutely able to suspend my sense of disbelief. I think a priority of Jon's was to always have people on the show who got along with the Muppets. It didn't matter how famous you were; if you couldn't get along with the creatures, forget it. For me, the Muppets allowed me to be a child again. They were just what I needed."

Among the highlights of the Collins appearances was the operatic, alphabetic duet she sang with Snuffleupagus. To a mock-Mozart score, Collins (in a floor-length off-the-shoulder gown) and Snuffy (in a jaunty feathered beret) run through the twenty-six consonants and vowels, their highs and lows offered to an unseen, adoring audience. Lifting the shy, shuffling character's elephantine "snuffle," Collins danced a mini-minuet, adding a greater sense of gaiety to this *Marriage of Snuffalo*. It was a vintage *Sesame Street* lesson in music appreciation, at once a parody and a celebration of classical propriety.

Collins has also credited *Sesame Street* for extending the depth and breadth of her fan base. "People come up to me at concerts and tell me how much they loved the Yes and No song I did with Bert and Ernie. They were little children when it first aired, teenagers in the early 1990s. They grew up and started coming to my shows," she said. "For them during a critically important time in their childhood, *Sesame Street* was the best of all television. It was intergenerational, which we performers loved. It had this magical ingredient that brought kids and adults and grandparents together. All of the age groups appreciated the humor and the artistry."

Muppets

In the show's first decade, the menagerie of Muppets expanded with the widening curriculum goals. Some characters sprang from Jim Henson's doodle pad, others from the typed page. But in every case, the Muppets that clicked best with viewers were the ones that intrigued the writers and challenged the puppeteers.

Take, for example, the number-obsessed Muppet with a monocle, that wonderful, vampiric Count Von Count. Head writer Norman Stiles came forward with the idea for a Dracula who craves counting with the same single-focused passion that drives Cookie Monster. The builders in the Henson Workshop gave the Count a lavender-fleece skin, bat-shaped ears, a flat black hairpiece, and a red spade tongue, outfitting him in caped formalwear.

Puppeteer Jerry Nelson provided all the rest. "Norman came to me one day to say he was working on a vampire character with a jones for counting." The most famous of Draculas, Bela Lugosi, provided the inspiration for the Count's exaggerated Eastern European accent, one in which *V*s are pronounced as *W*s and vice versa. "I love to count wegetables," Count Von Count would say, making an entrance to theater-organ music, lightning flashes, and thunder cracks. Nelson said he played the Count as scarier and hypnotic when the character debuted in 1972. As the years passed, the character became *Sesame Street*'s batty-but-benign uncle. Some first generation viewers didn't get the Lugosi takeoff until they were old enough to watch late-night horror movies and recognize the significance of the pipe organ, villainous laugh, and distinctive accent.

Another notable debut was the trundling elephantine wonder that is Aloysius Snuffleupagus, a towering full-size Muppet that takes two puppeteers to operate, front and rear, like an old-time costume of a barnyard horse.

Dulcy Singer said that she believed the idea for Mr. Snuffleupagus began with a Henson sketch. She and longtime writer Tony Geiss agreed that the character was always envisioned as Big Bird's imaginary friend, a fine idea while it lasted. Snuffy looked like a wooly mammoth whose tusks hadn't grown in yet. He was designed with wide, moony eyes (with luxurious lashes) and an elongated snuffle, a floor-length appendage that he used to conduct music and blow-dry his shaggy coat. In the early years, sad-sounding Snuffy was a less pessimistic Eeyore, a slow-motion galumphing cave dweller whose signature phrase was "*Ohhhhh*, dear." Nelson provided the original voice, while taking up the rear was a lanky puppeteer just out of his teens, a gung-ho guy who was only too happy to assume the physically demanding task.

Nelson first spied Richard Hunt during the training workshops for *The Great Santa Claus Switch*, a CBS Christmas special featuring the Muppets. "Jim had a video camera set up so the trainees could practice in front of a monitor, which provides a mirror image," he said. "It's the opposite of what you think, and it takes some getting used to, since your body is doing the opposite."

The eighteen-year-old Hunt demonstrated an almost manic talent at the workshop. "Richard had a boundless energy when he first came, like a little puppy wanting to do this, wanting to do that," recalled Nelson. "We sat on him pretty good at first. But he had this creativity, and this sense of what energy was required to compel a production in a needed direction. Some of that came from growing up in a theatrical family that encouraged his early interest in performing."

Hunt made his national television debut quite unexpectedly while seated in the Peanut Gallery during a live broadcast of *Howdy Doody*. "I dressed Richard and his sister Kate in blue velvet pants and white shirts," said their mother, Jane Hunt. "As Buffalo Bob was saying good-bye at the end of the show, Richard walked right up to him and said, 'Would you like to see a magic thhhrick?' He talked funny because he had fallen down and knocked out a front baby tooth.

"Buffalo Bob said, 'Not now, sonny. We don't have time.' But Richard had already pulled out the little props that came from a box of magic tricks someone had given him. And just at the instant the show was about to fade to black, Richard completed the trick. It was like abracadabra-please-and-thank-you *poof!*"

Though he was born in the Bronx, Hunt's family moved to Closter, New Jersey, nine miles from the George Washington Bridge, when he was in elementary school. "Richard had no fear . . . and no shame," his mother said. "The kids at school sensed that he was different and made fun of him. He used to steal money out of my pocketbook to buy candy to give away at school, and eventually everyone became his pal."

Puppetry was an active interest for a kid from a home where five children made the best of modest circumstances. Jane made a puppet theater for Richard out of a discarded cardboard box used to ship an appliance and purchased a set of Steiff puppets from a consignment shop.

By the time Hunt was ten years old, after he had already appeared on *Howdy Doody,* he and his family had come to know both Cosmo "Gus" Allegretti, the gifted puppeteer from *Captain Kangaroo,* and Burr Tillstrom of *Kukla, Fran and Ollie.* "My husband and I knew Gus from our days at Marietta College in Ohio," Jane Hunt said. "We remained friends when we all ended up in New York, and Gus used to come over to our house to do the kids' birthday parties. He'd bring his puppets and perform by going behind our upright piano."

By the time he graduated from high school, he was determined to catch on at *Captain Kangaroo.* "Richard just decided that was what he had to do," his mother said, "and so he went over to the CBS studio where the show originated, hoping to talk with Gus. It was a bit of a shock, but Gus went nuts. He took Richard outside and said, 'Get out of here! Bob Keeshan is the nastiest man in the world, and I don't want you anywhere near him. He's awful.'"

Instead of giving up, after that warning, Hunt reached into his pocket for change and made a pay phone call to the Henson Workshop. "I'm a puppeteer," he said "Can you use me?"

Jane Hunt cackled. "It's amazing when you think of it. On the very same day he was being shooed away from *Captain Kangaroo,* Richard called the Muppets. They told him about the upcoming training workshops, and you know the rest of the story."

Jerry Nelson said, "Richard just loved the Muppets and wanted to get involved with them as soon as he could. But like many talents who worked under Jim, he had to serve an apprenticeship. In his case, he did right hands for five years before he took on a character, and even then they were background characters."

When his chance came, Hunt's pent-up passion to perform could hardly be restrained. The list of characters he took on includes the following:

- The vain, clueless diva Gladys the Cow, the bovine bound for Broadway. In an early appearance, Gladys provided the punch line to a Sesame Street News Flash update on self-absorbed trust-fund baby Prince Charming. After trying the glass slipper on all three wicked stepsisters—and Cinderella—the siblings summon Gladys from their cottage. Her hoof is a perfect fit, and Charming is buffaloed.

- Forgetful Jones, the simpleton cowboy who couldn't shoot straight or, for that matter, keep anything straight. In a movie remake of *Oklahoma!* directed by Kermit (in a beret), Forgetful keeps muffing the opening number, replacing the stretched out "O" in the opening bars with a series of incorrect vowels. He sings, "*Aaaaaaaaaa-aik!* Lahoma . . ." as a chorus line of cows and horses clomp in time. With each blown take—"*Eeek*-lahoma" followed by "Eyek-lahoma"—Kermit becomes more unglued. When Forgetful finally gets it right, the stage director interrupts at midsong to announce that it's time for lunch.

- The piano-playing composer, Don Music, a tortured artiste who consistently needed assistance with lyrics from Kermit to complete an assignment. (The inside joke was Don had a framed photograph of Joe Raposo hanging on the wall and a bust of William Shakespeare on the piano.) As Don would reach an impasse—"Oh, I'll never get this song! Never, never, never!"—he would dissolve into a puddle of exasperation, banging his head on the keyboard.

- Hunt's most understated and complex character was construction worker Sully, the mute counterpart to Biff, an Archie Bunker–style blue-collar loudmouth who talked a good game but produced little. They made for a classic comedy team. Biff would encounter a problem, ask Sully's opinion, then interrupt before he could answer. While Biff would jabber away, Sully, who had brows but no eyes, would silently find a solution, often thanks to hidden talents.

  In a sketch about moving a piano that could have been written for Laurel and Hardy, Biff brags to Sully that he studied piano as a kid. It takes practice to master the scales, he says ("You know, do-rey-me-fatso-laddie-do?"), then proceeds to butcher the easiest of the lot, the all-white-keys C-scale.

  When Biff heads off to bring the truck around, Sully takes his place at the piano and plays Chopin's Prelude in A Minor, note perfect.

Hunt's characters had a persistent urge to succeed and a temperament that distinguished them as slightly out of the norm. They filled the screen with attitude and exuberance, with assistance from a writing staff that looked to use Hunt whenever and however possible. He was impossible to ignore or resist.

"He was just this zany guy who was so much fun to be around," said Ted May, a longtime director on *Sesame Street*. To May's astonishment, Hunt would ignore his script during downtime between segments while others studied their upcoming lines. Hunt would continue reading the *New York Times* as the director counted down the seconds, dropping it with just enough time to grab his puppet and hit his mark. He'd pull it together and perform flawlessly.

Whenever children were on set, Hunt would seek them out. "Richard was wonderful to Jason," said Emily Kingsley, mother of the child with Down syndrome. "They had a wonderful relationship."

Muppet designer Bonnie Erickson said "Richard was the master of the grand gesture. There was not a single trip we took where he wasn't the Pied Piper with every child on the plane. He would always try to sit next to them and get them to sing or he'd create a show, keeping everyone in stitches. I never saw anyone make friends faster than Richard."

Hunt was extraordinarily generous. Regardless of the number of diners around the table, he would pick up the check and wave off objectors. With his first paycheck from Henson, he bought a color television for his parents and siblings, the family's first set.

He could provide helpful assistance to colleagues, no easy trick around hypersensitive performers. Caroll Spinney credits Hunt with helping Big Bird become a more confident dancer. "Richard once said to me, 'Pretend Big Bird thinks he's the greatest dancer in the world, and just have him imitate what he thinks great dance is.'" When Spinney adopted that attitude for Big Bird, his struggles disappeared. "After that, I would say to choreographers, 'Just show me what kind of dance you want, but don't expect me to duplicate it,'" Spinney said. "Since then, Big Bird has danced onstage with the Rockettes at Radio City."

While he had a fundamentally generous personality, Hunt was no angel. In fact, his mother, who adored him as much as he adored her, said, "Richard could be a son of a bitch."

His critical comments often went unfiltered, but like insect bites, their sting never lasted long. He ran notoriously late, a venal sin in a business where time is money. And he could be downright nasty to people whom he didn't feel like accepting.

"Richard hated me at the beginning," said Marty Robinson, who, like Hunt, served a term as the hind end of Snuffleupagus. "To him, I was just some new asswipe kid, a Muppet geek who was wet behind the ears and a totally suspicious newcomer. He was a guy who had paid his dues, and he took exception to anyone coming in who might have been expecting anything more than what he got. If he didn't accept you, he'd just torture you on the set. It was nothing under-handed. In fact, it was always open and out there, and always with a certain amount of humor. If you came to the show with any whiff of ego at all, with an attitude that you could be as funny as any of those other guys, he would tear you apart. People would say to themselves, 'Hey, I'm a good puppeteer. Why am I doing right hands?' And he would say, 'Fuck you. I did right hands for eight years before they put a puppet on me. Do you want to do right hands for eight years?'" (The inglorious but necessary task of operating the rod that controls the arm of a character that is not being manipulated by the main performer is called "working the right hand." It is a rite of passage aspiring Muppeteers must endure, the apprenticeship that will one day lead to a character of their own to perform.)

Then Robinson carefully observed Hunt for a year, at a distance. "Richard was expansive and a big guy. The crew adored him. They knew that when he stepped into the studio, somebody was going to be made fun of. No one was safe around Richard, including Jim. He didn't edit his opinions, and I'm not sure that served him politically. He never let people think marvelous thoughts about themselves. He was always around to remind you where he came from. He always told Jim the truth, even when it was painful. Jim would be surrounded by people who were always saying, 'Yah, great idea! Brilliant!' Richard was the one who was saying, 'What are you doing? Is this what you really want?' He would call him on stuff, acting as devil's advocate."

Spinney recalled that Hunt, at times, "would tease Jim to the point where it was embarrassing. Jim would walk across the set, and Richard would say out loud in front of me, 'Here comes that rich bastard millionaire.' I don't know why he would say stuff like that. Sometimes my wife and I would look at him and say, 'What's wrong with you?'"

A breakthrough in Robinson's relationship with Hunt came after a year, when Hunt attended a performance of *Little Shop of Horrors*, the deliciously twisted stage adaptation of Roger Corman's horror-comedy from 1960. Robinson, a puppet builder as well as performer, had created the outrageous man-eating plant Audrey II, the insatiable scene stealer of the off-Broadway musical. Robinson was the unseen manipulator behind

Audrey II, which starts as a sprout and after devouring a number of human victims, grows more than two stories tall. In his *New York Times* review, Mel Gussow refers to Robinson's creation as "a pistil-packing vampire."[1]

"Richard loved musical theater," Robinson said, "and when he learned that I was doing something that was totally separate from the Muppets, something that he totally appreciated, that was when I started to be okay. It helped that my girlfriend at the time was Ellen Greene, who was the star of *Little Shop*. He adored her, as we all did, and he and Ellen went on to become very close."

During the period when Robinson was playing the front end of Snuffy, the writers created a puppy love-story line for him. It was art imitating life, as the puppeteer had as big a crush on Sonia Manzano as Snuffy did on Maria. "I was able to work out feelings through Snuffy," Robinson said. "They wrote some really nice scripts about lovelorn Snuffy, and it wasn't much of a stretch for me to play. We all had crushes on her."

Robinson's best-known hand-and-rod puppet arose out of desperation. "Telly was a minor character until Caroll Spinney got suddenly sick one day and couldn't come in. Waiting for him, of course, was an entire Big Bird script to do, and we were all looking at each other like, *What do we do now?* It was like, 'Hey, here's an idea. Let's give Telly something to do!'"

When puppeteer Brian Muehl perfomed Telly, he was a gruff-sounding, obsessive worrier, the mope Muppet. "Every monster has his mania, but Telly was a little too depressive and very hair trigger for me back then," Robinson said. "He used to consider Oscar his best friend and, of course, Oscar just tortured him mercilessly, which put him on this spiraling ring of self-loathing that was a joy for Oscar to behold. It was a classically sick, sadistic, masochistic relationship, and I much prefer him in his present state. After I took him over in 1984 he evolved. He gained a lot more range in his reactions and he's stronger. He can't be destroyed quite so easily and has good friends. His main thing now is that he believes totally in whatever he's into. And he can turn on a dime and that doesn't belie what he was feeling before. He can go from great joy to great sorrow and it's all totally genuine."

Considering that most Muppets start out as bath mats with appliqués, it's fairly miraculous that they seem to have more dimensionality to their personalities than do most human characters on television. That richness of characterization dates back to Jim and Jane Henson on their knees at WRC in Washington, back to the days when reception was fuzzy and the home screen color spectrum was gray, black, and white. They understood that viewers would suspend their sense of disbelief if they saw pieces of themselves in the characters. Forgetful Jones had a foible, and he was therefore funny and as recognizable as the elderly neighbor next door who always seemed surprised when the paper boy came to collect on Fridays. The Count had an obsessive need, and who doesn't? Telly fretted, Oscar kvetched, Ernie teased, Bert was anal, and Grover, like most of us, was, if not always a superhero, certainly above average.

There was a brief period during which Cookie Monster had neither an obsession nor a permanent name.

What he did have was Muppet ancestors, Henson characters who bore a resemblance to the bottomless sack with googly eyes. The first Cookie look-alike was used in a 1966 TV ad for some crunchy snacks called Wheels, Crowns and Flutes. The spot never ran, and the snack-snatching puppet known as Wheel Stealer went into hibernation for a year. He reemerged first in an IBM training film entitled *The Coffee Break Machine* and then later on *The Ed Sullivan Show*, as a saw-toothed monster who is as curious as he is voracious. Instead of simply admiring a piece of scientific equipment that only a government technocrat could love, the monster decides to eat it, component by component. It isn't until swallowing the "recorded analytic program readout" (which continues to drone on inside his belly) that we learn the machine is programmed to self-destruct. In the tradition of the Wilkens coffee commercials, the punch line is "*Kaboom!*"

The third incarnation of the character was the charm. In the weeks leading up to *Sesame Street*'s launch, as the production team was shooting segments at a furious clip, Jon Stone was handed a half-baked script. The premise was promising—a blue, baggy monster and his wife vie for cash and prizes on a quiz show—and though the sketch began well enough, it ended with a thud. "We read through it and Jim and Frank looked at me as if to say, 'We're supposed to perform *this*?'"

"Yes," Stone said, sweeping his arm and turning his right palm up, as if to say, "It's showtime, boys." Stone knew that if he could improvise an ending, Henson and Oz would embellish it. And so, yet again, the resourcefulness of the man who had once typed a makeshift résumé on a Manhattan sidewalk was put to the test.

"My mind was racing," Stone said. "In desperation I blurted, 'Okay, here's what we can do. The monster and his wife win the game like the script says. But when he gets the question right, the emcee will say, 'Your prize is either two weeks in Hawaii, all expenses paid; a free car; a new house and twenty-five thousand in cash, or . . . a cookie!'

"Jim and Frank went along and we began taping. When the critical moment of decision arrived, they really got into it. The husband monster was tortured by the emcee's offer. He looked at his wife and then to heaven for assistance and growled in his monstery voice, 'Oh, boy. Tough choice.'"

Then, using what would become Cookie Monster's Tarzan-in-the-jungle speech pattern, eliminating articles and substituting "me" for "I," the husband turned to his spouse. "You probably want house and car. Right?"

"Well, yes, dear," the wife patiently responded. "But you know how you like your cookies."

Stone said, "The monster glowered for another moment, and you could almost hear the gears grinding in his shaggy head. Then he raised himself up to his full height and bellowed his decision: 'Cookie!'"

At that moment "a star was born," Stone said.

Well-behaved (if sometimes insistent) children got Cookie Monster immediately. After all, he was a lot like them. "All of his monomania . . . would not stop him from caring about someone else," said Norman Stiles, a two-time *Sesame Street* head writer who began in 1973. "He's not going to knock over anybody to get the cookie. He's going to try to get around them to get the cookie. He's going to beg for the cookie."[2]

Adults recognized in Cookie Monster their own single-minded quest to satisfy needs, the id in all its "me-me-me, now-now-now" urgency. (In fact, during one of the annual *Sesame Street* wrap parties, outrageous affairs all, the puppeteers introduced Nookie Monster, a distant relative whose incessant carnal cravings had nothing to do with snickerdoodles.)

Technically, Roosevelt Franklin's skin was magenta, as anyone with a color television during the early years of *Sesame Street* could have told you.

But the innards of this Muppet—who had a wild explosion of Don King hair and often spoke in rhyme—was joyfully, exuberantly, indisputably black. Roosevelt was added for season two to answer criticism from some members of the black community that the Muppets of Sesame Street lacked soul, in the James Brown sense of the word. They also argued that any show directed at the inner-city would be negligent—and, perhaps, fraudulent—without a share of black humor, idioms, and vernacular.

And so, with a push from Matt Robinson, who created the character, a series of classroom scenes were fashioned around a child so clever and advanced that they named the school after him. Dialogue and song lyrics for Roosevelt, described in *Look* magazine as "a nitty-gritty black boy with a matriarchal mother and bullies on his block," were distinctly, unmistakably, and unapologetically attuned to the street. In *Newsweek*'s 1970 cover story on *Sesame Street*, executive producer Dave Connell said Roosevelt Franklin is "certainly not a white kid hiding in black skin. We do black humor, just like Irish humor and Jewish humor. It would be patronizing not to do it."[3]

"Matt created a delightful group of black puppet children, led by a feisty, funny Roosevelt," said Jon Stone. "His buddies had names like Sam Sound Brown and Hardhead Henry Harris and always referred to each other by their entire names. Matt had a great ear for the syntax and flow of black speech as well as a unique comedic gift, wrote most of the scripts for these sketches, and supplied the voice for Roosevelt."

Each of the bits would open with a shot of the imposing school's courtyard (which looked like a minimum security prison) and a student chorus singing, "Hail to thee, our alma-mamma, Roosevelt Franklin [at which point the horns chime in with a *dahdup duh-dah*] Elementary School!"

Spitballs and paper airplanes invariably greeted Roosevelt as he entered his classroom. In one pithy episode about household dangers, Roosevelt peeks into the frame as a classmate says, "Sumpin' must be up."

Roosevelt, as ever in his yellow-and-pink-striped turtleneck, asks the class the meaning of that day's spelling word: P-O-I-S-O-N.

"Baaaaaaad news!" they say in unison.

In another sassy segment, Roosevelt gives a geography lesson on Africa, referring to one of those window-shade-style display maps that always hung above classroom blackboards. With a jazzy beat provided by Danny Epstein brushing on the snare drum, Roosevelt disabuses the students' preconceptions—borrowed from Tarzan movies—that the continent is just one big jungle.

"All this," he says, pointing north, "is a desert."

"All this," he says, pointing to the southwestern coast, "is a whole bunch of beaches . . . and water . . . and fishin' places."

"All these," he says, "are big cities with buildings . . . and lakes . . . and parks . . . and schools."

Roosevelt says, "And up here there's oil," and the students, in call-and-response style, repeat "Oil!" "And down here, there's diamonds." ("Diamonds!") "And down here is gold." ("Gold!")

He finally turns to the class and says, "Now do you know what Africa looks like?"

Classmate Hardhead Henry Harris, perpetually in sunglasses, volunteers. "I know what Africa look like, and I know what Smart Tina look like, too," referring to the know-it-all who sits one desk ahead. "She look like a African queen, with diamonds and gold all around her. And dig it, she has a smile like the desert sun and eyes like the cool waters of a lake. And she tall like a building in the great city. And she got feet . . . like an African elephant!"

As the class erupts and another squadron of paper airplanes flies across the classroom, Roosevelt says, "I'm not going to sit around to hear what she says to him. I'm going to dismiss y'all."

Along with the actress-singer Rosalind Cash, Matt Robinson recorded "My Name Is Roosevelt Franklin," an LP of original material that included a black-pride confessional entitled "The Skin I'm In."

"Matt loved Roosevelt Franklin and was extraordinarily proud of that character," said Dolores Robinson, his wife at that time. "Roosevelt was who he really was, an alter ego. In private, Matt was never that shy. He loved to sing and imitate Ray Charles, and there is a little bit of Ray in Roosevelt."

At the height of the character's popularity, however, objections began to arise over the portrayal. "Matt's pride in his race and his anger with racism all came out in Roosevelt," Dolores Robinson said. "That's what those people heard and objected to. He was too black for them."

"There was often considerable conservative pressure with the Workshop," Stone said. "Several African American executives, particularly Evelyn Davis, a CTW vice president, and Lutrelle Horne, an administrator in the International Department, decided these characters fostered a stereotype and insisted on terminating them."

Joan Cooney was caught in the middle. "There was an argument about whether he should speak black English or not, whether children should be taught the King's English," she said. "I loved Roosevelt Franklin, but I understood the protests. I understood both sides. If Matt said it was okay, and the community said it was okay, and white people said it was okay, then it was okay with me. I wasn't wholly comfortable, but I was amused. You couldn't help but laugh at him. We knew that it was going to be a bit controversial, and it seemed to go away for a while, but then we heard from the Evelyn Davises, from the upper-middle-class of the black community."

Though small in number, the naysayers ultimately carried the day, despite what Stone said was "vigorous opposition" from the show's black performers. "The conservative faction prevailed, and Roosevelt Franklin bit the dust," he said.

Dulcy Singer, Stone's right hand, saw the decision for what it was: a cave-in that threatened the integrity and independence of the very creators who gave the show authenticity and a comedic sensibility in tune with the times. "At the beginning we could take so many more chances because nobody noticed us," she said. "We were the new kid in town. Then once the show became successful and more and more people were watching it, we were getting more and more mail. Management began to veto things that they wouldn't have the first season. And then more and more people were entering in and giving their opinions. It was always, 'No, this isn't good,' not 'Yes, let's do more of it.'"

"I suppose that's the way of the world," she said. "You become more cautious as you become more successful, and it came just as we were in a position to take more chances."

In 1970, unemployed actress Fran Brill was living in the Dixie Hotel on Forty-second Street, making the audition rounds without much success. "I had been in a Broadway show called *Red, White and Maddox* that closed after forty-one performances. The show, which originated in Atlanta and moved to New York, satirized segregationist Lester Maddox, then governor of Georgia.

"I used to watch the first season of *Sesame Street* to cheer myself up at the end of the day, followed by *Mister Rogers' Neighborhood*. I used to think, *Y'know, I've never played with a puppet in my life, but I could probably do all these voices and accents and whatever.* I had just broken into doing voice-overs and I saw an ad in *Backstage* that said Jim Henson was looking to train people for an Ed Sullivan Christmas special. So I called Jim Henson one day—and he picked up the phone—it was that small an organization at that time—and I said, 'I'm an actress, I've just come to New York and I have never really played with puppets but can you use me as a voice person?'

"Jim said, 'Well, we don't do it that way. The puppeteers do their own voices. But, you know, why don't you come on over?' It was that incredibly casual and easy."

Brill arrived at the Henson Workshop to find "Jim, Frank, a trunk full of puppets, and a big mirror and some scripts," she said. "We just played around with the puppets for a while and something clicked. It was just one of those wacky things where somebody with absolutely no expertise in the area got a break. Maybe it was my sense of humor. Maybe they knew I was an actress and could do all these voices and sing. . . ."

Henson invited Brill to attend an upcoming two-week training program in puppetry. "There were lots and lots of people the first week, and we all learned the basics. After he let some people go the second week, the remaining group of newcomers performed the group of monsters called Frackles in *The Great Santa Claus Switch*."[4]

The two standouts from the training week were Brill and Richard Hunt. Both showed enough promise to prompt Henson to ask if they would be available to work on *Sesame Street* for season two.

Brill said, "Oh, I'm an actress . . . I don't know."

Henson responded, "Well, just see if you can give us a few weeks out of the year."

She agreed, and that was the pivotal moment of her professional life. "The truth is I was doing whatever I could to pay the rent in those days, working industrial shows, doing lingerie modeling. But now, looking back on it, I was really just out of college and got a job with the Muppets!"

Brill began the mandatory period of Muppet servitude on *Sesame Street*, arriving on the scene at a time when people outside of Henson's circle began to wonder if he would ever break up the all-boys' club that was the Muppets. "They really didn't need a woman because the guys who perform in falsetto were hilarious, but the pressure was on in the seventies," Brill recalled. "Girls back then didn't think about puppeteering. They thought about being an actress or a comedienne, but to be a puppeteer was not on anyone's wavelength."

Blending in with the corps of players "was the most challenging thing in my life," she said. "You had to be one of the guys but you were not one of the guys, and there was a pecking order. You had to be mindful of what your place was. For a while there were some strong-minded women who came in, and they began to tell people what to do and how to do it." Brill sliced her index finger across her throat. "It was like 'Off with their heads!'"

Brill succeeded by embracing aspects of her femininity, and when her chance came to develop a character, during the heyday of women's lib, she reached for "a little pink puppet" and named her Prairie Dawn. "They put her in a blond wig [and a] party dress and asked me to create a . . . very feminine girly-girl. I came up with this innocent, pretty sound."[5]

Given generous time to develop the character, Brill and the writers filled out Prairie Dawn's levelheaded, patient personality. In most cases, Muppets season slowly before they mature.

"The whole Muppet thing works best when people are free and open and feel like nobody will criticize you. And Jim was incredible like that. He'd expect you to do the best you can, but he also knew where you came from. If you weren't a born puppeteer he didn't expect you to do incredible moves. Some people are incredible puppet manipulators, but they only have one voice that they end up using over and over and over. Some people aren't fantastic at the manipulation but they can do all these different voices and characters. And then there are more than a couple who can do everything."

From time to time when James Taylor is out on his annual summer swing of outdoor music pavilions, a voice from the audience will call out "Jelly-man Kelly!" The shout-out inevitably ripples through the seats, triggering a memory for a part of the singer-songwriter's fan base that had its first exposure to J.T. on *Sesame Street* in 1983. "Television *is powerful*," Taylor said with a smile.

Accompanied by jazz virtuoso Howard Johnson on tuba, Taylor introduced a sing-along song about a man who loved his jelly most on toast. His gal, Jenny Mulhenny, was a fireman's daughter who loved to boil water. A brigade of five preschoolers joined in for the chorus ("Oh! Can he come home, Jenny? / Can he come home, Jenny can he come?") and some nonsense lyrics ("Yaka yaka yaka yaka huh-uh no!").

Equally inspired was a 1983 rooftop duet with Oscar in which Taylor tweaked the lyrics to "Your Smiling Face." Its good-natured, happy vibe heaped misery upon the misanthropic puppet.

Oh, whenever I see your grouchy face
It makes me want to smile because I like you—just a little bit.

Oscar peeks out of his can.

And when you give me that nasty little frown
Turns me upside down.
Something about you, Oscar . . . I don't know.
Isn't it amazing that a grouch could make me feel this way?
But a face that looks so rotten can't be forgotten in a day.
But it looks so rotten.

Oscar picks up the refrain:

I thought I saw silly smiles before from the folks downstairs at Hooper's Store.
But yours makes me the maddest.
And that's when I feel gladdest.

Taylor described his three *Sesame Street* appearances—he sang his cover of Gerry Goffin and Carole King's "Up on the Roof" with his band in 1983—as "magical days. It was wonderful to get caught in the energy on that set. In television, the relationship with the audience is abstract, a cerebral thing. But because the creative team at *Sesame Street* somehow invented a world, the audience always seemed to be there. There was no barrier to break through between rehearsal and performance. It was like everything was happening all the time, and it was great to be part of that vitality, humor, and spontaneity. Elsewhere on television, there was a corporate Novocain that crept up and killed spontaneity. Television doesn't trust spontaneity because it's not reliable.

"The wonder of *Sesame Street* is that it has never tried to wrap children up in cellophane," Taylor said. "It's as if the show has been saying, 'Come on and join the real world,' helping children relate to that world. I mean, what other children's show ever dared to have a character like Bert, whose job it is to be boring? It's not the sort of thing you'd think would play to children. But it's all part of an artistic endeavor; it suggests to its viewers other ways of seeing themselves, and in that way, it's mythic. They created Cookie Monster, with his insatiable appetite, and wide-open Big Bird, characters that were accessible and that children could use.

"To me, art is a matter of people presenting usable models that people can adapt. Art blazes a trail through a territory that nobody else has walked on. But after the artist has walked on it, there's a way to go through it. Kids particularly need to find a vision of themselves that works in the world, a way in which they can tell themselves, 'Yeah, there's a place for me. I can go through and make it.' They need to know this daily, and in time it all comes together. And it's not only about children, it's about us as grown individuals and how we see ourselves, how we react and what kind of internal myths and self-images we construct for ourselves out of what's available. It's what our culture is. I find it amazing how much *Sesame Street* has offered of that essential process, and what a wide range of people it offered it to, a hugely inclusive group.

"Always," he said, "in a joyous way."

Chapter Sixteen

S ometimes life is like the movies, a story in three acts.

It was just that way for the founders of *Sesame Street*, who found themselves dealing with a series of challenges in the 1970s, all the stuff that constitutes the middle stage of any drama.

Though it would be difficult to divine exactly when act 2 began, the one thing that distinguished it from act 1 was easy to spot: things got complicated.

Raposo was both a delight and a distraction to Joan Cooney. Her "bandleader," as he referred to himself in correspondence to her, could alternately be a sweetheart or a pain in the ass, sometimes both within the same five-minute period.

No one ever begrudged him his musical talent, both as performer and composer, but certain of his colleagues often found him an arrogant, obsequious, petty, puffed-up braggart. "There was never enough love that one could bestow on Joe, in the eyes of Joe," Cooney said.

If Olympic gold was handed out for name-dropping, Raposo would have spent half his life on the medal platform. His casual conversations would be peppered with references to starlets and statesmen, the important people of the world who were forever seeking his counsel and consideration.

Raposo once approached Chris Cerf with a dilemma: "I just don't know what to do," he said. "I've got a terrible decision to make."

"What is it, Joe?" Cerf said.

"Two of my best friends are running against each other for president: Jimmy Carter and Ronald Reagan. I just don't know what to do."

"Vote your conscience," Cerf advised him.

To love Raposo was to accept his incessant need to impress. Cerf and Cooney accepted it as the gaudy foil wrapping around the gift of his friendship. Unlike some name-droppers who give the false impression they mingled with the glitterati, Raposo did actually know Barbra Streisand, Frank Sinatra, and Walter Cronkite. "Joe was the first man to kiss me on the cheek," recalled Cronkite.

It took even a strong stomach for show-business excess to tolerate Raposo at his worst. In collaborative endeavors, he was all first-person singular, self-absorbed, self-enamored, self-aggrandizing. His most enraging selfish acts invariably made their way upstream to Cooney's desk, and she would have to soothe the wounded.

Raposo clashed with anyone who dared encroach upon his perceived turf. Chief among his targets was Jeff Moss, a *Captain Kangaroo* veteran who succeeded Jon Stone as head writer. Beyond script writing, the sometimes combustible Moss was a gifted poet, composer, and lyricist. Raposo, a Harvard graduate, perceived the Princeton-educated Moss as a rival and threat, and Moss did little to dissuade him.

The classic en garde moment between the two came on a day when Moss skipped into the studio with the lead sheet for a new song he had written for mischievous Ernie. Moss had previously written a perfectly delightful waltz for Oscar entitled "I Love Trash," recorded with panache by Caroll Spinney and later included in the original *Sesame Street* cast album. (Raposo and Moss famously feuded over who would get the most songs featured on that album.)

Moss's new tune, a little ditty entitled "Rubber Duckie," gave Ernie the opportunity to sing the praises of his main squeeze, a yellow bath toy that often accompanied him on dry land.

Left behind by Moss in the music room for Raposo to orchestrate and score, Cooney's "bandleader" finally got around to giving it a run-through on the piano. When he was done, Raposo reached for a pencil, said music coordinator and house band drummer Danny Epstein, scribbled something on the music, and headed off for parts unknown. Epstein picked up the composition to see that his boss had written "Ho-hum" across the top of the lead sheet. "It wasn't exactly nasty," he said. "There was some style to the insult, a certain classiness. After that, Joe and Jeff really went at it, banging each other over the head, but always in an Ivy League kind of way."

Raposo fairly seethed with envy when "Rubber Duckie," sung by Jim Henson in the 1920s *vo-do-de-o* style of Rudy Vallee, rocketed to No. 11 on the Billboard Top 40 chart in 1971. "He went nuts," Epstein said.

The success of that song not only boosted Moss's bank account but his standing as a songwriter. He went on to write a small library of songs for *Sesame Street*, including the evocative gem "I Don't Want to Live on the Moon." Moss's lyrics, and his later books of children's rhyme, beautifully reflected the interior life of children. Raposo's could, as well, but too often his work was dashed off on the backs of envelopes while a taxi was delivering him to the studio. Some of Raposo's lyrics had a hollow ring, which was rarely the case with Moss's.

There was money to be made in songwriting, and Moss wasn't the only contributor to the show who cashed in on such opportunities. Among the others were scriptwriters Tony Geiss and Norman Stiles, and multitasking Chris Cerf. Still, more than anyone, with the obvious exception of Jim Henson, Raposo got rich from *Sesame Street*. But unlike Henson, he always seemed to find a way to rub it in. One day, after receiving notification by mail of song royalties totaling five thousand dollars, Raposo marched around the CTW offices, waving the check for all to see, a scene that made Epstein bury his face in his hands.

Raposo was the fortunate beneficiary of an early strategic decision regarding the music rights to *Sesame Street*'s catalogue. Because Cooney and her advisers wanted to interest top composers and lyricists to write for the show, and because CTW was a nonprofit entity just finding its way financially, it was decided to allow songwriters to own their work.

"Prior to *Sesame Street*, no kids' songs done on television ever realized much in the way of royalties," explained CTW public relations vice president Bob Hatch. "So the producers thought, *Heck, if this will make Jeff and Joe write all the harder, let's let them have it,* and they did well. But the Workshop got a lot of ink—and a lot of mileage—from the airplay of songs like 'Rubber Duckie.' It helped sustain the level of public interest in the show. That's not exactly nothing."

Raposo's best-regarded song for *Sesame Street* has an air of intrigue around it. This much we know: it began when Jon Stone approached Raposo with a request. "We need a song for the frog," he said. As he had many times, with many songwriters and many songs, Stone walked Raposo through the curriculum goal for the composition and made lyric suggestions. Only Stone and Raposo were in the room when the contemplative song for Kermit was mapped out, but members of Stone's family have insisted that it was presumptuous of Raposo to claim that he alone wrote "Bein' Green." The sheet music has always indicated "Words and Music by Joe Raposo," and thus the enormous royalties generated by the song have always belonged to him. Jon Stone's failure to call Raposo on claiming full credit kindled one of the worst marital disagreements Jon and Beverley Stone ever had.

Raposo's second wife, the New York television personality Pat Collins, refutes the Stone version of events and insists her husband deserves sole credit for the music and lyrics. They read:

It's not that easy bein' green,
having to spend each day the color of leaves,

*when I think it could be nicer bein' red, or yellow, or gold,
or something much more colorful like that.*

*It's not that easy bein' green,
It seems you blend in with so many other ordinary things,
and people tend to pass you over
'cause you're not standing out like flashy sparkles on the water, or stars in the sky.*

*But green's the color of spring, and green can be cool and friendly like,
and green can be big like an ocean, or important like a mountain, or tall
    like a tree*

*When green is all there is to be, it could make you wonder why.
But why wonder, why wonder?
I am green, and it'll do fine. It's beautiful, and I think it's what I want to be.*

Raposo quickly arranged the song for the *Sesame Street* house band, and Jim Henson sang it in the wee hours of a recording session. Epstein said that Henson's very first take was "magnificent," but that an audio engineer's error ruined the acetate for the track. "Jim didn't blink," Epstein said. "He just sang it and sang it until we had a take that came close to the original. But I'm telling you, as someone who heard it, the first take was the keeper."

Kermit's melancholy performance, a song as soliloquy, inspired an array of interpretations. Some heard it as a contemplation of racial difference. Some heard it as a plea for tolerance of difference, or a lament about the same. "It was taken as a civil rights song, but it wasn't that," said Cooney. "It wasn't meant to be about black people. It was meant to be about people who are different in more ways than just race."

Pat Collins, who would have known better than anyone, said the song was "simply about being comfortable in your own skin, being comfortable with who you are. There wasn't a lot of thumb sucking involved. Joe just went off and wrote it. But over time, as is the case with many good songs and poems, people identify with it on different levels. Ray Charles once told Joe that he wished that he had written 'Bein' Green' because it spoke to his experience." Charles made "Bein' Green" part of his repertoire.

While Collins has dismissed notions that the song was autobiographical—an attempt to explain what it felt like to be a Portuguese kid of modest means from Fall River, Massachusetts—she said that another of his *Sesame Street* songs, the sing-along simple "Somebody Come and Play," came straight from Raposo's childhood experience.

Somebody come and play.
Somebody come and play today.
Somebody come and smile the smiles,
and sing the songs,
it won't take long.
Somebody come and play today.
Somebody come with me and see the pleasure in the wind.
Somebody come before it gets too late to begin.

Somebody come and play.
Somebody come and play today.
Somebody come and be my friend,
and watch the sun till it rains again.
Somebody come and play today.

"Joe was an only child, and he never had enough playmates," Collins said. "For the first six years in school, nearly all of his classmates were orphans. His parents sent him to the neighborhood Catholic school, which was right across the street from his house. They thought it was a good school, but it was primarily a church school for kids without parents. They couldn't come over and play after school because they all had to go back to the orphanage at the end of the day. His parents were only too happy about that because it meant Joe would spend more time studying piano in the afternoon. His mother, the former Mary Victorine, nailed shut the window in the practice room so that he wouldn't open the window and go out and try to play baseball with the other neighborhood kids. She and her husband, Joseph D. Raposo, saw a child who was gifted, and they were correct."

"And so, I see 'Somebody Come and Play' not as a song of regret or self-pity," said Collins, "but a song about an only child looking to toss the ball around before the sun goes down. It's about begging for pals to hang out with, kind of saying 'If this day goes by, maybe we won't have another quite like it.'"

One Saturday, out of the blue, Jim Henson called Joan Cooney at home. Clearly agitated and sounding almost brokenhearted, Henson said, "You have ruined my life."

This was strange, coming from a man who was enjoying heretofore record levels of personal prosperity, professional achievement, and spiritual fulfillment. "We had had disagreements," Cooney said, "but the tone in

Henson's voice was one she had not heard before. It seemed a mixture of exasperation, disillusionment, and fear.

Henson then asked a question for which there was no answer: "Why did you have to be so successful?"

The remark wasn't meant as ironic flattery; he was being sincere. The question hung in the air a moment before he completed the thought. "I am now living my worst nightmare."

As far back as the days of *Sam and Friends*, as Henson established the Muppet brand, he had insisted his satiric and anarchic puppetry was primarily meant for adults. While he did nothing to discourage children from watching, and they did so in droves, Henson's subsequent television commercials and appearances on mass-audience shows such as *Today* and *Tonight* were written and performed with a sophistication and wit that often went right over the heads of children, just as the subtext of Burr Tillstrom's *Kukla, Fran and Ollie* did in the 1950s.

Puppetry was a means to an end for Henson. His goal was to be on television, and then later, to conquer the movies. Prior to *Sesame Street*, Henson's business was evolving just as he had imagined it might. Rowlf was trading quips with Jimmy Dean on the entertainer's prime-time show on ABC, and Henson's more abstract Muppets were frequently featured on *The Ed Sullivan Show*. But Henson would find it galling every time Sullivan would lead in to an appearance by saying "And now for the kiddies out there, Jim Henson's Muppets . . ." He was grateful for the exposure, but the categorization defeated his marketing strategy. In his mind, he was not, and never would be, a children's entertainer, though he embraced the idea of being a *family* entertainer. That was an important distinction, one that Sullivan—and others—could not appreciate. What Henson wanted to re-create for television with the Muppets was the experience from his childhood of listening with his parents and brother to Edgar Bergen and Charlie McCarthy on the radio.

Henson had an advantage and an insight that was lost on others, a vision that was the result of his European walkabout. It was there he did his de facto graduate work in the art and commerce of puppetry, visiting countries where the art is taken far more seriously than in the United States. He returned home determined to become America's counterintuitive puppeteer, a satirist who reinvented an ancient art form for the television age. He would be Burr Tillstrom—and then some, discarding the mock proscenium stage and the puppet theater for a more direct presentation to the home. He would, to the best of his ability, eschew daytime television, seeking after-dark opportunities, whenever and however possible.

But then came the entreaty from Joan Cooney to join in the noble cause of educational television. Its appeal was undeniable to compassionate, color-blind Henson, whose own young children were enjoying advantages denied to the less fortunate. Henson, a suburban commuter in hippie's clothing, poured bountiful energy into *Sesame Street* for its first few years, before backing away slightly to allow his company to manage the day-to-day dealings with production of the show.

By 1972, after the initial shower of accolades, there were times when his involvement with the show began to feel like a trap. Having worked so persistently to establish a broader identity, here he was, being hailed as America's most amusing babysitter. It felt hopeless at times to be reduced to that, and Henson began to resent *Sesame Street* at the same time he was grateful to it. By 1972, revenues were just beginning to flow in from *Sesame*'s licensed products, creating a reservoir of reserves. That cash enabled Henson Associates to grow from a boutique operation into a bona fide enterprise.

Still, there were days when Henson felt he had sold his soul, and it was on one of these despondent days that he picked up the phone to call his client and colleague.

Cooney can be a cool customer, in the best sense, and she became especially adept at handling uprisings among the oft-temperamental men under her employ in the early seventies. "They all submerged their egos for that first year and a half, before *Sesame Street* debuted, then all hell broke loose," she said.

"Joan had this enormous magic and force of personality," said David Britt, her chief lieutenant in the executive ranks through the mid-1990s. "She got these very strong characters to not only come to work for her but to work *together*. And most of them didn't necessarily get along very well."

Henson was the least of her problems, but on the day he called with what she described as a *cri de coeur*, he jumped right to the top of her priorities. It was only after Cooney had allowed him to vent that she responded. "It was a lengthy, anguished phone conversation, and I picked up a certain restlessness in his words. Together, we worked through whatever the problem was that prompted the call, and I have no memory of what that was, other than Jim was feeling trapped in preschool television. But I recognized he was someone who resisted entrapment and would want to fly away if caged. I said to him, 'You are going to break out of this. Something is going to happen that will provide new opportunities for you. You need to have the patience and belief to see what I'm saying is true.'"

What she could not have known on that weekend day was that just streets away, in the darkened Henson Workshop, amid the bales of fabric and pull-out drawers of eyes and noses, were scribbles and doodles and documented daydreams about a prime-time variety show starring the Muppets. Henson had long hoped that he might interest the networks with such an idea, stowing away ideas for what would one day become the world's most successful syndicated television series, a comedy colossus called *The Muppet Show*. After turning their backs on it, America's three commercial television networks watched in awe as Henson's half-hour series, informed by English music hall comedy and vaudeville, circled the globe.

Henson's despair over being viewed as a children's performer would never entirely dissipate, but Joan Cooney's reassurance on a down day was just what he needed, and he relaxed.

"I said to Jim, 'Whatever happens, we must stay together for the sake of the children,'" Cooney recalled.

"And we did."

Tim and Joan Cooney did not have children, but during the final turbulent years of their marriage they acted as de facto foster parents to an inner-city black child.

In 1970, Tim was working for Fight Back, a civil rights organization that helped blacks find work in New York's multi-billion-dollar construction industry. The group's storefront headquarters was situated in a typical block in Harlem, a mix of apartment houses, churches, hair salons, corner bars, and the kind of neighborhood shop that featured a candy counter, stacks of daily newspapers, and, in some cases, a back room to bet on the numbers. Next door to Fight Back was such an emporium, operated by an enterprising black woman.

Often when Tim stopped by for a paper he would see the woman's adorable six-year-old grandchild, Chauncey Raymond Gilbert. To everyone but his grandmother, he was known as Raymond. She monitored his welfare as best she could, as her reckless daughter was incapable of providing much stability to Raymond and his siblings.

Over time, Tim befriended Raymond. "He was so smart," Cooney said. "Tim thought there was something exceptional about him, and they took a shine to each other."

The Cooney apartment became a happy refuge for a little boy from troubled circumstances. While he could be a delight, Raymond was often a challenge. Trouble just seemed to follow him.

The Cooneys started taking him along on trips to their weekend home in West Hampton Beach. "Everybody was welcoming of this cute little kid, but he began to steal from the neighbors, pocketing money if it was left around," Cooney said. "When he was about eight years old, I half kiddingly asked him, 'Exactly when did your life in crime start?' He thought for a second, and went, '*Mmmm*. I guess it was when I was four and stole from a grocery store.' The way he said it was without feeling, as if he were describing a way to beat the system.

"Raymond cried easily if he got caught or if you scolded him, but otherwise I found him completely affectless," Cooney said. "I saw this conscienceless side of Raymond." The Cooneys hoped Raymond would become more responsible and rule abiding. "It was typical of Tim and me—and of a lot of other white liberals in the 1970s—that we thought we might make a difference, that a miracle might occur, that it was worth taking such a long shot on that particular kid."

The Cooneys arranged to have Raymond enrolled at Saint Christopher's-Jennie Clarkson, a well-regarded residential program for troubled children, located in suburban Westchester County. "Luckily I knew a psychiatrist for the school, and he got him in. It was a huge break because we couldn't afford a private institution, and this was absolutely free and wonderful. It was a therapeutic situation but it was also an accredited school."

After a year Raymond's mother came back into the picture. "He was there [at the school] for at least a year and doing better when his mother decided she wanted all of her children to be with her. She was living in Las Vegas, having a child a year with different men." Raymond withdrew from school and moved to Nevada.

"That was the beginning of the end of possibilities for him," Cooney said.

"Tim always built defeat into whatever he was doing, and it was so typical of him that he would be drawn to a child like Raymond, someone you'd invest all that time in and get nowhere. Tim never would have found a promising child in Harlem that we *really* might have helped. It would always be someone that you weren't going to win with."

In the late 1970s, Raymond returned to New York, no less a stranger to difficulties than when he left. Tim warned Joan against seeing him, fearing she might be at risk. "That was fine with me, because by the time Raymond was seventeen or eighteen, he had already been in prison," Cooney said. "Tim said that to kids like Raymond, prison was an initiation; you went to prison to enter the big time."

Raymond dealt in stolen goods and became a recidivist, doing time at Riker's Island and an upstate penitentiary. During his third prison stint, he obtained a college degree. "But he could not stay out of trouble," Cooney said, "From the time he was a child he was surrounded by petty crime and dysfunction."

Out of prison and back fencing goods, Chauncey Raymond Gilbert was shot dead on a New York street, well shy of his thirtieth birthday.

In the years leading up to the launch of *Sesame Street*—and the ascendancy of Joan Ganz Cooney—Tim Cooney had bolstered his wife's confidence and made things happen for her with his connections and convincing charm. But as Joan evolved into a celebrated figure—almost a three-name brand like Mary Tyler Moore—Tim began to withdraw into alcoholism, depression, and rage. On the one hand, he was immensely proud of *Sesame Street* and was thrilled that it was assisting poor children. On the other, "It made him feel unimportant," Joan Cooney said. "His tendencies toward self-destruction were made much worse by my success, although he loved what I was doing and would help me by reading over and editing press releases and speeches that I would give. He wanted the success for me, but he became less and less visible in his own mind.

"But Tim was never going to permit himself to succeed, no matter what had happened to me. I don't know what would've happened had I not succeeded, except that we would've been living hand-to-mouth."

At his wife's insistence, Tim saw a specialist in alcoholism and went on Antabuse, the first medication approved by the Food and Drug Administration for treatment of the disease. The drug interferes with the normal metabolic processes of the body. When a person consumes alcohol, it metabolizes into acetaldehyde, the toxic substance that causes hangover symptoms. As the hours pass, the body oxidizes acetaldehyde into acetic acid, which is harmless. Antabuse stops the oxidation of acetaldehyde, resulting in a build-up of the substance that is five to ten times greater than what normally occurs when a person drinks. The result is a barrage of symptoms that can range from copious vomiting and throbbing headache to congestive heart failure.

Amazingly, Tim found a way around it. "Antabuse controlled Tim's impulse drinking for eight or nine months, but then he secretly planned a drunk. He knew he could no longer just stop in a bar on impulse, and he knew he had to wait three or four days for the drug to pass out of his system." It was almost as if he circled a date on a calendar when he would cave. "It was unbelievably hopeless," Cooney said. "He just couldn't give it up. His tragedy was that he had no desire to be sober and he never hit bottom. Alcohol really destroyed that part of his brain that might have saved him."

When the Cooneys separated in 1975, Joan, recognizing that Tim had no visible means of support, instructed her lawyers to draw up an agreement that would provide food, shelter, and transportation for a man who hadn't held a paid position in years. "I don't know what would've happened had I not supported him," Cooney said. "I guess he would've ended up in a homeless shelter. I did what I had to do. All I wanted was a peaceful end to the marriage. And I knew that wasn't possible if I didn't sign a document saying I'd support him for the rest of his life. And, in fact, that document provided for a weekend house for him. I signed a car and a garage over to him. I was borrowing five thousand dollars a month on a bank loan to live. Every night I was doing the arithmetic of how do I get through to the next month. But I was happy to give him whatever he wanted. He was kicked out of his apartment house at one point, and I just quickly paid the landlord for the damage he claimed had been done. I found a broker, got a new apartment, and moved him in fast. I never wanted any of this to be public. I didn't want it in the papers that he'd been picked up on the streets as a homeless person. And it would've been newsworthy because he was a former city figure and my husband."

Cooney hoped for a respite from the demands of her personal life, but that longed-for peace never came. In August 1975, nine months after separating from Tim, she spotted a tiny pulsating bead on the left side of her chest, above the breast. "The lump was up in the muscle, just a twitching little thing that was less than a centimeter. But I could see it in the mirror. I could be in a slip and see it. At the time I was seeing a doctor every six months because my mother had had breast cancer at fifty-seven. And I had my own history of benign tumors, for which I had several biopsies that required hospital stays. I found a surgeon I loved, and when I came up with this lump, I lightly said, 'You'd say it's benign, wouldn't you?' And he said, 'No. I wouldn't say that at all.' I couldn't believe this tiny thing could possibly be cancer or dangerous." It was determined to be both.

"The doctor said chemo and radiation were too dangerous and that, being forty-five, I was too young to consider it. He said I could easily get leukemia by the time I was sixty or sixty-five, which a lot of people did. Susan Sontag and I were talking back then because we were both being operated on at about the same time. Her cancer was so widespread, she decided to go to Paris to see a doctor who was blasting women with chemotherapy. My doctor said, 'He's going to kill her.' But that doctor saved her and she lived till she was seventy-one or seventy-two.

"I had a radical mastectomy, a ghastly operation for a very small cancer," Cooney said, without a trace of bitterness or self-pity. "Nowadays it would be a lumpectomy, I would be on radiation, and it would be over."

Her estranged husband took the news hard. "Tim was absolutely *there* for me," Cooney said. "He came every morning and brought me the papers and asked me what needed to be done, going back to the apartment to feed the cats and the dog. It was the most decent and level he had ever been, even though he was quite jarred by my cancer. He needed me very badly in every way. He was sobered, as it were, by the thought that I might not live. I don't think he was thinking, *Oh my God, I may lose my means of support.* It was more that I was suddenly a needy figure.

"When I came home after about ten days, my sister came to stay with me," Cooney said. "Tim disappeared."

During her convalescence, Jim Henson arrived one day with a filled Cookie Monster cookie jar. "What he said was so typical," Cooney said. "I had asked him many times during the first five years of the show, 'What if something happens to you? What happens to your company? What happens to us at CTW?' And now here he was at my apartment, looking at me.

"You asked me what would happen, and then you go and do this," Henson said with a slight smile. "What happens?"

"Nothing," Cooney said. "I'm going to be fine."

"I just remember that stark look he had," Cooney said. "It was kind of like 'You had the nerve to ask me and then pull this stunt.'"

"I had Bob Hatch put out a memo to the staff that I had been operated on [and] returned to work quickly. I was supposed to stay out several weeks, but I started coming back for half days very early on, maybe after ten days. I had one interest: showing that I wasn't sick and that CTW wasn't going to miss a beat. I needed to feel normal again, back in the saddle, but there was a lot of depression. Work saved me."

Cooney's mother, Sylvia, had lived to see nearly eighty. "She had a fainting spell two years before her death that cut off oxygen to the brain," Cooney said. "I believe she died as a result of the radiation she had had for her second mastectomy."

"My doctor said, 'Trust me, you're going to be fine,' but I had many scares afterward, and many operations. But, after each one turned out benign, he'd say, 'I'm telling you, you can't have a recurrence. We can't ignore what's happening, but it's almost impossible for you to have a recurrence for breast cancer.'

"I never thought a lot about death, but I thought about my body having been assaulted."

Nothing in Tom Kennedy's experience at CBS and the Public Broadcasting Laboratory had quite prepared him for dealing with the federal government as CTW's vice president for finance and administration. Being pelted with demands while being bound in red tape was its own peculiar brand of torture.

"The government sent out directives about everything, including one about hiring criminals, ordering that we had to hire people with records. I was getting it up to here, and it reached a breaking point. I went down to a CPB meeting in Washington one afternoon. There must have been twenty people there from the Office of Education and public television. They wanted to know why we weren't hiring the mentally handicapped. The blood was boiling up inside me and I said, "The truth is I have been trying to hire the mentally handicapped. I've been searching and searching and I haven't been able to find them. Now I suddenly realize why I can't find them. They're all working for the government or CPB."

Things only got worse.

In 1974, CTW was informed that it was going to be the subject of a federal audit. "The head auditor from Washington sits down and has two thick books under his arm," Kennedy said. "They contain press clippings about all the organizations he has shot down, this hospital, and that hospital. 'I just want you to know we are competent,' he said.

"I said, 'Have you people done anything on auditing television?'

"'Oh yes, we've done this before,' he said.

"I said, 'Do you assign people who are familiar with television? Because it *is* different. We spend money different than a research project does. And this is not a research project, even though it says on your books that it is. Can you assign people to it who have had experience in television?'

"'Absolutely,' he said. "So he introduces the guys who are going to do it. I said, 'What projects have you handled?' One of them was a fifteen-thousand-dollar audit of an audio-visual project at Harvard. The other had done something similar, maybe it was twenty thousand dollars. And they were going to audit the Workshop as experts. I just blew up. I knew it was going to be a disaster. They sent a bunch of nincompoops who couldn't be talked to and couldn't be reasoned with. They had no idea what television is about. They never heard of anybody spending fifteen dollars for lunch. They spent a dollar and a half. They asked, 'How come Joan Cooney makes more money than congressmen make?' They spent about a year trying to find things wrong. And they leaked everything to the press because that was the game plan they always had. They didn't care if it destroyed the Workshop. You just had to hope their arrows didn't get you in the back."

It was an exhausting waste of time and energy. "The fact of the matter is they never collected fifty cents because none of it was ever substantiated.

They were an impossible lot. I was going to take them on when I left the Workshop but I was preoccupied with my own problems; my wife was dying. But I really thought that something should have been done about the way those auditors functioned," he said.

"They were not functioning in the best interest of the country."

For Cooney, tussles with Washington became part of the landscape. Some were more trying than others, if not as time-consuming.

"In 1978 Congressman Lawrence H. Fountain of North Carolina had an aide who worked for him who hated public broadcasting. And he fed a story to Jack Anderson, the investigative reporter and columnist, that we had misappropriated money, which is very different from misapplied funds. Misapplied means you have to straighten that out but it's not a crime. Misappropriated is a crime. Bob Hatch and I went down to see Congressman Fountain, and we all lit up cigarettes as we walked in because he was from the tobacco state. He pulled his aide back a little bit but that guy was a real enemy.

"Then we heard the *National Enquirer* had a reporter on it who was talking to everyone. I knew exactly what it was going to be: a big story in the supermarkets that would say 'IS BIG BIRD A THIEF?' You'd have to read through the whole story to find out no, he's not."

Cooney understandably was very worried, and, perhaps fortunately, she wore her anxiety on her sleeve. "It was right around the time I started going out with Pete Peterson. In fact, on our first date he asked me how things were going at the Workshop.

"We are having the scariest situation with the *National Enquirer*," Cooney told him.

Peterson seemed unconcerned. "I'll kill the story."

Cooney said, "You'll do *what*?"

Peterson soothingly said, "Just understand. It's over."

"Well just how will you do *that*?" Cooney asked.

Peterson explained that he had attended MIT with Generoso "Gene" Pope Jr., the owner of the *Enquirer*. "We are very close, old friends, and I am trustee of his estate. I'll just call and tell him to kill the story."

Peterson's secretary called Pope's secretary, asking that CTW be added to a list of untouchable topics for the *Enquirer*, "which included the CIA, Mafia, and Pete Peterson," Cooney recalled with a smile.

A day or two later, Cooney walked into the CTW office and said to Bob Hatch, "It's dead."

"What's dead?" he asked.

"The story is dead," Cooney said, in as businesslike a way as she could muster.

It was, she recalled, a great moment. "Hatch was almost having a nervous breakdown over what had been happening because Fountain had red flagged our funding request and time was running out."

A CTW lawyer with ties to Joseph Califano pulled off a minor miracle on the day the funding proposal was being considered. With time slipping away, Califano agreed to freeze the clock at midnight, allowing aides to work through the night to craft an acceptable compromise. "What they said after the dust settled was 'Okay, we'll give you the grant, but you will have to undergo an audit,'" Cooney recalled.

Northern Calloway and his piano accompanist Alan Menken were en route to a weekend booking, passing the time onboard the jetliner playing chess.

"Pawn to king 4," Calloway said, sliding his piece along the surface of the travel set's board. "You know, I've already beaten you."

Menken, a decent player, half smiled. "Okay, man," he said. "Bring it on."

Calloway's response was insistent. "No, no, no. You don't understand. I see every move ahead of me," he said. "I'm going to beat you."

Menken thought it beyond boastful that anyone would make such a pronouncement, especially after only one move. "*Um*, you've got to make moves in order to beat me," Menken said. "I may have some good answers for those moves."

But Calloway, growing indignant, would not hear any of it. "I . . . have . . . already . . . beaten . . . you," he fumed, turning his body toward the cabin window and studying the sky.

The first signs that Calloway was becoming increasingly delusional and hostile came at moments like this, when a cheerful mood would darken over a perceived contest of some sort. "He would need to be right about something, just some little, insignificant fact," Menken said. "And if you disagreed with him it would become a violent argument. The supposed antagonist would realize he wasn't joking and would back off. His colleagues never felt terribly in danger but began to suspect that he was unbalanced."

Once, while riding around with Menken and a drummer and bass player who occasionally joined them on the road for children's shows, the subject turned to Mozart and his contemporaries. Who was the most forward-thinking composer?

"We were merely talking to pass the time," Menken said. "But then Northern started screaming and cursing, becoming completely unglued, because his opinion was not shared by everyone else in the car. The others would try to laugh it off as if it was some sort of joke that had gone over the top. But I sensed that it was not a joke, and that the topic needed to change." Menken recalled that "Northern would bounce back extremely fast because he was operating at a frequency that was frankly another frequency."

In those days, Alan Menken was just beginning to make his way as a songwriter, filling assignments that came his way for *Sesame Street*. "It was pathetic money, but it still had some prestige to it," Menken said. "It was on the air and I was getting some royalties." Both Menken and Calloway were managed by Scott Shukat, whose idea it was to pair the two for an open-ended series of weekend appearances. "Northern needed someone to play *for* him and *with* him," Menken said. "It was an extremely portable thing. Northern sang and I played the piano. We were booked by this little company called NAMCO, owned by Fran and Barry Wiesler. They were just trying to break into Broadway musicals back then."

"Northern and I would go show up at an airport, fly somewhere, and put on our show. Northern had been married briefly to a beautiful show-girl, but it did not last. And he came out of that quite a ladies' man. He would hit on these women who came to the shows, and these attractive young white mothers would pick him up. And we'd go into these cities, often in the South, and Northern would be charming these white women. Sometimes I was his 'beard,' playing the role of a respectable suitor walking down the street with a woman. But she, of course, would be going to the hotel to be with Northern.

"Northern's behavior over time began to get pretty intense, and then somewhat erratic, and, in time, I came to understand that he was manic-depressive, or what is now bipolar disease. But unbeknownst to me, he was also snorting a lot of coke.

"It all reached a peak when we were met by a young woman in Nashville. There had been a big power outage with no power in the city. So we went off to sit at a coffee shop, where Northern had this breakdown, crying about how much emotional and mental turmoil he was in. He was having terrible nightmares and wasn't sleeping.

"We did the show and, as was Northern's pattern, he got involved with that woman. It was strange and intense, and it was almost the kind of thing where I felt like I should protect her. He had become very aggressive with his flirtations, almost out of control."

Menken and Calloway's relationship ruptured in the years that followed. "I had stopped working with him and my career had taken off,"

Menken said, starting with my first musical, *God Bless You, Mr. Rosewater*, and then *Little Shop of Horrors*. Northern watched all of this and was feeling competitive with me. He considered himself a songwriter and was a talented man. And he felt that because I was white and he was black is why I had succeeded, and that Scott was favoring me as a client. It was tense and unpleasant to deal with Northern, and then he sued Scott for money he felt that he deserved that Scott had not gotten for him. It was a horrible thing for Scott to go through, and he was completely exonerated. Scott Shukat was the most scrupulously honest manager I've ever known. He was embarrassingly honest. I mean he literally took me away from his own business managers and sent me to the business managers I'm with now, who are the best in the business, specifically to make sure there was not even a hint of conflict of interest."

Along with the late Howard Ashman, Menken went on to write the soundtracks for three modern-day Disney animated classics: *Beauty and the Beast*, *The Little Mermaid*, and *Aladdin*.

Calloway went on to fall off the edge.

Chapter Seventeen

J on Stone wasn't a man's man—he had few cigar-chomping, belt-sanding instincts—and while he wasn't entirely a ladies' man, the ladies did find him attractive and witty and appealing. Many succumbed to his charms.

If Bert and Ernie adored him, Big Bird (and the man inside him) was less enamored. Stone was at times cruel and punishing to Caroll Spinney, whose preference was to read over his lines on the morning of taping rather than commit them to memory overnight. Stone attributed this practice to laziness and unprofessionalism, Spinney to a desire to approach material fresh.[1] Spinney, by nature sensitive and always eager to avoid conflict (not unlike Big Bird himself), was often victimized by Stone. When Stone would strike, Spinney would respond by walking in circles, wounded and perplexed.

Stone's superiors, with one notable exception, found him at times to be a grating, unpleasant, defensive, unyielding, superior pain. He mostly felt the same way about them. He was capable of carrying grudges, ridiculing those who dared challenge his authority, refusing to suffer fools gladly.

That he could also be lovable, tender, brilliantly funny, tireless, resourceful, imaginative, and instinctive rounded out the edges of an emotionally complex and moody man, without whom there would not have been *Sesame Street* as we know it. Stone's supervision of the show defined his professional life and determined his legacy. That *Sesame Street* flourished during its adolescence, blossoming in the period from its tenth anniversary in 1979 to its twentieth in 1989, can be attributed to Stone's dedication to its content and to nurturing its spirit. Talent came and went in that ten-year span, but Stone—and his handpicked No. 2, Dulcy Singer—provided the constancy, the good taste, the adventuresome reach, and the great good humor that not only kept the show alive but thriving.

As a parent, Stone knew when to say no. He always kept a No. 2 pencil perched in his beard while at work in the studio. If a script met with his disapproval, he would extricate the pencil and then slash away at the pages, rewriting on the fly rather than allow a substandard tag line—called the "button"—to fall flat.

As a parent, Stone also knew when to say yes, allowing the puppeteers to extemporize and embellish comically when they knew they were on a roll. He created a studio environment where people were allowed to be their authentic selves, an almost homelike atmosphere that was welcomed by celebrity guests who came by for one episode and then wished they could stay for another. That the *Sesame Street* set has traditionally been completely informal is largely attributable to a man whose preferred style of dress included a fishing vest with pockets and vents everywhere.

As a parent to his daughters, Polly and Kate, Stone was nothing like his own father, a clinically cold obstetrician and medical faculty member at Yale who shipped his two sons off for the summer to a farm in New Hampshire. There was no denying Dr. Stone's brilliance, either in the operating room or when he would retreat to his study to solve mathematical problems or to play classical music on the piano. "My grandfather was not a man who loved children," said Kate Lucas, Jon's youngest daughter. "He was very much an intellectual and liked quiet in the house." Though he was wealthy, money was never spoken of in a household where appearances and proper manners mattered.

Jon was musical and athletic as a child, but he was also dyslexic. He struggled academically, and his father sent him to boarding school at thirteen, in the hope that it would shape him up.

He once shared a crushing story from those prep-school days with daughter Kate. "My grandfather only went to one of dad's football games, and on that day Dad rushed the kicker and blocked a punt with his chest. He saw stars and got knocked over, but the first thing that entered his mind was that his father was there to see it. But my grandfather had gone out of the stadium to make a business call and missed it. The disappointment of that stayed with my dad his entire life."

Family lore has it that Jon's father was pleased when his son was admitted to Williams College in Massachusetts, but displeased with his choice of major. Few undergraduates during Stone's four years at Williams declared music as a concentration.

One day years later, when Stone was completing his final year of graduate school at Yale Drama, his father was delivering twins across town in New Haven. As nurses bundled the first infant to emerge from the womb, Dr. Stone mentioned to colleagues in surgery that he was feeling peculiar. He stepped out into the hallway and fell dead from a massive coronary.

"My dad had a complicated childhood," Kate said. "He adored his mother and she adored him, but he clearly knew his father preferred his brother over him. A lot of times that pattern of rejection can continue into the next generation. But my father was the complete opposite of his father in terms of the way he loved his children. Polly and I were so lucky growing up to have a dad who was so wise. You could pick up the phone and tell him any problem in the world. He would listen and give you wonderful advice. Over and over he told us that we were his world, which kids need to hear. He told us we could do whatever we wanted to do in the world, and encouraged us to follow our dreams."

Without the slightest tinge of resentment, she said, "*Sesame Street* was his third daughter," the vessel into which he poured so much of his essence. She speaks of the show the way a younger sister looks up to an older sibling. And she believes that what her father often said about *Sesame Street* is true: that Kate and Polly had as much to do with the success of the show as anyone else. They were *Sesame Street*'s in-house, on-demand focus group, and just by being kids they contributed innumerable ideas for skits and sketches, and in one instance, a triumphant holiday special in 1978, *Christmas Eve on Sesame Street.*

The program was a tuneful, tasteful, at times heart-tugging imagining of the hours leading up to Christmas, a day somewhat spoiled by Oscar's rather sour and persistent skepticism about Santa Claus.

In a manner reminiscent of spiteful older children tormenting younger ones—the cynical neo-nonbelievers who pick on the faithful, who don't deserve to have their fantasies shattered—Oscar taunts Big Bird, raising doubts that Santa will deliver presents to buildings that may have rooftop vents but not chimneys. Stone and his cowriter, Joe Bailey, wrote script pages that reflected a plausible dilemma for an urban child, acted out by worrisome, restless Big Bird, who goes missing on Christmas Eve. Like a preschool child who wanders off in a department store, Big Bird is oblivious to the worry he is causing by stationing himself on the rooftop of Gordon and Susan's brownstone. As a snowstorm grows in intensity, Big Bird remains at his frigid post, on the lookout for Santa.

Panic sets in when word hits the street that Big Bird is gone. That's when Maria, behaving as any frantic adult might, pulls Oscar out of his trash can—by the scruff of his little green neck. What transpires is a startling reprimand that sounds surprisingly lifelike.

Oscar (*getting unceremoniously yanked*): Whaddya doin', Maria?
Maria: I hope you're satisfied! You had to start all that stuff about Santa and tiny chimneys and you've upset Big Bird so much he's gone!
Oscar: Well, I didn't know he'd do anything dumb like that! I was only teasing him.

Maria: *Teasing* him! Telling him that Santa isn't going to be bringing any-body any presents because he can't get down a tiny chimney? Now you call that teasing?

Oscar: We'll . . . he'll come on back. He's part homing pigeon. Besides, what's the big deal? He lives outside all the time anyway.

Maria (*slapping the fingers of her right hand into the palm of her left*): Now look here, Oscar. The nest is something different. That's his home. He's got an electric blanket there. He's got heating pads. And he's around all the people that he loves. But here it is, Christmas Eve, and he's out there somewhere in this big city and it keeps snowing and it's getting colder and he could be in serious trouble unless we find him. (*On the verge of tears*): So what are you going to do about it?

Oscar, shamed, regretful, and suddenly resolute, goes off in search of Big Bird, after getting his comeuppance from Maria, the one adult on *Sesame Street* who gives as good as she gets. Before he trudges off, his feet sticking out of the bottom of the can, Oscar can't resist one little tweak.

"Come on, hurry up, skinny," he calls out to Maria. It is at that moment the script reminds us that the grouch is at his orneriest around those he cares for the most.

The script allows for another powerfully relatable moment, after Big Bird decides he's had enough of waiting in the cold and comes downstairs to "warm up for a minute" at Gordon and Susan's place. Gordon has been trying to soothe Patty, a scared child who had been playing with Big Bird and reported him missing. She runs to Big Bird's side as he enters the foyer, giggling with joyous relief. That's when the questions begin from the sur-rogate parents.

Susan (*concerned*): Big Bird, are you all right?

Big Bird: I'm all right, except for my [frozen] giblets.

Gordon (*agitated*): Big Bird, where have you *been*?

Big Bird: Well, I went up on the roof to see if I could see Santa Claus, and then I fell asleep. *Brrrrr.* It got so cold I decided to come down and warm up. Then I'm going right back up—

Gordon (*firmly, with finger pointed*): Oh, no, you're not. You're just going to come in here and thaw out. *That's* what you're going to do.

Gordon all but pushes Big Bird into his apartment, where gifts deliv-ered from Santa are laid out under a tree decorated with baubles, tinsel, and candy canes. Not only did Santa arrive, he even left something for Cookie Monster.

The Christmas special features a second story line, borrowed affection-ately from O. Henry. Ernie is trading in his rubber duckie to get a cigar box for old buddy Bert's paper clip collection. Bert, in turn, is trading in his paper clips to Mr. Hooper for a pink soap dish for Ernie's use as a bathtime perch for duckie. Mr. Hooper, recognizing sacrifice and devoted friendship when he sees it, returns the duck and the paper clip collection, wrapped as gifts to his good customers Bert and Ernie, who sing "Have Yourself a Merry Little Christmas."

To watch that scene now, preserved on home video, is to be reminded how remarkably gifted were Jim Henson and Frank Oz, two real-life col-leagues and friends, at playing puppetry's Odd Couple. It is a tribute to their artistry that Bert and Ernie seem so emotionally valid and kinetic to the viewer, even though somewhere within the rational folds of the brain we know they are but extensions of shirtsleeves, two arts-and-crafts proj-ects, "dollies to wiggle" as Stone used to say.

Any sentimentalist looking for a reason to test his or her tear ducts would do well to insert *Christmas Eve on Sesame Street* into the video player and replay Bert and Ernie's rendition of a Christmas classic. It will remind the viewer that love and friendship are binding forces of the universe that transcend time and space. The relationship that existed between Henson and Oz, brothers, creative collaborators, and interlocking souls, was down-right enviable. They shared something holy and fragile, illuminated by laughter and held tethered by trust. God blessed them; but Jon Stone, a mere mortal, brought out their best.

"If there was one project to put in a time capsule and send off to space, to let the Martians know what *Sesame Street* was like, it would be that Christmas special," said Sonia Manzano. "Jon had a way of touching the exact pulse, the exact concerns of the child. He was not afraid."

Dulcy Singer, who produced the special, said "It was Jon's baby from the beginning. If you want to see his soul, watch *Christmas Eve on Sesame Street*."

Stone's now-adult children see aspects of their childhood in Vermont and New York reflected in the special. "When my sister and I were lit-tle, we would write a letter to Santa after dinner on Christmas Eve," said schoolteacher Polly, an interior designer by avocation. "We'd leave the letters with cookies—and a glass of scotch—by the fireplace. One year I asked Santa what his favorite poem was. My sister asked him how he got down that skinny little chimney. So the idea for Big Bird's dilemma in the special came from Kate, who was teeny at the time.

"The next morning came Dad's response—or should I say Santa's response—in a letter for each of us. To me he wrote, 'Roses are red, violets are blue, aba-ca-chu, I've got the flu.'

"To Kate he wrote, 'Well, I suck in my gut and I point my toes and *whoosh*, down I go! Getting up is a different matter.'"

Paul Firstenberg was CTW's executive vice president in 1978 when *Christmas Eve on Sesame Street* was produced. One of his more baffling decisions (which included selling off interests in cable television that would later be valued in the hundreds of millions) was to sign a deal that same year for *A Special Sesame Street Christmas*, with independent television producer Bob Banner. Banner, whose roots in variety television went back to the Garry Moore and Dinah Shore shows of the 1950s, had a track record of working with Henson and the Muppets from his days producing the prime-time *Jimmy Dean Show*. CBS bought the idea even though there was one in the works for PBS. When executive producer Singer questioned the wisdom of competing specials, Firstenberg said, "If we proceed with two shows, maybe one will make it to air." Said Singer, "Can you imagine the mentality? He had a complete lack of understanding of the show."

Firstenberg's low-budget network special featured a bizarre lineup of creaky B-list talent, including cloying host Leslie Uggams and nearly exhumed entertainers Ethel Merman and Imogene Coca. All three had been early guest stars on *The Muppet Show*, before top-name talent began flocking to the syndicated show after its first season. Adding to the surreal mix of the Christmas special were guest appearances by Henry Fonda and that breakout boy soprano from the Jackson 5, Michael Jackson.

It was a painfully obtuse hour built around a shaky story line that cast Oscar as *Sesame Street*'s resident Scrooge. It was an hour trimmed in treacle and about as far afield from the educational objectives of *Sesame Street* as one could imagine.

It should be noted here that an honest appraisal of Jim Henson's network television work with the Muppets must account for a good number of unworthy, unfunny, unbecoming, unwatchable appearances of which *A Special Sesame Street Christmas* was one. On balance, the good far outweighs the bad, and much of what Henson brought to television approached greatness. But his taste was not impeccable. He made plenty of television that *Muppet Show* balcony critics Statler and Waldorf would have booed off the stage, and quite rightly.

By November 1979, after *Sesame Street* had been broadcasting for a full decade, some nine million American children under the age of six were watching it every day. A study that had been reported the previous year indicated that 90 percent of children in low-income inner-city households regularly tuned in. Overall, four out of five households with children under six saw the show over a six-week period.

Writing in the *New York Times*, Fred M. Hechinger extolled *Sesame Street*'s virtues and cited its detractors upon its tenth birthday. "On its way to the top, *Sesame Street* was denounced by the Soviet Union as a tool of American cultural imperialism and by the British Broadcasting Corporation as an instrument of American hucksterism. It has been accused by American pedagogical critics of harmful side effects, ranging from shortening children's attention span to causing epileptic fits."[2]

That *Sesame Street* continued to be discussed so seriously was merely an indication that, after ten years, it still really mattered. And surviving ten years of television, a medium in which shows often don't last ten weeks, was a significant achievement. By 1979, the first viewers of *Sesame Street* had already reached puberty.

Bert and Ernie, on the other hand, didn't age a bit—or change out of their white turtleneck or striped polo very often. They just continued to needle and nag, talk to each other in bed, and feed their obsessions.

While the rest of America spent the next ten years looking inward, perhaps in vain, *Sesame Street* would spend the eighties turning outward, expanding its young viewers' world. In its second decade on television, the real-life experiences of the writing staff, cast, and crew provided a foundation for the series.

To look back at that period is to appreciate the profound effect that life-cycle events had on the show, offstage and on. There was birth and death, love and loss, courtship and calamity, pleasure and pain, all from a little show whose aims at first were simply to test television's ability to stimulate the brain. That it would also touch the heart was not its original intention, but as each year passed, *Sesame Street* became as much an emotional pathway for children as an intellectual one, and just in time. For this was the period when the children of baby boomers were riding in back of Chrysler minivans, with yellow BABY ON BOARD warnings slapped on the windows. Big Bird plush toys were along for the ride, belted in, naturally.

But by decade's end, the family would need to make room for a squeaky-voiced Muppet monster whose incessant laugh would make many a driver grip the steering wheel.

A bizarre report crackled across the police radio airwaves in Nashville in the early hours of Friday, September 19, 1980. Dispatch was issuing an alert that an African American male had been spotted running in the Green Hills area of the city, buck naked except for a T-shirt.

It was Northern Calloway, fleeing from a brutal assault but seemingly unaware of it—or the trail of property damage he wreaked on Graybar Lane.

Calloway had randomly ransacked several homes. At one stop he destroyed a family's collection of fine crystal; at another, he broke a lightbulb in his bare hand; at a third he snatched a book bag belonging to a first-grader. Along the way he hurled a rock through a car window, shattering it, and smashed a few headlights.

Calloway was delirious and agitated when police found him in a garage. "He was yelling and screaming," said Metro Officer James D. Murphy. "We couldn't talk to him. He said he was the CIA and to call [President] Jimmy Carter."[3]

Police learned that before the rampage, Calloway had been visiting a woman, a twenty-seven-year-old marketing director, at the Villager Condominiums on Hillsboro Road. During an appearance at the Nashville Performing Arts Center the previous week, Calloway had become smitten with Mary Stagaman.

Pursuing single or married white women he met on the road had become a habitual and daring sport for Calloway, but this escapade was tragically different. Calloway had snapped.

Police discovered that Stagaman had been battered about the skull and torso with an iron rod and was admitted to the intensive-care unit of Vanderbilt University Hospital, where she was treated for head injuries and broken ribs. She remained hospitalized for two months.

A *Nashville Banner* report quoted police as saying that "the beating was so severe, the iron rod was destroyed."[4]

Calloway recalled little of the night he was arrested and said he had no memory of beating Stagaman. He was admitted to a psychiatric facility in Nashville following the assault but was allowed to return to New York under a doctor's supervision. Noted Nashville criminal attorney Lionel Barrett took on Calloway's case.

In September 1981, a year after Calloway was charged with aggravated assault, the actor pled guilty by reason of insanity. District Attorney General Tom Shriver said that an agreement had been reached between the state and Barrett to bypass a grand jury indictment and to turn evidence over to a criminal court. The deal allowed the court to retain jurisdiction over Calloway's psychiatric treatment if a jury found him not guilty by the insanity plea. Doctors called in by the state had already determined that

Calloway was insane at the time of the attack and rampage on personal property.

During the intervening year, Calloway had received outpatient psychiatric care in New York and had returned to work on *Sesame Street*. Executive producer Dulcy Singer believed that with proper psychiatric treatment—and a promise that Calloway would conscientiously take his daily dosage of lithium—the actor could rejoin the cast.

For some reason, the incident in Tennessee was largely ignored by the mainstream press in New York and the supermarket tabloids. "I don't why, but the story never gained any legs," said CTW executive David V. B. Britt. "It wasn't so much an institutional crisis for CTW as it was a crisis for the show."

An understandable wariness shadowed Calloway upon his return to the set, especially among those who had detected volatility long before the assault in Nashville. "He always had an interesting gleam in his eye," said publicist Bob Hatch. "The ability to raise hell was not far beneath the surface. I never saw it in action, but I knew that it was there. And he got away with as much as he did because he was so damn talented."

The promise of his early years on *Sesame Street* diminished in the 1980s. "Lithium took Northern's zest away, and he became heavily sedated and put on a great deal of weight," Singer said. "Then I learned that he was doing cocaine—at the same time he was taking his maintenance drugs. At that time, Northern became totally unreliable. He couldn't remember his lines at all, and we'd have to do a dozen takes for every scene he was in. I had called his psychiatrist any number of times in an attempt to tell him what was going on with his patient, but the doctor just totally dismissed it. The doctor felt he was protecting Northern, but I think stupidly."

Shortly after appearing in the fifty-sixth annual Macy's Thanksgiving Day Parade, on November 25, 1982, Will Lee became ill and was admitted to Lenox Hill Hospital. The seventy-four-year-old Lee, not one to miss the parade, had braved the cold to take his accustomed perch on the float.

Lee had been in fine shape that production season. He had taped a good number of segments in November and had been regaling everyone with tales from his days as a near-destitute actor in the 1930s, sharing a cold-water flat that by rights should have been condemned. He liked to discuss his days in Yiddish theater with the CTW research director, Dr. Lewis Bernstein, a gentle man and a gentleman. Because Bernstein wore a yarmulke atop his skull, Lee would rattle on in Yiddish. The researcher didn't have the heart to interrupt him or disclose that he understood very little of the language.

Lee had played a range of roles in his theater career but had never found the level of popular success on the stage that he had in the television studio playing Mr. Hooper. At times, he would be put off when his fellow actors would extemporaneously wander beyond the script. His acting training—and his respect for writers—made it difficult for him to venture beyond what was there on the page. To that end, he would often run lines with his cast mates, helping them internalize the words that had been so thoughtfully crafted for them to interpret.

When cast and crew learned of his hospitalization, people drew in their breath. How could they tape episodes of *Sesame Street* without Mr. Hooper, the mainstay of the neighborhood? Since his first, somewhat enigmatic, appearance in episode 1, Mr. Hooper had become many things to many young children: a surrogate papa, pawpaw, pop-pop, gramps, and granddaddy, not to forget *abuelo, dedushka, dziadek, grand-père, nonno, pappaus, yee-yee,* and *zeidy.* Mr. Hooper was the guy in the apron at the far side of the generation gap, his half-lens glasses slipping down his nose.

That his establishment carried his name was of no small significance. The quirky variety store, with its signature soda fountain, was a projection of Mr. Hooper's personality onto an idealized social institution. Even children knew you couldn't walk away from a local 7-Eleven with a newspaper under your arm and a Slurpee in one hand, promising the cashier, "I'll be back to pay for it tomorrow." But your credit was good with Mr. Hooper because not only did he know you, he knew your *mother.*

Will Lee played Mr. Hooper with such certainty and naturalness he made adults suspend their sense of disbelief. When celebrity guests would arrive at the *Sesame Street* set for a taping, they often would walk into Hooper's store and look around, wishing they could buy something to bring home. Even people paid to engage in make-believe wanted to hold on to the illusion, and when they found the shelves lined with props, they left with the only thing in stock: mild disappointment.

Bob McGrath went to visit Lee in the hospital and was stunned to see how gravely ill his cast mate had become. "He was not passing water," McGrath said, "and I told him that if he minded the doctors and urinated, I would make sure *Sesame Street* would be made possible by the letter *P* upon his return to the set." That might have been the last line any actor fed Will Lee, a line as funny and smart as *Sesame Street* itself.

Lee suffered a fatal heart attack on December 7, 1982, at the Upper East Side hospital. A memorial service was held eight days later at the New

York Shakespeare Festival Theater on Lafayette Street. He left behind a sister, Sophie Lubov, in Florida.

Lee's sudden passing, which occurred toward the end of a production season, was no small issue for everyone associated with the show. In the months that followed, as another season was being written, the production team and research staff resolved that the part of Mr. Hooper would not be recast. Instead, the character—and, by extension, the actor who played him—would be memorialized on the show in an episode that would take on the tricky business of explaining death to a preschool audience.

It was left to head writer Norman Stiles to find an age-appropriate means to convey the finality of death without causing children undue fear or confusion. The result was a truly memorable episode, one of the show's best.

To assist him in dealing with such a sensitive topic, research director Bernstein convened an advisory group of psychologists and religious leaders to provide guidance. "It's what we call a curriculum bath," Bernstein explained. "We bring in the experts to allow the writer to soak in expertise. We in Research bring in people to provide the information, and then the artistry of the writer takes over, as they integrate what they've heard.

"We ended up with an entire episode that dealt with the life cycle, about the naturalness of birth and death. The psychiatrists who advised us said that we needed to be mindful that children, like adults, need to find a sense of closure, even though they don't yet know what the word *closure* means. We tried to make a show about beginnings and endings, leading to a segment that said Mr. Hooper had reached an end point.

"That death was a part of life was the lesson we needed to impart, but we had to sidestep religious matters, as best we could. So we decided that all religions deal in human memory, to one degree or another. We decided to say that while Mr. Hooper was not here anymore, we will always have that part of him that lives within the heart, that we have our love and that it will always stay.

"And at the same time, we wanted to establish that sometimes, for adults and children, expressing your feelings is hard to do."

Stiles went to work, crafting a script that allowed Roscoe Orman, as father-figure Gordon, to lead the way. It was the first of several brilliant choices. The second was to enlist Richard Hunt, who, as Forgetful Jones, kicks off the first scene a-whoopin' and a-hollerin', but for reasons he suddenly can't remember.

By questioning him, Gordon not only helps Forgetful recall what factors led to his jubilant mood, but establishes the show's conviction that talking about emotions can not only be helpful, but even entertaining. "Let's see if we can figure it out," Gordon says. "Let's think real hard . . . about what was happening when you were feeling happy."

Forgetful says, "The sun was shining . . . a breeze was blowing . . . and then the trees started swaying, sorta like dancin', back and forth . . . and then my heart started a-beatin' in time with the trees dancing, *ba boom-boom, ba boom-boom* . . . I started yellin', 'Well, all right,' 'cause I was happy. Can you imagine me forgettin' simple things that make me happy?"

Later, Big Bird forgets something that made him sad. The scene unfolds in the courtyard as Gordon, Susan, Bob, Maria, Luis, David, and Olivia are enjoying coffee, café style. "Hey, I've got a great idea," Big Bird says to the audience. "Why don't we watch the grown-ups for a while?" Somewhat to his dismay, Big Bird sees that all they are doing is talking. "Well, I was hoping you were going to be doing something more interesting," Big Bird says. "That's okay. I can make even listening to you guys exciting. What I'm going to do is I'll listen to what you are saying, and from what I hear I'll try to guess what you're talking about. And I'll do all that while I'm balancing on one leg!"

The adults resume discussing Leandro, a son born to the Williams family, whom everyone seems to know. The baby—who may or may not resemble his father—will be coming with his parents to *Sesame Street* later in the day. Susan turns to Big Bird and says, "You should be able to guess by now. Put all the clues together. We were talking about the baby, we said what his name was, we said what he looked like, and we said that he and his mother were coming over here today."

Big Bird says, "Right, right. You're talking about Mrs. Williams and her baby named Leandro and that she's coming here today. What are you going to talk about now?"

"Well, how about politics?" David asks.

"Hey," Big Bird says. "Not even standing on one leg could make that interesting."

"He's got a point," Maria says.

The segment establishes a truism of communal life: that sometimes kids can figure out what adults are saying, even when they seem uninterested.

After two brief inserts we return to the courtyard, where the adults are now discussing a female political candidate. David assures us that she is against "big spending, big business, and inflation. She says when she gets into office there will be enough money for government, social programs, and the space program."

Bob says, "Hey, it sounds great. What's her name?"

"Alice in Wonderland," Gordon answers.

Big Bird arrives with surprises, and from here we need to examine every word:

Big Bird: Hey, it's time for your presents. I've just drawn up pictures of all my grown-up friends on *Sesame Street*. And I'm going to give them to you. I'm going to be an artist when I grow up. (*The drawings are passed out and admired.*) And last, but not least, *ta-da.* (*He shows everyone a drawing of Mr. Hooper, in his half-glasses and bow tie.*) Well I can't wait till he sees it. (*Awkward silence and glances all around*) Say, where is he? I want to give it to him. I know. He's in the store.

Bob: Big Bird . . . he's not in there.

Big Bird: Then . . . where is he?

Maria (*looking around and then rising to talk directly to Big Bird*): Big Bird, don't you remember we told you? Mr. Hooper died . . . He's dead.

Big Bird: Oh yah. I remember . . . Well, I'll give it to him when he comes back.

Susan: Big Bird . . . Mr. Hooper's not coming back.

Big Bird: Why not?

Susan (*standing now, stroking Big Bird's feathers*): Big Bird, when people die, they don't come back.

Big Bird (*sorrowfully*): Ever?

Susan: No, never.

Big Bird: Well, why not?

Luis: Well, Big Bird . . . they're dead. They can't come back.

Big Bird (*trying to comprehend*): Well, he's got to come back. Who's going to take care of the store? Who's going to make my birdseed milkshakes and tell me stories?

David: Big Bird, I'm going to take care of the store. Mr. Hooper . . . he left it to me. And I'll make you your milkshakes and we'll all tell you stories . . . and make sure you're okay.

Susan: Sure, we'll look after you.

Big Bird (*shuffling away with his head down*): Well . . . it won't be the same.

Bob (*choked with emotion*): You're right, Big Bird . . . It's . . . It's . . . It'll never be the same around here without him. But you know something? We can all be very happy that we had a chance to be with him . . . and to know him . . . and to love him a lot . . . when he was here.

Olivia: And Big Bird, we still have our memories of him.

Big Bird: Well, yah. Our memories . . . Memories, that's how I drew this

picture . . . from memory. And we can remember him and remember
him and remember him as much as we want to . . . But I don't like it.
(*On the verge of tears*): It makes me sad.
David: We all feel sad, Big Bird.
Big Bird (*asking once again*): He's never coming back?
David: Never.
Olivia: No.
Big Bird (*a little angry*): I don't understand. You know, everything was
just fine. Why does it have to be this way? Give me one good reason!
Gordon: Big Bird, it has to be this way . . . because.
Big Bird (*quieting*): Just because?
Gordon: Just because.
Big Bird (*admiring his drawing*): You know, I'm going to miss you, Mr.
Looper.
Maria (*smiling, as tears run from the corner of her eye*): That's *Hooper*, Big
Bird. *Hooper*.
Big Bird (*as the cast surrounds him*): Right. (*Fade to black.*)

"When we finished that scene there wasn't one of us whose face wasn't
streaked with tears," Caroll Spinney said. "Jon Stone said, 'Let's do another
take, just in case,' but there was nothing wrong with that take. It was perfect."

Comically curmudgeon cameraman Frankie Biondo was left uncharacteristically speechless. "It was really, really sad, and really, really touching,"
he said, for once not kidding.

The episode aired on Thanksgiving 1983, a year after Will Lee's final
appearance in the Macy's parade. It was scheduled on that holiday to allow
maximum exposure for families at home.

It was a landmark broadcast, *Sesame Street*'s most noble and affecting
hour, and a bravura performance by Caroll Spinney, who arrived at the studio for the day of taping knowing his lines cold. Jon Stone, directing that
day, could not have asked for more. Prompted by Singer, Stone had called
Spinney the night before, just to make sure the puppeteer was preparing.

There had been a time, long before, that Spinney had failed to arrive
at the studio with some illustrations Stone had expected. "I just got overwhelmed and busy," Spinney said, "but Jon was furious, and he never forgave me. From that point forward, in his eyes I was unreliable."

Spinney himself drew the caricatures that Big Bird handed out to the
cast members during the segment on Mr. Hooper's death. In a final scene,
Big Bird has the drawing he did of Mr. Hooper, now framed, just above
his nest on Sesame Street. The camera lingers on the drawing for a second

before Luis comes knocking to ask Big Bird if he would like to see the Williams baby.

Big Bird gets the last line, closure, as it were. "You know, the one thing is about new babies, one day they're not here and the next day, here they are!"

By the way: *Sesame Street* came to us that day sponsored by the letter *J*, as in Jeff, Jim, Joan, Joe, and Jon, and by the number *5*.

In the minds of *Sesame Street*'s young viewers, puppets and people are interchangeable characters, coming and going as episodes pass like highway markers. As Mr. Hooper's store faded into the distance, a new landmark came into view. It was Elmo, the twice-orphaned Muppet.

In 1985, Elmo was but a bit player among the Muppets, just one of the background characters the Henson puppeteers refer to as AMs, short for Anything Muppets. Essentially they are like naked mannequins waiting to be dressed for the department store window, or Mr. Potato Head before the eyes, nose, and assorted appendages are added. Whenever a need arises for a onetime-use character—or a gaggle of anonymous puppets for a crowd scene—Henson's backstage "Muppet wranglers" reach into a trunk and grab AMs. They're the Muppet equivalent of a chorus line. And just as it can happen in musical theater, when a director spots a pretty face, sometimes Anything Muppets are plucked from the pack. So it was with Elmo, who may have stood out simply for being an arresting shade of cherry lollipop red.

Lost in the mists of time is which production member said, "Let's write something for it." In fact, even how Elmo came to be named is no longer known.

But this much we do know: puppeteer Brian Muehl performed Elmo three or four times, using a sweet, whispery voice for the character. It did not stick.

Soon after, Muehl, a veteran of the Swiss pantomime group ensemble Mummenschanz, left the Muppets to pursue acting and writing. When he departed, his characters were divvied up. Marty Robinson got Telly; Barkley the dog went to a young gymnast; newcomer Kevin Clash got Dr. Nobel Price; and Richard Hunt inherited Elmo. Hunt, who gravitated to more flamboyant, theatrical characters and avoided cute ones, took an immediate dislike to Elmo.

"Richard loved opera and partying," said Clash, "and he often came in with a hangover. With an aching head, he would give away parts to the young puppeteers, literally throwing them at us. Richard saved his energy for the hipper, more established characters, and he just hated doing Elmo.

Norman Stiles, our head writer, would say in disgust, "What is Richard *doing* with that character?"

Legend has it that Hunt entered the Muppet greenroom one day, holding Elmo upside down by his rod, as if he were carrying a dead buzzard by its claw. "I was the only puppeteer there," Clash recalled. "Richard said, 'You know what? Have you got a voice for *this?*'" With that, Hunt sent Elmo flying across the room.

That flight, not unlike Lindbergh's, proved life altering for Clash, who had wanted nothing more from the age of nine than to be a featured performer for Jim Henson's Muppets.

While other children were playing ball on the streets of his boyhood home of Turner Station, Maryland, a historic African American community south of Baltimore that natives sometimes call Turner's Station, Clash was making puppets from remnants out of his mother's sewing basket. Like Henson, Clash fashioned one of his first characters from the lining of a discarded woman's coat. That was just the first of many parallels in the lives of two men who learned the rudiments of television production through puppetry, while working as teenagers for local stations in the Baltimore-Washington corridor. Both demonstrated sketching and cartooning talent at an early age and a fondness for Walt Disney animation. Both were collectors of scraps and found objects, discards and junk that were recycled and refashioned into small whimsical creations. In both cases, whatever aspects of their personality were hidden behind a veil of shyness and reserve exploded in performance, even as children.

Kevin was one of four children born to George and Gladys Clash. George, himself by nature a quiet man, was a welder for the Reynolds Metals Company and a neighborhood handyman. Gladys ran an in-home child-care center in their two-bedroom, one-bath house at 17 Pittsburgh Avenue. "There were always children around who weren't my brothers and sisters," Clash said with a laugh. "Kids just gravitated to my parents."

Like his father, Kevin could draw and illustrate with uncommon flair. "I really didn't get interested in reading until I discovered *TV Guide*," he said. "Chapter books at school seemed so long to me, and I hated to get called on during reading, but I really was interested in reading about celebrities in *TV Guide*, and I really enjoyed TV as a child."

His favorite program was the *CBS Children's Film Festival*, the showcase of international films that was hosted by Kukla, Fran, and Ollie and written by Jon Stone and Tom Whedon. "I remember seeing *The Red Balloon* for the first time on that series, and loving it," he said. *Sesame Street* did not debut until Clash was nine, but he watched it along with the day-care kids at home. Like many older boys who passed by the screen as their younger siblings watched, Clash found Maria "sexy and attractive. I liked her even more when she wasn't around that David."

Clash was twelve when he built a finger puppet named Mondey, who resembled Mickey Mouse. "I wanted, in some ways, to go into this fantasy world because of my shyness," he said. "When my mother would send me to buy bread, and I saw a person walking toward me, I'd duck and find another way to get to the store."

In early adolescence he built a wisecracking puppet inspired by a school friend named Tony Bartee. The puppet, who took on the name Bartee, had egg-shaped L'Eggs panty hose containers for eyes and a wig that had belonged to Clash's grandmother. "The more he made, the better he got," said Gladys, a loquacious and animated nurturer.

Gladys took plenty of criticism from neighbors who were forever questioning why her teenage boy was staying indoors by the Singer sewing machine while the other kids in the neighborhood were out playing. "My parents never put a negative twist on [my interest in puppets]," Clash said. "They never persuaded me to go out and play sports if I chose not to. Peers teased me, but when I got into high school and was doing variety shows and heckling them, it was completely different."[5]

George paid little heed to what anyone but his wife had to say, and she always had plenty. The day-care mother was only too happy to have Kevin entertain the kids, not that that was anyone's business. Sometimes when a tot with soggy drawers had no other change of clothes, she'd slip the trousers off a puppet and onto the child.

George built Kevin's first puppet stage and carted his son around to Baltimore-area performances. Kevin's first paid gig, at thirteen, was at a neighborhood recreation hall. He earned $2.35. He gradually built a reputation as a capable performer, but sometimes he gave away candy to ensure a full house.

By age sixteen, when he was a sophomore at Dundalk High School, he was being paid twenty dollars for a half-hour performance at a church-hall social or at a private home for a birthday party, and thirty-five dollars for the full-hour show. Kevin invested a portion of the proceeds toward purchases at hobby shops and fabric stores, accumulating storage containers filled with fur, felt, and foam rubber.

In the years before Baltimore's decaying waterfront was transformed by the shops and promenades of the urban makeover known as Harbor Place, Kevin would entertain on downtown streets, using his array of handmade puppets to lip-synch to recordings played on a portable tape machine. Mama and son skunks would sing Helen Reddy's "You and Me Against the World." He'd spin a tune by Earth, Wind & Fire and have two puppets dance the Bump or he'd bring out a firefly character to sing Debby Boone's "You Light Up My Life." Throughout, Bartee, whose skin was made from orange terrycloth, would banter with passersby. "Like my hair?" he would ask, before yanking off the wig. "Here. You can have it."[6]

Clash once told his hometown morning newspaper, the *Baltimore Sun,* that Bartee "can tell people off, especially the cool dudes. He won't get hurt, and I won't get hurt, either. He's the one person—I mean thing— who can get away with it."[7]

Kevin's confidence grew, and when he was in tenth grade, appearing at the Dundalk Heritage Festival, he was spotted by Stu Kerr, a peripatetic television personality and weather forecaster in Baltimore who had been host of local children's programs and a slew of cheaply produced studio shows like *Dialing for Dollars.* Coincidentally, Kerr and Bob Keeshan were friends, dating back to their days together as postwar pages at NBC Television in New York. Keeshan would occasionally book Kerr on *Captain Kangaroo* to play Scoop, a scatterbrained newsman.

At the time he met Clash, Kerr was developing *Caboose,* a new railroad-themed kids' show, in which the host would play a train conductor. He invited Clash to come along for the ride, and over the next two years the young puppeteer learned to perform on the job, unknowingly replicating the same technique Henson developed at WRC in the 1950s.

But when he began getting roles in musical theater productions at predominantly white Dundalk High School, things changed.

Clash's pleasing baritone was developing a round richness by age sixteen. During the winter of his junior year, he snagged the role of Sky Masterson, the romantic lead in a spring musical staging of *Guys and Dolls.* In his 2006 memoir,[8] Clash recalled his sense of triumph in landing the part that Marlon Brando had in the 1955 film adaptation. "I was floating on air," Clash said. "This was a dream role—to have some great acting scenes and perform show-stopping songs like 'Luck Be a Lady' and 'My Time of Day.' I was also especially pleased that Sky's love interest, Sarah, was going to be played by a girl who was a friend of mine. Vanessa and I were in music and drama classes together, and she was bright and talented, with a remarkable voice."

The exhilaration was short-lived, thanks to a phone call Kevin received a few days after the cast list was posted outside the high school's music room and rehearsals had begun. Dundalk High has traditionally drawn its student body from a largely blue-collar swath of southwestern Baltimore County. Racial tensions were always under the surface, and a cafeteria melee that broke out between whites and blacks at the school made headlines in Baltimore in the 1970s. "It may have had more to do with drugs than race," said Clash, who was given a ride home that day by the school's drama teacher after the students were sent home at midday.

On Father's Day, 2006, Kevin, Gladys, and George Clash sat around an outdoor patio table in suburban Baltimore County. Theirs is a family that values respect and tolerance, hard work and sacrifice, laughter, and gratitude for every blessing. Though Gladys had a framed photograph of Angela Davis atop the family's RCA television set, she was hardly a black-power militant in the sixties. But she was prideful, as was her husband, and they raised their children to be comfortable in their skin and to stand second to no one.

That explains why a sadness—and a cool, residual anger—still crosses their faces when they recall what happened when the handsome star of their household, the shy child who mustered his courage to perform without his puppets, picked up the receiver on that day in 1976.

On the line was Vanessa, the student chosen to play Sister Sarah, the Salvation Army missionary who parries with inveterate gambler Sky in *Guys and Dolls*. After nervously stumbling over small talk, Clash's cast mate lowered the boom. "You know, in the musical you and I have to kiss . . . We can't do that."

Vanessa's mother, coaxing in the background, prompted her to ask Kevin to step down from the role. Clash's heart sank at the bold attempt to undo a decision that wasn't hers to manipulate: "What she was really saying was, 'We can't kiss in front of everyone at school because you are black and I am white.' "

Gladys, too, was listening nearby. "When my mom heard 'step down,' she went off, pouring words into my ear," Clash said. "I could barely take in everything she was saying, but I knew that the fury in her was coming out." It was up to Kevin to clarify things. "I told her I was not the one with the problem, she was," he said.

Gladys wanted Vanessa to put her mother on, but the parent refused. "I wanted to remind her that this was not about loving her daughter or Kevin coming for dinner like Sidney Poitier in that movie. This was about acting," she said. "Kevin could have been asked to kiss a block of wood, but the situation was that he was playing a part that required the leading man to kiss the leading lady."

Vanessa, who eventually gave up the part to take a role in the chorus, apologized months later. The role of Sarah was taken up by an African American, a student who already had a crush on Clash. "She had no problem with the kiss scene," Clash said.

Gladys Clash and Stu Kerr were the adults who figured most prominently in Clash's development as a performer, but there was a third.

Clash first came to know of Kermit Love after watching an episode of *Call It Macaroni,* a syndicated children's program that won a George Foster Peabody award for Westinghouse Broadcasting in 1975. Narrated by children, the documentary series explored extraordinary occupations, like that of Love, a costume designer and marionette maker.

To Clash, the fully bearded Love seemed like a modern-day wizard, and he was determined to meet him. Gladys, not one to be deterred, began calling the local station in Baltimore that aired the monthly show, asking for a contact name and number for Love. To no one's surprise, she not only got through to him but convinced Love to meet with Kevin during an upcoming school trip to New York. He did, and a lifelong bond was formed.

Not long afterward, Kerr began to talk up his young puppeteer find to Bob Keeshan, who saw a tape of Clash at a children's convention in New York. While still in high school, Clash took a meeting with the executives at *Captain Kangaroo.*

"He was kind of young, but we saw genius right away," Keeshan told *Newsday* in 1998. "He was always a great puppeteer and actually an incredible craftsman." Keeshan sent two emissaries to Baltimore to investigate the menagerie of eighty-nine puppets Clash had built, which were crammed onto plastic shelves in his parents' bedroom. The producer and writer chose five puppets for the show, and Clash began to make frequent appearances during the final two, barely seen, seasons of *Captain Kangaroo* on CBS. Almost cruelly, the network scheduled it at 6:00 a.m., allowing the show to wither and die at an hour when its viewers were either barely awake or still asleep.

In addition to doing puppetry, Clash played a college student on *Kangaroo.* "It was the worst costume," he said. "Penny loafers and an argyle vest. It was pretty embarrassing."

Said Keeshan, "We would see how really difficult it was for him to get out from behind the puppets, how he hated to be on camera himself. What's magic about him is how he just becomes so incredibly reverse of what he is in real life when he gets behind a puppet. [With a puppet] he's outgoing and funny as can be, and outrageous. Without the puppet, he's just a nice laid-back young man."

Clash was determined to join the Muppets, and Love was just as determined to help him. When a call went out for extras to work the *Sesame Street* float in the 1979 Macy's parade, he recommended Clash. The nineteen-year-old arose in the middle of the night in Baltimore to get to New York in time to perform Cookie Monster, waving to the throngs along Broadway. As the parade dispersed in late morning, he hopped a southbound train back to Thanksgiving dinner in Maryland, exhilarated at having met Jim Henson, however briefly.

For a dizzying spell of time, Clash worked twenty-one-hour days in New York, juggling responsibilities for *Kangaroo* and Love's syndicated children's show *The Great Space Coaster*.

"I would do *Great Space Coaster* in the morning, then from 2:00 p.m. to like 6:00 p.m., I would do the *Captain*, and then from 6:00 p.m. to midnight I would prerecord *Great Space Coaster*, and then from midnight to 6:00 a.m. I was building puppets for the Captain. Then I would have to go in at 8:30 in the morning. Fortunately I was young and healthy."[9]

It was right around that time that he got a call from Jane Henson. "Jim, Frank, and Jerry were in London doing *The Muppet Show*, and they needed puppeteers for *Sesame Street*," Clash said. They had a special assignment in mind for the six-foot, 180-pound, athletically built puppeteer: the hind end of Snuffleupagus.

"Both Jerry and Richard Hunt had done that job, and it just tore their backs up," Clash said. "It was my turn, I guess."

Clash also performed an array of characters, without much distinction, until Hunt literally tossed Elmo into his arms. As Hunt walked away, Clash began experimenting with a falsetto voice that he had used from time to time. "But I really didn't find Elmo's soul until I took a trip home to Baltimore, back to the kids in my mother's care. That's where I found his innocence, his positiveness, and his sweetness."

Teen actress Alison Bartlett—now known as Alison Bartlett O'Reilly—auditioned for a one-day part on *Sesame Street* and nailed it, despite herself. "It was 1985, and I was a student at LaGuardia High School with a bad attitude," she said. "I almost didn't take the audition, and I said to my agent, 'Thank you, but I'm *not* going to get hired for *Sesame Street*.' By that point I was already typecast as the tough kid, the Jodie Foster roles, and I had just played a girl who had been found in an alley."

Unbeknownst to O'Reilly, Jon Stone had seen her two years before on Broadway, playing a teenage drifter in David Rabe's *Hurlyburly*.

"My agent said, 'We need to get something on your résumé other than the roles you've been doing,' and I reluctantly agreed to go," she recalled.

"A bunch of girls were there, and I did the compare-and-despair thing, sitting around thinking *Why am I here?* I was in jeans and T-shirt and felt completely as though I didn't fit in, building walls around myself to hide my insecurities and prejudgments. Then, about two seconds from leaving, they called me in."

Stone and Lisa Simon were there, as was Marty Robinson, performing with Telly. Though there was a script, the emphasis was on improv, and O'Reilly quickly got into the spirit of the Muppet interplay.

"Jon struck me as a ghetto Santa Claus, and I liked him immediately," Bartlett said. She got the part, arriving at the studio prepared to play one of Gordon's students named Gina. She gets lost on the way to a science project meeting on the roof of 123 Sesame Street. The script called for her to get directions from a pair of Honkers, the brightly hued, slightly crazed creatures who communicate only through trumpetlike protrusions growing out of the tops of their heads.

"Everyone in the studio but me was clued in that Marty Robinson and Kevin Clash were going to put me through a kind of fraternity initiation," she said. "They tortured me while we were shooting, pulling at my knapsack, honking away in my ear, high-fiving each other. They were just trying to see how I would react, but I'm a New Yorker, and I'd been through a lot worse harassment than that. Growing up in Brooklyn helped."

Gina became a recurring role. "At first she was this feisty, kooky, kind of tough, innocent kid, a questioning type who was hyper and a bit confused," she said. "I was all over the place with her, nervous and jittery. But she had a spunky spark to her that they liked."

It was only after the actress was working on *Sesame Street* for a while that she shared this childhood memory with her cast mates: when she was four, Alison and her big sister Holly stood bundled up along Central Park West watching the Macy's Thanksgiving Day Parade. A home movie shows her wide-eyed and shivery, in a fur coat and muff. But it also shows fate stepping in. "All of a sudden, you see the *Sesame Street* float come into view in the movie, and then Will Lee and Northern Calloway hop off the float and come toward us to shake our hands."

Northern Calloway was becoming increasingly unreliable around the time O'Reilly joined the cast. He was appearing in fewer and fewer scenes because of his inability to remember and deliver lines. All of the sparkle that had characterized his studio work in the 1970s had dulled; all of that talent had become buried and burdened.

Dulcy Singer had compassion for him and did what she could, but from the mid-1980s on, Calloway was becoming less and less a part of *Sesame Street*. A low point came in the 1987 production year, when a story line was developed for Maria and Luis that would lead to a wedding on *Sesame Street*, a first for the show. In real life, then thirty-seven-year-old Sonia Manzano had recently married, and the idea of thirtysomething Maria falling in love with Luis, a tenderhearted Hispanic man she had gotten to know and trust over time, appealed to the producers and writers. As TV relationships go, the match was more than plausible.

But the news of this development was devastating to Calloway, who had for so long played David as Maria's boyfriend. He thought that if any character should marry Maria, it should be his. But it was never a serious consideration. "It was my idea to do the marriage and I played it cautious," Singer said. "I thought it would be better to do it with Luis because I didn't want to open up another kettle of fish. It was enough to get a wedding on the show and have a family without opening ourselves to more difficulties. And I thought it would be a good and helpful thing to show a stable Latino family."

Singer turned to Jeff Moss to script the wedding episode and provide the words and music, a decision that led to another of *Sesame Street*'s finest hours. Once again, Jon Stone directed.

Intense, tenacious Moss turned in an operetta that was as romantic as it was revealing, seven melodious minutes of soliloquy in song and spare dialogue that played out on the brownstone's rooftop deck, with a silhouette skyline as backdrop. It simultaneously reviewed and expanded the back stories of Luis and Maria, briefly introducing the bride's mother and the groom's proud father, seated in the open-air congregation. Among the other attendees were Gordon, Susan, Mr. McIntosh (stage manager Chet O'Brien), Gina, David, Bert, Ernie, the two-headed monsters, the Count, Cookie Monster, Oscar (in a shmutzed tuxedo), Telly, and Big Bird, who whispers "You look beautiful," as Maria enters in an off-the-shoulder white gown (with just a hint of cleavage).

A Hispanic priest addresses the bride and groom and explains marriage in terms simple enough for preschoolers to comprehend yet elegant enough for adults to appreciate.

"When two people get married, what they do is make a promise to each other," he says. "Luis and Maria are making a promise today, a promise to share their lives together, a promise to help one another and care for each other and love each other for the rest of their lives. They are celebrating this promise in front of you, the people they love most, their friends and their families."

The service dissolves and up comes an intro, a segue to lyrics that touch on the inner dialogue of the participants: the beaming groom ("Look at her. Isn't she wonderful?"), the bride with a late case of cold feet ("It's altogether possible I've made a major error. My hands are cold, my forehead's hot. It's either love or terror"), the equally jittery little red ring bearer ("Don't drop the rings, Elmo. Please, Elmo, don't drop the rings"), the heart-heavy ex-boyfriend ("Isn't it funny? I've seen her each day of my life. Now she's becoming . . . become Luis's new wife. I'm not used to thinking of her as anyone's wife"), the wistful bachelor and best man, Bob, turning to maid of honor Linda ("Sometimes I wonder how I would feel being married. If I were married, would it be to someone like you?"), the longtime girlfriend, Linda, dreamily responding in sign language through a video thought balloon ("Sometimes I wonder how I would feel being married. I wonder if you wonder, too. I wish I knew"), the newly adoptive parents Gordon and Susan with junior attendant Miles ("Look at him. Isn't he wonderful?").

Luis and Maria exchange vows and rings, and the priest concludes, "I now pronounce you husband and wife."

From the back row, Big Bird blurts out "Yay!" and Gina closes his beak to allow the bride and groom to kiss.

Just as the Mr. Hooper memorial had been writer Norman Stiles's masterpiece, the wedding episode was Jeff Moss's.[10]

Together, they are the poles that held up the canvas tent that was *Sesame Street* in the 1980s, a reflection of the sometimes silly, sometimes sad, always surprising, relentlessly spinning cyclical circus of life.

Chapter Eighteen

The nineties were a time of transition on *Sesame Street,* as the original architects and builders of the enterprise faced changes in the cultural landscape, trials on the show, and their own mortality.

"Everything that can happen to a family happened to those of us who worked on *Sesame Street,*" said Dulcy Singer, who weathered her share of challenges as executive producer of the show during a period when its dominance in preschool television was threatened.

She had many tense days and difficult messages to deliver, but the worst moment came on an afternoon in early January, just eight days into the new decade. On January 9, 1990, the Ossining, New York, police raced to Stony Lodge Hospital, a sixty-one-bed psychiatric facility in suburban Westchester County, where Northern Calloway had flown into a violent rage, striking a staff physician. Police described Calloway as "agitated and troubled" as they arrived and slowly maneuvered around him, not wishing to make matters worse with sudden movements. Calloway clearly did not want to be handcuffed, and a scuffle ensued. The more Calloway struggled, the more danger he posed to himself and others.

Finally, as he was being subdued, he went into a frightening seizure and then dropped to the floor.

What followed came as a shock, even to the hospital's trained staff: Calloway, just forty-one years old, went into cardiac arrest. He was transported by ambulance to nearby Phelps Hospital, where he was pronounced dead on arrival.

It fell to Singer to break the news of Calloway's death to *Sesame Street*'s cast and crew. "The hardest one to tell was Alison Bartlett," Singer recalled. "She loved Northern. When she came on the show, they worked in Hooper's Store together. He mentored her."

Though still a teenager, Bartlett weathered Calloway's ups and downs as tactfully as anyone on the set, even as she had good reason to be wary of him. He showed up unannounced one day at LaGuardia High School and proposed to her.

It was because of that incident—and another in which Calloway bit music coordinator Danny Epstein—that the actor had ultimately been dismissed. He finally ran out of second chances with a corporation that by all rights could have severed ties with him after his rampage in Nashville.

"We had to let him go because things got so bad," Singer said. By the late 1980s, Calloway had become useless on the set and a burden. "He would stand around for a scene and look like he had potato chip crumbs on his face," said Caroll Spinney. "I wondered why the makeup people didn't wipe around his mouth. He was so out of it he didn't check the mirrors, so that he'd look good for the camera. The last time they really used him he had only one line to say, because he couldn't remember a second sentence. They'd shoot one sentence at a time and then change the camera angle."

"In the early years of the show he had so many interesting, wonderful ideas, and he really cared about his character," Singer said. "After the incident in Nashville, I had a hard time with the front office, convincing them that we should keep Northern on the show. But it was apparent to me that he was extremely ill, so I fought to keep him," Singer said. "You don't fire people because they are sick."

It ultimately fell to Singer as executive producer to dismiss Calloway.

"I called Northern's psychiatrist to find out the best way to break the news to him, but the doctor saw me as a villain and was little help," she said. "Two of us met Northern at a restaurant because our bosses had suggested we meet in a public place. Northern actually took it well, thanking me for all the opportunities he had." Singer was relieved that Calloway did not cause a scene.

The Westchester County Coroner's Office in Valhalla performed an autopsy on Calloway. Cause of death, listed in the coroner's report for Case No. 1990-0079, was exhaustive psychosis, now more commonly referred to as excited delirium syndrome (EDS). A chemical analysis revealed traces of antipsychotic drugs Carbamazepine and Thorazine in tissue, but no evidence of cocaine or recreational drugs of any kind. Most who succumb to EDS have been under the influence of illegal stimulants.[1]

Calloway was laid to rest following a sparsely attended memorial service in Ossining. It had been some time since his colleagues from *Sesame Street* had seen or heard from him. Most grieved the loss in private.

"When something happens in the news I often think, *I wonder what Northern would think of this?*" Sonia Manzano said. "You know, somehow, he lives on. He was a man of tremendous energy and potential. He could sing, he could dance, he could tell jokes, he could write music, he could produce," she said, followed by a long pause. "But he always wanted it *now*."

Today Manzano is married and mother to Gabriela Rose Reagan, who played Maria's daughter, Gabi, for two seasons on *Sesame Street*. Her daughter is now about the same age Sonia was when she first stepped onto the *Sesame Street* set. Manzano smiled conspiratorially, with one eyebrow raised, when she spoke of how she and Calloway broke a television barrier back then, almost on a whim.

"When I first auditioned for *Sesame Street,* the script had it that David and Maria were up against tenement doors making out, like a scene out of *West Side Story,* she recalled. "The initial shooting scripts weren't written that way. So it was Northern and I who decided that David and Maria would go steady. We played it up that way, taking it as far as we possibly could. Jon did not encourage it, but the writers picked up on it right away. Maria and David gave *Sesame Street* that added dimension of teen romance."

Better that fans of *Sesame Street* remember Calloway just that way, as the handsome charmer who helped out Mr. Hooper in the store and had a thing for the Latina who used to curl up with a book on the fire escape that ran up the side of a brownstone on Sesame Street.

"I once gave a speech at a university and a professor in her late thirties came up to me," Manzano recalled. "She said, 'You and Northern were the J. Lo and P. Diddy of my generation.'"

When no one was looking, Northwestern University freshman Stephanie D'Abruzzo tore a full-page ad out of a stray copy of the *Chicago Tribune* and went happily on her way back to the dorm. May 16, 1990, had just gotten even better for the diminutive communications student from Pittsburgh.

The ad she had taken heralded fabulous news for a would-be puppeteer: the Muppets were going to have a permanent presence at Walt Disney World, a place where the public could celebrate their zaniness. D'Abruzzo, an irreverent brunette with a huge singing voice, thought she just might venture down there to see them in performance someday. And perhaps there would be an internship possibility.

During her first year living at the Communications Residential College at NU, D'Abruzzo had gained the freshman fifteen—"and then some," she said. She had become slightly self-conscious about her appearance. "I had a bad late-eighties and then an early-nineties perm," she once told her hometown *Pittsburgh Post-Gazette.* "It was obvious early on [in college] that looks mattered. I was a character actor who didn't look right for character parts.

"When I would watch the old Bugs Bunny cartoons or *The Muppet Show,* I realized how multilevel the humor is. Watching old *Sesame Street* and *Muppet Show* episodes, I began to think [puppetry] was a great way to do character work without it mattering what I look like."[2]

It helped that she already had a repertoire of comic voices that allowed her to play "any size, shape, sex, or species."[3]

"As I went back to my dorm room that day, I saw that the message board on the door had a note from my friend Ryan. It said, 'Sorry about Jim Henson.'" D'Abruzzo didn't know what to make of it.

"The previous week, there had been a bit of a campus hoax, where it had been widely rumored that Steve Martin had died. In an age where most students did not have televisions in their rooms, and with no Internet handy, such pranks were easy to pull off in the vacuum of a then relatively Luddite college campus. So that's where my mind headed: some sicko had started a new rumor. After all, there was no news of Jim Henson dying in the *Trib* that I had just swiped. But it didn't take long before I learned that the horrible news was true."

A friend on campus who had interned at the Jim Henson Company the previous summer called his friend Craig Shemin in New York to verify the report. Shemin, then working in the public relations department at Henson, had been fielding nearly every call that had come into the building that morning. The rest of the company was in shock behind closed doors.

D'Abruzzo walked around Northwestern in a daze, as well. "Whether I wound up going to classes that day remains a blur," she said. "I do remember that I instantly signed up to use the dorm's screening room for the rest of the day and into the night, and invited friends to come and watch Muppet movies and *Muppet Shows* and *Sesame Street* and anything else Muppet-related that we could dig up on VHS."

In silence that night, the group watched a PBS special produced by Children's Television Workshop and directed and hosted by Jon Stone.

"There is a tradition at Northwestern of painting this large rock that sits in the center of a cluster of South Campus buildings," D'Abruzzo said. "Organizations do it to promote events and whatnot. I thought that maybe I should paint The Rock as a tribute to Jim that night. But no one was available to help, and it is a *really* big rock. Whole fraternities and sororities stay up all night to paint it. So my friend Kathe and I got some street chalk and did some sidewalk art. We drew a picture of Kermit and Ernie with the caption 'Thanks, Jim.'"

The following week D'Abruzzo saw snippets of the Henson memorial on the evening news. "The dorm lounge had bad reception, and the news only devoted about fifteen to thirty seconds to the story," she said. "I didn't know any of those people who were singing and waving foam butterflies, but like many of them, my tears fell for a man I did not know."

It's a sorrow that Jim Henson didn't live to meet D'Abruzzo, a third-generation Muppet performer. In her he would have found the rarest of the rare, a self-made female puppeteer who not only nailed a range of inspired voices and mastered the physical challenges, but snagged a Tony nomination for *Avenue Q*, a musical that simultaneously spoofed and saluted *Sesame Street.*

Jim Henson and Jerry Nelson had been shooting the breeze in Central Florida one day, watching a video playback of a scene just taped at the Walt Disney Studios in Orlando. "I said to Jim that I was hoping I could retire soon," Nelson recalled.

With that, Henson recoiled. "You are *not* going to retire," he said firmly.

Nelson, slightly taken aback, turned directly to his boss, a bit surprised. Nelson was just getting to a point in life where there was enough money coming in to consider slowing down a bit. Plus, he had lost a daughter to cystic fibrosis and had been carrying the weight of grief for many years.

Henson had generously given his colleagues a percentage on such projects as *Fraggle Rock,* the allegorical HBO series that used puppets to examine the symbiotic relationship between species. After Nelson had spent so many years working away from home on *The Muppet Show* and subsequent Muppet movies, his nest in Cape Cod, a cozy retreat near Provincetown, was beckoning him and his wife. The good life awaited, but Henson wanted to hear none of it.

"They'll be wheeling us out of here," Henson then said to Nelson with a laugh. "In my case, it's getting closer to that."

That comment would take on a haunting quality after Nelson and a group of colleagues returned to New York from Florida in the spring of 1990. David Rudman, a young puppeteer from Chicago who was new to the Muppets, remembered that Henson had looked ill and drained while they were shooting a Disney World ad in Orlando.

When the performers reunited in New York to loop the commercial, Henson failed to appear. That their leader would be a no-show was an extraordinary event, and the puppeteers waited around for hours. "Nobody knew where he was," Rudman said.

Henson also failed to appear later that day at a party to promote a PBS special that would air the following night.

Back home in Chicago, Rudman was awakened by a late-night call from Richard Hunt, alerting him that something was seriously wrong with Henson. "Richard said he was on the way to the hospital and that he'd call me as soon as he learned anything more," Rudman said. "Around 2:00 a.m., Kevin Clash called, saying, 'Get back here to New York right away.'" Rudman took the first flight out of O'Hare and sped to the Henson Workshop, where his colleagues had begun gathering in the early morning hours. By then, Henson was gone.

"Everyone was walking around like zombies," Rudman said. "We started talking about a memorial service right away. It helped everyone get focused."

Joan Cooney was told of Henson's death at dawn. She called Dulcy Singer around 7:00 a.m. "I was in a sleepy daze," Singer said. "I didn't know that Jim had been sick, so my first reaction was disbelief. Jim had been such a workaholic. So many times I'd seen him work with the flu. People told me he had toughed out a case of walking pneumonia the year before in London. He had the most powerful will, and I don't think he listened to his body. He just went ahead and worked his way through illness."

Later in the morning, Emily Kingsley was driving into Manhattan from Westchester County for a writers' meeting at CTW when she heard a radio report of Henson's death. "I almost drove off the road," she said. "It turned out that all of us had heard the news on our way to work, and so, in a spooky way, we all experienced it together."

Puppeteer Fran Brill was recording voice-overs at the Young & Rubicam advertising agency when a casting director broke the news. "For years, I couldn't talk about that day," she said. "But now I believe that if Jim somehow could have been informed about how he died, he would have said, '*Hmmmm*. Interesting.' He would have just accepted it, taken it with a grain of salt, and not wondered about choices he had made along the way. He would not have said, 'Gee, I wish I had gone to the doctor.'

"I remember once on the set I saw Jim's back was wounded," Brill continued. "I said, 'Jim, you're bleeding from the back,' and he said, 'It's no big deal.'

"Jim just didn't do the doctor thing."

Bernie Brillstein's eyes still glistened and his voice cracked with emotion when he talked about his client of thirty years. "I'm convinced Jim knew he was going to die," Brillstein said, shaking his head. "Would a man of fifty-three—who felt he wasn't going to die anytime soon—write out instructions for his *funeral*? Instructions that were meant to be read *aloud*? Not only did the letter he wrote to his kids mention who he wanted to speak at the memorial, he also indicated his preferences for the *entertainment*." A little ruefully he added, "My bet is that Jim felt his kids would do it wrong, and he didn't want to leave anything to chance."

Other members of Henson's corps of advisers were also mystified by the letter left behind. *Muppet Show* executive producer David Lazer said, "Jim copied me on that letter. It was a premonition and it spooked me. Why else would a man who was so vital, who loved life so much, who loved being happy and making others happy, write a letter that was so serious in intent? I had only heard him mention mortality twice in the years I had known him. We were flying to Los Angeles at a time when his son John was about to face a serious operation, but we had a deadline to meet. Jim turned to me and said, 'If anything were to happen to any of my kids, I don't know how I could handle it.' That was a big statement from someone who never talked about mortality. The only other time was the letter.

"This was a man who loved having a good time at the gambling clubs in England. He threw *major* costume parties. This man loved fun and it showed up in his characters in their happy and innocent outlook. His values were not materialistic. Even though he liked to dress up and eat in nice places, he was one with the universe. He could look at a sunset and it would feed him. It was as if someone else got a million-dollar check. Jim was about harmony with people and in nature. There is a *reason* why the Muppets are different colors, shapes, and sizes. He never had a racist thought in his head. He celebrated everyone's differences. Some of the characters are cranky, some are this, some are that, but they all are pals together. They stick together in adversity. That's a lesson I learned from Jim just by being around him."

Brillstein said, "Jim loved being Jim, and he could show it, especially during the later years out here in Los Angeles, with his Missoni sweaters and his flowing hair. Who would figure Jim Henson to be a guy who would rent a yacht? But I took him on a cruise one year and he took me the next, celebrating our twenty-fifth anniversary together. Jim had a love for aesthetic things, for beautiful things and beautiful women."

In his office, Brillstein, who died in 2008, had a Muppet version of himself encased in glass, a one-of-a-kind gift from a man who would spend weeks working on a surprise for someone he held dear.

During the memorial service, Frank Oz provided a hard-to-top example. One Christmas season, Henson had approached Oz backstage during the season the Muppets were featured on *Saturday Night Live*. "It was just prior to dress rehearsal and the other guys had gone off to lunch. Jim and I were just hanging around the halls. He came up with a camera and Jim said in his quiet, enthusiastic way, 'Frank, I need to go in a dressing room with you . . . and if you could take off all your clothes, I could take a picture of you naked.'

"I said, 'Whoa! What?'

"And he said, 'I really need to take a picture of you naked.'

"We discussed this for a while . . . and I said, 'All right.' So we went into the dressing room and I took off all my clothes, buck naked. Locked the door, of course. And he said, 'Now pose. Put your hands over your genitals,' which I was glad to do. He said, 'Bend over [forward] and look into the camera in a state of shock,' which was not difficult at that time. So I bent over and he took some photos of me. I got dressed and we did the show."

Some days later Oz received a sculpted wall hanging that was entitled *Bert in Self-Contemplation*. It featured Bert with his arms holding a ledge filled with tiny toy Berts and photo miniatures of Henson Workshop employees. Henson had painted layers on the artwork, "like earth striations, which I gather were like the layers of Bert's mind, his soul," Oz said, "and within those layers he painted beautiful textures." When he picked it up to admire it, Oz noticed that Bert's pupils had been cut out, offering an invitation to look through, like a hole in a fence. "You look inside Bert's brain . . . and there I am, naked," Oz said. "I *knew* he had a good reason."

Trust is the mortar of every lasting relationship; if Jim Henson had yours, there wasn't anything he wouldn't do. Brillstein and Oz, two connoisseurs of funny, were Henson's wing men.

Henson trusted Joan Cooney, as well. They exchanged truths and confidences with ease and reliably read each other's moods. "Laughter permeated Jim's work, and that which he adored most was his work with the Muppets," Cooney explained. "This is not to say that Jim did not have his down moments and darker side. His darker side wasn't readily apparent, but without it he would not have made his fantasy-adventure films *The Dark Crystal* and *Labyrinth*. Both did not do well at the box office and were critically panned.[4] Jim had a long fall after *Dark Crystal* failed to meet audience expectations. I can tell you that he was seriously depressed, and we were worried about him."

Cooney said moviegoers sensed "a lack of sophistication" in Henson's tackling of serious themes. "Jim had a very serious, earnest side, but there wasn't much nuance there. The nuance was all in the comedy."

The program for the Henson memorial was prepared in five days. Martin G. Baker, an Englishman who produced, coproduced, or executive produced *The Muppet Show, Fraggle Rock,* and *The Jim Henson Hour,* coordinated the logistics. Duncan Kenworthy, vice president of production at Henson Associates and director of the London-based Henson Creature Shop, told the *Washington Post* in June 1990 that working on the two-and-a-half-hour memorial "was the most moving experience I've ever had. Someone said, 'It's the only memorial service I'd ever been to that you could take on the road.' It was a wonderful microcosm of us. There we were, disagreeing in many ways, having very strong views, trying not to say, 'What would Jim have done?' There was a lot of disagreement, but in the end, we came up with a service that was a real achievement. That's the best hope for the future—that you can have strong creative talents, and unanimity."[5]

"Martin Baker produced it as if he were producing any big show," Craig Shemin recalled. Although the Henson family turned down CNN's request to broadcast it live, the service was videotaped for posterity, in keeping with the meticulous and comprehensive regard the Jim Henson Company has for its history.[6]

"The service was a spontaneous outpouring," said Shemin. "Very little of it was scripted." In preparation for it, clusters of employees assembled fabric butterflies on wands to hand out to attendees. The gesture was undertaken not only to honor the spirit of Henson's more fanciful work but almost to provide a kind of "background" character for the scene. "Those type of butterflies had been used on many of Henson's productions," Shemin said. "Jim was forever working some character in the background. He was just as likely to have picked up a butterfly as anything else."

Shemin, who handled guest relations for the six hundred to seven hundred invitees, said the feverish preparations proved a godsend, "Everyone was so numb, we all were looking for something to do."

By the time the guests were escorted to the pews, Shemin realized he had no seat of his own. "But the florist who provided all the weekly arrangements for the Henson company and had done the flowers for the memorial service had put aside two folding chairs in a side closet." Craig and the florist extended a row and sat together.

The Muppet performers were seated together for the memorial service—"house right," recalled Fran Brill. Respecting Henson's wishes, the puppeteers wore no black. Brill chose a purple and white dress.

The colleagues had worked through countless challenges before, but nothing approached having to muster their strength to get through this day. "There was a lot of emotion, a lot of embraces, a lot of Kleenex," said Brill. "I cried from the beginning of the memorial to the end. I had never been inside St. John the Divine before, and the overwhelming majesty of the place—and the sight of the huge crowd that came to honor Jim, people who were strangers to him—moved me deeply. The enormity of Jim's influence, how beloved a figure he was to so many people all over the world really hit me.

"At one point we all got up onstage to sing 'The Rainbow Connection,' and I just mouthed the words because I couldn't stop crying. I remember being in awe of Louise Gold, a wonderful British puppeteer who had worked on *The Muppet Show*, who sang 'Bring Him Home,' that beautiful song from *Les Misérables*. She never lost her composure, I don't know how she did it.

"And, of course, after many had spoken about Jim, there was a long silence, as if the next scheduled speaker had missed their cue," Brill recalled. "But then there was a murmur in the body of the church and everyone began to realize that in the great distance behind the altar Big Bird was slowly walking toward us. As he walked, he looked left and right at the congregation, as if he was a bewildered child. It was exactly what a six-year-old would do. The murmur from the congregation grew and grew as more people saw him approaching. It took quite a while for him to get to the front. When he finally reached the spotlight he began to sing . . . and it was breathtaking."

Big Bird was never so three-dimensional as he was that day in the cathedral, so crushingly wounded by loss but so brave. Just as he had for the taping of the episode on Mr. Hooper's death, Caroll Spinney dug down deep and came up with a performance steeped in melancholy. As he began, Big Bird seemed slightly baffled and dazed at first, perhaps because the artist underneath all those yellow-dyed feathers was an artist who owed his livelihood to Jim Henson.

Being hired to perform Big Bird and Oscar had been the break of a lifetime. Although it took more than ten years of struggle for Spinney to be compensated at a level commensurate with his abilities and his characters' renown—his salary was shamefully low by show-business standards—he did begin to thrive financially in the 1980s. But more than that, Spinney met and married the love of his life thanks to *Sesame Street*.

This occurred after his first wife left him, with the three Spinney children in tow. "She done run off," Spinney said. "She hated that I was in television, even after I got Big Bird and accomplished just what I had dreamed of doing as a kid. I was on the best children's show on television, just as I had predicted to my mother so long ago. But [my wife] used to say, 'I wish to God you weren't in show business.' I embarrassed her. When she left, I was devastated. My little boy Ben was just a year old, and I had a bad, bad spell living without my children."

But at an album recording session in 1973, Spinney spied a young woman from the CTW research department who had been enlisted to watch over some children called in to sing. It wasn't the first time that he had been attracted to her, and twice before he had asked Debra out—once at her desk at CTW, another time at a CTW Christmas party—only to learn she was married. The third time, it was Debra who approached Spinney, who re-created the scene in his 2003 memoir. "She seemed to know me, though I didn't know how. She told me that since her marriage had recently ended, she was living with her family on Long Island. I was about to go on tour for the show, but I promised to call her when I got back. Three months later I met her [at CTW] and we walked toward Central Park. We held hands on our way to the Tavern on the Green. Before we finished dinner, we both knew in our hearts that we would be married. Thirteen days after our first date, we were walking down Broadway when, at Sixty-second Street, I was completely overpowered with the most fantastic, wonderful feeling. I stopped and blurted out, 'You will marry me, won't you?' And she said 'Y-y-y-yes.' I spun her around and kissed her. I was already more in love than I'd ever been in my life. And it's been that way ever since."[7]

Bernie Brillstein had the misfortune of being listed next in the memorial service order after Big Bird. "Jim told me to never follow the Bird," he said, to a ripple of laughter and applause. He then began in earnest.

"In a business where the one who shouts the loudest usually gets the most attention, Jim Henson rarely spoke above a whisper. You had to lean in to hear him most of the time, but it was always worth the effort. David Lazer and I knew how loud his whisper was. He was a man with a vision, and though his greatest appeal was the simplest of human emotions, the purest of ideas, he was not above using advanced technological means to achieve his goals. My friend Jim was by most definitions a genius, but not like Edison suggested. Edison said genius was one percent inspiration and ninety-nine percent perspiration. With Jim, I think it was about fifty-fifty. His ability to create whole worlds of people and things is well documented, and we'll have that legacy forever. But after coming up with the concept, he'd work tirelessly on every phase of the process to see that it was the best that it could possibly be.

"As a rule, perfectionists are a real pain. They drive the people around them crazy in their single-minded search for excellence. But Jim inspired people to be better than they thought they could be, to be more creative, more daring, more outrageous, and, ultimately, more successful. And he did it without raising his voice. That whisper will stay with us for a long time. Now we'll just have to listen a little harder."

The five Henson children stood in a semicircle around their mother, a good ten paces behind. The Henson daughters and sons were informally dressed in shades of blue, green, and tan, intentionally eschewing somber colors. Jane Henson wore a draped, muted monochromatic outfit consisting of a full-length taupe skirt topped by a long-sleeve, softly patterned blouse and vestlike duster, a flowing, multilayered ensemble. Without introducing herself, she began her remarks with a sentence that seemed like the answer to an unasked question. "I did ask for a lot of flowers," she said. "They came from Connie, our corner florist."

Addressing the congregation without notes, Jane Henson was at once grounded and a bit floaty, her remarks vaguely spiritual, but not in a traditional sense.

"Each flower is chosen because it's a perfect flower, designed by a perfect maker," she said. "Each flower holds a complete message that Jim would want to share with you, its beauty, its perfection, its differences, its beginning and its end. I don't want to pretend that I know what happens after this life, or that Jim knew what would happen after this life, but he had great plans."

Her observation elicited knowing laughter from those who were aware of Jim Henson's fascination with mediums, psychics, and astrologers, and his belief that it is entirely possible for the earthbound to receive messages from the next world. He consulted seers and considered their prognostications.

"I sure hope that somebody [up there] knows we are doing this down here because [Jim] is probably pretty busy," Jane Henson said, offering thoughts on who in the afterworld might be available to work on an ethereal project. She included Don Sahlin, the inventive prankster who designed Bert and Ernie; puppeteer Burr Tillstrom, the television pioneer and entertainment businessman who knew enough to own the trademark to Kukla and Ollie; Bil Baird, who proved early on—with no less a figure than Walter Cronkite on the CBS Morning Show—that television provides such a suspension of disbelief for viewers, it allows people and puppets to engage in parody, satire, and commentary; and Rufus Rose, the marionette builder who sculpted the original Howdy Doody. With a single flourish, she offered a short history of puppets in twentieth-century pop culture.

"Maybe more than anything else," she continued, Jim would want to reconnect with his mother, his brother, and his grandmother, Dear, "who he always credited as being his greatest inspiration."[8]

Looking briefly toward her now adult children, she said, "He stayed with us long enough to have given us certainly everything we need . . . if we are strong enough to carry on. Mostly," she added, "I just think now that it's only us, his family. These are only his kids, I'm only his wife. They had messy rooms, I burned the dinner. He didn't come home. The dog died. Whatever . . . all this stuff. It's only us."

After a brief pause, she got back on track. "Sometimes, because everyone else was working, I would be used for interviews," she said. "The press would ask did you ever have any idea it would get this big? And what I didn't know is that it had *gotten* this big. I just didn't know."

There she stood, thirty-plus years removed from the *Sam and Friends* days when she performed on her knees at WRC.

The University of Maryland coed who had long ago caught Jim Henson's eye could have grown as a performer but left the Muppets to raise their children in Connecticut, and her role in life became decidedly maternal. At some point in her marriage, what was once a fully entwined relationship unraveled. Jane was left abandoned in the suburbs while Jim Henson circumnavigated the globe. For reasons known only to husband and wife, they opted to remain legally separated for a long spell. At the time of Jim Henson's death, though, divorce seemed a certainty. Henson had already bought out her half of the business.

Why Henson called for her when he was so desperately ill is a mystery. "One of the biggest puzzles of my life has been why Jim sent for Jane at the end when he was trying to get a divorce from her," Joan Cooney said. "I guess when he was that sick he kind of wanted mommy or something. But he had no use for her, for years, and he certainly wanted out. Sending for her allowed Jane to become the widow Henson. That was the most unforgivable thing. It gave her an identity that she hadn't had in years."

Jane Henson had alternately reasserted her role as wife and caretaker, and then later, as cofounder of the Muppets and keeper of the flame. That was something that none of the women Henson dated could claim.

Looking out into the grandeur of the packed cathedral, a scene reminiscent of a state funeral, she expressed gratitude for the turnout. "The reason you're touched is because Jim touched some special place in you that knows all of the light and all the truth and all the love that there is to know. And I hope that you will take whatever it is he has given you to let it help you to enjoy life to the fullest. Because he *always* did, but *always* with a little pain and a little sorrow that gave it richness."

By eerie coincidence, tributes to two patriarchs of *Sesame Street* occurred within days of each other, one before a convocation of thousands, the other before a television audience in the hundreds of thousands. It had been fifteen months since composer, arranger, and lyricist Joseph G. Raposo died from complications of non-Hodgkin's lymphoma, cancer of the immune system, at Lawrence Hospital in Bronxville, New York, just three days shy of his fifty-second birthday.

Unbeknownst to nearly everyone, including those in his circle, Raposo had been living with the disease for ten years and had secretly undergone chemotherapy. "The diagnosis came while I was about a month pregnant with our son Andrew," said Pat Collins, a genial television presence in New York who reviews theater and film. "Joe had some lumps under his arms and in the groin, so he went to his doctor, who referred him to a specialist. I remember that day of that appointment vividly, sitting across from the doctor's desk. When he said it was non-Hodgkin's lymphoma, our first question was 'What does that mean?' You could immediately read from the doctor's face it was not something you want.

"Joe said, 'Pat is pregnant. Will I live to see this child graduate high school or college?' The doctor didn't respond, and Joe said, 'I really want an answer.'

"The doctor said, 'No, you won't.'

"Joe pressed him. 'Will I live to see him be in the first grade?'

"And the doctor just said, 'Joe, this is a very tough thing.'

"That was the moment we decided to move forward. It was Joe's desire and wish from day one that no one know about the diagnosis. We decided that our business manager, the guy who paid the bills, had to know, but that was it. We were living in Bronxville, and I went to elaborate lengths of establishing an account at a pharmacy near Carnegie Hall, where our offices were. We filled prescriptions there because Bronxville's a little place where people talk, including pharmacists. I thought if we really wanted to keep a lid on this, we'd have to be smart and cover our bases.

"Joe's words were 'I do not want to be seen as a patient.' Anyone who has had a relative, a dear friend, or a pal involved in a battle with a disease recognizes how the world thinks: 'There goes so-and-so. Isn't it terrible that he has cancer?' And then they either cut you more slack or start treating you differently. Joe said, 'I'm having none of that.' After everyone learns you have a disease and says all the appropriate things about how terrible it is, they think, 'Is he going to be able to finish the season? Will he finish this album or movie? Is he going to be alive when we perform this at Lincoln Center?' Joe's a great guy and we're gonna miss him, but we can't use him because by the time X is going to happen he might not still be here.' Pretty soon everyone is done working with you. Joe wanted to make sure that he could keep going and not be marginalized. No matter how many days you have left, you want to make every one of them count, and Joe was not a person who would crawl into bed, pull up the quilt, and never come out again.

"He used to go in for chemo really early in the morning at a place on the East Side, before too many people were around. Most people going through it lose weight and look gaunt. Joe, who struggled with weight issues all his life, used to say to me, 'I'm the only son of a bitch on chemo who is not losing weight. You'd think I'd at least get that out of it.'

"Near the end of Joe's life, Jim Henson got me aside and said, 'There's something very wrong with Joe. You've got to tell me what it is.'

"I said, 'I love you, Jim, but no, I don't. You're right that he does have some issues, but you've got to ask him. You can't have me tell you.'

"He said, 'I can't.'

"I said, 'Well, I don't know, then. It's kind of a standoff, isn't it? All I can tell you is he's obviously living with what he's got. That's all I can tell ya, babe.' And that was it.

"People did know he had something, but no one would cross that line to ask him. The only person he ever told was Walter Cronkite. They would go sailing a lot and one day when he came back from one of their little trips on the *Winnie*, he said 'I told Walter because I just had to tell someone. If you can't trust America's most-trusted man, who could you tell your secrets to?'"

Cronkite appeared in the PBS tribute to Raposo, a video love letter entitled *Sing: Sesame Street Remembers Joe Raposo*. "He was the first man to kiss me on the cheek," said Cronkite, who, one imagines, was an unlikely candidate to return the favor. "[Joe] was simply this guy who lived on the very top of life."

It was jarring at first to see Jim Henson on screen, given that footage of his memorial had just aired on the six o'clock news. Henson said, "I think of Joe as a big warm teddy bear . . . always with a hug and a big smile."

Liz Smith, the doyenne of gossip columnists, said, "[It] was so typical of him to open his loving arms and give you an expansive hug and self-confidence where you didn't deserve to have it."

Raposo took some posthumous, good-natured ribbing, as well. "Joe was such a name-dropper," Henson said. "He was the only person that could work into the conversation all the important people that he had seen in the last six months . . . *and* Barbra Streisand's telephone number."

Such harmless talk kept Raposo's ego balloon aloft, as Cerf explained: "It was one of these magical gifts, I guess, is that it would be annoying with other people, but with Joe it was just, 'Oh my god, he's not going to say it is he?' And he did! Somehow you loved him for it.

"I got a phone call at maybe one in the morning. It was Joe, incredibly excited. He said, 'You'll never guess where I am.'

"I said, 'No, I probably won't.'

"I'm in Frank Sinatra's car!" he said. Sinatra at the time had a mobile telephone installed in his limo, a luxury afforded few in the pre-cell-phone era. Raposo had dialed up Cerf when Sinatra stepped away. "You're the first person I called," he crowed.

"I was thrilled for him," Cerf said, "but it turns out he had called everybody else, too. It was a very Joe Raposo moment."

Joan Cooney once recalled receiving a postcard from Raposo. "He [had been] staying at one of Frank Sinatra's villas in Palm Springs. On one side of the card was an aerial view of Sinatra's estate, and he had circled one of the little houses and written 'That's my room.' That was quintessentially Joe."

Raposo contributed four tracks to Sinatra's *Ol' Blue Eyes Is Back,* a 1973 comeback album that brought the singer out of a premature retirement. The project met with mixed reviews, and some critics dismissed Raposo's "You Will Be My Music" and "There Used to Be a Ballpark" as schmaltz. For a time, Raposo was in Sinatra's good graces, back when the crooner thought the composer was a *paisan,* not Portuguese.

There were tears aplenty when Raposo passed, and a lot of elbow nudging when all of the people behind those dropped names came forward to say they were honored to be his friend. Pat Collins has a theory about it. "Joe wasn't bragging so much as he was sharing a kind of joy. He didn't name-drop to impress the listener, but to remind himself that he was not in a waking dream. He actually knew the likes of Sinatra and Cronkite and Richard Rodgers, pretty heady company. He was like a kid who loved baseball who grew up to hang around with Hall of Famers. Joe did not fawn over the famous. It was his pleasure to be in the company of the truly gifted. It was his respect for that rare combination of innate talent, hard work, and perfectionism."

Joan Cooney saw two sides of Raposo. "He could be the most difficult person imaginable with me," she said. "Other times we were lovey-dovey and close. Everything would be going fine, and then he'd suddenly erupt over something, like some obscure publishing-rights item. He actually quit *Sesame Street* cold over a music-publishing rights issue, an esoteric thing that I didn't even understand. After a few years, he wanted to come back, and so we made a date to meet for lunch at Twenty-one. I came into the restaurant a little bit early because of the sensitivity of the situation. The maître d' asked, 'Is your person here?' and I said, 'No, he isn't here yet.' Well, Joe had actually come in earlier and sat at a table in the back, instead of at one in the front where I could have seen him. I sat and he sat for forty-five minutes. Finally I told a waiter I was going to take a quick look round the tables because it did not compute to me that he would be late. You can imagine how awkward this was after this terrible rupture and separation. It haunts me to this day. Even though Joe came back to the Workshop, we were never close again."

Yet Cooney remained a fan and is always quick to praise his portfolio of work for CTW, hundreds of compositions that brightened *Sesame Street* and *The Electric Company*. Yet for all of his success and accolades, Cooney believes Raposo was bedeviled by insecurity.

"There was not enough adoration in the world to meet Joe's expectations," Cooney said. "You couldn't fill his needs. He had the weakest ego of any person I have ever known. It needed to be fed all of the time. He was an only child who was worshiped by his parents, and I always thought that resulted in ego strength. But sometimes it can be the opposite. He was jealous that Jim got so much attention after we went on the air, jealous that the Europeans and Latin Americans wanted adaptations done because the Muppets were such a sensation.

"And yet, Joe was a great genius," Cooney said. "One way you can tell a true genius from a near genius is in their need to keep creating. With geniuses, the urge is unstoppable."

To move forward in our story, we need to take a step back.

In early 1989, Jim Henson had invited Joan Cooney to lunch at a restaurant at the Sherry-Netherland Hotel, where he kept an apartment. He had news to share.

"I want you to know that I am going to sell the company to Disney," he said. "I want the kind of creative freedom that I'll have there without the burden of fund-raising."

Cooney, not at all shocked, told him how pleased she was for him. She then provided some news of her own, saying, "The timing is incredible, Jim. This is not known yet, but I will be stepping down in November as CEO of the Workshop."

One could almost sense seismic plates shifting underfoot. "We were both talking about big life changes together," Cooney said.

In August of that year, news of the sale created a crackle of excitement. Trumpeting a deal that executives described as "a business association made in family entertainment heaven,"[9] Disney announced that it had signed a letter of intent to purchase the Muppets, reportedly for $100 million to $150 million. As part of the deal, Henson agreed to a fifteen-year consulting role and a production pact that guaranteed his services to Disney exclusively.

It had made perfect sense to Cooney that Henson had decided to turn over the classic characters from *The Muppet Show* and the subsequent Muppet movies—along with the library of Henson television work, minus *Sesame Street*—to the Burbank, California–based entertainment conglomerate. (The deal did not include Henson's production company and the core creative talent who worked in the United States and in the London offices of the Henson Creature Shop.) Jim Henson and Walt Disney had this in common: both were small-town boys who knew how to establish the characters they created and tap into the collective unconscious. Even without the colossal resources that were ultimately at Walt's disposal, Henson had successfully propelled Kermit into an orbit few characters ever reach. Keeping him there for generations hence would be a business worry Henson would no longer have to shoulder if he sold to Disney. Plus, he could still be around for the fun part: providing Kermit's voice, movements, and expressions as a paid performer.

"Jim was fine with turning over the classic Muppets to Disney because he was tired of running the company, tired of having to raise money for every project," Cooney explained. "Plus, Disney was promising to back any movie project Jim wanted to do. That was huge."

"Jim didn't run his company like a good businessman," Cooney added. "He could never fire anybody, couldn't accept any plan for downsizing that was drawn up for him by his advisers. Jim feared that he couldn't face people afterward, so he just kept them on." Beyond that, Henson's movie projects had run notoriously over budget. Had it not been for the steady revenue streaming in from *Sesame Street* licensed products, the Jim Henson Company might have collapsed of its own weight.

In Henson's proposed business model, the *Sesame Street* revenue would have continued to pump perhaps seventy million dollars annually into his company while remaining out of Disney's reach.

It may have been naive for Henson to think that Disney would overlook that small matter. Any prospective buyer would have wanted all of the Muppets to be part of such a deal, and it didn't take long before the executive team at CTW began to worry that with a swipe of the pen, Michael Eisner could catch Henson at a weak moment and "have his hand on our windpipe," Cooney said. "At the time, CTW was doing better than Disney in reaching the preschool audience. If Disney could have convinced Jim to include the trademark to the *Sesame Street* characters, they easily could have limited our products on the shelves and tamped us down. They could have decided to do just about anything to us because their power would be so great."

But from all indications, Henson insisted from the start of talks with

Disney that the *Sesame Street* characters were off the table. Eisner, who could be charming and seductive, hoped he could soften Henson's resolve, as Disney lawyers—over a year's time—tried to answer messy questions over ownership of some of Henson's fringe characters and older properties.

Henson also worked on "Here Come the Muppets," a live stage show for the theme park.

At one of their final lunches together in 1990, Henson had tried to put Cooney's mind at ease, assuring her of his intention to not only keep Eisner at bay but to change his will to allow for the *Sesame Street* trademarks to be transferred to CTW upon his death, on condition that his heirs would continue to receive the same cut he always had from licensing and merchandising deals. Cooney later said CTW would have agreed to those terms, in perpetuity.

It was at that time, Cooney said, that Henson had also unburdened himself about misgivings about going forward with the Disney deal. "What really caused him immense grief, and I think contributed to his lack of physical resistance was the contract provision dealing with his personal services. Jim would have been exclusively theirs for the rest of his life. He would be permitted to work on *Sesame Street* for two weeks a year, but that was it. Jim wanted to sign only a five-year deal for his personal services, not fifteen, and Disney said no. In fairness, Disney was about to pay him $150 million, and for what? But Jim was feeling like a caged bird, physically and personally trapped. He just wanted to fly away. You want to say that was what killed him."

At one point, Eisner appeared to back away from his gambit to get Big Bird. Cooney and David Britt attended what was billed as "a peace lunch" at the Henson Workshop with Henson and Eisner. "In that period, Jim was on the phone with me almost daily about his concerns over the Muppets of *Sesame Street*," Cooney said, "He said to me at one point, 'If they don't give this up, it's a deal breaker.' He told them that and they finally dropped it, or so it seemed."

Cooney said Henson went into the initial discussions thinking "Eisner would be a male Joan Cooney." But it wasn't Eisner who was giving him headaches so much as it was the Disney lawyers. Before the peace lunch, Disney had asked Jim to ask us at CTW if we would agree to not build a theme park within a hundred miles of any Disney Park. [In 1980, CTW had opened Sesame Place, a theme park just north of Philadelphia that was populated later by walk-along *Sesame Street* characters.] Cooney immediately agreed to the stipulation. "That's easy," she said. "We weren't about to put a park anywhere near a Disney attraction."

Everyone was prepared to make nice at the peace lunch. "It was going so well," Cooney said. "Michael was absolutely being just his most charming self. He can be so much fun, and so funny. But then, out of the blue, he said something that stopped Jim cold. David Britt and I completely missed it, but he made some reference to the *Sesame Street* Muppets. It may be that we were feeling so comfortable, so happy to be out of the deal, we didn't catch it. But Jim turned to Michael and said, "You did it again!"

"Michael said, 'I did what?'

"Jim said, 'You mentioned *Sesame Street*.'

"Michael said, 'Jim, I'm so sorry, I didn't mean to.'

"But damage was done at that moment," Cooney said, "and it remained a real issue with Jim deep down."

"You kids get out of the way!" warned Joan Cooney, uncharacteristically livid. "I've got an elephant gun and I don't want to hit anyone here."

Cooney was confronting Cheryl Henson and her four siblings, heirs to a company their father built from his fertile imagination and decades of toil. Mere months after Jim Henson's death, Michael Eisner and a squadron of lawyers were negotiating with Henson's survivors in an attempt to close the deal that had been interrupted by catastrophe. Cooney's metaphorical elephant gun was aimed square at the bridge of Eisner's nose.

"The Henson children faced a really tough period after Jim died, and they were holding firm, absolutely committed to protecting what he wanted," Cooney said. "We at CTW felt threatened and committed to doing everything we could to make sure the *Sesame Street* Muppets would never be included in a sale to Disney."

Cooney had only her reputation as a truthful person to back up her assertion that Henson had disclosed a plan to transfer trademark of the Muppets he created expressly for *Sesame Street* to CTW upon his death. That his passing occurred only weeks after their conversation compounded an already difficult situation.

"No agreement had been signed, and Disney was doing its best to finish the deal," Cooney said. "You have to remember that $150 million was still on the table, and now Disney no longer had Jim Henson's services. So they went back to the old thing of 'We want the *Sesame Street* Muppets as part of the deal.' The Henson kids were unwilling to revisit that in any way, and that led to Disney's attempt at a takeover of the Henson Company. I don't know how they intended do that, but their plan was to hold the contract hostage and break the will of the Henson children."

Cooney, by that point, had had quite enough. She ruefully recalled the decisive moment, with a nod to a former adversary. "Nixon said that when you are dealing with an enemy, the enemy must believe you are a madman and not know what you are going to do next."

She summoned David Britt and gave him instructions to call Eisner with the following message: if The Walt Disney Company continued with its takeover attempt, Children's Television Workshop, a nonprofit institution, would be forced to seek immediate redress from the attorney general of the state of New York. With her sterling reputation and well-woven connections in government, Cooney would have been received by the attorney general the following day.

Mere hours passed, Cooney said, before she received a handwritten note from Eisner. "It was very short and to the point, saying that the Workshop was best prepared to control the Muppets of *Sesame Street*. He signed it and that was it. In effect, it was good-bye and good luck.

"I called Cheryl Henson and read her the note over the phone. Cheryl said, 'Well, we won!' And I said, 'No, you didn't. This is not a hello letter. It's a good-bye letter.' And I was right. Disney walked away from the deal, but they started showcasing the Muppets in Disney World, anyway, without paying any fees. It was outrageous, but Michael thought he could get all that was on the table for nothing."

A vitriolic and vicious lawsuit ensued, pitting Henson's company against the corporate giant. In this case, the mouse was the cat.

The Hensons contended that Disney was guilty of trademark and copyright infringement, and an "outright theft of Jim Henson's legacy."

In a counterclaim, Disney insisted it had "an implied license" to use the Muppets, suggesting that Jim Henson's handshake with Eisner represented an ironclad agreement, and that Henson's work on *Muppet∗Vision 3D*,[10] a wide-screen, 70-millimeter movie experience to be housed in a ninety-million-dollar complex being built at the new Disney-MGM Studios in Orlando, now called Disney's Hollywood Studios, was a tacit acknowledgment that the Muppets were part of the Disney brand.

Disney settled the copyright suit on April 30, 1991. The lead-in to Victoria F. Zonna's report in the *Los Angeles Times* reflected the shock of seeing the powerful Disney company humbled. "Mickey Mouse ate a big serving of crow Tuesday as Walt Disney Co. settled its copyright dispute with the heirs of Muppets creator Jim Henson by apologizing to Henson's family and buying a license for a pair of Muppets attractions at Disney World in Florida."

Disney had insisted on a ten-to-twelve-year license to allow the Muppets to perform in the stage show and to unlimited showings of the 3D film. They ultimately agreed to eighteen months for exclusive use in theme parks east of the Mississippi, with an option to renew.

Richard Hunt was driving over the George Washington Bridge with his older sister Kate one night in the late 1980s, his hands on the wheel of an old Checker cab that had been painted black, Hunt's idea of a dream vehicle.

"It was pouring rain as we were heading into New Jersey and onto the Palisades Parkway when Richard told me about his illness," Kate said. "I was the first person in the family with whom he shared the news." Almost as suddenly as Hunt blurted out that he was HIV positive, the car "went into a spin and we ended up on the guard rail of the highway. Richard simply said, 'Well, I guess I wasn't supposed to die *today*,'" she recalled.

Hunt developed full-blown AIDS and surived for five years, outliving a partner who had died in his arms of the disease. After spending his final days at the Cabrini Hospice in Manhattan, Hunt succumbed on January 7, 1992; he was forty. Most of his ashes were taken to a home he owned on Cape Cod.

A memorial service was held February 2 at the Cathedral of St. John the Divine, the same holy space where twenty-one months earlier he had eulogized Jim Henson. On that day Hunt and his Muppet colleagues Jerry Nelson, Kevin Clash, Dave Goelz, Steve Whitmire, and Frank Oz had performed magnificently, providing a fitting finale. With only piano accompaniment, they'd sung a medley of Henson's favorite melodies, from the well-worn ("You Are My Sunshine") to the semiobscure (Randy Newman's "Simon Smith and the Amazing Dancing Bear"). The performance spanned the decades, touching mostly gently on *The Muppet Show* and the Muppet films that followed.

"*The Muppet Show* years were Richard's happiest times," his sister said. Certainly, Hunt reached his artistic apogee in London during the five seasons of *The Muppet Show*, where he brought to life Beeker, the petrified lab assistant; Janice, the stringy blond Valley Girl lead guitarist from the Electric Mayhem Band; Sweetums, the yellow-eyed, twin-toothed ogre who had no need for hair plugs; and Scooter, who opened every episode with a knock on the guest star's dressing room door. "Fifteen seconds to curtain, Miss Minnelli."

Scooter reflected more of Hunt's soul than any other character, in his desire to please and provide, and his eagerness to set things right backstage.

"My brother overcame a difficult childhood," Kate Hunt said. "He had a father who drank too much and parents who yelled at each other all of the time. There was very little money. I'd say Richard's comedy gift came from a place of pain. He knew from the time he was young that he would have to be successful to take care of his family, and he did that to a fault."

Hunt's generosity is the trait friends and colleagues cite most often as his defining characteristic. He was as generous of spirit as he was with the folding money in his wallet.

He was in many ways unforgettable, even for the likes of Forgetful Jones.

Joan Cooney characterized Lewis Freedman as "the grandfather of *Sesame Street*" upon his death at age sixty-six in the early summer of 1992.

At the fateful dinner party in 1966, it was Freedman who turned the conversation to television's untapped potential. And it was Freedman, along with Cooney, who arrived at Carnegie Corporation with a sketchy idea for a television program that would teach as it entertained preschoolers.

Among Freedman's successes across forty-five years as a television producer and programming executive was a series of sixty-second historical sketches that ran on CBS during the yearlong celebration of the nation's two hundredth birthday. Those "Bicentennial Minutes," narrated by Walter Cronkite, won an Emmy, a Peabody, and high praise from fifth-grade teachers across the continent.

For the longest time, *Sesame Street* remained the undisputed heavyweight champion of preschool television. But in the immortal words of Bud Brown, Joan Cooney's effusive social studies teacher, change is the only constant. By the early 1990s, *Sesame Street* might have been overripe and a bit too sure of itself. How could it *not* have been, after twenty-plus seasons of ratings dominance and so great a surfeit of Emmys that CTW could have used them as doorstops?

But half a continent away from Manhattan, in unremarkable Allen, Texas, a suburb of Dallas, a tiny entrepreneurial start-up company was about to introduce its own paradigm to the world of preschool television and the culture at large. The idea for it came, as did *Sesame Street*, from a university-trained teacher. In the 1980s, former-teacher-turned-stay-at-home mom Sheryl Leach was dismayed at the narrow range of choices available at the video store for her two-year-old son, Patrick. Nothing seemed to hold his attention. While driving on the freeway one day, Leach had her eureka moment: why not bypass the store-bought, packaged tapes and whip up a homemade one? If it can work with baking brownies, why not videos?

How hard could it be? she wondered?[11]

That accounts for most of the prehistory of Barney, except to add that Leach's father-in-law owned a video studio and put up a million dollars to finance production of three Barney tapes. The stories in those initial episodes weren't written so much as they were typed, and the production values were just a cut above cable-access.

Barney was initially envisioned as a teddy bear, but he developed into a pudgy purple six-foot-tall dinosaur, sprouting tiny arms and yellow toenails and affecting a singsong vocal delivery that proved a siren song to small children. Most adults ran for cover while their children stared at the screen in rapt wonder.

Distribution of Barney tapes started out with his creators selling them one-by-one to teachers at Texas preschools and day-care centers. Word soon grew, and Barney began appearing at video outlets near and far. To adult eyes the features seemed amateurish and low budget; to children, born video illiterate, they seemed magical. Perhaps it was the bright Playskool hues of the show, or the familiar nursery rhyme tunes plucked for free from the public domain, or the ring of well-scrubbed children chirping away, or the simple directness of Barney himself, a plush toy come to life whose most complicated conviction was "I love you, you love me, we're a happy fam-a-lee." Whatever it was, it proved an elixir for the sippy-cup crowd.

Barney's big break came one Super Bowl Sunday, not with an appearance at a domed stadium (that would come later) but in the home of then four-year-old Leora Rifkin, daughter of a programming executive at Connecticut Public Television. In a manner not entirely different from Lloyd Morrisett's observing daughter Sarah so many years before, Larry Rifkin stood amazed while Leora played and replayed a Barney tape. He phoned the Lyons Group, the company name listed on the video packaging, and soon afterward a deal was struck to produce thirty half-hour episodes of *Barney & Friends* for PBS. The national exposure turned Barney into what the *Boston Globe* once described as Toyrannasaurus Rex, a merchandising behemoth. *Business Week* predicted in 1993 that Barney would move three hundred million dollars in toys and millions more in a bonanza of books, baubles, and bedsheets, more than two hundred licensed products in all.[12]

Barney enjoyed gargantuan commercial success but throughout his purple reign on PBS, he has been a piñata for the television press. The *Washington Post* once described the show as "so saccharine it can send adults into hypoglycemic shock." The *New York Times,* in a review headlined "Of Dinosaurs Why Must This One Thrive?" said, "Next to Barney and his friends, Sandy Duncan is a flesh-eating succubus."[13]

He was not without supporters, however. The *National Review* harrumphed that the Barney backlash was pablum fed by the liberal press and swallowed whole by baby boom parents "appalled at Barney's uplift." It described the series as "wholesome without relief . . . [U]nlike *Sesame Street,* set in a scene of urban decay, Barney entertains from a suburban schoolyard, swept clean of graffiti and trash. None of Barney's friends lives in a garbage can, and none grunts hip-hop. The pace is slow and lingering, a technique at odds with *Sesame Street*'s barrage of spastic, quick-cut graphics that prep the kids for the countless hours of MTV awaiting them in adolescence. And instead of *Sesame Street*'s multicultural insinuations, Barney's message revolves around the importance of brushing teeth, exercising, and even—this is how deep it goes—chewing with one's mouth closed."[14]

Regardless of whether Barney was an abomination or a fascination (Barney made *People*'s list of 25 Most Intriguing People of 1992), the show took a big bite out of *Sesame Street*'s ratings. David Britt, installed as Joan Cooney's successor as CEO in 1990, took heed. He assembled a SWAT team of executives to shake up *Sesame Street,* summoning Emily Swenson, executive vice president and chief operating officer; Marjorie Kahlins, group vice president for programming and production; Dr. Valeria Lovelace, research director for *Sesame Street*; and Franklin Getchell, vice president for programming and production.

As an agent of change, Getchell had a reputation for rampaging self-promotion and arrogance, at least among *Sesame Street*'s writers and producers. His track record as an executive producer included both success (the well-regarded science series *3-2-1 Contact*) and failure (the quirky HBO series *Encyclopedia*). After *Encyclopedia* was canceled, Getchell had hoped to land a job as a producer for *Sesame Street.* Unimpressed with his producing credentials, *Sesame* offered a spot on the writing staff, though he would first have to write an audition script, like anyone else. When Getchell turned it in, it was summarily rejected.

A few weeks after he was turned down by *Sesame*'s producers, however, Getchell became their boss, when Britt promoted him to replace Alfred Hyslop, who had reigned as vice president for programming and production (1980–88).

In his memoir, Jon Stone recalled the reaction around the studio: utter disbelief.

Stone, who had long since stepped down as executive producer to be more hands-on in the studio, heard the tom-toms beating, as did his successor, Dulcy Singer, who clashed with no one until Getchell came along. "Getchell was determined to put his own personal brand on the program," Stone wrote. "He made it abundantly clear to Dulcy and me that there were going to be big changes, that those changes were going to be his, and that he would not tolerate insubordination."

Increasingly, management perceived Stone and Singer as resistant to change, and they knew it. "They thought we were comfortable old sticks-in-the-mud who were opposed to any change whatsoever. It was an entirely absurd assumption: what was discerned as resistance to all change was in fact resistance to ill-conceived, unresearched, damaging change. We were never asked about modification. We were told."

David Britt's reading of the situation was that "Jon was being pressured to do things differently, for good reason. Research demonstrated that our viewing audience was growing younger and younger, yet the show was still being written and produced for older preschoolers. We actually didn't press him as hard as we should have, considering the change that was so evident to us. Jon couldn't give himself any distance from it, and things got ugly."

In part to blunt Barney's cut into ratings and in part to reinvigorate *Sesame Street* for its twenty-fifth anniversary season, Britt's management team, with the blessing and encouragement of Joan Cooney, came up with an urban renewal plan they called Around the Corner.

With an investment north of two million dollars, the executives planned an expansion of the landmark set design to include a never-before-seen cul-de-sac around the corner from the brownstone stoop at 123 Sesame Street. A group of new characters—human and Muppet—would populate a neighborhood that would be painted and lit considerably brighter than the original facades. A focal point would be the Furry Arms Hotel, operated by dim-witted Muppets Ingrid and Humphrey. A grande dame puppet named Sherry Netherland would reside there. At the end of each broadcast, an announcer would plug the hotel, saying "Guests of *Sesame Street* stay at the elegant Furry Arms, whether they want to or not." Nearby would be a dance studio, a home-based day-care center, and a playground, a new array of spaces that seemed less like Harlem and more like any gentrified up-and-coming neighborhood in America.

Adding to the determined upbeatness would be a trio of singing rodents called the Squirrels (Crystal, Darlene, and Rhonda), and comic actress Ruth Buzzi, best remembered for *Rowan and Martin's Laugh-In,* would join the cast as Ruthie, the proprietor of the Finders Keepers thrift shop, a kind of precursor to eBay. Typical items for sale in Ruthie's shop would be Jack and Jill's pail and Cinderella's glass slipper.

Significantly, a circle of trained child actors would now have a continuing presence on the show. The long-held tradition of using untrained children on the set, behaving as they would on a real street, would come to an end. That was not the way they did things on *Barney*.

Rather than impose changes she did not believe in, Dulcy Singer resigned before production commenced on the twenty-fifth season. She was replaced as executive producer by Michael Loman, a sitcom writer from California who had worked on *All in the Family, Happy Days,* and *Valerie.* CTW had commissioned a headhunter to identify outside candidates for the job, but Loman came in over the transom. He heard about the opening and pitched himself so successfully that he beat out other more qualified candidates, even though he had had no experience in children's television.

The producers and writers, long accustomed to a line-of-succession policy, were enraged that their preferred candidate, Lisa Simon, was passed over. Simon had worked well with Getchell and was prepared to institute change. But as with many executive searches in the 1990s, the flash of the new trumped familiarity and fidelity.

Accommodating the new set forced CTW to find a new production facility that had the necessary height, width, and floor space, and *Sesame Street* accordingly relocated to the massive Kaufman-Astoria Studios in Queens, a Hollywood-worthy motion picture and television production facility.

CTW was about to spend serious money with these changes, but they hoped to make it back by capitalizing on the letter *Z*.

After a few years away from *Sesame Street* to pursue theater roles, puppeteer Fran Brill returned to the series in 1993, in time for the major public relations and marketing push tied to the twenty-fifth anniversary. Without knowing it, unreasonable expectations were about to be heaped upon the puppeteer with the introduction of Zoe.

Adding characters had always been the province of CTW's creative team, a process that took time, trial, and patience. But this time around, CTW executives abandoned the tried and true, choosing instead to adopt a model more in tune with what the bourgeoning cable networks for children favored. In this about-face, the producers and writers would not lead the charge, but rather specialists in marketing and product development, in tandem with the research department at CTW.

Zoe was like a plush toy in search of an identity, a carefully considered product that would be tested for its appeal with children in focus groups. Every aspect of its development was controlled and strategic. The decision to make Zoe a bright orange, for instance, was deliberate. That color would not only contrast with Big Bird and Elmo on the TV screen but stand out on the shelves at Target, where Barney and his friends were making bar code scanners beep as never before.

The zest to create Zoe was considered almost Frankensteinian by the writers working on the other side of the building from the execs, the outward sign of the widening schism developing between the creative and business sides. But Zoe was carrying additional burdens. Even before she made her television debut, she became a standard bearer for feminists at CTW who had grown tired of waiting for a breakout female Muppet. The women wondered, quite understandably, why the most beloved *Sesame Street* characters—Big Bird, Oscar, Bert, Ernie, Grover, Cookie Monster, Snuffy, Telly, the Count—were males performed by males.

Any number of female characters had been added through the years, including the always hilarious Grundgetta, Oscar's trashy girlfriend. Though Grundgetta was originated by Brian Muehl in 1982, the prodigiously talented Pam Arciero had picked up the character and run with it in 1985.

There also was Prairie Dawn, Fran Brill's terribly earnest, earthbound pragmatist in an ash blond human-hair wig. Prairie was the Muppet most liked by librarians.

Bit player Gladys undoubtedly may have been the funniest of the female characters. But Richard Hunt's dairyland diva rankled feminists more than any other character. She was, after all, a cow.

The charge to promote Zoe was led by Dr. Valeria Lovelace, a social scientist who directed research for *Sesame Street*. Lovelace was the first activist research director. She vowed early in her tenure that research would no longer passively provide guidance to the production department but instead develop an active agenda for researchers to pursue and promote, a list of objectives that would be forced upon the creative team that had for so long driven the show. "She had little interest in the selfless role Research had played in the past," Stone said. "She felt Research should be an entity of its own and be considered, within the corporate structure of CTW as well as in practice, at least equal to Production."

For the producers, writers, and performers, Lovelace became an object of ridicule and derision. They nicknamed her "Maleria" and rebuffed and mocked her at every opportunity. One instance that became legendary involved a script about a showbiz sharpie named Walt Dizzy, in search of an actor to play a chicken in an upcoming production. Telly, badly bitten by the acting bug, obsesses about the part, practicing *clucks* and wing flapping. Alas, Elmo gets the role, but Telly lands another and all is well on *Sesame Street*. The script was heading into production when Lovelace put a halt to it: after reading the script, Research had concluded the material was unsuitable to air on the grounds of racism. "The part of a chicken should only be played by a chicken," was their conclusion, Stone said. "Someone who wasn't a chicken shouldn't play the part of a chicken. When the writers and producers realized that Valeria wasn't kidding, they explained that the whole art of acting is pretending to be someone other than who you are in real life, otherwise you wouldn't mount a production of Hamlet unless a real Danish prince happened to show up at the audition. Norman Stiles suggested with a straight face that we air the piece as written and see how much mail we get from outraged chickens."

Lovelace, an African American who had successfully pushed through a curriculum on race relations in 1992, was now determined to push Zoe into a starring role, with or without buy-in from the writers.

David Britt sanctioned the moves and the power shift, holding true to his contention that the production team—notably Stone and his acolytes—had become calcified and resistant to innovation, blind and deaf to the seismic changes that were under way in children's television, heralded by *Barney & Friends*. He believed Stone not only dismissed as nonsense the purple dinosaur who had encroached on *Sesame Street*'s success but was contemptuous of households where children tuned in the show. "You know the old line that's attributed to Hitler in the 1940s, when everything was going to hell: 'I'm beginning to wonder if the German people are worthy of me'? Jon's version of that was 'Well, when the kids don't respond anymore, they're not worthy of having *Sesame Street*.' He really had his picture of the show that was frozen in time."

Fran Brill was accordingly handed a mandate: make Zoe a star that little girls will relate to and the products team can bank on.

Zoe received a mighty gust of public relations support. Encamped in Pasadena at the annual Television Critics Association summer meeting, TV columnists were hand-fed a Zoe-is-the-answer agenda. Writing in *TV Times*, the Sunday listings guide inserted into the *Los Angeles Times*, reporter Jack Matthews wrote, "Valeria Lovelace, who has headed research for eleven years, says the new characters are usually 'the babies of writers,' but this year most were created to facilitate the show's curriculum. 'We usually move into the process when the character has been created and can go out and test them. We've been in the loop much earlier with these. . . . Every year we have created a female Muppet character, but they haven't been successful. This year we're trying to create a star who will be a very good role model for girls, in terms of taking initiatives and goals.'"[15]

The *New York Times* reported that CTW was "counting on Zoe to fill an embarrassing lacuna that has dogged the show since its creation in 1969: the lack of a strong, female Muppet." Lovelace said in the piece, "Little girls need to have role models on the show . . . [to] see them and say, 'That's like me.'"[16]

In advance of the twenty-fifth season debut, *People* magazine got closer to the truth than its editors may have even realized. "Political correctness has created a monster on *Sesame Street*," it declared. "Hoping to bring more positive female role models to children's television, the folks at that august address have a new resident who is indeed perfectly PC—perpetually cute, that is. [Zoe] is scruffy, wide-eyed and the color of a radioactive orange Popsicle. Only three, she is already pegged to be a star—the first female supernova of the show."

Brill was quoted extensively about a character that she had hardly had a chance to play with and develop. It was like asking a new mother to ruminate on the personality and potential of a one-month-old. Worse, the talking points she had been handed came from the public relations department, not the trusted corps of writers who understood the rigor behind character development.

"Before this time, writers were never driven by merchandising," Brill said. "It was always, Go write for the character and see what develops. This was just the opposite, and you shouldn't put out product before people have a chance to know who the hell you're talking about. Zoe got burned with that. Also, before Zoe we weren't designing puppets for their attractiveness. The Muppets are ugly when they're just lying on the floor unanimated. They're bath mats with big eyes. But when they're animated, that's a whole other story. Zoe marked the first time a character was created without it being a play-around puppet first. The very first thing I ever did on camera as Zoe was horrible because she hadn't grown out of something that I had nurtured and developed. I was sort of doing this Carol Channing voice that was just too much. Over time I pulled her back because it wasn't coming from anything within me.

"Jim Henson never used the word *cast* in discussing how he found the right person for a Muppet. Some people are more in tune with a puppet; it just depends what happens to your creative juices when you put it on. The classic story was Kevin Clash with Elmo. In my case, it was the opposite. Someone said 'Let's create this female blockbuster equivalent of Elmo. What color should she be? What color do we not have in the palette? Let's see, Big Bird is yellow, Oscar is green, they went through all the colors, like going through a box of Crayolas. Oh, she's got to be orange!' Well, a year or two later we had this merchandising person say to us, 'If only Zoe had been pink. It would be so much easier to sell her because girls love pink.'"

A pink Muppet? That, too, would come to pass.

Sam and Carol Gibbon had no intention of canceling their annual poker game with Dave Connell.

It was May 4, 1995, when the couple drove to River Edge, New Jersey, to join Connell and cronies Jim and Pat Thurman.

Dave's daughter, Jan, and son, Alan, also were there, monitoring their father, who had been diagnosed with terminal cancer. He chose to die at home rather spend another day in a hospital or move into a hospice.

"My dad had just started having a series of strokes, and the end was near," Jan said. "One of the things Alan and I did before the card game was read *Ferdinand* to my dad, his favorite children's story."

The Thurmans and the Gibbons settled in around a table in Connell's bedroom. "They got comfortable chairs and had drinks and told jokes and had a great time," Jan said. "It was a beautiful tribute to their shared friendship."

Sam and Carol went back in time the longest with Connell, to the first decade of *Captain Kangaroo* and the formative years of *Sesame Street*. The apotheosis of their creative partnership was *The Electric Company*, the sketch-comedy reading series that probably had as much or even more developmental impact on children in its day than *Sesame Street*. The pity is that because funding for the series dried up and it had no marketable characters to turn into plush toys or imprint on bedsheets to generate a revenue stream, production ceased in 1977 after 780 half-hour episodes.[17] On that day in Washington when Joan Cooney had convinced Barry Goldwater that CTW could wean itself off federal assistance, she had unwittingly made a kind of Sophie's Choice: *Sesame Street* would survive, *The Electric Company* would not.

Bright guys who never took themselves too seriously, Gibbon and Connell became visiting faculty members at the Harvard Graduate School of Education. They had gone through a lot together and were permanently bonded by their shared love of comedy. After all, these were the guys who created an *Electric Company* word sleuth named Fargo North, Decoder.

"When we were little, Dad would stop off at Sam and Carol's in Englewood Cliffs on the way home from work for a drink," said Jan Connell, who worked in the television industry before opening a psychotherapy private practice in Warwick, New York. "Dad would get tanked until we were in bed, because he didn't feel like dealing with it all. Then he'd come home after my mother had done everything, which was not very nice. But, at least, he admitted he wasn't a model father and husband back then. I don't think my parents ever got along. My father was very focused on work; there was not much room left for marriage. Like a lot of other businessmen at that time, he was very active sexually. Nowadays, you'd call it a sex addiction, and there would be trouble to pay in the workplace. But back then, with the discovery of birth control, there was sexual freedom that didn't exist before, and STDs weren't widely thought about. A lot of those guys were not saints, and they did it with secretaries and assistants and whoever was willing. Whenever there is the kind of tension and power that exists in the studio, all that intellect and talent, there's a huge sexual energy attached to it. Plus, they were never home. The irony is, while these men were out trying to educate the world, their wives were left at home to raise the children they brought into the world."

Jim Thurman's friendship with Dave Connell—"as close as a marriage," said Jan Connell—had begun when they conspired on *Roger Ramjet,* the syndicated cartoon lampoon of air force flyboys and cold war jingoists that enjoys a second life now on DVD and YouTube clips. Thurman had also worked with Connell on *Sesame Street, The Electric Company,* and CTW's vastly unappreciated math show for preteens, *Square One TV.*

As a quintet, the two couples and Connell enjoyed the best of times together. Their same-time-next-year card game—with its extended cocktail hour—was so well established a calendar highlight that the Thurmans and the Gibbons made a pact to honor the date for the 1995 poker game, around Dave's deathbed, resolving that it was better to laugh than to cry. They played Spike Jones music continuously, in the hope that Connell's brain was still processing the sublime silliness of it all.

Weeks before, when Connell was slipping in and out of coma, Thurman sneaked a flask into his hospital room. "Dad was barely able to drink a little water. But in came Jim with scotch," Jan said. "He looked at me, like for permission, and I shrugged, 'Who cares if he has one at this point?' Dad would dribble the water down his chin when the nurses tried to give it to him but every drop of scotch went down."

Connell had first been diagnosed with bladder cancer in 1987 and underwent chemotherapy. The bladder was removed and he had seven decent years. Jan said, "One day he called me out of the blue and said, 'I need to get to the hospital.' They took a chest X-ray and saw he was full of tumors. My uncle said, 'Who's going to take care of him? You or me?' I said, 'Me,' but I had no idea what it entailed. I went with him to every treatment, every transfusion, every hospitalization. I cooked and cleaned. But that's when I really got to know him in a different way. If I hadn't had the last three years with my dad, I might have had some regret. But nothing went unsaid." Before he became too ill to continue, Connell had been at work on a memoir of his years in children's television. When he stopped, Jan set up a camcorder and taped conversations with her father.

Alan Connell, a onetime producer for CBS News in New York, also grew closer to his father in adulthood. "Dad was there for the big things in life when we were kids, but I didn't know him as a person, his likes and dislikes, until we were much older. He learned to water ski with me—in his forties. I feel lucky I had that opportunity.

"His advice to me when I got married was this: 'I screwed it up, don't you screw it up. You've got a great woman there.' He realized he sacrificed a lot for his professional life. As a result of that, I have focused more on my personal life rather than my career."

Jan said, "In those last years, we tried to get him to spend some money on himself, but he was financially anorexic. His pants were worn thin, and he had slippers with duct tape on them. The only material things that mattered to him were a nice home and a good car. His last one was a Lincoln."

To the end, Connell had the executive producer mindset. "My dad was obsessive-compulsive and rigid," she said. "He had to make sure everything was in its place and working the way it was supposed to. Everything was timed and scheduled: you got up at this time and read the paper from this time till that time."

Connell even picked the appropriate moment to check out. "He died at Bloody Mary time," Jan said. "Right at eleven forty-five."

That Connell was not awarded a Lifetime Achievement Emmy is the academy's disgrace. As it was, he was nominated for twenty Emmys and won five across a career that spanned five decades. There likely has never been anyone in the history of children's television who has compiled a record of achievement equal to his, as executive producer of a string of enriching, progressive, and groundbreaking series: *Captain Kangaroo, Sesame Street, The Electric Company, Out to Lunch, Square One TV,* and *Mathnet.* He also was executive producer of CTW's animated adaptation of *The Lion, the Witch and the Wardrobe.* And, yes, there are those 156 episodes of *Roger Ramjet,* too.

Later in the summer of '95, a caravan of cars arrived at Sebago Lake, in the forest green mountainous region of Maine west of Portland. "That's where dad was happiest," Jan said. "and so we took him to Maine."

Jim Thurman kissed Dave Connell's ashes, "and then he threw them into the water," Jan said. "Dad would have loved it."

Connell, another *Sesame Street* patriarch to die of cancer, was only sixty-four when he passed on May 5, the morning after the poker game.

Thurman died in 2007 after a short illness. He was seventy-two.

Evelyn Payne Davis, the town crier of *Sesame Street*, died of lung cancer in the winter of 1997 at the age of seventy-five.

Though her name never ran on the credits and she won no Emmy statuettes, her influence on *Sesame Street* was profound. The show simply would not have been the initial success it was without her audacious promotion of the series in Harlem and in Appalachia, in churches and recreation halls, in the black press, and on small radio stations. She was unstoppable.

Beyond her work as a vice president at CTW, she organized voter registration drives as president of the New York Coalition of 100 Black Women and helped establish child-care centers in prisons, allowing inmates to work on educational goals with their visiting children. "Kids deserve to see their parents in a setting that doesn't scare them," she said. Davis was survived by a son and stepdaughter.

A neighbor who lived down the hall from her in Gramercy Park told the *New York Times* that the community outreach worker used to entertain neighbors while seated at the piano, imitating Billie Holiday. She also played one-string bass with a broom tied to an overturned washtub.

She could, whatever the circumstances, make people listen.

One day Jon Stone entered the studio in a daze. He had not been feeling well and had just returned from a visit to the doctor. Upon seeing writer Emily Kingsley, he turned to her and said, "I've got ALS, Em. Lou Gehrig's disease."

Kingsley hardly knew what to say, nor did anyone else once word spread that Stone had amyotrophic lateral sclerosis, a progressive disease that disrupts nerve cells in the brain and spinal cord. Although there can be some variance, the course the disease most often follows is a slow deterioration of muscle activity followed by paralysis and death. It is a miserable way to depart this earth, and Stone suffered no shortage of misery.

He continued to direct episodes of *Sesame Street* for as long as he could, first using a bicycle to get around the studio, then later a bright red motorized cart that had been Muppetized. As a token of their affection, the puppeteers commissioned a hand-tooled cane for his use, embellished with carvings of the Muppet characters.

Everyone in the studio vowed to keep his spirits up. One high point came on a day when a stagehand quietly wheeled Stone's bike to safety, replacing it with a look-alike that was missing its wheels, chain, and seat. Stone was convinced his bike had been vandalized, and vowed revenge when the prank was revealed, amid howls of laughter.

There was a great moment with the cart, as well. "My dad took the cart everywhere," said Polly Stone, who took care of her father in Manhattan until his last days. "It used to drive him nuts that people who knew him for years would see him in the cart and not comment on it, like somehow it was off-limits conversationally. But kids were fascinated by it. We were out in the park one July day, and there was a kid who stood right dead center in front of the cart. 'Why you on that thing?' he asked. Dad just looked at him, 'When it's warm and there's no snow, I can't use my reindeer.' The kid's eyes got wide and he totally disappeared."

Stone's emotions got the best of him as the disease progressed, and he made a terrible blunder one night in Oneonta, New York. At the time, Stone had been dating a professor of music business at the state university there, and she invited him in to guest lecture. He spoke frankly and pejoratively that night about his displeasure with the changes imposed on *Sesame Street*, disparaging the leadership at CTW for, essentially, dumbing down the show. Whether Stone realized that a reporter from a local newspaper was sitting in on the lecture is unclear, but the Associated Press picked up the reporter's story and it landed on the desks of the very people Stone had just criticized.

"Polly and I know that our dad would have laid down his life for us," said Kate Lucas. "That's how much he cared. And I think that's how much he cared about *Sesame Street*. He wasn't going to say, 'Well, we had twenty-five good years and at least we have those old shows.' He was going to fight pretty hard, and it cost him. The reporter's story blew things wide open. When CTW saw it, it was viewed as grounds for firing because there was a clause in his contract about upholding the values of the show. Dad had been such a troublemaker for them for not toeing the line, they were just looking for an excuse. But the people who were running the show on a day-to-day basis were still loyal to Dad, the puppeteers, the actors, the people behind the set, they all loved him. He was by then the grandfather of *Sesame Street*.

"If they fired him, it would have terminated his health insurance, which was unthinkable to someone who is in that condition. Dad threatened to go to the press if they fired him, to talk to anyone who would listen. And so they came up with an ugly compromise where they kept Dad on salary, kept his position where he was paid very well, kept his health insurance, but banned him from being on the set. His directing days would be over. Dad never cared about money. If he had, he would never have stayed at *Sesame Street*. He had so many opportunities to leave through the years, to go off with Jim and Frank and make millions."

Despite the rancor and the bitter departure, Joan Cooney kept in touch with Stone and agreed to deliver a tribute to him when he was honored by the ALS Foundation with a lifetime achievement award in October 1996. In accepting the award, Stone said, "When Lou Gehrig made his famous speech at Yankee Stadium, you know the one: 'I am the luckiest man, luckiest man, luckiest man on the face of the earth, the face of the earth, the face of the earth.' But when he did that, nobody heard him say he had the vaguest idea what amyotrophic lateral sclerosis was. That was July of 1939, and it's now fifty-seven years later and still nobody has the vaguest idea. They have no idea how debilitating it is, how fast moving it is, how lethal it is. And when I mention to people I have this disorder, they nod their heads and assume that it's some exotic strain of the Asian flu. It's an unfamiliar disease. That's why your contribution is so tremendously important, to raise the consciousness of people to this disease . . . to compete for research dollars with those giants among charities . . . with much more powerful public relations.

"I just have one last thought for the evening, and that is (and I don't want to offend anybody with this) it seems to me that Lou Gehrig has really borne the cross of his disease now for fifty-seven years and deserves a rest. He was such a great athlete that he shouldn't have a lousy, rotten, crummy disease like this named after him. So I propose tonight that we rename the damn thing Marv Throneberry disease."

In his final year, Stone got to work on committing his life story to paper, told in 209 pages of funny, poignant, biting prose. Doing so enabled him to disgorge a lot of bile that had built up over what he felt was a dismantling of *Sesame Street*. He didn't live long enough to see that the Around the Corner set was ultimately dismantled. Viewers soundly rejected the turning away from the core characters that had made the series so successful for so long. The only major character to survive the debacle was Zoe, and that was largely on the basis of Fran Brill's talent shining through.

Frank Oz remembered a visit to Stone in his final months. "Jon and I would occasionally meet for breakfast when he was still well enough to go out in his scooter. But I could see him getting worse and worse. The next time he'd have an oxygen tank, and then the next time he couldn't hold his fork. That, along with the bitterness of what happened to him at *Sesame Street*, was very, very difficult to take."

Something quite wonderful happened as the end neared, though. Beverley Stone, long divorced from Jon, started coming to his apartment one night a week to give Polly a night off from watching over her father. "We used to watch *Mad About You* together and laugh," she said. The Paul Reiser character reminded her of a young Jon; the Helen Hunt character reminded him of the young Beverley.

Stone was hospitalized on his final day. Beverley and Polly arrived with his memoir manuscript. "I'd planned on starting to read it the day before, but Polly told me he wanted some of it to get read when I got to the hospital. He hadn't read it for a while. As we went along, I said, 'Jon, wait a minute. It didn't happen that way. *This* is how it happened.' Then I turned the page to the chapter with a heading MISS RHEINGOLD. Jon looked at Polly and said, 'Now we're going to get it.'"

Jon Stone, the soul of *Sesame Street,* died on March 30, 1997. He was sixty-five.

A video shown at a memorial service included a lingering shot of an empty director's chair with Stone's name in script across the cloth back support.

Norman Stiles was relaxing at home on a weekend before Labor Day, 1998, when Jeff Moss phoned with a request: "He asked if I would be available to attend an upcoming meeting of the *Sesame Street* writers," Stiles said.[18] At the time, Stiles wasn't working on the series, "but I did not ask why he wanted me there. Jeff's voice sounded strained and his breathing was labored."

Moss said, "I'll be speaking for half an hour, and I'd really like you to be there . . . at twelve thirty, *sharp.*" He was one to take appointment times seriously.

Stiles assured his friend and colleague he'd be there—punctually.

It wasn't the first time Moss had invited Stiles to a writers' meeting without providing much explanation; it happened once before in 1969, when Stiles was vying for a staff writer's position on the new series *Sesame Street.*[19]

"I had just concluded a one-month audition period during which I and another prospective writer named Tippy each wrote a script a week," Stiles said. "I had been unemployed for over six months, with no other prospects, and I really wanted and needed the job. But only one of us was going to be hired. I didn't know whether I had the job or not. I just assumed a decision hadn't been made yet, or I would have been told. Silly me. I didn't know Jeff yet. I didn't know he preferred to use a kind of

Jeff Moss code to have people *infer* things rather than use a direct, simple approach. Jeff began to talk about new plans for the *Sesame Street* season and what would be written first, the schedule, things like that. So when the meeting ended, I just had to ask, 'Do I have the job?'"

"'Do you see *Tippy?*' he asked. Jeff was a little impatient, though there was a twinkle in his eye when he said it."

Years later, on that late summer day, Stiles sensed his days of pretending nothing was wrong with Moss were about to end. "I had known for about two years that he was ill, but I wasn't supposed to know," Stiles said. "Only a slight few knew the secret from the beginning. He had me fooled for the first few years, but as the symptoms became more obvious and consistent, it slowly began to dawn on me that maybe there was something more serious going on than he was letting on. I thought about asking him directly, but I didn't. I respected Jeff's decision not to tell me, and I really hoped, down deep, there was really nothing to tell. Then, a mutual friend confirmed my dark suspicions. She told me that Jeff was seriously ill. She couldn't tell me exactly what was wrong with him, but the gist was that it was life threatening, and that I couldn't say anything to Jeff, and I couldn't tell anyone it was she who had told me. As a matter of fact, she said the whole conversation never happened."

Moss could be stubborn, even with those he trusted and respected, including his pal Bernie Kruger, a noted oncologist. When Moss turned fifty, Dr. Kruger began urging him to get a colonoscopy, but he kept putting it off. By the time he did submit to the test, it was too late. The cancer in his colon, and resulting spread of the disease, required eleven operations and procedures. Only when his prognosis became grim, when he was confined to a wheelchair and on portable oxygen, did he decide to disclose his illness to the people he worked with for so long on *Sesame Street.* The day he did was one that shocked and saddened the denizens of One Lincoln Plaza.

In his prime, Moss was a force of nature, a wiry, strong, wild-haired, sometimes combustible, not always lovable, but dependably brilliant television writer, playwright, poet, composer, and onetime actor. (As an undergraduate at Princeton, Moss had performed in the fabled Triangle Club campus musicals.)

Moss flourished in the 1990s as he had at no other time in his life, and the upswing can be traced to a day in 1989 when Dr. Kruger set him up with Annie Boylan, a single mom who was seeking Mr. Perfect. Moss met his match in Boylan, a quirky, bighearted woman who had attended ten universities without completing a degree (thought to be an intercollegiate record).

Married once, to the actress Marian Hailey, and childless, Moss was open to a relationship.

"He took me out the day *before* Valentine's Day," Boylan said with a comedic pause. "It was Friday the thirteenth."

Moss arrived with a single rose, which Boylan carried around with her for most of the evening, But at one stop, she lost track of it. For reasons she could not entirely explain to Moss, she was distraught over her carelessness.

"Jeff would not have known it, but my sister Annie was a major flower person, and she was so upset at losing the rose," said Annie's sister, Molly Boylan, a longtime *Sesame Street* staff writer who got her start in television after being mentored by Moss. "Somehow, she knew this guy was going to be important to her. I know, because back then she used to run all of her potential boyfriends by me for approval. She called me after that date to say how well it had gone and that she wanted me to meet him as soon as possible."

The morning after the date, a messenger arrived at Annie Boylan's door with a single red rose and a card. It read: 'I think you dropped this.'"

Jeff and Annie married and in 1991 had a son, Alexander. Becoming a father to Alex—and stepfather to Jonathan—provided Moss a chance to be the kind of parent his father never was to him and his sister.

"Jeff did not grow up as the center of his household, although he was the golden boy, always at the top of his class, athletic and talented," Annie Boylan said. "Jeff's father was the actor Arnold Moss, a man with a huge ego. His mother, the actress Stella Reynolds, gave up performing to write for soap operas." There was room for only one star in the Moss household.

"Jeff was up against his dad his whole life," Annie Moss said. "His dad really never thought much of Jeff's work on television because it was for children, and how important could it be if it was work meant only for *them*? The only time Jeff's dad ever told him he loved him was when Jeff's musical, *Double Feature*, opened on Broadway, because that was the world Arnold Moss knew. But Jeff told me that when his father said it that night, his immediate thought was 'too little, too late.'"

Jeff Moss wrote the book, music, and lyrics for *Double Feature*, and it had the smell of a potential hit two years prior to its Broadway opening. Tommy Tune was its choreographer and Mike Nichols its director when the musical was being shaped in Connecticut in 1979. But Moss adamantly rejected Nichols's ideas to improve the four-character play, and Nichols, whose credits included a number of successful stage productions as well as the films *Who's Afraid of Virginia Woolf?*, *The Graduate*, and *Carnal Knowledge*, walked away from the project. Tune, no fool, followed Nichols out the door.

"Jeff would never back down, and he went toe-to-toe with Mike Nichols," said his sister-in-law Molly Boylan. "But *Double Feature* had gotten great reviews in New Haven and everybody had high hopes for it. But [then theater critic] Frank Rich destroyed it with the meanest review I've ever read."

Rich's opening line in the *New York Times* of October 9, 1981, read: "You know a musical is in trouble when act 2 opens with a song asking 'How's It Gonna End?' and you're still waiting for the show to begin."

With the closing of *Double Feature*, Moss matched Joe Raposo in 1986 and his Broadway disappointment, *Raggedy Ann: The Musical Adventure*, which closed after five performances. The two were the best of competitors.

Chris Cerf, who met Moss in 1964 on a miserable bus ride to Fort Dix to begin their army basic training, said the two composers once famously wrestled for position over a *Sesame Street* record album. "Jeff and Joe were determined one would not have any more songs than the other, but the producer decided the album was going to have an odd number of tracks. This was a *very* difficult problem to solve, but Jeff finally agreed that Joe could have more songs as long as Jeff's name was in a box on the back of the cover. Jeff took a lot of ribbing to add things like that, and rightly so, but he was such a perfectionist and a brilliant writer of both lyrics and music, and he had such a sensitivity and pride about his work, you could forgive him. The word that comes to mind is *integrity*. He would never change anything just because it was easier to let it go or because he thought he could get an easy laugh or if maybe things would go better for him if he makes changes."

What difficulties he may have caused were forgotten on the day in September 1998, when Moss arrived at Children's Television Workshop at 12:30, sharp. "His coming to that meeting and, in a way, saying good-bye and letting us say good-bye, was one of the most generous things I've ever seen in a human being," said Joan Cooney. "His generosity just took my breath away. He told us that he had been sick for five years, and he spoke so movingly about what his career at *Sesame Street* had meant to him and what we meant to him. When he finished, we stood and applauded for a long time. I wanted that to just go on forever, that moment.

"Then people got up and spoke spontaneously about what a privilege it had been for all of us to know him. And then we got to hug and kiss him and tell him how much we loved him. And then, a few days later, he was gone."

On his last day on earth, Jeff Moss completed another song. "It was entitled 'You and You and Me,' said Annie Boylan. "He was so prolific, and he never stopped. I remember once saying to him that maybe there would be a time when we could retire to an island like St. John, and Jeff said, 'Not on your life. I am going to keep working until they put me six feet under.' And so he worked on the day he died."

Moss died on September 24, 1998. He was fifty-six.

Ten years later, Princeton University announced a ranking of its twenty-six most elite graduates. Jeff Arnold Moss, Class of 1963, was listed, among F. Scott Fitzgerald, Woodrow Wilson, James Madison, John Foster Dulles, and Richard Feynman. An accompanying profile of him, written by journalist Todd S. Purdum (Princeton '82), mentioned that Moss "racked up fourteen Emmys and an Academy Award nomination, and helped teach hundreds of millions of children worldwide a good bit about what it means to be human."

One morning in 2002, Rosie O'Donnell was queued up at the Target checkout. "I looked like a wreck," she recalled, just another mother making a trip to the store. "I had no makeup."

Ahead in line was a toddler, facing his mother. Upon seeing O'Donnell, the child began to point and jabber. "Over and over he was saying, 'Elmo-freh, Elmo-freh,'" O'Donnell said. "The mother, a little mortified, starting shushing the child and reminding him it wasn't polite to point and to not talk to strangers. But there was no stopping him, and the mother was having a hard time understanding what had gotten into him. I said to her, 'Hey, it's okay. He's trying to let you know something.' Then, to the child, O'Donnell said, 'You're right, honey. I'm Elmo's friend from TV.'"

The shopper, a bit embarrassed, admitted, "Rosie, I wouldn't have recognized you."

"I know, but your two-year-old son did."

Elmo's appearances during the heyday of O'Donnell's syndicated daytime talk show, which ran for 1,193 episodes from 1996 to 2002, were singularly responsible for his overtaking Big Bird as the signature character for *Sesame Street* and for the frenzied success of an interactive Christmas toy.

"I first came to know about Elmo through my niece," O'Donnell said. "I'd go visit my sister and the TV would be tuned to *Sesame Street* for her little girl. I found myself watching along with her, because I loved the show from way back, but this new Elmo character was just so funny. A few years later they asked me to do a guest spot on *Sesame Street*. And, all of a sudden, there was this huge, handsome black man at my feet. I looked down at him and I went, "Are *you* Elmo?"

"Hi, I'm Kevin," he said.

"Okay," O'Donnell said. "First, you're a genius. Second, I cannot believe you look like you do. I did not have that image of you at all." (Clash says people often think he should be short, bald, and wearing glasses.)

"Kevin started improvising, just sitting there with me and I would forget that he was down below, you know? And I'm one of those people who can play pretend with a child for hours on end. So Kevin and I just clicked."

For the Christmas season of 1996 Tyco launched an Elmo doll that was the culmination of years of microchip research and development in the toy industry. Embedded within it was sound-and-motion technology that could make Elmo seem to giggle when his tummy was tickled, leaving him shaking in a convulsion of laughter. "Oh boy, that tickles!" was Elmo's big line.

"Tyco sent a Tickle Me Elmo to my home and another to the studio," O'Donnell said. "Sure enough, my son, who was one and walking at the time, would grab it, fall on it, hug it, laugh with it. It was the cutest thing I ever saw, and so I started talking about it on the show."

The rest was toy industry legend. Priced at $29.99, Tickle Me Elmo debuted in July with an expected sale of 400,000 units. But after Rosie's plug, and subsequent appearances on the show by Clash and Elmo, the four factories in southern China manufacturing the doll were running at full capacity. Boeing 747s were shuttling between Asia and North America in the months leading to Christmas, troop transports ferrying Elmos by the tens of thousands. In excess of one million dolls were sold, but countless other sales went unfulfilled because supply never caught up with demand.

O'Donnell forged a friendship with Clash, working together on charity events and special appearances. "It's like dancing with Baryshnikov to do acting with him," she said. "You have to really be in the moment because he's an amazing improvisational artist, a special skill not many have. People who you think would be great on talk shows, either because of their personalities or their image or their ability to be funny on a sitcom, oftentimes are not. It takes a special kind of skill to improvise and Kevin has it in overload.

"But the amazing part of it is to see kids around Kevin when he is doing Elmo. They will totally forget that he's standing there. What he does is so innate. Every soul wants to play and make believe. The more you try and take it away from kids, the more they will pretend. From the beginning Sesame Street encouraged imagination and playfulness. It always felt like a show to me about freedom, and it has always spoken to children in a pure and truthful way. Children are children, rich or poor, and there is a language of truth that is innate to these tiny, undeveloped beings that they can hear. *Sesame Street* had respect for its audience and respect for itself. They never cut any corners and they stuck to their democratic ideals."

It's hard to get fired from an unpaid internship, but Jeff Marx managed to do it during his term of service on *Sesame Street* in 1999. The story goes he wanted to write songs, not empty trash cans.

With this in mind, it would be logical to assume that the impulse to create an off-color musical satire of the series a year later, with rod puppets that look like second cousins of the Muppets who copulate onstage and sing of the virtues of Internet porn, was a vengeful act of disgruntled discards. But that explains nothing about the development of *Avenue Q,* the saltiest love letter ever sent to *Sesame Street,* penned by the clever songwriting team of Jeff Marx and Robert Lopez.

Avenue Q, originally conceived as a television series, gestated into a stage musical after myriad workshop sessions, rewrites, and an off-Broadway run. It debuted on Broadway to raves in 2003 on the final Thursday of July. Ben Brantley's review in the *Times* hailed the creators for demonstrating "that ambivalence, indecision, and low expectations can be the basis for a thoroughly infectious musical. . . . It is in its songs and performances that *Avenue Q* plays most piquantly on the contrasts between the world according to children's television and the reality of adult life. The nature of the twinkly songs, unfailingly tuneful and disgustingly irresistible, can be deduced from their titles: 'Everyone's a Little Bit Racist,' "Schadenfreude,' 'The Internet Is for Porn,' and 'You Can Be as Loud as the Hell You Want (When You're Makin' Love).' "[20]

Stephanie D'Abruzzo joined the project when it was still in development. Craig Shemin, then a writer for the Jim Henson Company and D'Abruzzo's husband of five years, recommended her to Marx and Lopez when they were searching for a singing female puppeteer to participate in an industry reading of their work in progress. By 2000, she was already a respected member of that circle of puppeteers who work on television projects in New York, including *Sesame Street.* "My first season of work on *Sesame Street* was the first year of Around the Corner," she said. "I did plenty of background birds at the Furry Arms Hotel. If Michael Loman hadn't come along—if they had simply maintained the status quo and only had the old characters and the old set—a new puppeteer would never have had the opportunity to perform. Around the Corner benefitted people like me."

When she got involved with *Avenue Q,* D'Abruzzo was in the curious position of simultaneously being on *Sesame Street* and its parody. Complicating that, she was performing diametrically opposed puppets in *Avenue Q,* the commitment-seeking kindergarten teaching assistant Kate Monster and Lucy the Slut, a singer with a major bustline and intentions for Kate's callow on-off boyfriend, Princeton. "The ingenue and the vamp," D'Abruzzo said.

The characters were designed by Rick Lyon, who got bounced from a puppeteering job at *Sesame Street* and, like Marx, used parody as a balm for any wounded feelings. On his Web site, Lyon posed the central question asked by the *Avenue Q* creative team: "What if a cozy, familiar kids' television show had to grow up? Not just the characters, but the subject matter, the songs, the attitude?"[21]

The cast also included *Sesame Street* puppeteers John Tartaglia and Jennifer Barnhart. Tartaglia, like D'Abruzzo, did double duty, performing Princeton and Republican stockbroker Rod, a repressed homosexual in love with his roommate, Nicky, played by Lyon.

Avenue Q won the 2004 Tony for best musical. D'Abruzzo, who was nominated for a best actress statuette, went on to do more than a thousand performances as Kate Monster.

People often tell her Jim Henson would have loved the show.

For season thirty, the Around the Corner set and sensibilities were abandoned, but ratings continued to erode for *Sesame Street* in the competitive environment of preschool television. At the same time, the mean age for the typical *Sesame Street* viewer was growing steadily younger.

In advance of a two-week workshop for producers and writers, an annual brainstorming event held before script assignments are handed out, executive producer Michael Loman called for ideas to refresh the show and solidify its core audience. "We were back into experimenting again," said veteran writer Judy Freudberg. "We had gotten mandates from the front office saying our ratings were in trouble. So we started trying to come up with a different way to do the show, tossing ideas around. The idea was to change it without losing what we had."

It seemed clear to the workshop attendees that the magazine format of establishing a street-based story at the top of the show and spacing out its development through the hour, with segments interrupting the narrative, was no longer ideal. The home-video boom of the 1980s and the explosion of new thirty-minute children's shows on cable clearly demonstrated that a story well told could hold the attention of children under the age of five for ninety minutes or more.[22]

"We felt that the gap between street segments was too long, and the kids were losing the story line. At the same time, Elmo's popularity had grown by leaps and bounds. I went home one afternoon and it just hit me: maybe we should do something *really* different. *Ally McBeal* was popular at that time, and it was so different than anything else on television. Thinking about that got me to wonder whether Elmo could have a segment that would be in an entirely different format. Maybe he could be the guide for the final fifteen to twenty minutes of the hour, the segment that audience research showed was the one in which kids were losing their way with the show. So, I brought that show-within-a-show idea with me during the final week of the workshop, thinking it would be killed. It was radical because we had never veered from that magazine mosaic and had never given any character more than another character to do."

Far from being rejected, it was added to a list of possible ways to revamp the series. Attendees split into work groups, and Freudberg joined five others to imagine what an Elmo-centric concluding segment might include.[23]

Over the course of a few days, with the backing of the main group, the basic conceits and constructs of Elmo's World evolved. They were refined over a month's time, but a breakthrough moment occurred when writer-animator Mo Willems proposed that Elmo could exist within a computer-generated universe that would have a stream-of-consciousness feel to it, looking like a child's squiggly crayon drawing come to life.

Not unlike the world inhabited by Pee-wee Herman in his sublime CBS Saturday morning series *Pee-wee's Playhouse* (1986–91), the furniture and electronics within Elmo's World would not be static. "They'd be stretchy and squashy," Freudberg said. And so a toddling table and a window shade that would snap open to unveil a new character that was, in fact, a throwback. For what was Mr. Noodle (played first by the late Michael Jeter, then later by Broadway actor Bill Irwin) if not a more Chaplinesque version of Buddy and Jim, the bumblers who tried to drive in a nail with a balloon? "Mr. Noodle, who never speaks, is all about trial and error," Freudberg said. "When you throw him a hat, he acts like he's never seen one before. Kids feel empowered watching him because they can do what he can't."

Baggy-pants Mr. Noodle—and his brother, Mr. Noodle—reflect the slapstick comedy of silent-film vaudeville. It is little wonder that Freudberg, with urging from writers Tony Geiss, Emily Kingsley, and Molly Boylan—found a way to pay homage to Jon Stone and Jim Henson by creating a character that would have made them laugh till they cried.

Epilogue

Once a month, Janet Wolf, Joan Cooney's longtime executive assistant at Sesame Workshop, makes a lunch reservation for six at San Domenico on Central Park South. "When they answer, it's always a solicitous '*Ohhhh*, a table for Miss Cooney. Yes, absolutely,'" Wolf says with a slight shake of her head. Sometimes, she notes, there are little reminders that behind the petite, polite, intellectually probing woman she has served so long "is a kind of command. Not that Donald Trump presence, like when you utter the name the world stops spinning, but when you do say 'Joan Cooney is on the line,' everyone always says, with a bit of reverence, 'Oh, one moment, please.'"

The monthly "Ladies' Lunch," a tradition inaugurated by Leslie Stahl of CBS News, summons a sextet of some of New York's most influential women in media. *Wall Street Journal* columnist Peggy Noonan, once a special assistant to President Ronald Reagan, is a member of the group, as is *Good Morning America* coanchor Diane Sawyer, *Vanity Fair* correspondent Marie Brenner, and syndicated columnist Liz Smith. "I'd love to be a fly on *that* wall," Wolf says.

Cooney, the smart sorority girl from Phoenix, arrives in tailored ensembles, flattering outfits that she wears for a season or two before donating to charity. A personal shopper at Saks Fifth Avenue makes choices based on her knowledge of Cooney's taste, designer preference, favored fabrics and colors. Cooney will arrive at the department store precisely at 10:00 a.m., look things over, and decide. She is not one to fritter away time or dither. She reduces small matters, like what to order for lunch during her 10:00 a.m. to 2:00 p.m. workday. The routine borders on ritual. For years she ate the same noontime meal: a tiny cup of cold bow-tie pasta accompanied by an even tinier cup of fruit salad. She allows herself one cracker and a glass of iced tea. In recent years she has added a small piece of dark chocolate, at Wolf's suggestion. "It's supposed to be good for you, and who doesn't like chocolate?" Wolf says.

Cooney keeps to her twice-weekly tennis dates and enjoys a set outdoors on summer weekends. She takes yoga classes, as well. At seventy-nine years old, she fairly radiates good health, the health of a cancer survivor who takes exquisite care of herself and those she loves.

Her office at One Lincoln Plaza is welcoming and drenched in diffuse natural light. As others have redecorated or refurnished at Sesame Workshop through the decades, Cooney has kept the same desk and credenza since 1969, an indication of her practicality and fiscal prudence.

Framed photographs, commendations, and mementos hang on the walls, a neat, asymmetrical arrangement of words and images that make a summary statement about her: she appreciates her life of privilege and position and the people who have walked with her, stride by stride.

In a corner near the far end of a table hangs the Presidential Medal of Freedom, awarded to Cooney in 1995 by President Bill Clinton. It is the highest civilian award one can achieve in this country; and among the recipients have been civil-rights activist Rosa Parks (1996), Supreme Court Justice Thurgood Marshall (1993), baseball legend and humanitarian Roberto Clemente (posthumously in 2003), and author Harper Lee (2007). Unless you were looking for the medal in Cooney's office, you could easily miss it.

Scattered about are dozens of *Sesame Street* plush toys and figurines, including characters not seen in the United States. There's a small shrine to Jim Henson and a late-sixties conference-room photo of Cooney with founding producers Jon Stone, Dave Connell, and Sam Gibbon all sharing a laugh.

Near a conference table where Cooney receives guests is a collection of black-and-white photos of her grandchildren, a brood born to the children of Peter G. Peterson, her husband since 1980. Peterson came into her life after a period when she was not sure she would marry again. Tim Cooney was enough to cure anyone of marriage.

"When I came on as Joan's assistant, she was very clear about something," Wolf said one day, with a chuckle: " 'My ex-husband comes with the job.' "

Over time, despite his being occasionally abusive to her over the phone, Wolf showed concern and compassion for Tim Cooney. He had few visitors when he was hospitalized in 1999, but Wolf arrived to cheer him. Two days later he was dead at age sixty-nine. She attended a memorial for him at a saloon on Second Avenue. "People got up and spoke," Wolf said. "I was there on Joan's behalf; she certainly was not going to show up for *that*. I went and reported the whole thing back to her."

In 2008, Peterson and Cooney moved into a grand apartment on Fifth Avenue that once belonged to Nelson Rockefeller. From their teak deck, one can see the expanse of Central Park to the west, lower Manhattan to the south, and deep into the uppermost reaches of Manhattan to the north.

Peterson recalled the early years of their marriage and "the ambivalence of children of divorce toward the *other woman*. Joan took more than she deserved of a kind of micro terrorism from my children, I guess you'd call it. They would go to great lengths to send her a message knowing that a certain piece of behavior would cause discomfort on her part, without being so explicit that it could be called rude. Before we got married, Joan used to have what she called 'sinking spells.' She had no children, and suddenly had to go from zero to five. And they were making life terribly difficult for her.

"Joan has [since] managed quite brilliantly to have achieved this wonderful nexus between family and friendship with the kids, without all of the psychological baggage of being their mother. So I think without exception the kids now adore her and they respect her enormously and feel very close to her. I call her the fairy stepmother."

"The grandchildren have had no problems with me from the day they were born," Cooney said, with a "thank goodness" glint in her eye. The older grandchildren call her "Joanie," while the younger ones call her "Doe." That came about after granddaughter Chloe, now twelve, tried to say "Joan" as a toddler and it came out "Doe." That endearment got picked up by friends, and sometimes Peggy Noonan will address an e-mail to Cooney, "Dear Doe."

Cooney and Chloe share an incredible bond. They took up piano together three years ago and now play duets, and have regular pizza-and-a-movie dates. "We see each other a lot," says Chloe Kimball, who credits *Sesame Street* for igniting a passion for reading. Big Bird was her favorite character.

In the early 2000s Chloe's grandmother began work on *The Roads to Sesame Street: A Memoir,* an autobiography that has been set aside for now. But as one pertinent passage recalls:

> One day, when Chloe was nine months old, I put her on my lap and turned on *Sesame Street*. She was immediately absorbed. Whenever Big Bird or Elmo came on the screen, she leaned forward, hugged the television set, and then patted the screen, trying to feel the feathers and the fur. She stayed transfixed for forty-five minutes.
>
> She began watching the show with her mother and nanny every day. I joined them whenever I had the time. I had viewed the show with many children in day-care centers to corroborate the results of our research, but I had never before watched it with a child I knew—especially one whom I

loved. I have no idea how *Sesame Street*'s playful way with letters and numbers actually stimulated Chloe's cognitive process, but before she was two she was counting the steps of the stairs at our house in the country.

Shortly thereafter, she was singing the ABC song and identifying letters and numbers on sight. She also displayed exceptional verbal and conceptual skills. One day, her nanny and I took her to see a *Sesame Street Live* show at Madison Square Garden. The place was packed with public school children from all over the city, and Chloe was one of the few white children there. For the first time, I saw with my own eyes how our original dream of reaching children from minority races and less-privileged homes had been fulfilled.

It was from watching *Sesame Street* with the grandchildren that Cooney concluded the series might benefit from having a new female character that could connect with an emerging generation of preschool girls who couldn't seem to get enough of princesses and fairies in pink. Cooney recognized that the cycles of pop culture had once again swung, and she wanted *Sesame Street* to tap into the zeitgeist. Doing so might keep things current on the *Street* and, who knows, might create another rush to Toys R Us, as happened in the 1980s, after CTW dumped unproductive millions from the nonprofit's endowment into a television project entitled *The Best of Families*.

"Not many people knew it, but CTW was very shaky in the mid-eighties," Cooney said. "Our boat was really rocking. David Britt and I decided we couldn't go beneath ten million dollars in the endowment and we were maybe at fourteen million dollars and falling. Things got so bad, I had David write up a plan that I hid in my desk for safekeeping. We called that plan The Little Workshop. It was a downsizing plan that would have shed everything except enough to keep *Sesame Street* going and make a modest income. But we'd have to cut costs to even do that.

"Just when things seemed so dire, along came a toy called Talking Big Bird, which used new interactive technologies. Money started rolling in, and it was the beginning of a real turnaround financially. Other things happened, but Talking Big Bird was like hitting a jackpot in Las Vegas on a slot machine. We just couldn't believe that the quarters kept coming out. Talking Big Bird was a miracle.

"My husband uses an expression: dumb luck beats careful planning every time. And I always said when things got bad, 'Oh, something will come in over the transom.' And it always has. The Workshop has really been stalked by good luck from the very beginning. Terrible luck in terms of the health of the principal people, terrible, tragic luck. But otherwise it has always been stalked by a certain amount of just dumb luck."

Cooney's pretty-in-pink brainstorm ignited the charge to create Abby Cadabby, another attempt to launch a funny, feisty female lead character. This time, though, Tony Geiss, a *Sesame Street* staff writer since the early 1970s, provided the essential constructs that led to development of a blond sprite with tiny wings and a magic wand that allowed her to call home to her fairy godmother.

Abby, performed by ingenious puppeteer-comedian Leslie Carrera-Rudolph, is thus television's first fairy godchild. She was announced with great fanfare and public relations puffery in the summer of 2006. Liz Nealon, who was for a brief term executive vice president and creative director for the Workshop, explained to the *New York Times* what niche Abby Cadabby was intended to fill. "We have our wacky and our gentle. But we wanted a female lead character. If you think about the *Mary Tyler Moore Show,* some girls relate to Rhoda, who's our Zoe, and some girls relate to Mary, who's a girly girl. And we didn't have that girl."[1]

Feminists fumed at this news, proving the more things change, the more they stay the same.

When Sarah Otley arrives home from her library job at the University of Maine, Farmington, she reaches for her knitting and settles in for some quality television viewing.

The former Sarah Morrisett is in her mid-forties now, married for eighteen years to a groundwater expert. She chases two cats, a dog, and that husband around a home they share ninety miles north of Portland. Sarah hasn't worn a tutu for some time now, but in 1985 she did earn a combined undergraduate degree in dance and computer science at Goucher College in Baltimore. Later she picked up a master's degree in health and fitness at Springfield College in Massachusetts. Suffice it to say that Sarah has found a felicitous balance between left-brain intellectual pursuits and right-brain creative endeavors.

What remains consistent all these years is her love of television. She and husband, Mike, enjoy the forensic sleuthing series that have defined prime-time network schedules in recent years. Sarah continues to marvel at her father, who in his late seventies remains Sesame Workshop's board chairman. After his retirement in 1998 from the presidency of the John and Mary R. Markle Foundation, Lloyd Morrisett became chairman of Infonautics, a public Internet company. Morrisett serves on the board of the Rand Corporation and is a member of the Council on Foreign Relations. He took up piano late in life and has the fitness profile of a man who could fly to Hawaii and compete in the Iron Man triathlon.

Regal twin portraits of Morrisett and Joan Cooney adorn the entranceway to the Workshop's corporate offices at One Lincoln Plaza, just five hundred steps away from the Marc Chagall mural at the Metropolitan Opera House. Together Morrisett and Cooney founded a mom-and-pop nonprofit that has set a global standard for educational media for children, and today adaptations of *Sesame Street* air in 140 countries. Productions thrive in such disparate locales as Egypt, South Africa, India, and Northern Ireland.

Cooney said, "Once, for a special on *Sesame Street*'s twentieth anniversary, Jim Henson asked me on camera, 'What's the biggest surprise you've had with the show?' and I said, 'Being in Israel.' The foreign productions have been thrilling, but being in Israel and the Arab world have been extraordinary.

"I said to Jim, 'My dream is one day they'll be at the negotiating table and someone will say something and it will start a Bert and Ernie routine and then peace will break out in the Middle East.'"

Children's television has come a long way since *Sesame Street* debuted on stations with snowy reception that required tinfoil balls affixed to the rabbit-ears antenna. Domestically, *Sesame Street* is a mainstay on PBS as it steams toward its fortieth anniversary in November 2009. On-demand episodes of the show are available for anytime viewing on PBS Kids Sprout, a digital channel offering round-the-clock preschool programming.

Gary E. Knell helped put the Sprout deal together with Comcast and HIT Entertainment in 2005. Knell succeeded David Britt as Sesame Workshop's president and CEO in 2000 and has presided over an especially fertile period in the nonprofit's history. Knell, a whip-smart lawyer with a Seinfeldian gift for observational asides, is one of three founders of the Joan Ganz Cooney Center at Sesame Workshop, a media lab launched in 2007 whose mission is to "catalyze and support research, innovation, and investment in digital media technologies to advance children's learning." Cooney and Morrisett are once again founders of an enterprise that links the theoretical with the practical. They intend to keep going until someone says stop.

In a sense, Bert and Ernie have an office these days at Sesame Workshop. After a series of developments that were as unlikely as they were fortuitous, the trademarks for the Muppets of *Sesame Street* now reside at One Lincoln Plaza, after a strange spell when the Muppets were the property of

EM.TV, an ill-fated German media company that nearly collapsed just as the Internet bubble burst.

"The Hensons made a strategic decision to sell their company in 2000," Knell said. "People were cashing out of all kinds of properties, especially brand names that had some relevance in the world. Anything that had a classic nature with a positive cachet was open game at the time. People were pushing me and the Workshop to take SesameStreet.com public, trying to figure out if we could collect hundreds of millions of dollars by creating a public stock offering of some kind or a private equity offering. There was a lot of money floating around and tons of ideas, good and bad. Can someone say 'Pets.com'?"

Charles Rivkin, president of the Jim Henson Company, flew to Munich in the summer of 1999 to meet with Thomas Haffa, CEO of EM.TV, then Europe's largest distributor of children's television programming. Unbeknownst to Rivkin, billionaire Haffa was almost groupielike in his adoration for the Muppets. Along hallways of the company were posters and photographs of Miss Piggy and Kermit. Haffa indicated his desire to own a piece of the Muppet franchise, but Rivkin said, "We're not for sale."[2]

Upon returning to the States, Rivkin discovered that the Henson heirs were open to investigating a sale of the company, after all, following ten difficult years of adjusting to life without their father, onerous estate-tax problems, and a changing landscape in family entertainment. Knell recalled, "The Henson kids basically said, 'Wow. Here's an opportunity.' In some ways it mirrored the outlook that their dad had years earlier. They asked themselves, 'Do we want to be running this business or would selling it allow us to do what we want to do best, creative work?' They decided to see what was out there and found there was a lot of interest.

"We had just started Noggin, a joint digital cable channel with Nickelodeon, and thought, *Gee, maybe we should buy the Muppets together,* thinking there was a way that we at the Workshop might centralize control over the characters. Nickelodeon could take over the licensing. Nick was already an aligned partner with the Workshop, so they would have a vested interest in allowing us to do our thing with the *Sesame Street* characters and could have aligned a strategy around the classic Muppets that didn't interfere or compete with *Sesame.* We fashioned a bid and things moved up to a fairly substantial level. But the amount that we established as the value for the Muppet franchise—$300 million—was less than half the amount it sold for. Our offer made everyone guffaw."

Thomas Haffa threw a mind-boggling $680 million in cash and stock at the feet of the five Henson children. Only eleven years earlier Disney had put up $150 million. The deal with EM.TV was consummated in February 2000. In Germany, as in the United States, properties were selling at prices that seemed unrealistically high.

Just about everyone at Sesame Workshop, Gary Knell included, read the news in the *Wall Street Journal* and swallowed hard. Had the Workshop not already had good business relations with EM.TV, there would have been even more stress. "They were our licensing agent in Germany," Knell said, "and we always got along fine."

But then, another development occurred in Germany, followed by more stories in the *Journal*. "Thomas Haffa and his brother Florian really drank the Internet bubble Kool-Aid," Knell said. "They began to view themselves as a mini-Disney, buying companies left and right. They were really on the march, and they saw the purchase of the Muppets as a way to put them on the map in the United States. But about a week after they did that deal, they put a billion dollars on the table to buy half of Formula One, the auto-racing circuit in Europe, from Bernie Ecclestone, who is one tough character. It was at that point—when they put down a billion—that I said to myself, *Uh-oh*. It was one thing overpaying for the Muppets, another thing striking a deal a week later for an enormous amount of additional money. All you would be seeing is enormous debt load. Everyone was asking 'How are they possibly going to absorb all of these management issues and make the economics work?' The dream lasted about two and a half days before they started running into problems. The financial community caught on pretty fast and the whole thing collapsed within six months.

"Here in America things weren't going so swell, either. EM.TV put a gal in place to run licensing at Henson, and the first thing she did was move into Jim Henson's old office in New York. You can imagine how *that* went over. It was a statement intended to mean, 'It's a new day,' but it was interpreted as a foreign power marching in to destroy a legacy. It was pretty ugly.

"Things began to spiral down fast, and we got caught in the middle of it. Here is the company that owns Big Bird and Elmo in freefall. Their stock goes from $110 to $2 in a matter of two months. Thomas Haffa called me while I was on the beach in Hawaii, during one of the few family vacations I had in that era. Haffa said, 'I'm going to sell the Muppets. You'd better come to Munich.' The next thing I knew we were discussing a purchase price. We knew we had to put something together pretty fast. We were afraid—especially in a fire sale—that they were going to sell the Muppets to God knows who. It could have been anybody who would not necessarily have the interests of *Sesame* on its priority list."

In a sense, Elmo's popularity helped save the day. To understand how, it takes revisiting that windfall Christmas season of 1997. "Tickle Me Elmo was a big hit . . . and the Workshop had a spike in its 1998 revenues," Knell said. "It was also a terrific year in the stock market." A $28 million increase, attributable to the toy's success and a rise in value to the nonprofit's stock portfolio, led the Workshop's executive team to move forward with a plan to invest in Noggin, a digital cable channel for preschoolers. Their partner was Nickelodeon, one of the MTV networks owned by Viacom. In 1998, the Workshop invested $25 million in the project, and, over time, the channel became a welcome destination for kids and parents.

With money in the bank, the Workshop was in a position to strike when the Sesame Street Muppets became available. EM.TV accepted an offer of $180 million. "Everyone, most especially the puppeteers, were thrilled that we were able to bring them home," Knell said. "It protected *Sesame Street* and allowed our international expansion to continue. Owning these characters has allowed us to maximize their potential. We are now in control of our own destiny."

To make the deal, the Workshop borrowed $100 million from Summit Bank and worked out a payment plan with EM.TV to pay the German company $7 million per year for ten years. The final $10 million came out of the Workshop's investment portfolio.

Within a year, the Workshop sold its half interest in Noggin to Viacom for a whopping $100 million, netting a $75 million profit after only five years in the digital cable business. "We used the net profit to pay back a large percentage of the [$100 million] loan and we prepaid that $7-million-a-year deal with EM.TV, significantly reducing the cost of our purchase price. [EM.TV] gave us a big discount because we paid in cash. I think we saved $20 million."

In May 2003, the Jim Henson Company bought back most of its assets from EM.TV for the bargain price of $89 million. Other suitors, including bids by Disney and by Dean Valentine, once head of UPN television, were turned away by Haffa.

Elation and relief among the Hensons ensued. Then, a year later, the damnedest thing happened: the Muppets were sold again.

After eleven years of making efforts to do so, The Walt Disney Company finally bought the classic Muppets on February 17, 2004, for an undisclosed sum. Brian Henson, cochairman and cochief executive of the Jim Henson Company, said "Michael Eisner's long-standing passion and respect for the Muppets give me and my family . . . confidence in Disney as a partner."[3]

"It all ended up in about as good a place as it could have ended up,"

Gary Knell said. "We own the *Sesame Street* characters and Disney owns the classic Muppets. You go back years earlier and you see it's exactly the way Jim wanted it."

We mortals toil away and wonder whether there is a grand plan to all that transpires or whether it just unfolds as it goes. Sometimes, as Joan Cooney so fervently believes, it seems like you're either lucky or you're not. Other times it seems like all the coincidences and collisions, the caprice and the serendipity, happen for a reason.

What if Richard Hunt had not thrown the skinny red puppet to Kevin Clash?

In 2009, it's hard to imagine a world without Elmo, a character so ubiquitous and inescapable that newborns seem to emerge from the womb with an Elmo doll attached to their umbilical cord. Many children say "Emmo" before they say "bye-bye." Elmo is the marketing wonder of our age.

But more than that, as *Sesame Street* approaches age forty, Elmo remains the embodiment of the show. He's an exuberant, inquisitive, trusting, embracing, innocent, playful, life-affirming star who long ago eclipsed Big Bird, although the eight-foot canary made *Sesame Street* the most influential children's television show the world has ever seen. Elmo simply renewed the mission and added effervescence, at just the right moment. As President John Fitzgerald Kennedy might have said, Elmo demonstrated "vigor."

The final lines of Kennedy's inaugural address come to mind. In it he concluded, "With a good conscience our only sure reward, with history the final judge of our deeds, let us go forth to lead the land we love, asking His blessing and His help, but knowing that here on earth God's work must truly be our own."

It may well be that Joan and Jim and Jon and Joe and Jeff and Lloyd and Dave and everyone else in the gang were doing God's work on earth.

Put a finger to your lips and say it as Jim Henson might: *"Hmmmmm."*

Acknowledgments

Writing a book is like eating an elephant.

When it's done, you want to unbuckle your belt, flop down on the couch, and belch. It's a lot like that woozy hour after Thanksgiving dinner, minus John Madden, the turducken, and the tower of dirty dishes.

And so, before I drift for dreamland, there are people to thank for helping me bag the beast. If an orchestra begins to play, it means I've gone on too long.

Street Gang grew out of an assignment during my seven years as a senior editor and Family Page columnist at *TV Guide*. During that spell I edited the work of J. Max Robins, a great white hunter of a reporter who covered the television industry. Max's lust for reporting was infectious and his energy contagious. As Melvin Udall (Jack Nicholson) said in *As Good as It Gets*, he made me want to be a better man.

Three additional former colleagues from *TV Guide*—Vashti Anderson (photo research), Abby Royle (transcription and research), and Maya Stanton (fact-checking)—provided exceptional service and support. Bravo, ladies.

Rutgers University undergraduate Padma Schwenzer assisted me in the summer of 2008. Her work was exemplary.

Literary agent Susan Reed convinced me to write this book, then promptly left the profession to edit *Golf for Women* magazine ("A Putter's Dilemma: Skirt or Culottes?"). Susan, now editor of *O: The Oprah Magazine*, turned me over to Mark Reiter, a triple-threat author, editor, and literary agent.

Viking editor Rick Kot, who is eight feet tall and speaks so softly you have to turn up the Miracle Ear to the turbo setting, guided me through the wilderness.

Rick's surefire assistant, Laura Tisdel, is the Annie Oakley of publishing; her aim is true and her spirit can-do. Plus, she looks great on a horse.

I devoted two years of research on *Sesame Street* before approaching Joan Ganz Cooney. The road to her office was paved, in part, by my *TV Guide* colleague Steve Battaglio, who passed a good word to an executive at the Workshop at just the right moment. Ellen Lewis, the Workshop's high-energy vice president for public relations, greased the skids as well.

In Joan Cooney I found the rarest of birds, a relentlessly honest and forthright public figure who, more often than not, is the smartest person in the room. That she doesn't flaunt it is only the least of her enviable attributes. Without her willingness to be tortured by my incessant questions—and without her opening the Workshop's archives—*Street Gang* would have died aborning.

The same is true for Sesame Workshop cofounder Lloyd Morrisett, that beacon of integrity and intelligence. Lloyd, who gave Children's Television Workshop its Y chromosome, informed this book in myriad and marvelous ways.

I met Harvard University professor John R. Stilgoe during my year in Cambridge as a Nieman fellow, and his influence was nothing short of transformative. At a confusing career crossroads, Professor Stilgoe cleaned my windshield and pointed me in the right direction, just like the men of Texaco once did on the byways of this great land.

When I was little, my parents used to say, "Turn off that TV and go find a nice book." They were only half right. I'd never have written this book had I not loved television; I got a lot of it. But because Seymour and Eleanor Davis valued reading, I also was the kind of kid who would trudge home from the Newport (R.I.) Public Library with a sack of books. I found the mustiness of the library intoxicating.

My self-taught, immigrant grandmother, Cecelia Meierovitz, read every newspaper she could get her hands on. By the time I was ten, I did, too. There's a connection.

The *Newport Daily News* hired me at fifteen to cowrite a weekly column ("Teen Scene") and cover high school sports as a stringer. From 1968 on, I was never without a job in journalism, including a stint as sports editor of *The Daily Tar Heel*, the student-run paper at the University of North Carolina at Chapel Hill. I covered basketball at the *DTH* and have often described coach Dean Smith as the greatest teacher I never had. Most of what I know about leadership came from watching him and listening.

John Walter, then managing editor of the *Ithaca* (N.Y.) *Journal*, not only gave me work in 1974, he urged me to apply to the master's in journalism program at Northwestern University's Medill School of Journalism, the smartest move of my life. John left us suddenly in the summer of 2008; he's probably editing Gannett's *Heaven Today.*

I thank:

My daughters, Meagan and Tyler, for their love, support, and patience, and for providing a reason anew to watch *Sesame Street.*

My brother (and lecture agent!), Robert Paul Davis of the American Program Bureau, and his brilliant wife, Susan.

My daughters through marriage, Amy Becton and Jill Smith, and my granddaughters through marriage, Brittany and Hope Smith.

Christine, Phil, and Bob Wilkinson, for their belief and encouragement.

Here comes that fat passage containing the names of people who would have gotten their own paragraph if paging had allowed: Juliann Barbato, Stephanie Baumoel, Francesca Belanger, Denis Boyles, Carolyn Coleburn, Jillian Davis, Lauren Davis, Alicia Durand, Holly Eardley, Robert Edelstein, Linda Ellerbee, Karen Falk, Sheila Feren, the Reverend Anne Gehman, Diana Goldstein, Kaitlin Gonser, Katherine Griggs, Pam Hacker, Rae Hammerman, Emily Kaiser, Marty Kaiser, Kate Lloyd, Arthur Novell, Nerina Rammairone, Steve Reddicliffe, Carole Remick, Joe Rhodes, Dan Roberts, Maurice Sendak, Emily Sklar, Dr. Barbara H. Sohmer, Steve Sonsky, and Melissa Tiers.

Finally, I thank the framers of the U.S. Constitution and those courageous Supreme Court justices who have upheld and protected the First Amendment. To borrow a phrase from magazine mogul and decorative arts doyenne Martha Stewart, it's a good thing.

Notes

The author is grateful and indebted to the interview subjects for this book: Nick Aronson, Marty Arnold, Martin Baker, Lou Berger, Dr. Lewis Bernstein, Frank Biondo, Linda Bove, Molly Boylan, Fran Brill, Bernie Brillstein, David V. B. Britt, Alice Cahn, Dave Campbell, Chris Cerf, Peggy Charren, Dr. Milton Chen, George Clash, Gladys Clash, Kevin Clash, Bob Colleary, Jill Colley, Judy Collins, Pat Collins, Joan Ganz Cooney, Mike Dann, Jim Day, Emilio Delgado, Cynthia P. Deutsch, Danny Epstein, Jason Epstein, Bonnie Erickson, Susan Erion, Anne Evans, Karen Falk, Judy Freudberg, Amy Friedman, Julian Ganz, Brian Garfield, Tony Geiss, Arthur Gelb, Dave Goelz, Linda Gottlieb, Louis L. Gould, Pam Green, Karen Gruenberg, Robert Hatch, Richard D. Heffner, Brian Henson, Cheryl Henson, Jane Henson, Don Hewitt, Jane Hunt, Kate Hunt, Al Hyslop, Eric Jacobson, Brown Johnson, James Earl Jones, Jim Jinkins, Jerry Juhl, Chloe Kimball, Emily Kingsley, Gary Knell, David Lazer, Sharon Lerner, Jerry Lesser, Loretta Long, Joan Lufrano, Sonia Manzano, Ted May, Joey Mazzarino, Mac McGarry, Bob McGrath, Alan Menken, Lloyd Morrisett, Mary Morrisett, Annie Moss, Jerry Nelson, Arthur Novell, Rosie O'Donnell, Roscoe Orman, Sarah Morrisett Otley, Frank Oz, Pete Peterson, Alaina Reed, Charles Rosen, David Rudman, Arlene Sherman, Cathy Short, Fred Silverman, Lisa Simon, Dulcy Singer, Stuart Sucherman, Nick Raposo, Marty Robinson, Charlie Rosen, Diane Sawyer, Josh Selig, Craig Shemin, Liz Smith, Caroll Spinney, Norman Stiles, Beverley Stone, Jon Stone, Polly Stone, John Tartaglia, David Tatum, James Taylor, Rosemarie Truglio, Tom Whedon, Steve Whitmire, Mo Willems, Vanessa Williams, Caroly Wilcox, Norton Wright, and Janet Wolf.

PROLOGUE

Interviews: The re-creation of the Jim Henson memorial was based on interviews with Martin Baker, Bernie Brillstein, Chris Cerf, Kevin Clash, Joan Ganz Cooney, Dave Goelz, Jane Henson, David Lazer, Frank Oz, Jerry Nelson, Marty Robinson, Dulcy Singer, Craig Shemin, Caroll Spinney, and Steve Whitmire.
Additional Sources: Sesame Workshop provided a videotape of the memorial.

CHAPTER ONE

Interviews: The dinner party re-creation is based on recollections gleaned from the author's conversations with Joan Ganz Cooney, Anne Bower Bement, Lloyd Morrisett, and Mary Morrisett. All factual references were confirmed by the sources.
Additional Sources: A splendid series of videotaped oral histories from the Academy of Television Arts and Sciences proved essential as background material for this book. Included in the collection are not only interviews with Cooney and Morrisett, but an array of personalities who figured prominently in developing and sustaining the Children's Television Workshop (changed in 2000 to Sesame Workshop) and *Sesame Street*. Unless otherwise noted, all quotes are from those recordings, the author's interviews, or *Children's Television Workshop, The Early Years: An Oral History* by Robert Davidson (CTW, 1993).
1. Familiar to early risers from Ogunquit, Maine, to Ojai, California, the "Indian-head test card," as it was known, was as old as television itself. RCA had created it for use

at the 1939 New York World's Fair, where television, a decades-in-the-making communications marvel, was finally demonstrated to the public. Visitors to the World of Tomorrow exhibit at the RCA Pavilion were left agog as they waved to a camera and instantaneously saw themselves. To them, RCA handed out souvenir cards printed with the phrase "I was televised." (Nearly seventy years later, rain-drenched tourists still wave goofily at *Today* show cameras outside NBC studios in Rockefeller Center.)

2. Freedman was a pioneer in refitting classics of the legitimate stage for television, most notably in the series *Play of the Week*, a forerunner of *Masterpiece Theatre* that aired on independent stations. Among his most notable credits were adaptations of Henrik Ibsen's *Master Builder* (starring E. G. Marshall); Eugene O'Neill's *The Iceman Cometh* (Jason Robards); and a Sidney Lumet–directed staging of *The Dybbuk* (with Theodore Bikel).

3. That neighborhood, a bastion of the elite, had been developed in 1831 by open-space advocate Samuel B. Ruggles. On property that had once been an Uptown farm, the development was patterned after the residential squares in London. Nineteenth-century brick houses and brownstones now line the historic district, which includes Theodore Roosevelt's birthplace. The greensward around which the neighborhood was built remains Manhattan's only private park. Residents—and guests of the Gramercy Park Hotel—are the fortunate few provided keys to the park's iron gates.

4. Under the watchful eye of Kennedy's bride, the former Jacqueline Bouvier, small, elegant portions of Verdon's nouvelle cuisine were served up to princes, potentates, captains of industry, and Washington's political and media elite. We, the people, followed suit.

5. Newton N. Minow, speech, National Association of Broadcasters, Washington, D.C., May 9, 1961, http://americanrhetoric.com/speeches/newtonminow.htm.

6. The author worked for a Head Start program in Dryden, New York, during the 1974–75 school year.

CHAPTER TWO

Interviews: Over the course of five years the author conducted twelve interviews with Joan Ganz Cooney at her Sesame Workshop office and at her Manhattan home. Another twenty-two conversations were conducted by phone. In addition, Mrs. Cooney, early adapted to new media, provided many prompt answers to queries by e-mail. She confirmed all factual material in this largely biographical chapter.

Additional Sources: Unless otherwise noted, all quotes are from the author's interviews, the Archive of American Television oral history DVDs, and *Children's Television Workshop, The Early Years: An Oral History* by Robert Davidson (CTW, 1993).

1. Mr. Tatum provided and confirmed factual material about Arizona during the Great Depression. He also provided documentary evidence about the Ganz family's history in Phoenix and the death of Sylvan Ganz.

2. *Life*, "Reflections," Spring 1990, 41.

3. Barbara Rowes, "Bio," *People*, June 13, 1977, 94.

4. *Life*, "Reflections," Spring 1990, 41.

5. Something quite foul was astir in Washington that year, led by Senator Joseph McCarthy of Wisconsin, a prophet of paranoia and a poisonous presence in the great hall's chambers. Under his hand, the House Committee on Un-American Activities had already begun its witch hunt for alleged Communist infiltrators and sympathizers. One victim of the McCarthy era's blacklisting of writers and performing artists would be Will Lee, a classically trained stage actor and teacher of actors who became Mr. Hooper on *Sesame Street*. During that shameful period in our history, Lee was stripped of his rights to appear onstage

solely for his interest and participation in unpopular political causes. But as Bud Brown might have asked of his ninth graders, why is it that the very people sworn to defend our constitutional rights are first in line trying to deny them?

6. "Boss Is Better," *Forbes*, June 1975.

7. Barbara Rowes, "Bio," *People*, June 13, 1977, 94.

8. Jacqueline Kaufman, "Success in the Media: Inventing the Right Niche," *Management Review*, October 1985, 17.

9. Barbara Rowes, "Bio," *People*, June 13, 1977, 97.

10. Of his newspaper Swope once said to *Sun* columnist Hayward Broun, "What I try to do is to give the public part of what it needs and part of what it ought to have, whether it wants it or not." Swope also said, "Pick the best story of the day and hammer the hell out of it. Don't forget that the only two things people read in a story are the first and last sentences. Give the blood in the eye on their first one."

11. About two months after starting at RCA, Cooney got a call from Lester Markel, Sunday editor at the *Times*. "He said I could write for the women's page, but that was easy to turn down," Cooney said. "I knew I wasn't going to get the kind of assignments I had at the *Republic*, and I wasn't about to go back to writing wedding announcements." Had she accepted the job offer, "I might have been Charlotte Curtis," she said years later, with a smile.

12. Though perpetually at odds with RCA chairman Sarnoff, who was always more concerned with the commerce of television than its content, Weaver institutionalized much of what Americans have come to expect from a network programming day. For the breakfast table, he concocted *Today*, an easily digestible mix of news, information, and entertainment. For a midday break, Weaver mounted *Home*, an ambitious and intelligently rendered magazine program for women. In prime time, Weaver pioneered the ninety-minute "spectacular," and at bedtime, he all but invented late-night TV, with Steve Allen's *Tonight* show. And yet, at the peak of his influence and success, Sarnoff dismissed Weaver, a stunning disappointment to those who served alongside him at NBC. Cooney, perhaps because she saw Sarnoff socially on the weekends and did not fear being fired for posing a blunt question, button-holed the General to ask why he terminated the network's programming genius. Cooney said, "I'll never forget his answer: 'He was spending me into bankruptcy.'"

13. All factual information in this section about Sylvan Ganz's death: "Sylvan Ganz Dies of Shotgun Wound," *Arizona Republic*, June 19, 1956.

CHAPTER THREE

Interviews: Substantial assistance for the portions of this chapter dealing with *Captain Kangaroo* came from Bob Colleary, Sam Gibbon, Beverley Stone, Tom Whedon, and Norton Wright, all of whom worked on the series. Gibbon, a onetime production assistant on *Howdy Doody*, provided background on that series. The author is indebted to two of Dave Connell's surviving children, Alan and Jan, for providing a bounty of documentary and anecdotal material about their father's career and personal life. This book is all the richer for their generous cooperation.

Additional Sources: Unless otherwise noted, all quotes are from the author's interviews, the Archive of American Television oral history DVDs, and *Children's Television Workshop, The Early Years: An Oral History* by Robert Davidson (CTW, 1993). Jon Stone's unpublished memoir was an invaluable resource for the biographical passages about him. All quotes, unless otherwise noted, come from this autobiographical work.

1. In the age before videotape revolutionized production, performers didn't blink at being asked to do back-to-back broadcasts, but never back-to-back-to-back shows. Children

in the Pacific time zone would settle for kinescopes of *Captain Kangaroo*–filmed versions of the show made from the image on the picture tube.

2. The Captain was originally imagined as a museum watchman, a job Keeshan's father once held.

3. Wesley Hyatt, *Encyclopedia of Daytime Television* (New York: Billboard Books, 1997), 89.

4. CBS press release quoted in Dennis McLellan, "Bob Keeshan, 76; Entertained Millions as TV's Captain Kangaroo," *Los Angeles Times,* January 24, 2004.

5. A good number of the biographical quotes used in this and succeeding chapters came from *Good Morning Captain: 50 Wonderful Years with Bob Keeshan* (Minneapolis: Fairview Press, 1996), a trade-paper trove of material for fans of the show. Keeshan and Cathryn Long coauthored the book.

6. Ibid., 10.

7. The Museum of Broadcast Communications, "Keeshan, Bob," www.museum.tv/archives/etv/K/htmlK/keeshanbob/keeshanbob.htm.

8. Dave Barry, *Dave Barry Turns 50* (New York: Ballantine Books, 1998), 44.

9. Buffalo Bob Smith, "Voices," *People,* Summer 1989.

10. Long before the advent of the media beat at newspapers and magazines, Jack Gould was covering the television industry and criticizing its programming, in a manner that was tough but fair, clear, engaging, and exactingly reported. Gould's career and gutsy body of work figure prominently in the history of *Sesame Street.* Today's media bloggers and critics would do well to read the instructive and provocative *Watching Television Come of Age: The New York Times Reviews by Jack Gould* (Austin: University of Texas Press, 2002), a collection of his work edited by his son Lewis L. Gould. This excerpt was taken from "Hail Howdy Doody! He Triumphs over Mr. X, Survives Mr. Y and Always Delights the Youngsters," 164.

11. Buffalo Bob Smith, as told to Cable Neuhaus, "I Remember Howdy," *People,* November 30, 1987.

12. Ibid.

13. Larry Wolters, "Mistress of 'Ding Dong School,'" *New York Times,* January 4, 1953.

14. "She Rings the Bell," *TV Guide,* October 16, 1954.

15. Wolters, "Mistress of 'Ding Dong School.'"

16. The Grady College of Journalism and Communication at the University of Georgia conducts an annual competition to determine the best in electronic media. *Captain Kangaroo* won in 1957.

17. J. P. Shanley, "TV: Antidote to Jumping," *New York Times,* October 15, 1955.

18. It is the author's fond wish that Jon Stone's memoir will one day be published and appreciated for its insights, heart, and great good humor.

19. Keeshan, *Good Morning Captain,* 44.

20. Ibid., 59.

21. Paul Gardner, "Little Musical Moves in Upstairs," *New York Times,* July 10, 1963.

22. Gerald S. Lesser, *Children and Television: Lessons from Sesame Street* (New York: Random House, 1974), 4.

CHAPTER FOUR

Interviews: Joan Cooney, Cynthia P. Deutsch, Linda Gottlieb, Lloyd Morrisett, and Richard Heffner provided essential testimony about this crucial stage in *Sesame Street*'s development.

Additional Sources: Unless otherwise noted, all quotes are from the author's interviews, the Archive of American Television oral history DVDs, and *Children's Television Workshop, The Early Years: An Oral History* by Robert Davidson (CTW, 1993).

1. Much thanks is due to Karen King, assistant curator at the National Public Broadcasting Archives at the University of Maryland–College Park, for providing access to hundreds of records documenting the development of the Children's Television Workshop and *Sesame Street*.

2. This was a historic moment in that it marked the first time the word *research* was used in the same sentence with the show that would become *Sesame Street*, perhaps the most vigorously researched, vetted, and fretted-over program on the planet. It would take a forklift now to haul away the load of scholarly paper devoted to the series over nearly forty years.

3. "Lifestyle," *American Home*, March 1971, 12.

4. "Bureaucracy Pruner, Timothy Conney," *New York Times*, January 17, 1966.

5. Edwin McDowell, "Doing Right by a Book," *New York Times*, March 22, 1985.

6. A six-paragraph report of the nuptials in the following Sunday's *New York Times* indicated the groom had graduated from Columbia College and the bride was a member of the Junior League of Phoenix. "Joan Ganz Married to Timothy Cooney," February 23, 1964.

7. Michele Morris, "The St. Joan of Television," *Working Woman*, May 1986.

8. *Carnegie Commission on Educational Television, Public Television: A Program for Action* (New York: Bantam Books, 1967), 95.

9. Joan Ganz Cooney, "A Report to the Carnegie Corporation of New York on the Potential Uses of Television in Preschool Education."

10. Ibid.

11. Ibid.

12. This passage is from a eulogy Joan Ganz Cooney gave as part of a Lewis Freedman memorial service on September 11, 1992.

CHAPTER FIVE

Interviews: Brian Henson, Cheryl Henson, Jane Henson, Lisa Henson, Karen Falk, Mac McGarry, Arthur Novell, Frank Oz, Craig Shemin, and Beverley Stone.

Additional Sources: The Jim Henson Company provided a DVD of clips from *Sam and Friends*. The La Choy dragon commercial is available for viewing online at www.youtube.com. Finally, one of the most insightful Henson interviews ever undertaken was conducted in 1982 by Judy Harris for *Cinefantastique* magazine. It is archived at the Muppet Central Web site, http://www.muppetcentral.com/articles/interviews/jim1.shtml.

1. The handsome coffee-table book *Jim Henson: The Works*, an upbeat appraisal of the artist's life and work by Christopher Finch, describes Dear as "a painter and voracious reader, as well as a prolific creator of quality needlework." According to the book, Dear's handiwork inspired the young Jim Henson "to appreciate the power of visual imagery and to value creativity."

2. It is unclear what family influences there might have been on his developing sense of humor, but it is certain the radio comedy of the 1940s played a significant role—especially the timing and repartee of mild-mannered ventriloquist Edgar Bergen and his sly, sarcastic dummy Charlie McCarthy. Bergen introduced audiences to McCarthy, his raffish, flirtatious ward, on the vaudeville circuit. But it was network radio that made the pining puppet a national sensation and "the woodpecker's pinup boy." Doing ventriloquism on the radio may not seem like compelling entertainment today, but for two decades, Bergen invested verisimilitude into a trio of former trees—Mortimer Snerd, the bucktoothed hayseed; Effie Klinker, the man-hungry spinster; and McCarthy, the debonair detonator of the double

entendre. (Northwestern University once awarded McCarthy an honorary degree as Master of Innuendo and Snappy Comebacks.) "I tried to imagine how they looked as they made their jokes," Henson said as an adult. "But I don't remember ever thinking of them as one man and his puppets." Many would one day say the same about him.

3. Don Freeman, "Muppets on His Hands," *Saturday Evening Post*, November 1979, 52.

4. Christopher Finch, *Jim Henson: The Works* (New York: Random House, 1993).

5. "You've Got to Believe," *Time*, January 2, 1950.

6. A sixth item in that same Laurent column mentioned Bil Baird, the puppeteer behind *Life with Snarky Parker*, a serialized cowboy farce that debuted in 1950 and barely lasted eight months on CBS. Wide-eyed marionette Snarky, sheriff of Hot Rock, bore a disturbing resemblance to actor Richard Benjamin. His trusty horse, Heathcliffe, did not. The series was produced and directed by Yul Brenner. Yes, *that* Yul Brenner. Laurent noted that Baird, "whose marionettes provide the action for music on the CBS Morning Show," spells his first name with a single letter ell. "Why not?" Baird said. "People never pronounce the second ell, anyway."

7. Jim Henson, interview by Judy Harris, 1982.

8. Finch, *The Works*, 8.

9. Laurence Laurent, "The Straight Man Totes the Load," *The Washington Post*, May 15, 1955.

10. Finch, *The Works*, 16.

11. Jim Henson, interview by Judy Harris, 1982.

12. Finch, *The Works*, 53.

13. Jim Henson, interview by Judy Harris, 1982.

14. Freeman, "Muppets on His Hands," 53.

15. John Culhane, "The Muppets in Movieland," *New York Times*, June 10, 1979.

16. Finch, *The Works*, 18

17. Jim Henson, interview by Judy Harris, 1982.

18. Ursula Keller, "'Muppets' Win Way," *Christian Science Monitor*, December 1959.

19. Finch, *The Works*, 19.

20. Ibid., 21.

CHAPTER SIX

Interviews: Conversations with Fred Silverman, Beverley Stone, and Tom Whedon informed this chapter.

1. King, Peter H. "Burr Tillstrom, Creator of TV's 'Kukla, Fran and Ollie' Dies," *Los Angeles Times*, December 7, 1985.

2. Sheldon Caswell, "Tillstrom and the Kuklapolitans," *Men*, August 1951.

3. Found in both "Kukla's Daddy," *Radio Mirror*, November 1949, and "A Burr Tillstrom Biography," prepared by NBC's promotions department in September 1961, www.richsamuels.com/nbcmm/kuklapolitans/tillstrom_biography_1961.html.

4. Max Wilk, *The Golden Age of Television—Notes from the Survivors* (New York: Delacorte Press, 1976).

5. Ibid.

6. Bill Fay, "Allison in Wonderland," *Collier's*, March 1950.

7. Wilk, *The Golden Age of Television*.

8. Unless otherwise noted, biographical information on Fran Allison came from "Allison in Wonderland," by Bill Fay.

9. Ibid.

10. Jerry Crimmins, "Burr Tillstrom, 68, Legendary Puppeteer," *Chicago Tribune*, December 8, 1985.

11. By then, Stone and Whedon had formed a two-man creative-services company, first puckishly called Talent, Ltd. It was later amended to Albatross Productions, at the behest of their agent, who feared some might not get the joke. In his memoir, Stone wrote, "My friend Charlie Rosen designed a logo for us consisting of the company name with a smug, smiling albatross leaning confidently on the capital *A*. Beneath and slightly behind the albatross was a huge egg."

CHAPTER SEVEN

Interviews: Caroll Spinney generously agreed to face-to-face interview time and follow-up phone conversations.

Additional Sources: An especially illuminating interview conducted by Michael Rosen for the Television Academy on May 12, 2001, informed this chapter, as did *The Wisdom of Big Bird (and the Dark Genius of Oscar the Grouch): Lessons from a Life in Feathers* by Caroll Spinney with J Milligan (New York: Villard, 2003). Unless otherwise noted, quotes came from the author's aforementioned interviews as well as the preceding two sources.

1. Spinney also created two animated films for children about a wombat and a crayon that comes to life. Entitled *Crazy Crayon*, the seven-and-a-half-minute shorts were drawn in black and shot on 16-millimeter film. Both were featured on *Captain Kangaroo* in the early 1960s.

CHAPTER EIGHT

Interviews: Joan Cooney, Gordon Howe, Lloyd Morrisett, and Cathy Short.

Additional Sources: Unless otherwise noted, all quotes are from the author's interviews, the Archive of American Television oral history DVDs, and *Children's Television Workshop, The Early Years: An Oral History* by Robert Davidson (CTW, 1993).

1. "Sidney Fields, "TV's A-B-Cer," *New York Daily News*, May 27, 1969.

2. Richard M. Polsky, *Getting to Sesame Street: Origins of the Children's Television Workshop* (New York: Praeger Publishers, 1974), 28.

3. Ibid., 30.

4. Alistair Cookie was played by Cookie Monster, who in turn was played by Frank Oz. One of the featured presentations introduced on *Monsterpiece Theatre* was *Me, Claudius*.

5. Eric Pace, "Fred Friendly, CBS Executive and Pioneer in TV News Coverage, Dies at 82," *New York Times*, March 5, 1998.

6. Schlesinger was quoted in Pace's obituary; ibid.

7. Polsky, *Getting to Sesame Street*, 35.

CHAPTER NINE

Interviews: Milton Chen, Joan Cooney, Mike Dann, and Lloyd Morrisett.

Additional Sources: Unless otherwise noted, all quotes are from the author's interviews, the Archive of American Television oral history DVDs, and *Children's Television Workshop, The Early Years: An Oral History* by Robert Davidson (CTW, 1993). Jon Stone quotes from his unpublished memoir.

1. Gerry Lesser recommended a trio of distinguished scholars from the University of

Chicago (Susan Stodolsky), Duke (Michael Wallach), and Harvard (Roger Brown) to join Carnegie's Barbara Finberg, USOE's Lou Hausman, Edward Meade of the Ford Foundation, freelance writer Linda Gottlieb, Cooney, and Morrisett.

2. Information on Johnson, PBL, and the Public Broadcasting Act of 1967 comes from Robert B. Semple, "Johnson Signs Bill Creating Nonprofit TV Agency," *New York Times*, November 8, 1967.

3. "PBL Debut Wins Praise, Cancellations," *Washington Post and Times Herald*, November 7, 1967.

4. Ibid.

5. Gould was particularly annoyed by the "tiresomely long" final segment, a satire entitled "A Day of Absence." In it, a southern town awakens to find its black residents have vanished. "A Noble Experiment: Nowhere to Go But Up," *New York Times*, November 12, 1967.

6. Harold Howe II, memorandum, January 3, 1968, Carnegie Archives, CTW files, New York.

7. Barbara Finberg, interview by Richard Polsky, Columbia University's Oral History Research Office, March 30, 1972, 9.

8. *The Children's Television Workshop: How and Why It Works* (New York: Nassau Board of Cooperative Educational Services, Research and Development Division, n.d.), 25.

9. James Day, *The Vanishing Vision: The Inside Story of Public Television* (Berkeley and Los Angeles: University of California Press, 1995), 107.

10. *CTW: How and Why It Works*, 20.

11. Roberta Brandes Gratz, "The New People," *Glamour*, January 1971, 104.

12. Ibid.

13. "Joan Ganz Cooney: Powerful Impact, Gentle Persuasion," *Successful Woman*, May/June 1986, 12.

14. *CTW: How and Why It Works*, 21.

15. "Joan Ganz Cooney: Powerful Impact, Gentle Persuasion," 12.

16. Ed Meade, interview by Richard Polsky, Columbia University's Oral History Research Office, April 17, 1972, 7.

17. Polsky, *Getting to Sesame Street*, 59.

18. *CTW: How and Why It Works*, 27.

19. Ed Meade, interview by Richard Polsky, 8.

20. "Joan Ganz Cooney: Powerful Impact, Gentle Persuasion," 13.

21. Polsky, *Getting to Sesame Street*, 56.

CHAPTER TEN

Interviews: Alan Connell, Jan Connell, Mike Dann, Sam Gibbon, Fred Silverman, Beverley Stone, and Polly Stone.

Additional Sources: Unless otherwise noted, all quotes are from the author's interviews, the Archive of American Television oral history DVDs, and *Children's Television Workshop, The Early Years: An Oral History* by Robert Davidson (CTW 1993); Jon Stone quotes are from his unpublished memoir.

1. Squeezed into the final paragraphs: a lukewarm mini-review of the "The Reluctant Dragon," a television adaptation of Kenneth Grahame's children's book, performed by Burr Tillstrom, Fran Allison, and the Kuklapolitans. Tellingly, Gould criticized both the small space in which Tillstrom worked as well as the clunky restaurant ads that had been inserted into the program by the players.

"[The program] illustrated the strengths and weaknesses of commercial television's approach to programming for youngsters," Gould wrote. "The adaptation . . . seemed cramped and static in the confining space in which the gifted Mr. Tillstrom had to work. And in his role as the dragon who wouldn't breathe a wisp of fire, Ollie was never quite his endearing self.

"The larger lesson exemplified by "The Reluctant Dragon," however, was the pitfall of trying to do children's television under prevailing commercial standards. In the advertising, Miss Allison, Ollie, Kukla and Beulah stepped out of the world of make believe to plug the wares and services of a restaurant chain. The element of illusion was instantly sacrificed and there occurred the distasteful gimmick of capitalizing on childhood involvement as an instrument of sales promotion.

"To use the young as a merchandising weapon against their parents is one of the blights of TV. Mr. Tillstrom, Miss Allison, Kukla and Ollie are performers; if they need guidance on where to eat, let them consult Craig Claiborne, not the sponsor of their appearances."

Jack Gould, "TV: Focus on Programming for the Disadvantaged Child," *New York Times*, March 22, 1968, 95.

2. Ibid.

3. Polsky, *Getting to Sesame Street*, 69.

4. Among its properties was Roger Ramjet, the crudely animated misadventures of a dimwit superhero (voiced by Gary Owens) who protected our way of life from the likes of Noodles Romanoff and N.A.S.T.Y. (the National Association of Spies, Traitors and Yahoos), his dastardly organization.

5. Dave Connell, interview by Richard Polsky, Columbia University's Oral History Research Office, January 24, 1972, 2.

6. The Ground Floor started serving patrons in 1965, the year after Black Rock was completed. The *New York Times* reported in 1983 that CBS founder William S. Paley had sampled most of the restaurant's dishes and supervised the decoration of the interiors before its grand opening.

7. We should note that George Dessart, the executive who suggested using commercials to sell letters and numbers, was considered the top candidate for executive producer before Dave Connell entered the picture. "I desperately tried to get George," Cooney said, "but that would have been a disaster. He resisted us, saying, 'That's not the job for me.' To his credit, he, too, understood I needed a volume producer."

8. From an address given before the Hollywood Radio and Television Society on October 13, ca. 1970–71.

9. Dave Connell, interview by Richard Polsky, 2–4.

10. Ibid., 4–5.

11. "20,000 Attend King Rites in Park," *New York Daily News*, April 8, 1968.

12. Ibid.

13. Arthur Greenspan, "A Hushed City Marks the Day," *New York Post*, April 9, 1968.

14. Lesser, *Children and Television*, 57–58.

15. Daniel Ogilvie quoted from Polsky, *Getting to Sesame Street*, 73. Originally appeared in Ogilvie's "Partial History of Sesame Street: Summer 1968" (1970). CTW archives.

16. *CTW: How and Why It Works*, 44.

17. Ibid.

18. Howard W. Reeves, ed., *Wings of an Artist: Children's Book Illustrators Talk About Their Art* (New York: Harry N. Abrams, 1999), 26.

19. Dave Connell, interview by Richard Polsky, 9–10.

20. Ibid.

21. Day, *The Vanishing Vision*, 155.

CHAPTER ELEVEN

Interviews: Joan Cooney, Danny Epstein, Sam Gibbon, Robert Hatch, Brian Henson, Lisa Henson, Charles Rosen, Toots Thielemans, and Tom Whedon.

Additional Sources: Sesame Workshop provided a DVD of the sales presentation. Unless otherwise noted, all quotes are from the author's interviews, the Archive of American Television oral history DVDs, and *Children's Television Workshop, The Early Years: An Oral History* by Robert Davidson (CTW, 1993); Jon Stone quotes are from his unpublished memoir.

1. Marvin Gaye's "What's Going On" wouldn't be released until 1971, but he and Tammi Terrell hit No. 53 on Billboard's Top 100 for 1968 with "Ain't Nothing Like the Real Thing."

2. "Sidney Fields, "TV's A-B-Cer," *New York Daily News*, May 27, 1969.

3. Stuart W. Little, "Children's Television Workshop," *Saturday Review*, February 8, 1969.

4. Cooney's quest to influence program managers was reinforced by CPB president John Macy at an April 9 press conference at the Waldorf. He called on public stations to assign the twenty-six-week series to a time slot that made the most sense for the preschool viewer. "I would not want to see these prospects for success and enrichment jeopardized in any way by the fact that the new series could not be seen at the right time on the right station by the largest number of American children," he said.

5. Philip H. Dougherty, "Advertising: The Message Is 'Give a Damn,' *New York Times*, May 16, 1968.

6. A brief historical note: When Stone was struggling to come up with a concept for the show, Dave Connell arranged to have a treatment completed by someone who was not intimately involved with the planning. Clark Gesner, an actor, author, and composer who wrote the music and lyrics for the Peanuts-inspired off-Broadway musical *You're a Good Man, Charlie Brown*, worked on the project in Princeton, New Jersey. His stark, futuristic concept featured a set constructed of white plastic and actors dressed uniformly in white. It was soundly rejected. Gesner, another veteran of *Captain Kangaroo*, later worked on *The Electric Company*.

7. Raposo and Epstein also provided live music for Jim Henson when the Muppets appeared on *The Ed Sullivan Show*.

8. Thielemans received residual checks for decades for his studio work whistling the Old Spice jingle. He also composed the jazz standard "Bluesette."

9. Brian Henson also appeared in a number film in which he counted dimes, nickels, and peas.

CHAPTER TWELVE

Interviews: Joan Cooney, Susan Erion, Brian Garfield, Robert Hatch, Loretta Long, Bob McGrath, Frank Oz, Dolores Robinson, and Caroll Spinney.

Additional Sources: Unless otherwise noted, all quotes are from the author's interviews, the Archive of American Television oral history DVDs, and *Children's Television Workshop, The Early Years: An Oral History* by Robert Davidson (CTW, 1993); Jon Stone quotes are from his unpublished memoir.

1. Dave Connell, interview by Richard Polsky, 21.

2. Her cohost was the estimable Dr. Alvin F. Poussaint, an Ivy League–trained psychiatrist who was born in East Harlem.

3. Brooks Atkinson, "'Waiting for Lefty' and a Program of Sketches and Improvisations by the Group Theatre," *New York Times*, February 11, 1935.

4. Also appearing in the special were Lesley Gore—"It's My Party"—as Little Bo Peep and the musical group The First Edition—"Just Dropped In (To See What Condition My Condition Was In)"—later Kenny Rogers and The First Edition.

5. The former Betty Toshiko was married to Chet for twenty-five years. The third of his three wives, she died in 1989.

6. Quotes from this and subsequent passages from Chet O'Brien were obtained with permission from *Tripping the Light Fantastic*, his unpublished autobiography completed in 1989. O'Brien's nephew, the California-based writer Brian Garfield, collaborated on the high-dish, laugh-loaded manuscript. Garfield generously provided additional material and reflections by e-mail.

7. The dialogue in this section was obtained by the author during multiple interviews with Caroll Spinney and from passages in an interview with him conducted by the Television Academy, as well as from his book, *The Wisdom of Big Bird*.

8. Spinney, *The Wisdom of Big Bird*, 22.

9. Apologies—and a deep bow—are offered to Rod Serling, from whose fertile mind sprang the greatest of all anthology series, *The Twilight Zone*.

10. Connell, Stone, and Gibbon thought that was nonsense, based on their years of experience on *Captain Kangaroo*. As a "teacher," Mr. Moose was every bit as effective as the Captain or Mr. Green Jeans. Children respond to a smart, funny script and a professional performance, whether it be from a sentient being or a sock with Ping-Pong-ball eyes. "When the suggestion was made to put Muppet characters right into the show, I thought it was just fine," said Palmer, the research scientist. Maybe it was because he had small children at home watching the Captain.

11. Barbara Delatiner, "NBC Special to Prevue 'Sesame Street' Series, *New York Newsday*, October 17, 1969.

12. The unions also granted an exemption for a commercial station in Ohio.

CHAPTER THIRTEEN

Interviews: Dolores Robinson

Additional Sources: Sesame Workshop provided DVDs of the first five episodes of *Sesame Street*. Unless otherwise noted, all quotes are from the author's interviews, the Archive of American Television oral history DVDs, and *Children's Television Workshop, The Early Years: An Oral History* by Robert Davidson (CTW, 1993); Jon Stone quotes are from his unpublished memoir.

1. The episode in its entirety is included in *Sesame Street Old School, Volume 1*, a three-disc boxed set released in 2006. *Old School, Volume 2* followed in 2007.

CHAPTER FOURTEEN

Interviews: Frank Biondo, Bernie Brillstein, Chris Cerf, Joan Cooney, Alan Connell, Jan Connell, Mike Dann, Jason Epstein, Emily Kingsley, Loretta Long, Lloyd Morrisett, and Norton Wright.

Additional Sources: Unless otherwise noted, all quotes are from the author's interviews, the Archive of American Television oral history DVDs, and *Children's Television Workshop, The Early Years: An Oral History* by Robert Davidson (CTW, 1993); Jon Stone quotes are from his unpublished memoir.

1. Leo Seligsohn, "Sesame Street," *New York Newsday*, February 9, 1970.

2. Jack Gould, "This Sesame May Open the Right Doors," *New York Times*, November 23, 1969.

3. "Sesame Street: Wunderkind," *Variety*, December 24, 1969.

4. Cecil Smith, "Sesame Street Geared to Preschoolers," *Los Angeles Times*, November 10, 1969.

5. Stefan Kanfer, "Who's Afraid of Big, Bad TV?" *Time*, November 23, 1970. *Time's* competitor *Newsweek* also weighed in with its glowing evaluation: "While the show is candy to children, it is as good for them as spinach."

6. Nixon letter courtesy Sesame Workshop Archives.

7. Miriam Jacobs, "Puppets, Jingles, Cartoons Spark Kids on Sesame Street," *Woodbridge (NJ) News Tribune*, April 30, 1970.

8. Leo Seligsohn, "Backstage at Sesame Street," *New York Newsday*, February 9, 1970.

9. Bereiter quoted in Robert W. Morrow's *Sesame Street and the Reform of Children's Television* (Baltimore: The Johns Hopkins University Press, 2006), 145.

10. Urie Bronfenbrenner, "Who Lives on Sesame Street?" *Psychology Today*, October 1970.

11. Lee Kottke, "Producer Answers Sesame Street Critics," *Chicago Daily News*, May 20, 1970.

12. Arnold Arnold, "Writer Attacks Sesame Street," *Hackensack (NJ) Record*, August 5, 1970.

13. Richard K. Doan, "Kindergarten May Never Be the Same Again," *Childhood Education*, July 1970.

14. Ron Powers, "Some Changes for Sesame Street," *Long Island Press*, July 16, 1970.

15. "Mississippi Agency Votes for a TV Ban on 'Sesame Street,'" *New York Times*, May 3, 1970.

16. "Mississippi Bars Sesame Street," *Chicago Sun-Times*, May 2, 1970.

17. "Mississippi Agency Votes for a TV Ban on 'Sesame Street,'" *New York Times*, May 3, 1970.

18. Harry Harris, "Capt. Kangaroo Had Ideas, 'Sesame' Gets Prizes," *Philadelphia Inquirer*, May 19, 1970.

19. Les Brown, "Licensing Credo of 'Sesame Street': You Can't Toy Around with Poor Kids," *Variety*, August 26, 1970.

20. Horne, an African American, was yet another *Captain Kangaroo* production veteran who signed on with CTW. In later years he was head of international production for *Sesame Street*.

21. Marvin Kitman, "Truly the Talleyrand," *New York Newsday*, June 24, 1970.

22. "Mr. Dann of Sesame Street," *Time*, July 6, 1970.

23. *Variety* article quoted in Kitman, "Truly the Talleyrand," June 24, 1970.

24. "BBC Doesn't Buy Sesame Street," *Washington Post*, September 8, 1971.

25. Reprinted in Lisa Grunwald, *Women's Letters: America from the Revolutionary War to the Present* (New York: Dial Press, 2005), 657.

26. Later Naomi Foner Gyllenhaal went on to become an Academy Award–nominated screenwriter (*Running on Empty*) and mother to actors Maggie and Jake Gyllenhaal.

CHAPTER FIFTEEN

Interviews: Linda Bove, Fran Brill, Chris Cerf, Judy Collins, Emilio Delgado, Danny Epstein, Brian Garfield, Jane Hunt, Kate Hunt, Emily Kingsley, Loretta Long, Frank Oz, Sonia Manzano, Jerry Nelson, Dolores Robinson, Marty Robinson, Buffy Sainte-Marie, Lisa Simon, Dulcy Singer, Caroll Spinney, Norman Stiles, and James Taylor.

Additional Sources: Sesame Workshop provided DVDs of *Sesame Street* episodes that featured appearances by Judy Collins, Buffy Sainte-Marie, and James Taylor. Videos also available on www.youtube.com. Unless otherwise noted, all quotes are from the author's interviews, the Archive of American Television oral history DVDs, and *Children's Television Workshop, The Early Years: An Oral History* by Robert Davidson (CTW, 1993); Jon Stone quotes are from his unpublished memoir.

1. In his *New York Times* review, Mel Gussow refers to Robinson's creation as "a pistil-packing vampire." "Musical: A Cactus Owns 'Little Shop of Horrors,'" *New York Times*, May 30, 1982.

2. Elizabeth Blair, "Cookie Monster: A Sweet, Sensual Id, Unfiltered," *All Things Considered*, February 10, 2008, National Public Radio, www.npr.org.

3. "TV's Switched-on School," *Newsweek*, June 1, 1970.

4. The CBS special, which aired December 20, 1970, was written by Jerry Juhl, with music from Joe Raposo. Art Carney starred. In addition to Fran Brill (performing the Frackle named Snerf), the Muppet players included Jim Henson, Frank Oz, Jerry Nelson, Richard Hunt, John Lovelady, and Marilyn Sokol.

5. Srianthi Perera, "She Loves Her Life on the 'Street,'" *Arizona Republic*, December 27, 2007.

CHAPTER SIXTEEN

Interviews: Chris Cerf, Pat Collins, Joan Cooney, Robert Hatch. Sharon Lerner, Alan Menken, and Nick Raposo.

Additional Sources: Unless otherwise noted, all quotes are from the author's interviews, the Archive of American Television oral history DVDs, and *Children's Television Workshop, The Early Years: An Oral History* by Robert Davidson (CTW, 1993); Jon Stone quotes are from his unpublished memoir.

CHAPTER SEVENTEEN

Interviews: Dr. Lewis Bernstein, Linda Bove, George Clash, Gladys Clash, Kevin Clash, Emilio Delgado, Bob McGrath, Sharon Lerner, Dr. Loretta Long, Kate Lucas, Sonia Manzano, Alison Bartlett O'Reilly, Roscoe Orman, Dulcy Singer, Caroll Spinney, Norman Stiles, Beverley Stone, Polly Stone, and Vanessa Williams.

Additional Sources: Sesame Workshop provided a DVD of the episode in which Mr. Hooper (Will Lee) was memorialized. Unless otherwise noted, all quotes are from the author's interviews, the Archive of American Television oral history DVDs, and *Children's Television Workshop, The Early Years: An Oral History* by Robert Davidson (CTW, 1993); Jon Stone quotes are from his unpublished memoir.

1. It proved to be a source of tension that literally followed both around the world, rupturing in Asia during the taping of the special, *Big Bird in China*.

2. Fred M. Hechinger, "About Education: 'Sesame Street' After 10 Years," *New York Times*, November 6, 1979.

3. Marah Nichols, "'Sesame' Actor Found Innocent," *Nashville Banner*, January 29, 1982.

4. Ibid.

5. Scott Moore, "He's Got the Whole World in His Hand," *Washington Post*, December 1, 1996.

6. Sandy Banisky, "Puppets Are Stars of His Show," *Baltimore Sun*, April 16, 1976.

7. Gerri Kobren, "A Turner Station Puppeteer Joins Captain Kangaroo," *Baltimore Sun*, September 21, 1980.

8. Kevin Clash with Gary Brozek, *My Life as a Furry Red Monster: What Being Elmo Has Taught Me About Life, Love and Laughing Out Loud* (New York: Broadway Books, 2006).

9. Diane Werts, "He's Elmo! The Man Behind the Cheerful Red Muppet Is a Serious, Organized Guy Who Has Been a Professional Puppeteer Since 10th Grade," *Newsday*, February 19, 1998.

10. Moss mixes fantasy and reality in ways a viewer could not have known. In real life, Sonia Manzano and Linda Bove had forged a sisterly bond during their years together on the set. Manzano, who had begun writing for the show by the mid-1980s, wove her colleague into segments, allowing the deaf actress to express her full range of acting abilities. It made complete sense that Bove would play Manzano's maid of honor. Also, the young actor playing Miles is Roscoe Orman's real-life son, also named Miles, and the light of Orman's life.

CHAPTER EIGHTEEN

Interviews: Martin G. Baker, Annie Boylan Moss, Molly Boylan, Fran Brill, Bernie Brillstein, David V. B. Britt, Chris Cerf, Stephanie D'Abruzzo, Danny Epstein, George Clash, Gladys Clash, Kevin Clash, Pat Collins, Alan Connell, Jan Connell, Judy Freudberg, Tony Geiss, Sam Gibbon, Linda Gottlieb, Jane Henson, Jane Hunt, Kate Hunt, Emily Kingsley, Kate Lucas, David Lazer, Sonia Manzano, Jerry Nelson, Arthur Novell, Rosie O'Donnell, Frank Oz, Marty Robinson, David Rudman, Craig Shemin, Dulcy Singer, Caroll Spinney, Beverley Stone, Polly Stone, and Mo Willems.

Additional Sources: Sesame Workshop provided DVDs of the Henson memorial and of the PBS special *Sing! Sesame Street Remembers Joe Raposo and His Music.* Unless otherwise noted, all quotes are from the author's interviews, the Archive of American Television oral history DVDs, and *Children's Television Workshop, The Early Years: An Oral History* by Robert Davidson (CTW, 1993); Jon Stone quotes are from his unpublished memoir.

1. Theresa G. Di Maio and Vincent J. M. Di Maio, *Excited Delirium Syndrome: Cause of Death and Prevention* (Boca Raton, FL: CRC Press, 2006), 1–3.

2. Rob Owen, "Q/A with Stephanie D'Abruzzo," *Pittsburgh Post-Gazette*, January 14, 2007.

3. Stephanie D'Abruzzo provided a recollection in writing about this painful day in her life. Her quotes in this passage were extracted from that remembrance.

4. Vincent Canby, reflecting a majority view among critics, drubbed *The Dark Crystal* in his *New York Times* review of December 17, 1982. He described it as "without any narrative drive . . . charm as well as interest." Canby likened Henson to comedians who yearn to do Shakespeare. "Henson . . . and Frank Oz, his longtime associate, have apparently dreamed of creating mechanical marvels more significant and timeless than the irrepressible Miss Piggy and her pals. The result is *The Dark Crystal*, which aims, I think, to be a sort of Muppet *Paradise Lost* but winds up as watered down J. R. R. Tolkien."

Roger Ebert is kinder to Henson is his review of *Labyrinth* in the June 27, 1986, *Chicago Sun-Times*. While the Pulitzer Prize–winning critic describes it as overly long and lacking narrative structure, he commends Henson for a film "that obviously was made with infinite care and pains."

Henson devotees and fantasy film enthusiasts regard both pictures as small masterpieces. Thanks to DVD reissues, they live on as something more than curiosities. This is especially true of *Labyrinth*, which starred an eerie David Bowie and an adolescent Jennifer Connelly. In 2001, Connelly won an Academy Award for *A Beautiful Mind.*

5. Kim Masters, "Disney's Muppet Miasma; Corporate Style, Henson's Death Complicates a Deal-in-Waiting," *Washington Post*, June 13, 1990.

6. The company keeps in its employ an archivist in Karen Falk, who goes about her work with the same fastidiousness one would expect from a curator at the Smithsonian.

7. Caroll Spinney with J Milligan, *The Wisdom of Big Bird*, 111–12.

8. Henson's father, Paul, married his sister-in-law after the death of his wife. He outlived two sons.

9. Richard W. Stevenson, "Muppets Join Disney Menagerie," *New York Times*, August 29, 1989.

10. There is no greater monument to Henson than this twelve-minute shower of soap bubbles, cream pies, cannonballs, puns, and mayhem, an attraction found both at Disney World and at Disney's California Adventure Park in Anaheim, California. It continues to astound and delight.

11. Michael Riley, "Stuuuupendous!" *Time*, December 21, 1992.

12. Stephanie Anderson Forest, "Wouldn't You Like to Knock the Stuffing Out of Barney?" *Business Week*, August 16, 1993.

13. James Gorman, "Of Dinosaurs Why Must This One Thrive?" *New York Times*, April 11, 1993.

14. "Barney Backlash," *National Review*, November 29, 1993.

15. Jack Mathews, "Counting to 25," TV Times, *Los Angeles Times*, November 21–27, 1993.

16. Erik Eckholm, "Move Over Grover. Here's Zoe," *New York Times*, August 20, 1993.

17. A PBS revival of the series was planned for 2009.

18. Background and quotes from this passage were adapted from a moving eulogy Norman Stiles offered at a memorial service for Jeff Moss.

19. Moss succeeded Jon Stone as head writer in 1969 once production of the series began in earnest.

20. Ben Brantley, "A Feeling You're Not on Sesame Street," *New York Times*, August 1, 2003.

21. Jake Tapper, "Is This Town Big Enough for Two Puppet Boulevards?" *New York Times*, July 27, 2003.

22. In the early-to-mid-1980s, the author's two daughters used to sit mesmerized in front of the home screen watching Disney classics on VHS. He referred to these bouts of tele-intoxication as "video benders."

23. Among them was Tony Geiss, Freudberg's writing partner on director Don Bluth's 1986 full-length animated film *An American Tail*, the best Disney film Disney never made. One cannot claim to be movie literate unless one has screened *An American Tail*. It may be coexecutive producer Steven Spielberg's least-appreciated triumph.

EPILOGUE

Interviews: Joan Cooney, Jason Epstein, Don Hewitt, Chloe Kimball, Gary E. Knell, Peter Peterson, Sarah Otley, Diane Sawyer, Liz Smith, and Janet Wolf.

1. Susan Dominus, "A Girly Girl Joins the 'Sesame' Boys," *New York Times*, August 6, 2006.

2. Karen Lowry Miller, "Just Call Him Grosser Vogel," *Newsweek*, March 6, 2000.

3. Gary Gentile, "Kermit, Miss Piggy Joining Mickey Mouse at Disney," Associated Press, February 17, 2004.

Index

ILLUSTRATION CREDITS

The photos in the insert on page 1 are reprinted courtesy of Lloyd Morrisett; page 2 (*top* and *center*), page 14 *center*, and the last photo on page 16 courtesy of Joan Ganz Cooney (page 2 *top* was photographed by Alexander Archer Photography); page 2 *bottom* and page 12 *top* with permission from CBS/Landov; page 3 *top* with permission from Hearst Communications and the University of Maryland Library, Special Collections; page 3 *bottom*, page 5 *center*, page 6 *center*, page 8 *bottom*, page 11 *top*, and page 13 *bottom* courtesy of Sesame Workshop Photo Archives; page 4 (*top* and *center*) and page 12 *bottom* courtesy of Pat Collins; page 4 *bottom* with permission from Maurice Sendak; page 5 *top* and page 10 *bottom* courtesy of Bob McGrath; page 5 *bottom* courtesy of Carroll Spinney; page 6 *top* with permission from The Jim Henson Company and with the cooperation of Sesame Workshop Photo Archives; page 6 *bottom* courtesy of Nick Raposo; page 7 *top* courtesy of Linda Bove (photographed by John Huang); page 7 *bottom*, page 9 (*top* and *center*), and page 10 *center* with permission from Bill Pierce; page 8 (*top* and *center*) courtesy of Anne W. Boylan; page 9 *bottom* and page 12 *center* courtesy of Martin P. Robinson; page 10 *top* courtesy of Jane Hunt; page 11 *center* and page 15 *bottom* courtesy of Emily Perl Kingsley; page 11 *bottom* courtesy of Dr. Loretta Long; page 13 *top*, © Al Hirschfeld, reproduced by arrangement with Hirschfeld's exclusive representative, the Margo Feiden Galleries Ltd., New York, www.alhirschfeld.com; page 13 *center* and page 16 *top* courtesy of Sesame Workshop Photo Archives with permission from Richard Termine; page 14 *top* courtesy of Fran Brill, © Christopher Little; page 14 *bottom* and page 15 *top* courtesy of Michael Davis.